# WITNESS THROUGH THE IMAGINATION

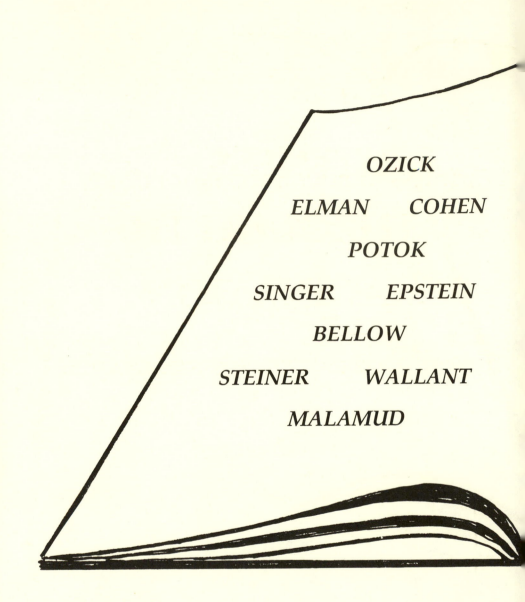

OZICK

ELMAN    COHEN

POTOK

SINGER    EPSTEIN

BELLOW

STEINER    WALLANT

MALAMUD

# WITNESS THROUGH THE IMAGINATION

## JEWISH AMERICAN HOLOCAUST LITERATURE

### S. LILLIAN KREMER

WAYNE STATE UNIVERSITY PRESS    DETROIT    1989

**Library of Congress Cataloging-in-Publication Data**

Kremer, S. Lillian, 1939–
    Witness through the imagination : Jewish-American holocaust
literature / S. Lillian Kremer.
        p.    cm.
    Includes index.
    ISBN 0–8143–2116–X (alk. paper). —ISBN 0–8143–2117–8 (pbk. :
alk. paper)
        1. American fiction—Jewish authors—History and criticism.
2. Holocaust, Jewish (1939–1945), in literature.  3. American
fiction—20th century—History and criticism.  4. World War,
1939–1945—Literature and the war.  5. Jews—United States—
Intellectual life.  6. Jews in literature.  I. Title.
PS374.H56K7      1989
813′.54′09358—dc19                                         88–34652
                                                             CIP

*Acknowledgments*

*Portions of this book previously appeared in somewhat altered form in the* Holocaust
Studies Annual *and the* Saul Bellow Journal. *Portions of Chapter 7 previously
appeared in somewhat altered form in* Studies in American Jewish Literature 6
*(Fall 1986), "The World of Cynthia Ozick," Daniel Walden, ed., pp. 24–43.*

*Quotations from* The Victim *by Saul Bellow reprinted by permission of the
publisher, Vanguard Press, Inc. Copyright © 1947 by Saul Bellow. Renewed
copyright © 1974 by Saul Bellow.*

*Excerpts from* The Pawnbroker, *copyright © 1961 by Edward Lewis Wallant,
reprinted by permission of Harcourt Brace Jovanovich, Inc.*

*Selections from* The Portage to San Cristobal of AH *copyright © 1979, 1981 by
George Steiner. Reprinted by permission of Simon & Schuster, Inc., and Faber and
Faber Ltd.*

*The author gratefully acknowledges permission from Richard Elman, Leslie Epstein,
and Cynthia Ozick to reprint excerpts from their works.*

This book is dedicated to my father, Joseph Kimmel, whose reports of pre-Shoah Jewish life in Poland and whose Holocaust losses sensitized me to the treacheries of anti-Semitism; to my sons, Michael and Ian, who have unselfishly used their energies to support threatened people; to survivors who have endured and taught us much; and to the blessed memory of the six million Jews who perished.

For the Jewish novelist of today, assuming he does not repudiate his Jewishness, there can be no theme more urgent and meaningful than that of the suffering of his people in the Nazi era. All plots and parables pale and sound trivial by comparison: his is the awesome privilege to identify with a tale, unique in its shattering power.

Elie Wiesel

# CONTENTS

5

# PREFACE

During the twentieth century, humanity has
exhibited unparalleled creative and destructive capacities. Germany—celebrated for its cultural and scientific achievements—embraced a political system and supported a technological program
designed to annihilate an entire people singled out by racial crite-
ria. The Germans and their accomplices murdered six million
Jews, filling mass graves with the corpses and ashes of tortured,
mutilated, starved, shot, and gassed victims. The victims—of all
ages, all social, educational, and economic strata, and every political
persuasion—were a population whose crime was being descended
from a Jewish grandparent. Unlike earlier massacres of ethnic populations, the Nazi endeavor was the first to technologically implement the systematic annihilation of an entire people. That the
*Shoah* is a focal point of Jewish history is self-evident. The Holocaust should be recognized as a turning point in world history, a
catastrophe that altered fundamental assumptions about the
human condition. Pre-Auschwitz innocence has been forever obliterated. We no longer harbor the beliefs about God, civilization, and

7

man that once assured us. Just as the Trojan War engaged the imagination of Homer and Virgil and the French Revolution inspired Wordsworth and Shelley, so, in our time, when the magnitude of horrors surpassed previous upheavals, has the Holocaust informed artistic sensibilities. It was inevitable that when the destructive efforts of politicians, bureaucrats, and technocrats were brought to an end, the historians, archivists, diarists, and artists would begin to document and interpret the Holocaust and explore the peculiarities of human nature revealed in the Holocaust. Some observers argue that the *Shoah* defies comprehension. Yet we may come closer to comprehension through the efforts of artists whose works incorporate and transcend representational reality, rather than through histories and eyewitness accounts. This book chronicles and analyzes the encounter between the American literary imagination and the Holocaust as seen through the perspective of ten Jewish-American prose writers, writers who by virtue of geography escaped the direct effects of the event, but nevertheless elected to bear "witness-through-the-imagination."[1]

*Holocaust* is the most widely used English term to designate the 1933–1945 war against the Jews, a war that began with the burning of books and culminated in the burning of human beings in the crematoria and lime pits of Nazi-occupied Europe. Although the word *holocaust* suggests an apocalyptic destruction, it also has an unfortunate sacrificial connotation suggesting a biblical burnt offering, which is "consistent with a prevailing Christian reading of Jewish history."[2] Although the sacrificial connotation of the word renders it morally objectionable for me, I use it since it is the most widely accepted term in common and scholarly usage. However, I occasionally employ the Hebrew word *shoah* and the Yiddish word *hurban* as preferable alternatives. Hebrew and Yiddish nomenclature refute the affirmative theological overtones of the Greek-derived *holocaust* and signify instead the rupture in the collective consciousness engendered by the destruction of one-third of world Jewry. The biblical word *shoah,* meaning ruin, calamity, desolation, was reintroduced in modern Hebrew to suggest the cataclysmic destruction of European Jewry that transformed conceptions of God, society, and man. The Yiddish term *hurban* shares the implications of *Shoah* and alludes to a long history of catastrophes.

Criticism of Holocaust literature is an emerging field of inquiry, and as might be expected, the most innovative work has concentrated on the vanguard of European and Israeli Holocaust literature. Now that American fiction has amassed an impressive and provocative Holocaust canon, the time is propitious for its evaluation. The impetus for this study came from admiration for the analyses of European and Israeli Holocaust literature by Lawrence Langer, Alvin Rosenfeld, Sidra Ezrahi, Edward Alexander, Alan Mintz, and David Roskies, and the complementary belief that American Holocaust literature had not received the critical explication and assessment it merits. Aside from Alan Berger's recent fine study *Crisis and Covenant* (1985), examination of American works has been limited to occasional chapters in books emphasizing European literature, short articles in scholarly journals, and brief reviews. This study differs from its predecessors in the scope of its analysis of the American material, and differs from Berger's in its focus on literary explication and the authors and titles studied. Berger examines literature as a vehicle for demonstrating the impact of the Holocaust on covenantal Judaism. I present a critical reading of themes and stylistic strategies of major American Holocaust fiction to determine its capacity to render the prelude, progress, and aftermath of the Holocaust.

In deciding what to include from a substantial body of literature, I selected writing that addresses the Jewish experience. Although Nazi crimes against humanity touched many non-Jews and included the mass murders of other peoples, this volume is limited to the particularity of the Jewish experience as interpreted by Jewish-American writers. Thus, although William Styron's *Sophie's Choice* and Jerzy Kosinski's *The Painted Bird* are of significant interest both for their treatment of the Nazi period and their stylistic strategies, they are outside the scope of this book. Another consideration for the selection of materials was the practical concern for length. Therefore, I omitted two superior novels, Norma Rosen's *Touching Evil* and Susan Schaeffer's *Anya*.[3] Rather than prepare an encyclopedic review of American Holocaust fiction, I have analyzed representative works of artistic merit that render the Holocaust in exemplary, innovative, and influential ways and that share common themes and rhetorical patterns. Included are works by critically acclaimed writers, meritorious works by writers whose reputations are still growing, and recent publications that await the critical attention and recognition they deserve.

The book includes an introductory chapter addressing the complexities of American Holocaust literature, its major themes and technical strategies. The following chapters address the Holocaust fiction of Saul Bellow, Bernard Malamud, I. B. Singer, Edward Lewis Wallant, Cynthia Ozick, Leslie Epstein, George Steiner, Richard Elman, Arthur A. Cohen, and Chaim Potok. Some chapters deal with a single work. Where the writer's canon includes several Holocaust titles, analysis is more extensive. The rich diversity of American Holocaust literature is revealed through the fiction set in ghettos and concentration camps, which focuses on victimization and accommodation to the Nazi hegemony in Europe, and the fiction set in postHolocaust America and Israel, which relates the past through physical and psychological survivors of varied national backgrounds, social strata, and generations.

The unifying critical approach is the textual explication of themes and literary method, occasional comparative references to international Holocaust literature, and a discussion of extra-literary Holocaust sources that have influenced the creative writers' treatment of the Holocaust universe. Among the common subjects and themes explored are the connections between historic anti-Semitism and Nazi genocide; dehumanization of victims; Holocaust era survival strategies; postwar survivor syndrome, including behavioral and attitudinal transformations ranging from despair and nihilism to spiritual regeneration and social restoration; Holocaust moral accountability; and theological, social, and psychological implications of the Holocaust. The recurrent devices and techniques found in this literature include the introduction of historic figures in the fictional universe; the introduction of the concentrationary universe character types—types hitherto unknown to American fiction; the juxtaposition of documentary realism with metaphoric and symbolic evocations of the "concentrationary world"; surrealistic nightmares; voluntary and spontaneous memories; the inversion of conventional literary forms; and the inversion of liturgical language to repudiate traditional literature's implicit premises of order and explicit philosophic and social affirmations.

While some of the sources I examine are well known, others have thus far had a limited readership. Consequently, some chapters include introductory material, while others assume reader familiarity with the texts. Fully half of the works focus on the preservation of Jewish cultural and religious identity and incorporate references to Jewish sacred studies and liturgies that demand thorough explication. For example, Cohen, Potok, Ozick, Bellow, and Singer employ explicit discussion of Jewish law and literature and include Judaic archetypes and allusions to religious sources that require exegesis. This group of novelists also allude to pre-Holocaust Jewish history, which needs explication. Similarly, Epstein's extraordinarily dense use of ghetto documentation requires reference to his research sources. My intention is to suit the critical method to the requirements of the texts rather than impose an artificial, unifying critical structure.

# ACKNOWLEDGMENTS

I am grateful to Richard Elman, Leslie Epstein, Cynthia Ozick, and Chaim Potok, who generously agreed to interviews. Their forthright responses to my questions about Holocaust fiction were vital to my understanding.

The Memorial Foundation for Jewish Culture has my gratitude for awarding a fellowship which freed me from teaching responsibilities in order to complete the manuscript.

Portions of this study have appeared in *Studies in American Jewish Literature, Saul Bellow Journal,* and *Holocaust Studies Annual.* I thank the editors for permission to reprint.

Finally, I wish to express a special note of appreciation to Eugene Kremer, who read manuscript drafts, and offered wise counsel and loving encouragement that sustained me through bleak periods of Holocaust research.

# INTRODUCTION

*The Holocaust Universe in American Fiction*

Historians, artists, and critics who contemplate the imaginative integration of the Holocaust in fiction recognize its pitfalls. Some critics argue that Holocaust literature unavoidably diminishes the suffering that victims endured. Some believe that only eyewitness accounts are valid. Hannah Arendt, who has written brilliantly on the nature of totalitarianism, believes the horror of life in the concentration camps can never be fully embraced by the imagination, "for the very reason that it stands outside of life and death."[1] T. W. Adorno's dictum, "No poetry after Auschwitz," has haunted many. Elie Wiesel and George Steiner have at various times identified silence as the deepest form of respect for the Holocaust victims. Yet the literary careers of both Wiesel and Steiner testify to the paradox of Holocaust-imposed silence and compelled speech. Six million Jewish victims must not be consigned to oblivion. The murdered must be mourned and remembered.

Representative of the immediate postwar American intellec-

13

tual response to the "age of enormity" is Isaac Rosenfeld's 1948
recognition of the problematics of Holocaust comprehension.

> We still don't understand what happened to the Jews of Europe, and
> perhaps we never will. There have been books, magazine and news-
> paper articles, eyewitness accounts, letters, diaries, documents cer-
> tified by the highest authorities on the life in ghettos and concentra-
> tion camps, slave factories and extermination centers under the
> Germans. By now we know all there is to know. But it hasn't helped;
> we still don't understand. It is too painful for the majority—besides,
> who wants to understand?[2]

Rosenfeld realized that mankind has, in the Holocaust era, surpassed its historic notions of good and evil, that the Holocaust
initiated a condition of "terror beyond evil."[3] In the same year,
Lionel Trilling addressed the inadequacy of literary response to
the Holocaust, even in light of growing knowledge of Holocaust
history. Trilling, like Elie Wiesel and the Yiddish poet Uri Zvi
Greenberg, recognized that there are no adequate analogues to the
Holocaust in history or literature:

> Society's resistance to the discovery of depravity has ceased; now
> everyone knows that Thackery was wrong, Swift right. The world
> and the soul have spilt open of themselves and are all agape for our
> revolted inspection. The simple eye of the camera shows us, at
> Belsen and Buchenwald, horrors that quite surpass Swift's powers, a
> vision of life turned back to its corrupted elements which is more
> disgusting than any that Shakespeare could contrive, a cannibalism
> more literal and fantastic than that which Montaigne ascribed to
> organized society. A characteristic activity of mind is therefore no
> longer needed. Indeed, before what we now know the mind stops;
> the great psychological fact of our time which we all observe with
> baffled wonder and shame is that there is no possible way of re-
> sponding to Belsen and Buchenwald. The activity of mind fails be-
> fore the incommunicability of man's suffering.[4]

Alfred Kazin speaks for many American Jews when he writes of the
intrusion of the Holocaust in his consciousness, describing it as the
"nightmare that would bring everything else into question, that will
haunt me to my last breath."[5] Few Jews have escaped some version
of Kazin's nightmare of himself, his parents, his family, his neighbors, and his friends: "fuel for flames, dying by a single flame that
burned us all up at once."[6] Kazin's nightmare is a manifestation of

George Steiner's observation that "Jews everywhere have been maimed by the European catastrophe, that the massacre has left all who survived (even if they were nowhere near the actual scene) off balance."[7]

During the late 1960s, a significant change occurred in Jewish-American Holocaust fiction. Early in the decade Holocaust delineation was virtually absent from Jewish-American literature, and by decade's end it was an ever present, though subdued, component of the fiction. In a 1966 essay on Israeli Holocaust fiction, Robert Alter lamented, "With all the restless probing into the implications of the Holocaust that continues to go on in Jewish intellectual forums . . . it gives one pause to note how rarely American Jewish fiction has attempted to come to terms . . . with the European catastrophe."[8] Three years later, Lothar Kahn observed "No Jewish writer . . . has written a book without the memory of Auschwitz propelling him to issue warnings, implied or specific, against the Holocaust."[9] The sixties marked the beginning of wide-spread American interest in Holocaust literature and the ensuing decades have witnessed the development of a substantial body of work.

The writers treated in this study did not directly experience the ghettos, camps, and killing centers. That innocence, however, does not deny them the privilege of writing about the Holocaust. Authority is not limited to those with personal suffering. Nor is authenticity guaranteed by personal suffering. Emil Fackenheim, who was incarcerated at Sachsenhausen, asserts that it was not until years later—when he read a study of that camp—that he felt he truly understood his own experience and what had occurred there.[10] Deception of the victims was such an integral part of the administrative policies in the camps that it is possible historical accounts could contain information hidden from camp inmates. Authority may be achieved from the will of the artist to learn and shape the material. Although the writers whose works I examine have not directly shared the Jewish experience in Europe in 1939–1945, they share the historic burden of Jewish history. Tradition commands all Jews to consider themselves figuratively present at Sinai to receive the Torah. Contemporary Jews increasingly feel that, geography aside, they were present at Auschwitz. American Jews carry the psychological burden of Auschwitz and Chelmno and Dachau and Bergen-Belsen and Treblinka and all the other Nazi death factories where their relatives died brutal deaths.

A year before the 1948 commentaries of Rosenfeld and Trilling, Saul Bellow's *The Victim,* a novel whose symbolic underpinnings are delineated in Holocaust images, was published. Although Bellow's approach is muted and includes only one overt Holocaust reference, he addressed the topic while focusing the novel on the related topic of anti-Semitism. Despite their psychological association with the *Shoah,* the writers in this study, with the exception of Saul Bellow, began to write Holocaust literature in the sixties after the Europeans. Perhaps as nonparticipants, Americans believed it would have been presumptuous to deal with subject matter they did not experience directly. Perhaps they believed it was too soon to approach the topic without the benefit of adequate historic analysis. Perhaps since Jewish writers had only recently gained acceptance by the literary establishment, they were unwilling to broach a topic as controversial as the Holocaust.

What accounts for the intensification of the treatment of the Holocaust in Jewish-American fiction at the end of the sixties and through the seventies and eighties? The trial of Adolf Eichmann in Jerusalem and the 1967 Arab-Israeli Six Day War appear to have stimulated American interest in the Holocaust. The Eichmann trial, the intellectual debate aroused by Hannah Arendt's analysis of the trial, and her "banality of evil" thesis again brought Holocaust crimes to the forefront of American Jewish thought. Several Israeli writers who "derived their authority from their participation in the War of Independence in 1948"[11] departed from customary national themes and finally confronted the Holocaust following the Eichmann trial.[12] The post-Eichmann transformation from Holocaust silence to expression in Israeli literature was paralleled in American writing.

The 1967 joint Arab attack on Israel and its concomitant Nazi-style threats to annihilate Israel provided another catalyst for the development of imaginative Holocaust literature. Since the 1967 and 1973 Arab-Israeli wars, petrol politics has helped fuel international anti-Israeli propaganda, and once again in the twentieth century a large segment of the Jewish people is threatened with extinction. The unthinkable is again thinkable and is the articulated policy of most of Israel's geographic neighbors. When Jean Paul Sartre linked Zionists with Nazis, and a coalition of Third World and Communist countries in the United Nations branded Israel a racist society, Jews were even more threatened by hostile forces. Nations that appeased Hitler in the thirties and forties acquiesce in the seventies and eighties to Middle Eastern terrorists;

anti-Semitism is, therefore, again on the rise, leading scholars and artists to renewed interest in the Holocaust. With the revival of Nazi rhetoric—even in America, where Jews believe they are safe and assimilated, just as German Jews believed half a century ago—many have been moved to think and some to write in the Holocaust framework. Whatever the reason, or aggregate of reasons, we now have in American literature an admirable body of fiction addressing the Holocaust. Although it is interesting to speculate about the confluence of causes that have generated American Jewish Holocaust literature in recent decades, from its historic inception the Holocaust has haunted the Jewish American imagination, and its expression was long overdue.

Historically the German annihilation of Jews is widely interpreted both as the logical outcome of a two-thousand year old European, anti-Jewish tradition nourished by the Christian churches and as a drastic new policy formulated according to a racial doctrine, which asserted that the superior Aryan race had to rid itself of the debasing presence of the inferior Jewish race. After 1933, hatred of Jews was raised to the level of law.[13] *Rassenkunde*—racial science—dominated Germany's intellectual climate and infiltrated every segment of national life during the Hitler era. Religion, science, philosophy, law, economics, and history recast their old premises to acknowledge the danger of the "Jewish poison." Historians generally concur that the success of the war against European Jewry is substantially attributable to the continent's historic Christian anti-Semitism as manifested in anti-Jewish edicts, expulsions, pogroms, and mass murders—all rationalized by the need to keep Christian Europe free from Jewish influence.

Determinist racial theory, contending that human destiny is decreed by nature and expressed in race and that history is determined by the iron fist of race, is bankrupt and has come to naught. As Hitler came to power, the emptiness of Nazi ideology was revealed in rule by brute force and by exploitation of conquered peoples rather than viable social, economic, and political philosophy. Perhaps for these reasons, novelists give minor attention to Nazi racial theory, focusing instead on the Christian attitude toward Jews throughout European history as a primary element in the success of Nazi propaganda and its *Judenrein* objectives. The causal relationship between historic Christian anti-Semitism and the Holocaust is a recurrent subject of American Holocaust literature. Rather than emphasize the distinctions between Christian and Nazi anti-Jewish policies, the novelists more often dramatize their similarities to demonstrate the acceptability of the Final Solution in Christian Europe. The writers also make clear the significance of the strategies of Christian anti-Semitism in the implementation of the Final Solution. Each of the authors treated in this study portray the major catastrophes of Jewish history in the Diaspora as annunciations of the Holocaust. Although the novelists acknowledge distinctions in the racial and technological aspects of Nazi genocide and Christian anti-Jewish persecutions, they persistently raise the moral implications of Christian anti-Semitism as a source of Western acquiescence to Germany's war against the Jews and as explanation for the zealous role of non-Germans in facilitating the slaughter of the Jews.

Like the handful of Christian scholars and theologians, such as Henry Cargas and Robert Drinan,[14] who have acknowledged Christian Holocaust culpability, the novelists allude to the similarity of Martin Luther's assertion, "next to the devil life has no enemy more cruel, more venomous and violent than a true Jew," and Hitler's statement in *Mein Kampf,* "I believe that I am today acting in accordance with the will of the Almighty Creator: by defending myself against the Jew I am fighting for the work of the Lord."[15] Like the historian who describes Hitler "reechoing the medieval Christian stereotype of the Jew as criminal, parasite, evil incarnate, aiming at world conquest,"[16] the novelists show the analogy between the church's historic efforts to protect the Christian community from Jewish teaching and the German desire for racial purity. Nazi rhetoric is perceived as latter-day racist revision of traditional religious bigotry. Parallels are drawn between the church and Nazi persecutions of the Jews, including the progression from book burnings to human burnings; visual differentiation of Jews from the general population by requiring identifying badges; prohibitions against intermarriage; exclusion from businesses, schools, and professions, and the social and cultural activities of the community; ghettoization; and finally mass murders.

The Holocaust gave rise to unique categories of fictional characters, often classified by their attitudes or job statuses in the concentrationary hierarchy. Wallant's Nazerman, a *sonderkommando* who had shovel the corpses from the gas chambers into the crematorium, is troubled by memories of brutal *kapos* who herded men to labor; others remember the lessons learned from the *muslims,* the living dead, who were unable or lacked incentive to practice techniques that might keep them from joining the ranks in the death selections, such as personal sanitation, a spritely walk, or rouging the cheeks in order to look healthier. Leslie Epstein takes the fullest opportunity to explore Jewish and German functionaries, the Jewish ghetto elder and his Nazi-instituted Jewish Council members, Jewish police, resistance smugglers, organizers, fighters, and ghetto workers. A recurring character in the fiction of Malamud and Ozick is the survivor-mentor, whose function is to instruct untutored and lapsed American Jews in the significance of Jewish history, ethics, and sacred literature—or in Potok's and Ozick's cases, to teach in American religious communities. A related role is Wallant's and Bellow's use of survivor as judge and critic of contemporary life. Not infrequently, in the worlds of Ozick, Potok, and Malamud, these survivor-mentors resemble stock figures in Yiddish literature and folklore, and *lamed-vov tzaddikim* (the thirty-six hidden saints), the Hasidic *tzaddik* (righteous model) or the *rebbe*. Malamud's last Mohican, a *schnorrer* (mendicant) survivor, teaches an American artist Jewish history; Potok's boy fashions an imaginary *golem* to fight Nazis, and Ozick invokes Rabbi Akiva's *Bene Brak*.

Typically Jewish-American Holocaust literature focuses on the Jewish victims of Nazism and consigns the Germans to verbal oblivion. Concentration on the victims rather than the perpetrators of the crime adheres to the archetypal tradition of Jewish commemorative liturgy, which mourns martyrs and relegates villains to a tangential reference at best, possibly stemming from the liturgical petition to "blot out the names of our enemies." Aside from the historic figures who administer Epstein's ghetto and Elman's references to Eichmann's contrivance of the Brand and Kastner negotiations in 1944, Germans remain peripheral ghosts in Jewish-American Holocaust literature.

Struggle for survival during the Holocaust and during the postwar era constitute significant parallel themes in American fiction. Although American Holocaust fiction devotes considerably less attention to the description and dramatization of Nazi brutality than the works of Europeans and Israelis who directly endured the Nazi terror, dramatic presentation, memory, and nightmare are devices Americans frequently employ to depict the horrors of starvation, disease, excremental filth, medical experimentation, sadism, deportations, and death selections. After witnessing the asphyxiation of his fellow ghettoites in a mobile gas chamber and their subsequent stripping of gold teeth and hair, Epstein's protagonist struggles to maintain his sanity. Elman's protagonist is deceived in his good faith negotiations to barter his property and wealth for the safe passage of his family out of Hungary. Unlike Epstein and Elman who set their novels in the Holocaust era, most of the writers in this study use recollection and nightmare to record survivors' endurance of Holocaust humiliation and pain. Wallant's protagonist dreams of the surgery he suffered without benefit of anesthetic, remembers witnessing his wife's rape and his countryman's electrocution, and recalls being forced to move the corpses of his family and friends from the gas chamber to the crematorium. Bellow's protagonist speaks of escaping from a mass grave and hiding in a forest from Polish partisans who preferred to complete the Nazi genocidal objective rather than have Jews survive in Poland. Singer's protagonist frequently recalls his concealment in a haystack, and Ozick's recalls his fugitive fears in a convent cellar and barn. Through direct dramatic convention and indirect retrospective revery, American fiction charts the history of degradation that characterized the survival struggle in Nazi controlled Europe.

The more common and extensive treatment of survival in American fiction is devoted to the problems of postwar survival trauma. After overcoming the horrendous difficulties in the ghettos and camps, survivors suffered from both physical and psychological wounds. Extended postwar physical and psychological debilitation appears in Bellow's *Mr. Sammler's Planet;* Wallant's *The Pawnbroker;* Singer's *Enemies, Shosha,* "The Cafeteria," "Hanka," and "The Mentor"; Malamud's "The German Refugee"; Ozick's *The Cannibal Galaxy;* Elman's *The 28th Day of Elul;* Cohen's *In the Days of Simon Stern;* Steiner's *The Portage to San Cristobal of A.H.;* and Potok's *In the Beginning* and "The Dark Place Inside." In addition to depicting the survivors' long-term, Holocaust-generated physical ailments, the writers focus on the depression that stems from the guilt many feel for outliving families and friends; the recurrent nightmares and memories of Holocaust indignities, betrayals, and torture; the loss of faith and rejection of obligatory duties and rituals; and the failure to resume prewar ambitions and professions. Malamud's literary critic loses the ability to communicate in his native language; Wallant's Cracow University professor becomes a pawnbroker; Bellow's artist degenerates into a painter and sculptor of the grotesque; Ozick's aspiring astronomer becomes a mediocre educational administrator; Singer's Talmudic prodigy descends to hack essayist. Others suffer identity and religious crises, impairment of the capacity to love and trust others, death or disorientation of the creative impulse. Many are trapped by their Holocaust experiences. Some continue to manifest wartime behavior, such as searching for places of concealment; others dream of revenge; and still others interpret postwar violence in light of Holocaust knowledge. Each of the survivor-protagonists manifests alienation and suffers unbidden memories, nightmares, and psychological disquiet. "More recent novels with immigrant-survivor protagonists are likely to stress the homelessness of the immigrant, his separation from Americans who have not experienced near-death and qualified rebirth as he has."[17] This phenomenon appears in the histories of Wallant's, Bellow's, Cohen's, and Singer's protagonists. Unlike the immigrants of American-Jewish fiction set in the pre-Holocaust period, the postHolocaust immigrants do not seek assimilation and acculturation, but continue instead to grapple with the European past and often labor to preserve their Jewish particularity, history, and tradition.[18]

American Holocaust fiction demonstrates the constant change in the human condition and the perspective wrought in the Holocaust crucible. Although all survivors suffer Holocaust trauma, some engage in a regenerative process that takes the form of rebuilding Judaism and the Jewish community in America and Israel. Central to the concerns of the religious survivors is the preservation and transmission of the Jewish past. Potok's yeshiva teachers and scholars try to build new centers of Jewish learning in America and Steiner's Israeli Nazi hunters try to bring Nazis to justice and retain the Holocaust in the historic record opposing forces that would diminish or deny its significance. In the fictional worlds of Cohen, Ozick, and Potok, preservation and transmission of the Jewish sacred legacy is essential to the witness's testimony. Enoch Vand begins to study the Torah and the Talmud, Joseph Brill develops a dual Hebrew/Western curriculum, and Bleilip returns to the orthodoxy he scorned. Potok's rabbis and writers are strengthened in their devotion to Jewish practices and learning; Simon Stern builds a survivors' compound on the Akiva model. Even prewar Anglophile Sammler manifests renewed interest in Jewish particularity and history. Singer's Communists, Socialists, and secular intellectuals often recant and return to the values of Jewish orthodoxy or ethics. In one way or another, these protagonists respond to the

Holocaust tragedy by revitalizing their Jewish identities and commitments. They become committed to "increased emphasis on Jewishness and traditionalism . . . [as] part of the postHolocaust sensibility."[19]

Wallant, Bellow, Singer, Steiner, and Cohen create survivor communities that function like a Greek chorus, amplifying the tragic hero's positions and commenting on the actions and opinions of the principal dramatic figures. This device has been particularly valuable for enlarging the Holocaust canvases beyond the protagonist's experience and in incorporating the diversity of Holocaust history and the national peculiarities and operations of distinctive ghettos and camps. Thus, through the extended survivor community, Wallant deals with the Buchenwald and Bergen-Belsen camps; Bellow with the Lodz Ghetto and Buchenwald, in addition to Polish forest partisan units; Singer with the Nazi occupations of Poland and Russia; Steiner with the German, British, French, and Russian spheres of influence as well as various ghettos and camps experienced by a team of Nazi hunters; and Cohen with the French, Austrian, and German experiences.

A minor theme in the fiction is the interpretation of the Holocaust in light of the establishment of an independent Jewish homeland in Israel, the second major event of twentieth-century Jewish history. Although the American novelists neither link the two events politically, suggesting that Israel's birth was an acceptable outcome of the Holocaust, nor suggest that the meaning of the Holocaust is found in the creation of a Jewish state, they often link the perils of contemporary Israeli survival to the threats in the Nazi era to European Jewry. Analogies are often drawn either in character dialogue or authorial voice between Nazi and Arab anti-Jewish rhetoric and propaganda. Bellow, Singer, Steiner, and Elman set portions of their Holocaust narratives in Israel and introduce Israeli Holocaust survivors who parallel Arab rhetoric, war, and terrorist policies to those of the Nazis and proudly contrast Israeli military assertiveness with historic Jewish diasporan passivity in the face of anti-Semitism. Even the non-Israeli Jewish characters in this fiction interpret Israeli political and military policies regarding security according to Holocaust history. Although the topic of Jewish immigration to Israel is generally given short shrift in American fiction, it is a concern of the Holocaust fiction, appearing as a political theme in Bellow's, Elman's, and Steiner's works, and as political and spiritual themes in Singer's and Potok's works.

A related subject of American Holocaust fiction is the post *Shoah* status of theodicy and Judaism. Called into question are the three pillars of historic Judaism: God, Torah, and the Jewish people. The Holocaust, more than any other event in Jewish history, taxes the Jew's faith in a just and merciful God and provokes questions about the nature of God, the covenant between God and Israel, and the nature of man. Since the covenant implies a moral partnership between God and His people, the Jew asserts his moral position in these protestations. Jews question the meaning of Jewish identity in our time, whether traditional Jewish responses to evil and persecution are still viable options, and what kind of Judaism is appropriate in the postHolocaust era.

Jewish novelists write as descendants of the biblical protestors and interrogators of divine purpose. Judaism has a tradition of theological protest dating from the biblical histories of Job, Abraham, Moses, and Jeremiah. Elie Wiesel uses the metaphor of a trial in *The Gates of the Forest*, a tale of four rabbis who convene a court in their concentration camp to confront God with His sins. The prosecutor announces his intent "to convict God of murder, for He is destroying His people and the Law He gave them from Mt. Sinai."[20] Not unexpectedly, the judges return a guilty verdict. Without the formal trial structure, I. B. Singer also incorporates the theme of judging the Almighty for Holocaust sins. Several characters in *Enemies, A Love Story* and the heroine of "The Mentor" try to convict the passive deity. Chaim Potok's Israeli Holocaust survivor and George Steiner's Nazi hunter also indict God of crimes against the Jewish people. Richard Elman's Yagodah, a secularist, asks the pertinent questions without the benefit of traditional Judaic learning.

Representative of the major Jewish Holocaust theological and philosophical responses are questioning and protest against God's inaction in the face of injustice. Contemporary theses promulgated by Richard Rubenstein, Emil Fackenheim, Eliezar Berkovits, and Irving Greenberg derive from the biblical and prophetic tradition. Although the moderns categorically reject *mi-penei hata' einu*, an explanation that posits catastrophe as just retribution for sin, they differ widely in their conclusions. Rubenstein argues that the only response to the death camps is rejection of God, posits the meaninglessness of existence in a universe in which there is neither divine plan nor divine concern, and proposes that the human condition reflects no transcendental purpose. Instead of a covenantal bond, Rubenstein urges a strong commitment to the survival of the Jewish people. Emil Fackenheim insists on reaffirming God and Judaism, arguing that to do otherwise would give Hitler a posthumous victory. Eliezar Berkovits accepts the uniqueness of the Holocaust in the magnitude of its destruction, but rejects the notion of a consequent unique theological dilemma, since Jewry has throughout its history suffered terrible persecutions and retained faith. Irving Greenberg accepts Holocaust-wrought vacillation between moments of faith and renunciation.

In *After Auschwitz: Radical Theology and Contemporary Judaism,* Rubenstein denies divine will and the world and history as manifestations of divine purpose. Rejecting God and the traditional Jewish theological framework, Rubenstein affirms instead the existential belief that people must create meaning and value. He argues further that with the "death of God," the significance of the community of Israel is more important: "It is precisely because human existence is tragic, ultimately hopeless, and without meaning that we treasure our religious community."[21] For Rubenstein the postHolocaust Jewish identity is fashioned in "the shared vicissitudes of history, culture, and psychological perspective."[22] One finds the characters expounding this view in "The Mentor," *The 28th Day of Elul, The Portage to San Cristobal of A.H.,* and "The Last Mohican."

In *God's Presence in History,* Emil Fackenheim rejects the Rubenstein thesis, countering that a more appropriate response to the Holocaust is to keep God and Israel together. Also rejecting the *mi-penei hata' einu* theory of retribution for sins, Fackenheim does not seek to explain the Holocaust because its enormity transcends all traditional explanations of suffering and evil. In his postwar reappraisal of Judaism, Fackenheim finds Jewish liberal belief in the perfectability of man invalid, but still affirms the orthodox position on the centrality of God in human history and the covenantal bond between God and Israel. Fackenheim's acceptance of the covenant is based on a reading of Jewish history that distinguishes central events as "root" experiences and "epoch making events":

> The most powerful incidents, such as those connected with the Exodus from Egypt and the giving of the Torah at Sinai, actually created the religious identity of the Jewish people. These creative extraordinary happenings Fackenheim calls "root experiences." [They] are

historical events of such a formative character that they continue to influence all future "presents" of the people . . . these past moments legislate to every future era . . . They belong to the collective memory of the people and continue to claim the allegiance of the nation. . . . [They] provide the accessibility of Divine Presence in the here and now . . . thus the Jew is "assured that the saving God of the past saves still."[23]

Distinguished from the "root experiences" are those occasions Fackenheim calls "epoch making events," which are not formative in that they do not create the essentials of Jewish faith.

but rather they are crises that challenge the "root experiences" through new situations, which test the resiliency and generality of "root experiences" to answer to new and unprecedented conditions and realities. For example, the destruction of the First and Second Temples severely tested whether or not the commanding and saving Presence of God could be maintained.[24]

The Holocaust is an "epoch making event." Yet Fackenheim contends "the Jew must still affirm the continued proximity of God in Jewish history . . . and he must affirm the present reality of the people's 'root experience' of a commanding God (at Sinai) now commanding Israel from within the Holocaust itself."[25] The religious Jews in the fictions of Potok, Singer, and Ozick share these thoughts without expressing them in Fackenheimian vocabulary. This view is at the heart of Singer's *Shosha*, Ozick's "Bloodshed" and *Cannibal Galaxy*, Cohen's *In the Days of Simon Stern*, and Potok's *In the Beginning.*

Fackenheim takes the Jobian position, "Though He slay me, yet shall I trust in Him," (Job 13:15) and his rationale is that Jews are under a sacred obligation to survive as Jews. Jews are "forbidden to despair of the God of Israel, lest Judaism perish" and Hitler be granted a posthumous victory.[26] For Fackenheim, the God of deliverance is affirmed in the establishment and maintenance of the State of Israel. What Auschwitz denies, Israel affirms and provides living testimony to God's continued presence in history. Bellow's Sammler and Malamud's Bok come to similar conclusions in secular terms and the religious devotees in the fiction of Potok, Ozick, Singer, and Cohen express these convictions in terms more closely associated with, although not necessarily derivative of, Fackenheim.

In *Faith after the Holocaust,* Eliezar Berkovits searches the tradition for concepts to help deal with the death camps. He joins Rubenstein and Fackenheim in rejecting the *mi-penei hata' einu* thesis, arguing that it is "an injustice absolute,"[27] but adds, "It was an injustice countenanced by God."[28] He arrives at this belief through the tradition's explanation of God's tolerance of evil known as *hester panim* (Hiding of the Face of God), postulating that occasionally God inexplicably turns His face from man and that such hiddenness is necessary for man to exercise free will, because only by withdrawing from history and abstaining from intervention in the human condition, despite great injustice and evil, does God facilitate freedom of choice. Thus, God suffers evil humanity while allowing the innocent and good to suffer. For Berkovits, this view of theodicy permits the Jew to continue to believe in the deity despite Holocaust reality.[29] Elman's Alex Yagodah arrives at a similar position at the close of his theological debate. Berkovits further insists that the Holocaust not be treated as an isolated event in Jewish history; he agrees that it must be analyzed within the framework of past Jewish experience. Although Berkovits acknowledges that the Holocaust, like previous persecutions of Jewry, poses questions about God's providential presence and moral perfection, he disputes the notion that it represents a novum in Jewish history whose essential distinctness creates a new problem for religious faith different from previous persecutions. The continued existence of Jewry in the face of its long history of suffering is, for Berkovits, proof that God exists despite His periodic concealment. The Jew must assess God not simply on the basis of His Holocaust passivity but upon consideration of all history, including the redemptive joy of rebuilt Zion, the "ingathering of the exiles," in the ancient homeland. Concurring with Fackenheim, Berkovits believes that just as Auschwitz is evidence of the self-concealed God, the rebirth of Israel as a Jewish state and its survival are evidence of "a smile on the face of God."[30] Illustrating this proposition, I. B. Singer's survivor-penitent, Shapiro, advances from denunciation of the silent God of the Holocaust era to his spiritual return to a loving God in the rebuilt Zion.

In the essay "Cloud of Smoke, Pillar of Fire: Judaism, Christianity, and Modernity After the Holocaust," Irving Greenberg inquires where God was during Auschwitz and whether His silence was another instance of hiding His face or whether He ceased to be the God of trust. Greenberg argues that even if we are able to retain belief in the caring biblical God after the Holocaust, such affirmation is problematic and inconstant, comprising "moment faiths."[31] Like Elie Wiesel, Greenberg acknowledges that since the death camps, there are times when "the flames and smoke of the burning children blot out faith," but these moments of doubt are interspersed with moments of faith. The tension between these polarities of doubt and faith constitute a major thematic interest in American Holocaust fiction and may be seen in the fiction of Bellow, Ozick, Singer, and Malamud.

The Jewish messianic and mystical interpretation that catastrophe requires greater human effort to repair in the face of the hidden God also finds expression in American literature. Lurianic kabbalists respond to Divine self-exile with a call for *tikkun* (a continual act of human repair and restoration) by means of proper *kavanah* (intention, devotion, meditation). Human assistance in the achievement of God's purpose is an intricate part of the kabbalistic response to evil. The view that the interruption of divine duty does not excuse human convenantal responsibility finds vital expression in the fiction of I. B. Singer, Bernard Malamud, Arthur Cohen, Cynthia Ozick, Saul Bellow, and Chaim Potok.

The moral dilemma of whether to speak or remain reverentially silent in tribute to the Holocaust victims is resolved in this fiction on the side of the sacred duty to bear witness. Unlike Israeli writers of the *Palmach* generation—those who fought in the War of Independence, who sought to write an Israeli rather than a Diasporan literature, who sought to separate themselves from the passive ethos of European Jewry, and who experienced the conflict between longing to forget the Holocaust and compulsion to remember—for the Americans, bearing witness and the act of Holocaust transmission itself are central Holocaust themes. After writing six novels on the Holocaust, Elie Wiesel explored the dilemma in *The Oath* and examined the possibility that it might have been better to have remained silent in the face of such evil. Silence might have been the more powerful witness. *The Oath* chronicles his conviction that if a single life is saved by telling the Holocaust story, he is morally obliged to speak, even if in so doing he violates an earlier oath to keep silent, as did the narrator. The novelists represented in this study do not grapple with the dilemma of speech or silence. They and their protagonists are morally committed to bearing witness. If there is any dissent, it is in the manner of articulation. Indeed, some survivor-characters assert that the essential purpose of surviving is to bear witness. So significant is the role of survivor-witness that characters are specifically designated as scribes, journalists, and teachers. Arthur Cohen's book is narrated by Nathan, the scribe who brings to his *hurban* narration the dedication of a Torahic scribe. His vision is panoramic, placing the Holocaust in the context of ancient and modern persecutions of the Jews. Bellow's Sammler abandons writing about aesthetics to concentrate on spiritual studies. On the occasion of the Six Day War, he is compelled to write a journalistic account of the event. Singer's writer-protagonists record the lives of the dead, chronicle *shtetl* memories to commemorate the Holocaust dead, or act as interpreters or facilitators through whom survivors may tell their histories. Cynthia Ozick's Enock Vand literally documents the Holocaust in his role as a U.S. government record keeper. In "The Suitcase," witness testimony is the vehicle for the direct confrontation of a Jew and German. In "Levitation" and *The Messiah of Stockholm* oral history is given. Steiner's Nazi hunters bear witness by bringing Nazis to trial. Malamud and Potok create survivor-mentors to transmit Holocaust history, Jewish values, and learning. Epstein approaches the issue visually creating an artist and two photographers who record for posterity life and death in the ghetto. As each writer bears witness to the uniqueness of the Holocaust, a dual sense of mission emerges. Not only do they attest to the historic record and commemorate the dead, each warns humanity of its capacity for genocide.

How does literature—an art form people use to bring order to chaos, to impose form on the formless, to explore the vagaries of human thought and emotion—give form and structure to the atrocities of a schematic, mechanized, and socially organized program of annihilation that denies the human values literature celebrates? To structure a creative response to a destructive force is an anomaly. Nothing about the Holocaust is aesthetic. It is a denial of the creative instinct. Just as the Holocaust was beyond normal human experience, so too the imaginative recreation of it demands, many believe, a language and literature somehow different from that which expressed pre-Holocaust suffering. The aesthetic problem is to find language appropriate to the Nazi universe, language to convey a bureaucracy of evil. Literature has long explored evil; it has traced the careers of Machiavellian villains such as Tamberlaine, Macbeth, and Richard III; it has treated obsessive megalomaniacs such as Ahab and Rappaccini, but never before has humanity, and literature, encountered evil in the magnitude of the Holocaust. Such desolation, it has been argued, required a new artistic style, a new language. "The difficulty," as A. Alverez suggests, "is to find language for this world without values, with its meticulously controlled lunacy and bureaucracy of suffering."[32] Although there may be no adequate Holocaust aesthetic, there is nonetheless the experience that demands artistic rendition and writers have struggled to create a language and literature to convey some measure of the Holocaust trauma.

The writer's problem is to devise a means of presenting material for which there is no adequate analogue in human history and a subject that many believe is beyond art. There is no archetypal or familiar model, no literary touchstone, no exemplar for Holocaust fiction. Documentary realism would be a mere repetition of the archivists and historians. Writers had to devise methods for fusing documentary matter with refashioned conventional literary models to convey the image of man and the social order wrought by the Holocaust. American writers learned from their European and Israeli colleagues and from the patterns of behavior and responses to extreme experiences described by diarists, archivists, historians, and social scientists and integrated the documentary material with artistic vision. American Holocaust fiction is a literature of hindsight. The creative writers immersed themselves in the voluminous testimonials and diaries that were retrieved from hiding places, ghettos, camps and those that were written after the war in the histories and documents published by Holocaust researchers. Survivors have provided materials novelists have diligently studied— eyewitness accounts of the genocidal capacity of humankind, as well as its capacity to endure.

In his description of Yiddish writers' responses to the catastrophe, David Roskies argues that they had "basically two approaches to draw upon from the fund of ancient and modern sources; one that imploded history, and the other that made the Holocaust the center of apocalypse."[33] A similar principle may be noted in Jewish-American Holocaust fiction, with Singer, Ozick, Cohen, and Potok on the first side of the equation and Malamud, Wallant, Elman, Epstein, Steiner, and Bellow on the second. Writers steeped in Jewish history could draw upon the centuries-long history of persecution suffered by European Jews. Because the Nazis followed church precedent with the imposition of yellow badges, the defiling of Torah scrolls, the burning of synagogues, the public humiliation of rabbis, the establishment of Jewish ghettos, the expropriation of Jewish property, and the mass expulsions and murders, and because the Nazis followed historic precedent in coordinating their violence with the Jewish calendar, some novelists invoke historic persecutions as referents and correspondents—albeit on a smaller scale—to the modern disaster. Writers sensitive to Jewish history commonly invoke the paradigms of destruction and desecration as imprecise evocations of Holocaust loss. Thus, Singer invokes the Chmielnicki and Petlurian Massacres and villains such as Pharoah and Haman; Cohen invokes the Spanish Inquisition and Ozick the plight of the Marranos and persecutions in the time of Akiva; and Malamud invokes the blood libel persecution. Representative of this approach is Arthur Cohen's vast compendium of Jewish history, his disjointed narrative style interrupted by essay entries, philosophic digressions, stories within stories, and parables, all used to create a background for viewing the Holocaust in the historic context of traditional European anti-Semitism. Andre Schwartz-Bart's use of Jewish history in *The Last of the Just,* from tenth-century persecutions through the Nazi slaughter, finds its counterpart in Ozick's *Cannibal Galaxy,* with its allusions to *midrashic* Akiva, Uriah, and Zechariah stories, her Egyptian references, and *Ta'anit* lessons. At the opposite extreme is Leslie Epstein who has little interest in traditional Judaism, but a deep interest in the Holocaust and a particular fascination with the personality of Chaim Rumkowski, the model for his ghetto elder. Aside from one scene evoking medieval, church-orchestrated anti-Semitism, Epstein essentially apprehends the Holocaust as its own archetype, and rather than compare it with other historic anti-Jewish persecutions, he introduces a catalogue of literary genres—the Greek satyr play, the medieval morality play, and Renaissance drama—to evoke the cultural context of evil; and he fuses that atmosphere with the Lodz Ghetto as a touchstone of Nazi reality.

History is a creative resource throughout American Holocaust fiction, reflecting the artist's primary loyalty to fact while allowing either the fusion or superimposition of specific events to convey an imaginative response. Incorporation of historic figures into the fictional context is a successful device in American Holocaust literature. Saul Bellow and Leslie Epstein examine the flamboyant and enigmatic elder of the Lodz Ghetto, Chaim Rumkowski; Bellow dramatizes in a brief vignette the simultaneous tragedy and absurdity of the Nazi universe, and Epstein structures his

novel around the career of the elder. Epstein fuses invented scenes
with episodes from the Warsaw, Lodz, and Vilna ghettos reported
in Leonard Tushnet's *Pavement of Hell*. He dramatizes ghetto starvation, slave labor, public beatings, the display of tortured bodies as
object lessons, public executions, and mass murders. Aside from
John Hershey's *The Wall*, it is difficult to identify American fiction
that is as heavily dependent and true to the histories and documents chronicling the ghetto experience as is *King of the Jews*.
Cynthia Ozick's description of the roundup of Parisian Jews owes
much to *Vichy France and the Jews*, and her fantasy about the recovery of the Bruno Schulz manuscript is based on the historic account
of one German's protection and another's murder of the novelist.
Similarly, Richard Elman's treatment of the Hungarian situation in
1944 reflects a close reading of the Hungarian section in Raul
Hilberg's *The Destruction of the European Jews*. Although his incorporation of historic figures is limited to references to the Joel Brand
case and the work of Rudolf Kastner and his unsuccessful negotiations with the Allies to exchange war supplies for the lives of thousands of Hungarian Jews, Elman's work focuses on the systematic
isolation of Hungarian Jews in 1944 through restrictive legislation
and deportations. Elman depicts rape, expropriation of civil rights,
and human branding. Despite its faulty chronology, Elman's medical examination and tattooing session suggests the same dehumanization that Primo Levi's *Haftling* 174517 feels, recognizing
"Nothing belongs to us anymore, they have taken away our clothes,
our shoes, even our hair. . . . They will even take away our
name."[34]

   Whereas Epstein and Elman dramatize these events because
their work is set in the European sphere during the Holocaust,
those whose narratives are set in America use symbolism, memory,
nightmare, or survivor dialogue to evoke the same events. "Perhaps," as A. Alverez noted, "the most convincing way [of delineating the concentrationary world] is that by which dreams express
anguish: by displacement, disguise, and indirection."[35] Illustrative
of the successful use of the dream device to create Holocaust reality
is Bellow's creation in *The Victim* of a disorientation and entrapment nightmare, which assaults the senses with an immediacy
and brutality that imitates Holocaust violence. Wallant also uses the
dream device in his nightmare series in *The Pawnbroker*: the transport dream in which parents helplessly witness their child drown-
ing in excrement, nightmares in which the protagonist is subjected

to surgical experimentation without the benefit of anesthetic, and others in which he is witness to an electrocution and his wife's enforced whoredom. Throughout *The Pawnbroker*, Nazerman's nightmare memories are juxtaposed with American ghetto scenes at key stressful moments to suggest the brutality and sadistic attitude of Germans toward their Jewish victims. Potok uses both dreams and a stream of consciousness reverie to convey an American's response to newspaper photographs of Buchenwald. Writers often turn to the dream device both to convey the displacement, confusion, indirection, and incoherence of the victim during the Nazi period and to serve as a barometer measuring the failure of the victim to repress the past.

In contrast to the indirection of dream and involuntary memory, direct speeches focusing on Nazi crimes are offered by Cohen's survivor-narrator, Nathan of Gaza, who records the history of starvation, disease, and illness among the inmates of Auschwitz; Ozick's Vand, who documents the various camp death tolls for American intelligence services; and Steiner's Nazi hunter, who iterates a long catalogue of Nazi atrocities in his prosecution of Hitler. Similarly, Sammler's recurring recollections of a massacre in front of an open mass grave serve as a persistent reminder of Nazi atrocities.

Although there is no equal in these works for the surreal quality of Jerzy Kosinski's *The Painted Bird* and Gunter Gras's *Tin Drum*, fantasy occasionally appears in American Holocaust fiction. Examples of the use of fantasy are found in I. B. Singer's "The Cafeteria," in which the ghosts of Hitler's henchmen are summoned; in "A Wedding in Brownsville," where the dead Jews of an East-European village are revived; Bellow's creation in *Mr. Sammler's Planet* of a mad scene dramatizing Bruch's Buchenwald-generated psychic disturbances; Ozick's levitation scene; Cohen's projection of a modern Spanish Inquisition; and Steiner's resurrection of Hitler.

Whereas some Europeans felt they had to disrupt conventional literary forms to write Holocaust literature, the Americans often used traditional Jewish and Western forms. Western forms often highlight the connections between Holocaust brutality and the civilization where the brutality took shape and was sustained. Illustrative of this method is Epstein's introduction of Greek, medieval, and Shakespearean models to render his themes of political corruption and radical evil. Conversely, in writings from the

Hebrew and Yiddish traditions, American writers found conventions and language appropriate to the unique Holocaust sufferings of the Jews. Ozick and Cohen introduce the Hebrew *midrashic* legend, Singer and Potok lamentation liturgy, biblical allusions, Hasidic implications of restoration, and covenant theology to place the Holocaust in the historic context of Jewish martyrdom. A comparative study of methods of Holocaust delineation reveals that Americans share the elegaic, lamentative tone and its parodic countercommentary commonly found in the writing of Jewish European and Israeli writers. Arthur Cohen, Cynthia Ozick, I. B. Singer, and Chaim Potok draw on traditional Hebraic responses to national catastrophe, invoking the collective Jewish memory. These novelists are knowledgeable heirs of the rabbinic literature; their touchstones are Jewish theology and history. Their characters are often located in communities whose values are ultimately Jewish rather than secular. They are more often firmly rooted in the Jewish cultural and religious contexts, and they express themselves in biblical, *midrashic*, mystical, and messianic themes when responding to the *Shoah*. They speak in authentic Jewish voices. Adherence to the collective history distinguishes the characters of these authors from the characters in the works of Elman and Wallant, who are generally secular and assimilated rather than religiously or culturally Jewish. In the Holocaust fiction of the latter, attention is focused on the suffering of the individual, whereas in the former, the suffering individual translates his plight into the collective experience, because he is much more attuned to Jewish history. Readers of Cohen's *In the Days of Simon Stern* and Ozick's *The Cannibal Galaxy* learn of the history of Jewish martyrology, as one also does in Andre Schwarz-Bart's *The Last of the Just*. Simon Stern and Joseph Brill understand that their destinies are tied to the Jewish people and to Jewish history. They are culturally bound to Jewish civilization despite their diasporan location. Bellow's Arthur Sammler, on the other hand, represents assimilated Jews arbitrarily subjected to catastrophe in Europe because of an accident of Jewish birth, who later choose Jewish association as part of their Holocaust witness. In Elman's trilogy, the characters consistently evidence their lack of Jewish education. Aside from Lilo's countercommentary prayer-parody, biblical allusion is superimposed by the novelist using the omniscient voice, rather than imaginatively integrated as in the fiction of Singer, Cohen, and Ozick. In place of Jewish cultural loss sustained in the Holocaust, Bellow, Wallant, and Malamud stress historic data, concentrating on the political, social, and psychological ramifications of the Holocaust.)

Among the most effective techniques Americans borrowed from Hebrew and Yiddish Holocaust literature is countercommentary. In *Against the Apocalypse*, David Roskies explicates the fascination of secular Jewish writers with collective catastrophe through the use of parody and the inversion of sacred texts, which emphasizes the subversion of God's principles in the historic context. Thus, the violation of the text mirrors the violation of the covenant. The prayer-parodies in the fiction of Singer and Elman reveal this attitude. Lilo's *Kaddish* achieves the same forceful expression of anguish that is rendered in the Yiddish and Hebrew writers' irreverent use of the sacred text, and it functions as they do: "to imitate the sacrilege, [to disrupt] the received order of the text in the same way as the enemy, . . . disrupted the order of the world."[36] Roskies offers an important distinction between those who use parody constructively and destructively, arguing that the use of parody is present in

> anger deflected through the hallowed texts, a highly mediated and ritualized form of anger. By making the text seem for a while crazy and corrupt, the individual sufferer expands its meaning, allowing subsequent sufferers to enter the breach.[37]

Generally the pattern that follows this inversion is an ode of defiant affirmation, which is clearly present in Lilo's passage, a passage whose sequence mimics prayer allowing her to maintain faith even as the promise is subverted. The angry commentators of the twentieth century share the dismay of the Hebrew poet who played on sound and sense, transposing the traditional petition "Who is like You, O Lord, among the mighty" (*elim*) (Exodus 15:11) to "Who is like You among the mute" (*illemim*) to register dissatisfaction with the silent God.[38]

A related phenomenon in Holocaust literature that Lawrence Langer and Alvin Rosenfeld have noted is the revisionary and antithetical tendency in European Holocaust writing to refute and reject literary antecedents. Langer demonstrates the Holocaust-wrought subversion of the *Bildungsroman* in Wiesel's *Night*, which inverts the traditional pattern of initiating a young boy into society; Rosenfeld addresses a similar reversal in Primo Levi's *Survival in Auschwitz*, which renders the concentrationary goal of dehumanization and debasement of prisoners. Rosenfeld reads these literary inversions as repudiations of the antecedent literature and culture, "a denial not only of an antecedent literary assertion but also of its implicit premises and explicit affirmations."[39] Perhaps because Americans were not victims, one finds little of that tendency in American writers who remain reluctant to parody literary forms in Holocaust fiction. On the contrary, American writers often use traditional forms and devices, in addition to subversion and parody, to dramatize the connections between the Holocaust and its antecedents in European culture. Leslie Epstein introduces a contemporary, wagon-staged morality play to correlate Christian and Nazi anti-Semitism and incorporates a Greek satyr play to expose Nazi corruption. Rather than suggesting disillusionment with traditional literary forms or the failure of literature to posit rational, humane, moral and ethical ideals, Epstein incorporates these celebrated forms either to emphasize German corruption or, as in the case of his superb production of a ghetto *Macbeth*, to dramatize the capacity of art to inspire human compassion in the midst of moral decay. Epstein's technique here is illustrative of Jewish American writers' shared antiapocalyptic vision. They write as witnesses against Nazism and witnesses for humanistic values normally associated with literature, even in an age of atrocity.

Whereas European survivor-writers bear witness in their literature to that which they encountered, American writers can only join their colleagues as "the generation that bears the scar without the wound, sustaining memory without direct experience. It is this generation that has the obligation, self-imposed and self-accepted . . . to describe a meaning and wrest instruction from the historical."[40]

# CHAPTER ONE

*Scars of Outrage: The Holocaust in* The Victim *and*
Mr. Sammler's Planet

Saul Bellow's nonfiction references to the
Holocaust are often pleas for the survival of a people and culture
and attacks on the pathology of anti-Semitism and its historic re-
currence. *To Jerusalem and Back* reveals a postHolocaust consciousness ardently defending the right to Jewish survival in a national Jewish homeland:

> There is one fact of Jewish life unchanged by the creation of a Jewish
> State; you cannot take your right to live for granted. Others can; you
> cannot. . . . Jews, because they are Jews, have never been able to take
> the right to live as a natural right. . . . The Jews did not become
> nationalistic because they drew strength from their worship of any-
> thing resembling Germanic *Blut und Eisen* but because they alone,
> amongst the peoples of the earth, had not established a natural right
> to exist unquestioned in the lands of their birth. This right is still
> clearly not granted them, not even in the liberal West.[1]

Bellow was at the forefront of American readiness to address
anti-Semitism in fiction. Throughout the canon, Bellow presents
the theme of anti-Semitism dramatically, allusively, and sym-

36

bolically.[2] The Holocaust is a subdued, ever present component in Saul Bellow's fiction. Although the Holocaust is rarely at the dramatic center, the works are rich in characters haunted by its spectre. When six million Jews were being methodically murdered, Bellow's literary response to the Holocaust was muted. His first novel, *Dangling Man,* published in 1944 at the height of the Holocaust, alludes, in a speech assigned to a German character, to the European folkloric conception of the Jew as the incarnation of evil. Set during the time of World War II, the novel's protagonist appears to be Jewish, although he is not so identified. Absent from the foreground of the novel, the Holocaust enters metaphorically through Joseph's dream of searching through a roomful of corpses, the result of a massacre. Similarly, Augie March, the all-American boy of Bellow's third novel, who has served in the U.S. Coast Guard, demonstrates no particular concern about the Holocaust. In contrast to Augie's peripheral Jewish identity, the historian Moses Herzog has a strong association with Jewish culture and history. During his visits to the Warsaw Ghetto, he finds "the stones still smelling of wartime murders."[3] Humboldt Fleisher refuses an invitation to present a lecture series in Berlin because he is fearful that former Nazis will kidnap him. He reasons that a year in Germany would be a constant reminder of "the destruction of the death camps, the earth soaked in blood, and the fumes of cremation still in the air of Europe."[4] It is in *The Victim* and *Mr. Sammler's Planet* that Bellow turns to substantive Holocaust exploration—symbolically in the former and realistically in the latter.

*The Victim,* Bellow's most comprehensive exploration of anti-Semitism, was published two years after World War II. Critical discussion of *The Victim* has rightly centered on the dynamics of interaction between Jew and anti-Semite. Perhaps because Bellow was ahead of his time, perhaps because his treatment was on symbolic and allusive levels, perhaps because readers were not ready to face Holocaust atrocities in literature, Holocaust matter in *The Victim* has passed virtually unnoticed in literary criticism. The Holocaust symbolism of the novel is itself a matter of complexity and is certainly of importance to the work's critical evaluation. Bellow's method reflects an historic pattern. Nazi persecution of European Jewry may be discerned as a product of centuries of European anti-Semitism. So, too, may the novel's Holocaust imagery be read as an organic outgrowth of its treatment of the complex nature of anti-Semitism.

Set against the backdrop of the Depression and World War

II, *The Victim* pits Jew and anti-Semite against each other. Victim and victimizer alternate roles. Asa Leventhal, a first-generation American Jew, and Kirby Allbee, a colonial descendant and anti-Semite, stereotype each other and suffer both their own and the other's prejudicial views. Asa Leventhal hopes to protect himself against society's ills, from the victimizing forces of the external world. Kirby Allbee, Asa's emotional double, forms a parasitic relationship with Asa, demanding compensation for an imagined injury. A few years prior to the action of the narrative, Allbee arranged a job interview for Leventhal with his boss. Rudiger was rude; Leventhal argued with him, and several days later Allbee was fired. A minor character suggests that Allbee recommended Leventhal knowing all along that his boss would react unfavorably to Leventhal, that he was in fact playing a trick on the Jew that backfired. Nevertheless, Allbee appears early in the novel to charge that Asa has vindictively destroyed him to avenge derogatory remarks he made about Jews, to blame Leventhal for his dismissal and subsequent downfall, and to insist on compensation. Convinced that the Jew is evil incarnate, Allbee uses diction evoking the stereotypical view of a Jew as a Shylockian, calculating avenger. Allbee's antagonism toward Jews stems from his feeling of being a member of an older order, one traditionally bred to rule and influence American society, which is being displaced by the descendants of non-English immigrants. Allbee sees himself as a pawn, "a victim of social determinism and social displacement."[5] Blaming the Jew for the Gentile's economic troubles has a long and treacherous history, including its Nazi variation during the pre-genocide period as an excuse for forcing Jews out of their professions and businesses and for expropriating their property. Allbee, as his name suggests, is a classic anti-Semite. He relates to Jews not as individuals, but as members of a group he hates, a people he considers to be at the root of evil, selfish and profit-seeking exploiters of Gentiles, avengers exacting a pound of flesh for a presumed injury.

Because Asa considers himself lucky to have escaped his role as society's victim, he is sensitive to Allbee's plight. Although Bellow never makes clear whether Asa was responsible for Allbee's sacking, Asa initially rejects Allbee's charge and asserts that alcoholism led to his dismissal and deterioration, but Asa then becomes obsessed with the issue and undertakes a probing self-examination. He did not plot to ruin Allbee, yet he acknowledges responsibility for the unintentional harm he caused by arguing with Allbee's boss.

His reaction to Allbee's irrational charges is reflected in the novel's epigraph from *The Thousand and One Nights,* which suggests that one is unavoidably responsible for one's actions, even if ignorant of their consequences, even if they cause unintentional and accidental harm to another. Asa, who "liked to think that 'human' meant accountable,"[6] takes Allbee into his home and puts up with Allbee's abuse of his generosity, but finally ejects him when Allbee brings a whore into the Leventhal bed. Returning to his victim's home to commit suicide, Allbee nearly kills Asa in the process. Thus, through a series of ironic inversions, victim and victimizer exchange roles. As Asa's *Doppelgänger,* Allbee has forced Asa to see himself in a manner he hoped to evade and becomes the agent through whom Asa heals himself. True to the Hebrew meaning of his name (healer or physician), Asa attempts to heal himself through introspection and his oppressor through charitable assistance.

The major dilemma of *The Victim* centers on the issue of moral accountability for intentional and unintentional consequences of one's acts. Although he does not articulate his position with reference to traditional Jewish sources, Asa's behavior coincides with Judaic law that declares that even if the person harms another unintentionally, compensation is obligatory. Thus, through the course of his education and healing, Asa learns the nature of unintended sin and acknowledges his responsibility to Allbee, who he has unwittingly injured. Leventhal's confrontation with Allbee may be interpreted as a trial of his Jewishness, "challenging his ability to be a *mentsch,* a human being, to act according to the Jewish moral code under difficult circumstances."[7]

Beyond the pathology of anti-Semitism revealed in the dramatic confrontation of the antagonists, Bellow probes polar Jewish responses to anti-Semitism. Unlike his immigrant father who is indifferent to gentile ridicule because he is secure in his own culture and rejects the gentile world as undesirable, Asa seeks social acceptance and is pained by anti-Semitism. Asa's father is typical of those Jews who wish to maintain their distinctive Jewish identity and social separatism. Asa wants to be the Gentile's equal in a gentile society; his father harbors no such interest. A dramatic counter to Asa's sensitivity to anti-Semitism is his friend Daniel Harkavy's acquiescence to it. Harkavy responds to an anti-Semitic insult by acting as though it had not occurred. In contrast to Asa's aggressive assertions and the elder Leventhal's efforts to debunk

his oppressors' charges, Harkavy suffers silently. Both Asa's hyper-
sensitive vigilance and Harkavy's imprudent disregard of anti-
Jewish bias are symptomatic of victimization. Asa chooses to see
enemies everywhere, and Harkavy to feign blindness.

Bellow uses the conflict between Allbee and Leventhal to reveal the diverse and intricate nature of anti-Semitism. He invests
Allbee with an amalgam of twentieth-century, anti-Jewish arguments: economic displacement, cultural pollution, and racism,
which had become dominant, but had not eliminated the religious
animosity common to earlier centuries. Consistent with the anti-
Semite's pathology,[8] Allbee repeatedly speaks of Jews as a people
apart, referring to them as "You people."[9] Viewing Jews as a
people divorced from and unable to comprehend normal behavior,
Allbee despairs of Jewish restraint of the sensual spirit in diction,
which emphasizes his prejudice against Jews in business: "You
keep your spirit under lock and key. . . . You make it your business
assistant, and it's safe and tame and never leads you toward anything risky. . . . What for? What's in it? No percentage" (*V*, 133).

Illustrative of Bellow's allusive treatment of the Holocaust is
his use of figurative language and imagery to relate Allbee's anti-
Semitism to the anti-Semitism of the Nazis flourishing in the years
preceding publication of *The Victim*. Allbee's language and imagery
correspond to the Nazi propaganda of the 1930s. A descendant of
Governor Winthrop,[10] he believes that leaders of American society
should be drawn from his class and should reflect its values, and he
is, therefore, distressed by growing Jewish influence in America.
Allbee's insistence on the inordinate Jewish presence in American
civilization is the counterpart of the Nazi charge that Jews were
gaining control of German life. "It's really as if the children of
Caliban are running everything. . . . The old breeds are out"
(*V*, 131). With masterful economy of means, Bellow not only conveys the social and political implications of Allbee's remarks but
also uses Shakespearean allusion to evoke the rhetoric of Nazism.
The Caliban reference implies the Third Reich's official classifica-
tion of Jews as a subhuman species.

Not only does Allbee object to the imposition of Jewish
culture on American life, he also echoes the Nuremberg Laws of
1935—which forbade persons of more than 25 percent Jewish
blood to play the music of Bach, Beethoven, Mozart, and other
"Aryan" composers—by insisting that Jews ought not interpret
American music and literature. This belief is revealed at a party

when Allbee admonishes a Jew for singing an American spiritual: "You shouldn't sing those old songs. You have to be bred to them.... Sing a psalm, ... any Jewish song. Something you've really got feeling for" (*V*, 44). His exclusive attitude is reiterated during a later argument about Jewish encroachment on American culture. Allbee despairs that a Jewish scholar has had the audacity to publish a book on the American transcendentalists, Emerson and Thoreau. He is certain "people of such background simply couldn't understand" (*V*, 132).[11] Bellow ironically juxtaposes Allbee's comments regarding the impropriety of Jewish interpretation of American literature and philosophy with a reference to the Hebraic Book of Job. Allbee's allusion to Job illustrates his arrogance; he does not hesitate in citing a Jewish source immediately after admonishing a Jew for interpreting American literature. Further, he superimposes his Calvinist view on the Jewish text. The Calvinist position of suffering as punishment for sin is at odds with the Jewish lesson of Job, noting that even the just suffer. Distressed by this blatant anti-Semitic insistence that the Jew, no matter how assimilated to the host culture, can never fully appreciate non-Judaic Western philosophy and literature, Asa passionately associates cultural anti-Semitism with the ultimate violent variety, referring overtly to the Holocaust: "Millions of us have been killed" (*V*,133). This outburst provides internal evidence of Bellow's intention to link Allbee's racial and cultural anti-Semitism to Nazism. Although Bellow employs this direct Holocaust reference only once, his symbolic delineation of the period's atmosphere, rendered in pervasive images commonly associated with the Nazi persecution of European Jewry, together with his juxtaposition of Allbee's convictions and those of Nazi propagandists, yields an absorbing holocaustal impression augmenting *The Victim*'s thematic exploration of anti-Semitism.

Bellow consistently foreshadows or follows anti-Semitic verbal assaults on Asa with a single or fused reference to the archetypal images of the Holocaust: the yellow badge of shame, the resettlement trains, and asphyxiation by gas. Furthermore, the historic context of the Holocaust in European history is suggested by yellow, a symbol of degradation imposed on the Jewish people by the medieval church. Bellow supplements his use of yellow as a traditional image of Jewish oppression with symbols peculiar to Nazi exploitation of modern technology in carrying out its genocide program. Asa's anti-Semitic induced depressions in crowded

American trains evoke the crowded transports of European Jews destined for resettlement in concentration camps and death camps. Lethal gas, perfected by the Germans as a weapon for mass murder, is the final element in the Holocaust image cluster. Allbee's aborted assassination of his Jewish victim using his kitchen stove is a grotesque parody of the Nazis use of gas chambers and crematoria to effect the Final Solution.

Yellow images consistently appear when Asa is oppressed by the anti-Semitic remarks and behavior of his employer, Mr. Beard, his sister-in-law Elena, and her mother. Asa travels by train and ferry to Staten Island in muggy air, dampness, and gloomy yellow light to be with his terminally ill nephew. He broods about Beard's characterization of Jews as taking unfair advantage of others while anticipating an unpleasant encounter with the child's grandmother, whom he believes regards him with "spite and exultation, as though he were the devil" (*V*, 159). Asa is convinced that the old woman is full of hate because "a Jew, a man of wrong blood, of bad blood, had given her daughter two children" (*V*, 61). Bellow objectifies Asa's anxiety during the ferry ride using fire and color imagery:

> scorched, smokey, gray, and bare white . . . the light over them and over the water was akin to the yellow revealed in the slit of the eye of a wild animal, say a lion, something inhuman that didn't care about anything human. (*V*, 52)

In this early passage delineating Asa's grief for the loss of a child and a Jew to the faith and people, Bellow begins the crucial juxtaposition of yellow with fire imagery, on realistic and symbolic levels. He transforms the life-sustaining sun, into a symbol of oppression, glaring and beating down on the shoreline towers. Moreover, the oppressive yellow of the exterior environment invades the novel's interior setting. The "yellowish, stiff web over the blackness of the window" (*V*, 60) in his nephew's sickroom provides the physical context for Asa's speculation that the child's grandmother regards the fatal illness as punishment for her daughter's marriage to a Jew. In the context of the Catholic funeral service, which effectively obliterates any sign of the boy's Jewish identity, Asa's mood is objectified in the imagist fusion of a yellow shine on the chauffeur's uniform and the smoke from the officiating priest's cigarette. Returning by ferry, Asa "caught a glimpse of the murky orange of the hull, like the apparition of a furnace on the water" (*V*, 163). *Yellow* and *smoke* are transformed to the more intense *orange* and *furnace* corresponding to Asa's deepening sense of oppression. Having established variations on the theme of anti-Jewish oppression in yellow tones, Bellow blends color and gas imagery to deepen the Holocaust analogy. He suggests Asa's mounting anxiety by blending yellow and gas imagery appropriate to the novel's urban environment and Holocaust mood: "the blink of yellow light in the middle of the street started him into a trot. An eddy of exhaust gas caught him in the face" (*V*, 134). Flight and asphyxiation, common Holocaust subjects, thus heighten Bellow's exploration of anti-Semitism.

Train imagery sustains the integration of realistic cityscape and metaphoric Holocaust landscape. Bellow portrays Asa's anxiety about the de-Judaization of his nephew by employing train imagery in conjunction with yellow and gas images: the "lead car with its beam shot toward them in a smolder of dust" (*V*, 213), and Asa felt the "concussion of the train" (*V*, 213). Asa ascends from the subway into the open air and breathes with difficulty. Bellow thus encapsulates yellow, train, and gas, the prototypical Holocaust images, in a single scene of anguish stemming from intimations of religious anti-Semitism.

In another train sequence, Bellow introduces a hallucinatory, Kafkaesque atmosphere through a dream—a device also frequently employed by European Holocaust writers as a means of suggesting the disorientation and dislocation of the victim, a disordered universe, and survival anxiety.[12] The dream contains multiple symbols that function on psychological and historic levels.

> He had an unclear dream in which he held himself off like an unwilling spectator; . . . He was in a railroad station, carrying a heavy suitcase, forcing his way with it through a crowd . . . flags hanging by the hundreds. . . . He had missed his train, but the loud-speaker announced that a second section of it was leaving in three minutes. The gate was barely in sight; he could never reach it in time. There was a recoil of the crowd—the guards must have been pushing it back—and he found himself in a corridor . . . It seemed to lead down to the tracks. . . . He began to run and suddenly came to a barrier. . . . Two men stopped him. "You can't go through," . . . "This isn't open to the public. Didn't you see the sign on the door?" . . . and a push on the shoulder sent him into an alley. (*V*, 150–51)

On a psychological level, the dream suggests the anxiety created by Allbee's intrusion into Asa's life. On a symbolic level, it suggests the Nazi transports of Jews to the death camps. Railroad station, flags, barriers, recoiling crowds pushed by guards, and sealed exits call to mind the Jews of Europe trapped in the Nazi net. The dream crowd is herded by guards, much as European Jewry was herded to the transports and into the gas chambers. By chance, Asa evades transport as American Jews escaped the fate of European Jewry. The holocaustal implications of Asa's dream are achieved in its content, diction, and frenzied rhythms.

The metaphoric implications of the novel's atmosphere, introduced in the first meeting between Allbee and Leventhal on a hellish summer night,—"a redness in the sky, like the flame at the back of a vast baker's oven" (*V,* 28)—establishes the persecutor-victim relationship of anti-Semite and Jew and simultaneously foreshadows the novel's climax: Allbee's failed effort to use Asa's oven to kill himself and the unsuspecting Jew. Asa's victimization is expressed metaphorically through cremation symbols. He imagines "he was like a man in a mine who could smell smoke and feel heat but never see the flames" (*V,* 226). While Allbee plays out the death scene, Asa suffers a tortured nightmare set in a surrealistic amusement park where he sees "round yellow and red cars whipping around and bumping together" (*V,* 245). The dream environment, visually disorienting and frenzied in atmosphere, conveys Asa's anxiety stemming from his forced association with Allbee. Roused from his chaotic dream world, Asa faces a nightmarish reality: "Gas was pouring from the oven" (*V,* 246). Gasping for air at the window, Asa observes that a "long line of lamps hung down their yellow grains in the gray and blue of the street" (*V,* 246). Thus, the novel's climactic confrontation of anti-Semite and Jew merges dream and Holocaust imagery to represent the Nazi dementia that Jewry had recently suffered and survived. The confrontation is a powerful Bellovian parody of Germany's sinister Final Solution— the gas chambers and ovens of Treblinka, Chelmno, and Auschwitz.

In Bellow's pre-1970 fiction, the six million were peripheral phantoms; in *Mr. Sammler's Planet,* they live. Unlike Europeans, Elie Wiesel and Tadeusz Borowski, who set their fiction in the Holocaust era and confront the reality of the concentration camp directly, the American novelist eschews the dramatization of atrocities and camp life. Instead, Bellow evokes the past through the haunting recollections of survivors and the examination of current behavioral and emotional disorders springing from wartime brutality. Although this literary method precludes depiction of the immediacy of Nazi horror, the lasting effect of the barbarism is powerfully conveyed. Holocaust survivors continue to suffer decades after their initial victimization. Wartime clamor echoes in their minds; tormenting visions reach across chasms of time and space, oppressing the victims. For the survivors, contemporary American reality is marred by the European disaster. Bellow focuses on the consequences of survival: death or distortion of the creative impulse, impairment of the capacity to love, and religious confusion.

Although Bellow turns from symbolic to realistic Holocaust presentation in *Mr. Sammler's Planet* when he evokes the period symbolically in the later novel, he returns to the color imagery established in *The Victim*. Postwar decay is linked to Holocaust corruption through a yellow-tinged landscape:

> Symbols everywhere, and metaphysical messages. . . . There was a yellow tinge to everything, a yellow light in the sky. In this light, bad news for Sammler, bad news for humankind, bad information about the very essence of being was diffused. Something hateful, and at times overwhelming . . . in this yellow despair.[13]

*Mr. Sammler's Planet*, like *The Victim*, is set in New York, and its urban landscape is similarly realistic and symbolic. Sammler, like Leventhal, lives in a city tinged in yellows of misery, disease, and decay. However, in *Mr. Sammler's Planet*, it soon becomes clear that New York is emblematic of a worldwide condition.

The novel's structural pattern is similar to that of other survivor-centered fiction, such as *The Pawnbroker, The 28th Day of Elul*, and *The Cannibal Galaxy*. All share three common characteristics. They begin and end in the postHolocaust period of survivorship and return through memory to the pre-Holocaust order and the Holocaust universe. Another structural pattern Bellow shares with Wallant is incorporation of a survivor community acting as choral voice commenting on, corroborating, or enhancing the protagonist's Holocaust experience and interpretation. Each of these works reveals the survivors to be so maimed by Holocaust experience that they regard themselves as fundamentally apart from those unscathed by Holocaust trauma.

Arthur Sammler, an aging introspective intellectual, and his daughter were retrieved from a displaced persons' camp and brought to America where they are emotionally and financially supported by his nephew, Elya Gruner, who harbors strong family loyalties. When the novel opens, Sammler has been living in New York for twenty years with Margotte, a niece whose "family had been destroyed by the Nazis like his own" (*MSP*, 18). He wonders if he has a place among the living and is convinced that he is marked forever and peculiarly distinguished from others who have no personal Holocaust experience:

> I am aware of the abnormality of my own experience. Sometimes I wonder whether I have any place here, among other people. I assume I am one of you. But also I am not. I suspect my own judgments because my lot has been extreme. I was a studious young person, not meant for action. Suddenly, it was all action—blood, guns, graves, famine. Very harsh surgery. One cannot come out intact. For a long time I saw things with peculiar hardness . . . by force of circumstances I have had to ask myself simple questions, like 'Will I kill him? Will he kill me? If I sleep, will I ever awake? Am I really alive, or is there nothing left but an illusion of life?' And I know now that humankind marks certain people for death. (*MSP*, 209–10)

World War II, a cataclysmic event in Sammler's life, marked the turning point in his Jewish identification. The son of a wealthy, assimilated Polish-Jewish family, Sammler eschewed Jewish parochialism and espoused universalism prior to the Holocaust. As a devotee of the Bloomsbury group, he and his wife enjoyed the company of the British intelligentsia. He was proud of his association with H. G. Wells and those who advocated and worked for a world society based on tolerance and a rational and scientific attitude toward life. After a twenty-year career in London as a correspondent for Warsaw journals, he returned to Poland to reclaim the family land. There he was received neither as Anglophile nor Pole, but as Jew. His personal happiness was shattered as were his utopian dreams. Engulfed by his ancestral legacy of persecution and forced to share the violent history of millions of Polish Jews, he was coerced into accepting his relationship to the Jewish people. Sammler's wife was killed in a mass murder, and Sammler barely escaped, suffering the loss of an eye and damage to his nervous system. These injuries plague Sammler throughout the novel, erupting periodically as migraine headaches that "put him in a postepileptic condition" (*MSP*, 28). Entering Jewish history involuntarily, Sammler achieves voluntary self-identification with the Jewish people in the aftermath of his Holocaust experience and reinforces it during the Arab Israeli Six Day War.

The Holocaust enters the novel through flashbacks, involuntary memories, shared survivor experiences, and current historic interpretation of the period. Rather than employ a single, extended Holocaust flashback, Bellow renders Sammler's war memories in moments of spontaneous recollection at stressful periods in the protagonist's life. An example of this is Sammler's decision to avoid using a city bus for fear of encountering a thief who knows Sammler spied him stealing and is now threatening him. Sammler descends into the subway and suddenly recalls his descent into the mass grave in Poland and his entombment in a mausoleum. Associating his current anxiety with his time of terror in Poland, his fear of the thief is manifested in a constriction at the base of the skull that suggests "the breath of wartime Poland passing over the damaged tissues—that nerve-spaghetti, as he thought of it" (*MSP*, 9). As he tries to escape from the pickpocket, the old man remembers how he fled from fellow Polish partisans who betrayed the Jewish resistance fighters in an effort to purge postwar Poland of its few surviving Jews.

> He knew something about lying low. He had learned in Poland, in the war, in forests, cellars, passageways, cemeteries. Things he had passed through once which had abolished a certain margin or leeway ordinarily taken for granted. Taking for granted that one will not be shot stepping into the street, nor clubbed to death as one stoops to relieve oneself, nor hunted in an alley like a rat. This civil margin once removed Mr. Sammler would never trust the restoration totally. (*MSP*, 47)

In a later passage, Bellow moves further back in time to Sammler's recollection of the mass murder scene in which his wife died and he was blinded. Although Bellow constructs the episode through a series of horrendous images that move the reader to indignation, he maintains artistic distance and refrains from overt moral judgment:

> When he and sixty or seventy others, all stripped and naked and having dug their own grave, were fired upon and fell in. Bodies upon his own body. Crushing. His dead wife nearby somewhere. Struggling out much later from the weight of the corpses, crawling

out of the loose soil. Scraping on his belly. Hiding in a shed. Finding
a rag to wear. Lying in the woods many days. (*MSP*, 86–87)

A more complete account of the graveside experience appears at
the novel's midpoint. Here the remembrance of Holocaust times
moves beyond physical description to include philosophic speculation and moral judgment. As Sammler examines his obsessive concern with the past, he hypothesizes that some Navaho or Apache
must have risen from a near fatal interment in the Grand Canyon
and put it out of mind. As a moralist, Bellow juxtaposes this speculation about a hypothetical accident with a calculated government
program of genocide. He adds a chilling reference to Adolf
Eichmann's discomfort at the swelling of fresh blood around his
boots at a similar mass grave. He thereby underscores the crucial
distinction between accident and the organized brutality European
Jewry suffered. Anticipating the remonstrance of those weary of
hearing about the Holocaust, Sammler asks, "Why speak of it?"
Bellow, like Elie Wiesel, reminds us that survivors need to bear
witness, to remind the world of its silent acquiescence and its active
complicity.

From this full account of Sammler's blinding and near
murder, Bellow moves to a description of the physical deprivation
and danger of his partisan experience. Freezing and starving, resistance fighters explode bridges, destroy rails, and kill German
stragglers. Having learned violence from his Nazi and Polish persecutors, Sammler disarms and kills a German soldier who begs for
his life. By this time, Sammler is a changed man. He is able to deny
mercy to an unarmed man. He is even able to take comfort in
killing the German.

In his final chapter, Bellow sketches the mass murder scene
with even greater physical detail. Concrete sensory images abound
in a vivid evocation of the landscape of death:

> The hole deepened, the sand clay and stones of Poland, their birth-
> place, opened up. He had just been blinded, he had a stunned face,
> and he was unaware that blood was coming from him till they
> stripped and he saw it on his clothes. . . . The guns began to blast,
> and then came a different sound of soil. The thick fall of soil. . . . A
> sound of shovel-metal gritting. . . . He had clawed his way out. If he
> had been at the bottom, he would have suffocated. . . . Perhaps oth-
> ers had been buried alive in that ditch. (*MSP*, 249)

Earlier passages stressed philosophic meditation and the psychological terror of the past; this passage focuses on the torment of anticipation. The emphatic, graphic portrayal of physical movement toward death and the initial rendering of the graveside scene contribute to the novel's structural unity. The Holocaust becomes the reader's preoccupation as Bellow reveals the experience in its diverse ramifications.

Sammler's disinterest in recovering his pre–1939 Anglophile identity is consistent with the views of survivors, that the Holocaust "put into question everything that we had believed before."[14] After Auschwitz, civilization could not, and should not, be the same. The apocalyptic experience of the Holocaust and its paralytic aftermath lead Sammler to seek spiritual understanding.

> He wanted, with God, to be free from bondage of the ordinary and the finite. A soul released from Nature, from impressions, and from everyday life. For this to happen God Himself must be waiting, surely. And a man who has been killed and buried should have no other interest. He should be perfectly disinterested. . . . What besides the spirit should a man care for who has come back from the grave? (*MSP*, 109)

This passage is consistent with Bellow's remarks in *To Jerusalem and Back:*

> The Holocaust may even be seen as a deliberate lesson or project in philosophical redefinition: "You religious and enlightened people, . . . you believers in freedom, dignity, and enlightenment—you think that you know what a human being is. We will show you what he is, and what you are. Look at our camps and crematoria and see if you can bring your hearts to care about these millions.[15]

Paralleling his exploration of the Holocaust experience is Bellow's continuing probe of the long-term effects of Nazism on its surviving victims. Bellow suggests the enormity of Nazi crimes and non-German complicity by surrounding Sammler with a community of survivors whose Holocaust-induced disorders are variations and reverberations of his own troubles. Sammler would fail if he tried to forget the Holocaust, because he is intimately involved with survivors who recall the trauma.

Sammler's son-in-law, Eisen, a painter, foundry worker, and metal sculptor, manifests his disturbance in violent behavior and the distortion of the creative impulse. Like Sammler, Eisen suffered for his Jewish identity after, as well as during, the catastrophe. The histories of Sammler and Eisen are marred by non-Aryan, anti-Semitic persecution. Each faced the hatred of his comrades-in-arms. Each was attacked by countrymen trying to rid Europe of the few Jews who survived the Holocaust. Sammler's escape from the massacre of Jewish partisans by Poles determined to "reconstruct a Jewless Poland" (*MSP*, 129) is paralleled in Eisen's deliverance from Russian soldiers. Wounded at Stalingrad, Eisen was traveling in a troop transport and was thrown from the moving train, "Apparently because he was a Jew" (*MSP*, 25). Speaking of the incident years later in Haifa, Eisen remarks, "Good fellows—*tovarishni*, but you know what Russians are when they have a few glasses of vodka" (*MSP*, 26). One may read this as ironic commentary or as a reference to the long history of Russian anti-Semitism, or as a reference to the European diasporan Jew's belief "that violence was for the *goy*," an attribute of the gentile male. In these accounts of non-German, anti-Jewish violence, Bellow adds his voice to those with the courage to condemn the active complicity of Christian and communist countries in the Nazi effort to rid Europe of its Jewish population. I. B. Singer and Leslie Epstein address similar situations.

A dehumanized creature of iron, Eisen is permanently damaged by the Holocaust and its aftermath. Physically mutilated in war, he remains a psychological cripple in peace. Eisen's painting reveals the trauma of his existence. His creative potential aborted; he has become a grotesque, a craftsman of the ugly. Sammler finds the art appalling, the work of "an insane mind and a frightening soul" (*MSP*, 62). The people in his paintings resemble corpses. Eisen also fashions metal medallions into traditional Jewish symbols: Stars of David, seven-branched candelabra, scrolls, and rams' horns with Hebrew inscriptions. The inscriptions he selects—*Nahamu* (comfort ye) and God's command to Joshua, *Hazak* (strengthen thyself)—defy those who would destroy him. The victim of homicidal maniacs, Eisen has become violent himself. He transforms his creation into a destructive tool when he uses sculpture as a weapon to thwart a criminal's attack on another person. Sammler has learned compassion from his ordeal; Eisen subscribes to a primitive code, kill or be killed.

Efforts to achieve the annihilation of Jewry did not cease with the end of the European Holocaust. Sammler was able to retreat into the world of books and spirituality after the war, reading historians and philosophers; Eisen had to continue to fight wars designed to destroy Middle-Eastern Jewry. In Israel, the silent endurer of Russian and German anti-Semitism has been "transformed . . . to the fierce freedom fighter, which is now the mark of the Israeli."[16] The image of the tough Jew is one Sammler has difficulty accepting. A diasporan Jew, he can accept the Jew only as a victim of other people's violence and others' indifference to that violence.

Sammler's daughter, Shula-Slawa, whose name indicates her identity conflict, suffers prolonged religious and cultural schizophrenia as a result of four years spent hiding from the Nazis in a Polish convent. Although Sammler is outraged by Shula's present-day antics and will not excuse them, he interprets her postHolocaust deceit as the direct result of her wartime deprivation. Shula, too, manifests the connection in regressing to her native tongue when confronted with criminal charges. Although Sammler recognizes the connection, he resents Shula's effort to exploit her victimization.

Sammler's postwar religious transformation parallels Shula's, yet is distinctly different. Her character reflects the plight of young Jewish survivors who were protected from the Nazi menace by Christian religious orders, but who subsequently experienced religious confusion stemming from indoctrination by their protectors. Long after the war, Shula's religious schizophrenia recurs, most poignantly during Easter season.

> Things that ought but failed actually to connect. Wigs for instance suggested orthodoxy; Shula in fact had Jewish connections. She seemed to know lots of rabbis in famous temples and synagogues. . . . She went to sermons and . . . lectures. . . . She became well acquainted with the rabbi, the rabbi's wife and family—involved in Dadaist discussions about faith, ritual, Zionism, Masada, the Arabs. But she had Christian periods as well. . . . Ash Wednesday was observed and it was with a smudge between the eyes that she often came into clear focus for the old gentleman. (*MSP*, 24–25)

Thus, it is obvious that Shula's interest in Catholicism, focusing as it does on the period when the observant religious ponder physical death and spiritual rebirth, is but another instance of her Holocaust trauma. In addition to religious confusion, this passage demonstrates Shula's obsession with survival as illustrated by its reference to Masada, the site where a band of Jewish zealots resisted the mighty Roman legions for two years before committing suicide. The survivor of the Nazi effort to annihilate Jewry remembers another fallen empire's attempt to destroy the Jewish people. That she dwells on the matter of Jewish persecution and survival in the context of Masada alludes to her postwar Israeli soujourn and that nation's embrace of Masada as a symbol of defiance and strength. It is symbolic of both Jewish vulnerability and hope.

Loss of religious faith or religious confusion, major themes in European and American Holocaust literature, appear not only in Shula's Jewish/Christian dichotomy and another survivor's apostasy but also in Sammler's Jobian probings. Although he is the descendant of Orthodox Jews, prior to the war Sammler had not been observant. Reared by assimilated parents, Sammler took pride in being a free thinker. Nevertheless, in his postwar analysis of his spiritual evolution, he identifies the Holocaust as the catalyst for doubts concerning God's purpose:

> During the war I had no belief, and I had always disliked the ways of the Orthodox. I saw that God was not impressed by death. Hell was his indifference. But inability to explain is no ground for disbelief. Not as long as the sense of God persists. I could wish that it did not persist. The contradictions are so painful. No concern for justice? Nothing for pity? Is God only the gossip of the living? (*MSP*, 215)

Temporary apostasy and atheism were not uncommon Jewish responses to the Holocaust. Questioning God's purpose is within the Jewish tradition. Sammler's assessment of God is strikingly parallel to Elie Wiesel's, "There is the same indictment of God for His failure to uphold the covenant, the same attempt to reject God completely, the same involuntary, unwelcome persistence to belief."[17] Sammler rationalizes his judgment against God from within the framework of religious doubt. During the war, he had turned from God; his exultation in killing a Nazi soldier dramatizes this. Sammler's return to God and the covenant is signified in his compassion for an Egyptian soldier killed in the Gaza. His response to the Egyptian, juxtaposed with his heartless response to the death of the German, serves as an index of the survivor's moral regeneration. The Sammler who rejoiced at the death of another person was the acculturated Bloomsbury littérateur dehumanized by Nazi and Polish anti-Semitism. Sammler explains his capacity to kill in relation to his spiritual loss, claiming he "would have thanked God for this opportunity. If he had had any God. At that time, he did not. For many years, in his own mind, there was no judge but himself" (*MSP,* 130). It is not until Sammler takes the Jewish way, responding to the human needs of his declared enemies, that he gains spiritual health and is convinced that he "was a man who had come back. He had rejoined life" (*MSP,* 264). His postwar spiritual condition can be best described as one that alternates between polar spheres: "between a knowledge of divine indifference as manifested by the Holocaust and intimations of divine presence in everyday existence."[18]

Unlike his earlier extensive reading in Western philosophy, history, and literature, Sammler tells us that in his seventies he focuses on Meister Eckhart and the Bible. He often quotes Proverbs and Ecclesiastes. Like the biblical text, *Mr. Sammler's Planet* focuses on the vanities of life, the ephemeral nature of life, the transitory coming and going of generations against the constancy of the earth.[19] Like Solomon, the aged Sammler "assesses his own life, evaluates human existence, and ultimately affirms his faith in God and man."[20]

Bruch, a Buchenwald survivor and acquaintance of Sammler's, evinces frustration in his determined effort to reject God and Judaism. Anger and spite seem to be Bruch's primary motives for denouncing God and faith. Although Bellow chooses to treat Bruch's "apostasy" ironically, he explores the significant implications of the Holocaust-inspired Jewish doubt of God. Bruch's grandstand "rejection" of God and Judaism is, in essence, an expression of his desperate disappointment in God's apparent indifference to the suffering of His people. In the end, Bruch abandons neither God nor religion; he merely changes denominations, rebelling against orthodox piety and strict adherence to Torah and adopting a more liberal form of Judaism. Unlike Sammler, who, for a time, denies God, Bruch simply shifts from Orthodox to Reform Judaism.

In addition to representing the crisis in religious identity, Bruch's character reflects the psychic wounds of Holocaust victims, demonstrating that the pathology of the Third Reich continues to claim its victims. He lives in perpetual suffering as a result of degrading experiences in Buchenwald. His illness takes the form of reenacting death scenes in his private theater of the absurd, repeatedly playing the corpse to the accompaniment of his own funeral chant. In his early years as a refugee, Bruch and another German-

Jewish refugee "used to hold Masses over each other, one lying down in a packing case with dime-store beads wound around the wrists, the other doing the service" (*MSP*, 56). The theater metaphor is also evidenced by Bruch's alternate routine in which he holds a pot over his mouth for an echo effect and rants in imitation of Hitler, "interrupting himself to cry 'Seig Heil'" (*MSP*, 56).

Although Bellow generally approaches the concentrationary universe indirectly, as do most American writers, he uses the Bruch cameo to introduce the Holocaust universe. The barbarous is juxtaposed with the ridiculous, suggesting the absurdity of Germany's assertion of Aryan superiority and Germany's efforts to degrade its Jewish victims as a prelude to their murder.

> Saucepans were offered to the prisoners for sale. Hundreds of thousands, new, from the factory. Why? Bruch bought as many pans as he could. What for? Prisoners tried to sell saucepans to one another. And then a man fell into the latrine trench. No one was allowed to help him, and he was drowned there while the other prisoners were squatting helpless on the planks. Yes, suffocated in the feces! (*MSP*, 56)

Repeated use of *pan, saucepan, pot,* and death references in the Buchenwald recollection and Bruch's contemporary behavior emphasize the causal relationship between the Holocaust experience and the character's abnormal postwar behavior. This verbal link also provides structural unity, reinforcing Bellow's established pattern of demonstrating that the Holocaust was the genesis of survivors' physical and psychological maladies. Further, the particular means Bellow employs to chart the debasement of the prisoner is an authentic representation of the excremental assault that characterized the concentration camp environment.[21] Conditions established by the Nazis were calculated to debase and humiliate prisoners. The stench of excrement mingled with the stench of crematoria smoke and rotting flesh in the camps. Buchenwald latrines consisted of open pits twenty-five feet long, twelve feet deep and twelve feet wide, with side railings on which prisoners could squat.[22] The latrine death that Bellow describes reflects that reported by prisoners. Apparently "one of the favorite games of the SS, engaged in for many years,"[23] was to throw men into the pit. Prisoners assigned to empty the overflowing pits with nothing but small pails often slipped in the slime: "The others were not allowed to pull the victims out. When work was done and the pit empty, then and then only were they permitted to remove the corpses."[24] This defilement was designed to generate self-disgust in the victims and to harden Germans who could then cope with mass killings, since their victims would appear subhuman.

Bellow indulges his penchant for symbolism and irony in his choice of names. In naming the character Bruch, Bellow deletes the vowel sound from *Baruch* (a popular Hebrew name meaning blessed) to convey the concept of disrupted or incomplete blessing. Life, which Jews are taught to value as a blessing, has in Bruch's experience been a curse at worst, and far from hallowed at best. Similarly appropriate for our consideration is the Yiddish noun signifying a disaster, a break, in this case aptly connoting the destruction of the Holocaust.

Elements of the absurd and the theatrical introduced in Bruch's Buchenwald memory reemerge in Bellow's Lodz Ghetto. The novelist introduces this episode with words and phrases such as *deformed, obsessed, abnormality, play acting, dramatic individuality, theatricality in people,* juxtaposing concepts of mental illness and theater as he had in the earlier Bruch section. Theatrical posturing, grotesque humor, and emphasis on the unnatural, insane existence characterize Bellow's recreation of Nazi rule. Eight years prior to Leslie Epstein's novel based on the career of Chaim Rumkowski, *King of the Jews,* Bellow treated the macabre in his own rendition of Rumkowski, the mad Jewish king of the Lodz Ghetto. Disorientation and the disruption of reason dominate the scene depicting chaotic life in ghetto, restructured as slave labor camp. Relying on historic records, the novelist incorporates details from Chaim Rumkowski's reign as Jewish elder, a Nazi-installed ghetto dictator. Bellow dramatizes Rumkowski as an elderly, corrupt, failed business man, "a distasteful fun-figure in the Jewish community" (*MSP,* 210). Amid tragic suffering, the bizarre Rumkowski dressed in ceremonial robes and rode through the ghetto in a dilapidated, but ornate, nineteenth-century gilded coach. In addition to the pageants and plays he organized in his own honor, he printed money and issued postage stamps bearing his likeness. This terror of the Jews, whose name is derived from the Hebrew word *chai,* meaning life, ironically presided "over the death of half a million people" (*MSP,* 211).

Bellow uses the Rumkowski passage for rare, direct, and critical moral commentary on the Nazi mentality. In Sammler's voice, Bellow notes:

> This theatricality of King Rumkowski evidently pleased the Germans. It further degraded the Jews to have a mock king. The Nazis liked that. They had a predilection for such *Ubu Roi* murder farces. . . . Here at any rate one can see peculiarly well . . . the blood-minded hatred, the killers' delight taken in its failure and abasement. (*MSP,* 211–12)

Historic authenticity is served in Bellow's characterization of Rumkowski as exhibitionist. This posture is qualified by speculation about Rumkowski's motivation for playing the mad king. Bellow controls the relatively short Rumkowski section by conveying his moral outrage in various ways. The parodic grotesque is offered in parallel with a stark, graphic portrait of human misery and degradation: "The ghetto became a labor camp. The children were seized and were deported for extermination. There was famine. The dead were brought down to the sidewalk and lay there to wait for the corpse wagon" (*MSP,* 211). Bellow follows an account of Rumkowski's nonsensical behavior with reference to an occasion when Rumkowski protested the arrest, deportation, and anticipated murder of his council. For this breach of conduct, he was severely beaten. Bellow's portrait considers the contradictory position of Jewish leaders who accepted the *Judenaltester* position. They had to cooperate with the Nazis to effect a small measure of relief for their constituencies. "Perhaps his secret thought was to save a remnant. Perhaps his mad acting was meant to amuse or divert the Germans" (*MSP,* 211). Rumkowski's ability to continue in his appointed role of dictator, arbiter of life and death for half-a-million people in the German spectacle, had its limits: "He voluntarily stepped into the train for Auschwitz" (*MSP,* 212). Although conflicting evaluations of Rumkowski's motives and behavior are given in survivor testimony, Bellow's conclusion that the ghetto master volunteered for "resettlement" is consistent with historic accounts, which indicate that he had the option of remaining in Lodz with the seven hundred people assigned to clean the ghetto. He chose, instead, to join his brother on August 30, 1944, in the last transport for Auschwitz.[25]

The Rumkowski passage takes readers beyond the normal

environment of literature and into the lunatic realm of the Third Reich, forcing them from comfortable illusions and compelling their contemplation of a severely disordered universe. Bellow creates the nightmarish quality of this episode through extended juxtaposition of comic, absurd detail with realistic scenes of suffering and death, of parodic ceremony with tyrannical oppression. Through Bellow's insightful association of bureaucratic functions with barbarism, and his refusal to acquiesce to the differentiation between the "banality of evil" of a bureaucratic functionary and radical evil, readers are shocked into a comprehension of the enormity of Nazi crimes.

Perhaps Bellow relies on images and scenes of the absurd because he concurs with George Steiner's conviction: "The world of Auschwitz lies outside speech as it lies outside reason."[26] Perhaps he abstains from documentary reference to the torture chambers, gas chambers, and crematoria because he believes that it would be presumptuous for an American to treat such horrendous events. Although he limits his description of the ghetto and excludes the concentration camp from his fiction, Bellow directly confronts the moral significance of the Holocaust; he forces readers to grapple with the fact that one of Western civilization's most reputedly enlightened nations implemented such obscenity and the rest of the world acquiesced in this barbarism.

Bellow's moral indignation finds voice in Arthur Sammler. The hero-survivor refuses to absolve the Nazis; he points ironically to the German facility designed for slaughtering innocent millions. When urged by his niece, Margotte Arkin, herself a refugee of the early period of National Socialism, to comment on Hannah Arendt's "banality of evil" thesis, Sammler rejects the historian's contention that Nazis of Eichmann's ilk were ordinary men, neither monsters nor pathological anti-Semites, but merely loyal Germans performing their duties. Moreover, he resents Arendt's conclusion that these Nazis' evil deeds emanated not from their own characters but from their positions in a totalitarian state. Sammler insists on the moral responsibility of the individual. These men were raised in pre-Nazi, Christian Germany and, therefore, should have harbored no confusion about the distinction between good and evil, no illusions about the connection between anti-Semitism and murder. Sammler's condemnation of the Nazi mentality, in this instance, is appropriately phrased in Judaic terms, stressing concepts such as the sacredness of life and the individual's moral responsibility:

> The idea of making the century's great crime look dull is not banal. . . . The banality was only camouflage. What better way to get the curse out of murder than to make it look ordinary, boring, or trite? With horrible political insight they found a way to disguise the thing. . . . Do you think the Nazis didn't know what murder was? Everybody . . . knows what murder is. That is very old human knowledge. The best and purest human beings, from the beginning of time, have understood that life is sacred. To defy that old understanding is not banality. There was a conspiracy against the sacredness of life. Banality is the adopted disguise of a very powerful will to abolish conscience. (*MSP*, 20–21)

A comparative analysis of the novel and an earlier manuscript version shows that Sammler's denunciation of Arendt's thesis is heightened in the final text.[27] To the moral indignation that was there from the beginning, Bellow added criticism of intellectual method:

> This woman professor's enemy is modern civilization itself. She is only using the Germans to attack the twentieth century—to denounce it in terms invented by Germans. Making use of a tragic history to promote the foolish ideas of Weimar intellectuals. (*MSP*, 21)

Bellow has since restated Sammler's views in his own voice, rejecting Arendt's concentration on a political explanation for evil, her vision of man totally conditioned by historic circumstance, and her relative neglect of man's moral understanding of evil.[28]

Arthur Sammler, whose name comes from the Yiddish word *sammlen* (to gather), is a Tiresias figure, a one-eyed observer and judge of the modern moral wasteland. He collects evidence of violence, corruption, and degeneration. As the horror of the Holocaust forced Sammler out of Bloomsbury complacency in 1939, confrontation with a black felon is the catalyst which propels him from postwar spiritual withdrawal into contact with the violence and excess of the Vietnam era. A victim of irrational cruelty, Sammler speaks for reason, order, tradition, and human dignity in the midst of chaos. He scorns intellectuals willing to be duped by theories such as Hannah Arendt's substitution of *banality* for *evil*, which he perceives as leading to dismissal of moral values and standards. Drawing on Jewish and humanist traditions, Sammler advocates reverence for the sacredness of life, communal responsibility, and ethical conduct.

Despite his blind eye and smoked glasses, Sammler is an acutely perceptive observer. Other characters solicit his judgment because "his experiences were respected. The war. Holocaust" (*MSP*, 73). Surrounded in his own family by a gallery of grotesques representative of modern licentiousness, Sammler strives to remain aloof from the imperfect. Despite his resistance, he is cast in the judicial role. Acceptance of that role and its attendant obligations to become involved with humanity are the subjects of Sammler's meditations and the manifestation of his Holocaust regeneration. Sammler grapples with characteristic Bellovian ethical questions: "What is the true stature of a human being?" (*MSP*, 212). "Where is the desirable self that one might be?" (*MSP*, 214). When, near the end of the novel, Sammler accepts the role of moral authority that his family has sought to impose on him, he concludes that disinterested isolation is immoral. It is Sammler's Holocaust experience that has offered the moral yardstick by which he rejects his innocent dreams of the 1920s as charming but naive, castigates the excess and romantic distortions of the 1960s, and affirms the values of God and soul. He seeks ethical wisdom and a reawakening of traditional values by which man can attain virtue: "Trying to live with a civil heart. With disinterested charity. With a sense of the mystic potency of humankind. With an inclination to believe in the archetypes of goodness" (*MSP*, 125–26). Sammler's eulogy for his benefactor is both a declaration of love for Elya Gruner and a commitment to the covenantal ethics and wisdom of the rabbis. His insistence that "each man knows the terms of his contract," implies affirmation of Judaic submission to God and the covenant. It is through the covenant metaphor that Sammler addresses Gruner's assumption of the responsibilities imposed on him and his acceptance of moral obligations. Affirming the Judaic reverence for creation, Sammler argues that God's will demands moral attitudes toward life, that human life demands an ethical code that sanctifies biology and leads to holiness, "the pain of duty makes the creature upright" (*MSP*, 201). Sammler's concluding prayer parallels the conclusion of Ecclesiastes and its iteration of the contract God makes with man.

Why Bellow chose to write a novel that brings the Holocaust to the forefront in 1970 is open to speculation. That Bellow has written implicitly and explicitly of the Holocaust in periods when Jewry's physical survival was severely threatened is evident from the publication dates of *The Victim* (1944) and *Mr. Sammler's Planet* (1970). A probable explanation is that he was motivated by the 1967 Middle-East crisis when Arab states threatened another Holocaust. That the novelist overtly associated Arab intentions in the Six Day War with the Holocaust is dramatically manifest in the text of *Mr. Sammler's Planet* and in Bellow's nonfiction, polemic voice. Bellow's association of the Holocaust with the Six Day War is an accurate reading of the Jewish psyche and in accord with the thinking of such novelists and scholars as Elie Wiesel and Nathan Glazer, who attributed worldwide Jewish reaction to the 1967 war in the Middle East to the similarity of Nazi and Arab anti-Semitic propaganda. The Arabs echoed Holocaust rhetoric, promising genocide to the Jews of Israel as the Nazis did to the Jews of Europe. Writing in his own voice in *To Jerusalem and Back* (1976), Bellow draws a direct parallel between Nazi and Arab rhetoric. Referring to his experience as a *Newsday* correspondent in the Sinai during 1967, Bellow describes picking up comic books prepared for illiterate Arab soldiers that contained "anti-Semitic caricatures of the Nazi type I thought had gone out with Julius Streicher and *Der Sturmer.*"[29] Bellow also notes the distribution in Arab countries of the infamous forgery, *The Protocols of the Elders of Zion.* Bellow writes eloquently and passionately in defense of Jewish survival in *To Jerusalem and Back.* Here he observes that when Israel's existence was threatened in 1967, nations remained silent as they had when the Jews of Europe were destroyed. Because the 1967 crisis and the Holocaust are linked in Sammler's thinking, he joins his fellow Jews in this hour of new peril. Offended by the cyclical persecution of Jews, the "maniacal push of certain ideas, themselves originally stupid, stupid ideas that had lasted for centuries" (*MSP,* 131), Sammler refuses to remain safely in New York reading newspapers and listening to radio and television coverage of the Arab threat to annihilate Israel while the rest of the world remains indifferent. His association of the Middle-Eastern war with the Holocaust compels him to be in the thick of danger: in Jordan, in Syria, in the Sinai, and in Israel. He travels to the Middle East as a journalist to report on the war for a Polish newspaper. His observations are taken from Bellow's own account of the conflict, "Israeli Diary," which the novelist compiled in the war zones for *Newsday.* Sammler's nausea and pity for the rotting Egyptian corpses can be found in Bellow's Sinai report of June 13, 1967; Sammler's references to the destroyed Russian equipment are taken from Bellow's inspection of the Gaza; Sammler's concern for the children at play is taken from Bellow's encounter at Al Arish.[30]

Sammler's pre-1967 visits to Israel were no more than tourist trips. He felt no particular relationship to the people or loyalty to the country. However, his trip to the land of Israel in its time of crisis signifies his full-hearted return to the people of his ancestors. When Israel's existence is endangered, Sammler experiences intense emotional connection to its people. That Sammler's only writing since World War II is concerned with Jewish subjects, such as his essay on Rumkowski and his articles on the Six Day War rather than any further work on H. G. Wells and the Bloomsbury set, suggests "how important the specifically Jewish past and future have become to the Anglophile, universalist Sammler."[31]

For Bellow, as for other Jewish writers, the State of Israel is of crucial importance to the identity and survival of world Jewry. Bellow's grave concern for the nation's survival is echoed by his protagonists, be they physical survivors like Sammler and Bruch, or psychological survivors like Herzog, Humboldt, and Citrine. In *To Jerusalem and Back,* Bellow speaks in his own voice about his concerns for Israel's survival as well as his pleasure in the young nation's accomplishments. In the fiction, Bellow's protagonists express only their anxiety and they do so repeatedly in reference to the Six Day War.

Alvin Rosenfeld, who views Arthur Sammler as a prototype of the Holocaust writer—a man "possessed of a double knowledge: cursed into knowing how perverse the human being can be to create such barbarism and blessed by knowing how strong he can be to survive it"[32]—points out that the very nature of Sammler's experience has enlarged his sight, that his vocation is "that of a seer, a man of unusual perception whose observations carry the ring of authority."[33] One may say the same of Sammler's creator. In the eyes of many readers, Saul Bellow has attained the stature of artist-seer. It is Bellow, after all, who has reminded us, after decades of the tendency for modern literature to be its own source and to be estranged from modern society,[34] that it is appropriate for the writer to accept the role of moral authority that society imputes to its men of letters.[35] Bellow's literary career is a testament to his vision of the writer as sage and guide. A distinguished moral voice in twentieth-century literature, he confronts central issues of our time with intelligence and courage. In *The Victim* and *Mr. Sammler's Planet* he has helped us understand the difficulties he described in "Distractions of a Fiction Writer": the enormity of inhumanity in our age.

> Man's hatred for himself has led in this century to the wildest of wars and demolition of the human image in camps and jails built for that purpose. Bodies stacked like firewood we have seen; and the bodies of the massacred exhumed for the gold in their teeth we have seen too.[36]

Despairing contemporary fiction's retreat to aesthetics, its tendency to be its own source, its acceptance of separation and estrangement, Bellow has consistently brought readers to the world, to engage and to question

> just what the reduction of millions of human beings into heaps of bone and mounds of rag and hair or clouds of smoke betokened, . . . the meaning of survival, the meaning of pity, the meaning of justice and the importance of being oneself, the individual's consciousness of his own existence.[37]

# CHAPTER TWO

## *From Buchenwald to Harlem: The Holocaust Universe of* The Pawnbroker

Edward Lewis Wallant's 1961 novel, *The Pawnbroker,* is a prototypical American Holocaust novel, establishing what have since become the standard devices of American Holocaust fiction. Wallant successfully moved the Holocaust from the shadowy realm of symbolism and allusion to the foreground of fiction, presenting it as a major component of theme, narrative, and character construct and making it the central focus of his survivor-protagonist's consciousness and experience. Similarly, his use of a survivor-chorus and the evocation of the Holocaust era through voluntary and spontaneous recollection and dream have become the primary means of Holocaust recreation in American fiction. The novel's structural pattern consists of a series of dramatic dichotomies: Holocaust-era Europe and America of the late fifties; Holocaust and postHolocaust conditions of a specific survivor; and the juxtaposition of Holocaust survivors with American ghetto dwellers. This contrapuntal arrangement sharply clarifies and focuses the raw Holocaust experience, one which remains incomprehensible despite its centrality to twentieth-century life.

63

The novel is set in ghetto Harlem and suburban Westchester in the summer of 1958, remote in place and time from Buchenwald and Bergen-Belsen. Nevertheless, the survivor-protagonist, forty-five-year-old Sol Nazerman, still bears physical and psychological wounds suffered at the hands of the Nazis. His body is witness to nefarious concentration camp medical experimentation, "A piece of his pelvic bone missing, two of his ribs gone, and his collarbone slanted in weird misdirection."[1] More complex are his psychological wounds, which are manifested in obsession with the past and alienation and withdrawal from contemporary relationships. A former professor at the University of Cracow and a devoted family man, Nazerman was deprived in Nazi-occupied Poland of everything that held meaning for him. To protect himself from further psychological pain he maintains an emotional barrier to keep people at a safe distance. He remains a man apart, reluctantly engaging in meaningful dialogue only when an antagonist provokes him. Although he still reads Checkov and Tolstoy, he generally denigrates his pre-Holocaust values and interests. He insists: "I do not trust God or politics or newspapers or music or art. I do not trust smiles or clothes or buildings or scenery. . . . But most of all, I do not trust people and their talk, for they have created hell with that talk" (*P*, 114–15).

That Nazerman's personal encounters are marred by the physical and psychological atrocities inflicted upon him in Europe appears in his rejection of those who would befriend him. Since Holocaust experience has taught him that the human bond may be arbitrarily sundered by a demonic external force, he passionately resists intimate connection with his current acquaintances: with his American relatives, with his mistress, with contemporary victims of American urban and economic blight, and with his fellow workers. Although Nazerman's temporal and physical location is New York City, his spiritual and metaphysical sphere is the Holocaust universe, his real associates the murdered Jews of Europe.

To convey the survivor's alienation, Wallant juxtaposes the pawnbroker's attitudes with those of his ghetto foil, social worker Marilyn Birchfield. Whereas Miss Birchfield persistently reaches out to Nazerman in genuine—albeit naive—friendship to resurrect the charitable spirit she perceives buried beneath the rubble of his European past, Nazerman resists and firmly demands privacy. It is through Wallant's sharp contrast of these Harlem outsiders—detached survivor-immigrant and engaged American do-gooder—

that we understand the severity of Nazerman's alienation. Marilyn Birchfield, reared in New England Protestant security, is, as her name implies, safely rooted in her native land and culture. As a social worker, she came to New York City to help disadvantaged youth, to touch the lives of others. Conversely, the uprooted European Jew came to be among strangers, to survive in a land that would allow him to live in peace. Whereas Birchfield strives to be of the community, Nazerman is content to have the solitude of the pawnbroker's wire cage. Particularly difficult for the social worker is Nazerman's antipathy toward the people who patronize his shop. Although Miss Birchfield grants the survivor "a great deal of sadness and grief" (*P*, 145), she is intolerant of his bitterness, thus evidencing her American innocence. Without enumerating the horrors of his past, Nazerman rebukes the self-righteous American and warns her that she will encounter the unbearable should she probe into Holocaust reality.

> People who have 'suffered' in your little world may or may not become bitter, depending, perhaps, on the state of their digestive system or whether they were weaned too early in infancy. . . . There is a world so different in scale that its emotions bear no resemblance to yours; it has emotions so different in degree that they have become a different species! (*P*, 146)

For Nazerman, Europe is a vast graveyard, where he witnessed one of the West's most civilized nations "Not at its worst," as some would say, but according to its victims "as it really is" (*P*, 210).

Juxtaposition of pre- and postHolocaust immigrants, contrast of those who sought economic opportunity with those who sought refuge from the hell of concentration and death camps, is Wallant's astute means of distinguishing the survivor-protagonist from other immigrants and an important contribution to American fiction. As an obsessed Holocaust victim, Sol Nazerman is philosophically and psychologically alienated from his bourgeois sister who escaped the European catastrophe by prewar emigration. Whereas Bertha came to America in 1928 in search of economic advancement and assimilation to the good life and can, therefore, reject postwar perpetuation of Holocaust trauma, Sol cannot dismiss the past because it is his present and will be his future. Free of her brother's history, Bertha concentrates on being an American. Her greatest satisfactions come from material acquisitions and the deluded conviction that her family has shed its Jewishness in favor of the American suburban ideal. Insensitive to the magnitude of her brother's plight, she would have him forget past degradations of the camps and get on with American prosperity. Sol's woeful presence is a grotesque contradiction of Bertha's carefully structured façade of well-being and conspicuous consumption.

In addition to distinguishing the Holocaust survivor from other immigrants, Wallant further enriches Nazerman's portrait by comparison with three other survivors: Tessie Rubin, Sol's mistress; Mendel Solowitz, Tessie's ailing father; and Mr. Goberman, a collector of funds for Jewish relief work. The survivor community acts as a Greek chorus whose comments and behavior provide a gauge by which to measure the protagonist. The survivor chorus has since become a literary model for other Holocaust novelists and is seen in the work of Saul Bellow and Susan Fromberg Schaeffer, among others.

The Holocaust experiences and sensibilities of Mendel Solowitz and Tessie Rubin echo and supplement Sol's history of physical and psychological suffering. Mendel's body, which prompts his physician to remark that he should have been dead many years ago, testifies to the torture he sustained, just as Sol's body shows how he was deformed in Nazi medical experimentation programs. Further, Mendel's Holocaust-induced gallow's wit corresponds to Sol's bitter harangues. In agony, on his deathbed Mendel greets his benefactor ironically—"it's a Jew—gas him, burn him, stick him through vith hot needles" (*P*, 61)—intimating the emotional scars he and Sol still share.

Instead of love, Sol and his mistress share a legacy of loss. Both are bereft of marriage partner and children, both harbor memories and visions of the murder of their loved ones. However, in contrast to Sol's Holocaust-wrought emotional withdrawal and bitter assertiveness, is Tessie's down-trodden docile passivity. A perpetual victim, her life is a series of Holocaust recollections and disabilities. As she ministers to her sick father, Tessie is haunted by Bergen-Belsen memories. The only relief she allows herself is rationalization that the dead are better off than the living. Since both Tessie and Sol are consumed by grief—one expresses it while the other suppresses it—their own relationship is void of joy, and is but a mere biological coupling of automatons. While this dispassionate union confirms Sol's emotional isolation, it sheds additional light on his character as a charitable human being. Although he fails as passionate and sensitive lover, he succeeds as compassionate financial benefactor and discerning defender of two weaker victims.

Central to the success of Wallant's survivor portraits is his ability to resist maudlin and saintly characters, and to present instead a gallery of complex human beings whose diversity suggests variations of survival. In addition to the complex and abrasive Nazerman, he designs a brilliant cameo portrait of a guilt-ridden survivor, Mr. Goberman. The least sympathetic of the survivor community, Goberman is a haunting, aggressive beggar, a professional refugee who assuages his own guilt by devoting his time to Jewish survival efforts. He plays on survivors' guilt, insisting that Holocaust survivors are themselves perpetually obliged to save threatened Jewish lives in tribute to their own escape from annihilation.

A pathetic figure, Goberman has become so deranged by his concentration camp experience that he hurls accusations and insults at the victims of Nazi crime rather than indict the perpetrators of the crime. In a grotesque parody of justice, Goberman confuses Holocaust survivors with their oppressors, demanding that the victims expiate their sin of outliving fellow Jewish Holocaust victims by helping Jews in current peril. He chides: "Their blood is on you. You must give me money for the Jewish Appeal or your name will go down with Hitler in Hell" (*P*, 89). In an effort to assuage his own guilt, Goberman capitalizes on the guilt and fear of others. An insidious pest, he threatens to reappear "like the Angel of Death to the Egyptians" (*P*, 89), not to avenge the enemies of the Jews but to plague the Jews themselves.

Not only does Nazerman reject Goberman's macabre inversion of innocence and guilt, but he implies that Goberman has no right to judge others. Goberman melodramatically bares his arm to show the familiar blue tattooed numbers and taunt the skeptic with his inventory of horrors.

> Inside my heart is more credentials, too. Go get a knife from the kitchen and open me up. I'll show you the stab wounds, the burnt pieces from the murders of my wife, my five children, my mother, my sister. . . . I'll show you credentials printed in red, in BLOOD! You want more? Chop open my brain, see there the pictures of the walking dead, the raped, the disemboweled. (*P*, 122)

Whereas Tessie Rubin is moved by Goberman's agony, Sol listens to the harangue dispassionately because he recalls Goberman as the dreaded concentration camp informer, a victim who collaborated with the Nazis in a desperate effort to assure his personal survival. Goberman's vociferous denial of Sol's charges lamentably intimates the awful probability of their truth:

> Not my own family, never my own family. What kind of person would say a thing like that? Here, look at me, see how I collect money for the Jews, how I bleed for them all over the world. Day and night I try to get money for their salvation. I scream, I threaten, I sacrifice my self-respect to do for them. And this, this is my reward! No one can say to my face that I . . . never in a million years would I have done a thing like that to my immediate family. Do you think that I could sleep at night, . . . How could anyone? It is beyond imagining that such a person could walk the face of the earth. . . . I . . . NEVER . . . SOLD . . . MY . . . OWN . . . FAMILY . . . NEVERNEVER-NEVERNEVER! (*P*, 123–24)

Silent about his own Holocaust suffering, Sol disdains Goberman as "a professional sufferer, a practicing refugee" (*P*, 124), an opportunist eager to turn a profit on disaster. Because Sol's personal degradation is free from the taint of betrayal of fellow victims, he is free from survivor guilt and urges Tessie to resist Goberman's efforts to induce guilt. The Goberman cameo is a sensitive dramatization of one of the most painful truths of the Nazi era, recognition that subjection to atrocity can transform ordinary human beings into amoral automatons, the victim can become the victimizer.

Just as the Holocaust experience may have transformed Goberman into a collaborator and finally into a guilt-ridden mendicant, so it accounts for Nazerman's ironic occupational metamorphosis from cultured professor to stereotypical pawnbroker. Claiming "A sense of kinship, of community with all the centuries of hand-rubbing Shylocks" (*P*, 8), the survivor of the world's most successful anti-Semitic endeavor ironically brings to the New World the Old World's anti-Jewish burden. Perversely spiteful is Nazerman's grotesque adoption of the "much maligned calling," the hateful role of moneylender long and ardently assigned to the Jew by Christian European religion, art, and politics. Nazerman's assumption of the pawnbroker role is symbolic of his own regression and historic referent for the limitations nations have traditionally imposed upon the Jew, a method whereby the despised second-class citizen provides services that the nation's favored citizens refuse to render for themselves. It is through the survivor's postwar, ironic assumption of the hated stereotype that the novelist plunges the reader into an imaginary Holocaust landscape.

August, the anniversary of the Nazerman family deaths and Sol's season of discontent, is the testing time in which the survivor's precarious armor of self-conscious indifference fails. Poignantly correlating the traditional month of lamentation in the Hebrew calendar with Nazerman's time of personal grief, Wallant traces Sol's August bereavement from midmonth to its awesome culmination on August 28. Sol's current torment begins with "a deep, unlocalized ache, a pain that was no real pain yet but only the vague promise of suffering, like some barometrical instinct" (*P*, 55). The reader initially encounters Sol on a pleasant "rosy" morning as he walks to work feeling "the sensation of being clubbed" (*P*, 5). Midsummer warmth and joy fail to penetrate the Holocaust survivor's inner chill and heartfelt despair. His vague feelings of discomfort then become objectified in the novel's urban environment.

Harlem is the "objective correlative" of Nazerman's fractured postHolocaust existence. Wallant's ghetto is both realistic and metaphoric, evoking the tormented mental state of a man remembering his brutalized family, a man in mourning for his slaughtered innocents. Dehumanizing and hostile aspects of the physical setting reflect the tormented protagonist's anguish. Dark images of filth, disease, and pollution objectify the survivor's weariness with life, his own sense of impending collapse. Paralleling the city's physical deterioration are Nazerman's physical manifestations of psychic malaise: "pressure in him, a feeling of something underneath, which caused the growing tremors on the surface of him" (*P*, 155). As the pawnbroker waits on the subway platform, his train approaches in a yellow beam of blinding light and thunderous roar, assaulting the passenger "like a projectile . . . rush[ing] to swallow him up" (*P*, 155). Stark, realistic urban imagery thus symbolizes Holocaust degradation and atrocity. The yellow light evokes offensive yellow identity badges; the city train suggests wartime boxcar transports carrying Jews to concentration camps and crematoria. Although the concentrationary world is repeatedly evoked by Harlem degradation, Nazerman's thoughts center on the earlier humiliation and remain aloof from contemporary suffering. For Nazerman, the significance of present misery is its value as Holocaust referent.

Although Nazerman survived the evils of fascism and the

infamies of Hitler for American peace and quiet, he is still forced to witness victims and victimizers. The daily life of a pawnshop owner exposes Nazerman to an American underclass at the mercy of the powerful and the corrupt; it exposes him to the oppressed, the impotent, the cynical, the ineffectual innocents the defeated and complacent, the selfish and well-intentioned. Although Wallant juxtaposes Harlem ghetto and European concentration camp, he judiciously distinguishes between the attendant human debasement of the American ghetto experience and government-sponsored genocide in the German concentration camps. To suggest, as some critics do, that "the conditions of the camps are repeated and perpetuated"[2] in the Harlem setting is unfortunate. German concentration camp and American ghetto are hardly analogous in magnitude and meaning. The Nazis and their collaborators intended to exterminate an entire people. American slum degradation, horrible and destructive as it is, does not represent an overt policy of genocide, as Auschwitz did. Although degree and kind of suffering are unequal, contemporary humiliation and pain precipitate Nazerman's free associations, nightmares, and spontaneous recollections of Holocaust horrors.

Representative of Wallant's skillful juxtaposition of Sol's past and present is his introduction of Mabel Wheatly, paramour of Sol's pawnshop assistant and local prostitute. Mabel activates Sol's memory of his own wife's imprisonment in a Nazi brothel barrack. As Mabel offers herself to Nazerman in an effort to finance her lover's business ambitions, memories of European dehumanization flood the survivor's consciousness. Sensitized by his wife's forced whoredom, Sol gives Mabel the money she would earn by the sale of her body, but he refuses to exploit her. A former victim, he refuses to victimize another, even a willing candidate. While Sol questions his assistant, Jesus Ortiz, about Mabel, he thinks of Ruth, his face, "lost in some nameless graveyard of thought" (*P,* 113). Although Sol tries to redirect his thinking, "to escape burial with things he had left behind forever," his face revealed graveyard horror, as at "something exhumed" (*P,* 113). Wallant's diction clearly suggests the ghastly living death of the Jewish women in the Nazi brothel barracks. Nazerman is so angered by his discovery that his silent business partner, Murillio, owns the brothel where Mabel works, that he resolves to extricate himself from a partnership with a man whom he now judges to be an agent of evil. Murillio's response to Sol's demand to be released from their business arrangement is a symbolic death threat, administered by a henchman who forces the barrel of his pistol into Sol's mouth.

Nazerman's futile attempt to escape his troubles through sleep is foreshadowed as he drinks a nightcap from a ritual memorial glass. The thoughts he tries to repress in his waking hours intrude as a nightmare. He dreams of being forced to watch a black-uniformed SS officer compel Ruth Nazerman to commit fellatio. As the grieved, shamed husband tries to turn away from the sordid spectacle, he is repeatedly struck and made to endure his wife's humiliation. As Ruth's "mouth stretched in soundless agony" (*P*, 169), Sol cries out for both. The parallel is complete: as the professional prostitute evokes memories of Ruth's victimization, the symbolic fellatio links Harlem whoremaster with Nazi tyrant, and the present again evokes the past. In another sequence of the rape nightmare, in a Goberman-like inversion of innocence and guilt, Sol's anguish for his wife is replaced by his own anger. In this instance, as the guard forces him to witness his wife's defilement, he thinks: "*How ugly, what a mockery of their love! Why did she do this to him? He felt like tearing at her horrid nakedness*" (*P*, 224). The husband's impotence is dramatized in his paradoxical condemnation of the Jewish victim and his failure to denounce the Nazi villain. In a world turned upside down by Nazi values, the absurd is the real, and a tormented husband may condemn his wife for infidelity because the ruling power imposes whoredom on her.

In addition to rendering the survivor's troubled psyche, dream and involuntary recollection further serve as vehicles whereby the concentration camp universe may be brought to the forefront of the postwar setting. Structural and thematic unity are achieved as Wallant repeatedly uses these devices to demonstrate the survivor's continuing trauma and as effective methods of recreating the concentrationary universe. In each instance Wallant has astutely prepared for memory and dream with a causal link to contemporary misfortune, whether as an evocative pawnshop event or survivor referent. Despite the protagonist's efforts to repress his Holocaust experiences, they will not be put to rest and forcefully invade his consciousness, either as flashes of spontaneous recall or nightmare. The conscious will to repress the Holocaust is consistently overpowered by the subconscious will or need to confront the horror.

In addition to charting the enduring emotional impact of Holocaust trauma through dream, Wallant also uses the device to outline Holocaust chronology: from the early stages of captivity in the boxcar transports, through the concentrationary experience, and the final destination at the crematoria. The setting of an early dream is the cattle-car transport of the Nazermans to Buchenwald. Amid the endless wailing of the crushed multitude, Sol's wife clings to their daughter who is pressed against her bosom, "held there without her arms, for the crush of the bodies held them all as in ice" (*P*, 38). Sol is incensed by his impotence to aid his children as they suffer the physical and psychological hardships of the long train journey through Poland. *"His son David squealed with a rodent sound of˙helplessness somewhere down near Sol's leg. 'I'm slipping in it Daddy, in the dirty stuff. I can't stay up'"* (*P*, 37). Pressed by two hundred other bodies, Sol is unable to save his son from falling into the excrement. The powerless parents can only watch as their son vomits and drowns in filth.

In one nightmare Sol recalls a Nazi object lesson for would-be escapees. Buchenwald inmates are forced to stand in the camp square and witness a crazed father, whose son had recently been gassed, being driven against a temporarily defused barbed-wire fence by guard dogs:

> *For a few seconds the dogs fell back, surprised at the deceptive quarry which had seemed so small. Rubin was screaming, one shining red figure of blood, only his mouth definable in all the torn body, and that so vivid because it framed the scream . . .*
>
> *Suddenly Rubin turned and flung himself up on the thorny wire fence, where he clung just out of reach of the snapping dogs. One of the guards waved toward the guard tower. There came the rattly crack of electricity. The bloody figure went rigid, pulled away from the horrid life of the wires, and then seized it and pulled it tight in a lover's embrace. Then the body went limp. And the ragged bundle of blood and charred flesh, caught like some wind-tossed rubbish on the wires, was no longer Rubin or anything else.* (*P*, 100–101)

The crescendo of atrocities mounts as Nazerman's dreams multiply and appear an increasingly vivid detail. The dream that follows is about Sol's own disfigurement, just as savage though executed by German scientists and physicians rather than their trained attack dogs.

> *He was flat on his back, staring at the glaring surgical lamp. . . . He heard the sawing of bone, and he knew that it was his bone . . . Then there came the*

*clunking sound of parts dropping into a bucket, the sounds of leakings and
drippings.*

    *"WHAT ARE YOU TAKING OUT OF ME?" he screamed, seeing himself
"boned" like some beast being prepared for someone's meal. "STOP, STOP," he
shrilled, visualizing so clearly how he would be as a soft, collapsed carcass of
flesh. "Shut up, Jew," a blue-eyed nurse snarled into his face. "Shut up or
we'll take your prick, too." . . . "All done," a doctor said. "It will be interesting to see how he functions now." A murmurous medley of voices sounded a
cold glee. "If he functions, if he functions at all, if you know what I mean."*
(*P,* 130–31)

Vocal and thematic echoes unite and reverberate from one
dream to the next. Sadistic pleasure taken from Jewish pain is
evident first as the concentration camp guards joke and laugh at
Rubin's disorientation and then as the medical team finds humor in
Nazerman's subjection to surgical experimentation. A bond of sadism seems to join prison-guard mentality and that of the elite
German medical community.

Tension resulting from the combination of the approaching
anniversary of the Nazerman family slaughter and recent under-
world threats on Sol's life is manifested in the greater frequency
and intensity of the victim's nightmares. His postwar anxieties multiply. He dreams of "*a mountain of emaciated bodies, hands and legs
tossed in nightmare abandon, as though each victim had died in the midst of
a frantic dance, and hollow eyes and gapping mouths expressing what could
have been a demented and perverse ecstacy*" (*P,* 197). Through a dream
the reader learns that Nazerman's camp job was loading corpses
onto a pile in the crematorium, a job that filled him with shame.
The degradation of such work was intensified by the horrible probability that he would recognize a familiar face, by the prospect of
finding his wife and child in the mass of bodies. To cope with such
labor, Sol averted his eyes from the heads of the corpses, seized "*the
dry, bone-filled limbs and heaved*" (*P,* 197). As he pulled at a body, his
spectacles fell to his feet and he finally concluded that he had to
look, to give the dead a modicum of respect. Accepting the risk of
discovering his own dead, he decided to bear witness, to affirm the
murdered millions. This crematorium dream is distinguished from
the earlier nightmares by its progression from graphic description
and registration of the protagonist's anger and humiliation for his
own suffering to compassion for other victims. There is also a
marked shift from a bitter to an elegaic tone, progressing Hebrai-
cally from expression of personal loss to collective bereavement.

In the ensuing fragment of the same dream, Wallant charts the bizarre transference of blame to the victim and thereby suggests the psychological distress experienced by many survivors who outlived their fellow sufferers. The innocent victim whose forced labor consisted of collecting bodies for the crematorium attributes sin to himself: *"The smell of the burning flesh entered him, and it was as though he ate the most forbidden food"* (*P*, 225). Whereas the initial reference to his camp job revealed pain and revulsion, the new reference to Orthodox dietary laws prohibiting the consumption of ritually impure food transforms other-directed pain to inner-directed guilt.

Thus, the Nazerman who disputed Goberman's effort to victimize the victim through guilt repeatedly suffers similar, albeit undeserved, guilt in his dreams. Powerful dream imagery, evoking the primary will to live and misconceived guilt for doing so at another's expense, speak eloquently to the survivor's dilemma.

> *The smoke of their bodies was blowing north when this hideous hunger hit him. He lusted for rich meats and heavy pastries, had an insane yearning for wine and coffee. He dug his claw like fingernails into his thighs to punish himself for not praying to that fleeting, greasy smoke. . . . And then this lust turned to a hunger of the loins, and he wondered at the monster he was, and pulled some of his hair out.* (*P*, 225)

To the demented victim of Nazi-inflicted horror, the instinctual human will to live, codified in Jewish law as a holy responsibility, is in the Nazi universe ironically perceived as sin, symbolized in his dreams as culinary and sexual gluttony—sins the Jew must repent and expiate.

The novelist uses a collage of elements from recurring nightmares to construct Nazerman's final dream. Tension is heightened by interrupting the nightmare with wakeful moments that focus on present difficulties. Wallant thereby develops an emotional crescendo and conveys the impact of the Holocaust as a brutal and persistent intruder in the survivor's postwar life. This final, intense Holocaust dream of a crematorium chimney belching all that is left of the Jews is visually reinforced by a contemporary Harlem street scene of echoing imagery. The Harlem sky "was burned to the pallid blue of scorched metal" (*P*, 226). In the survivor's perspective, urban misery is a forceful reminder of camp suffering: "All the repulsive faces appeared to melt before his eyes, and Sol imagined them dissolving to dark smudges on the pavement" (*P,* 226). The Holocaust experience is forever seared into Sol's consciousness; the streets of Buchenwald and Bergen-Belsen have followed him insidiously to the streets of Harlem.

Many critics interpret the relationship between Sol Nazerman and Jesus Ortiz Christologically, arguing that the sacrificial death of Jesus Ortiz during the pawnshop robbery is the cause of Nazerman's regeneration:

> The pawnbroker of limited vision, a hard and unfeeling heart, and nightmares of almost inhuman atrocities, teaches his mysteries of suffering and acquisition to the son, Jesus, who learns the lessons so well (finally) that through his own sacrifice, which is the ultimate leap of faith, he is able to motivate Sol into acknowledging human connection again and also afford Sol the possibility for his renewal of love and life. . . . Ortiz is the innocent to the end, the zealot Christ, trying to establish his kingdom.[3]

This assessment places excessive emphasis on the importance of one scene at the expense of the rest of the novel, reading it as the source of rather than an extension of Nazerman's continual regenerative commitments, including financial support of two families, moral support for an exploited prostitute, and dissolution, at grave personal risk, of his business partnership. These acts exemplify a spiritual rebirth in the Jewish manner of repentance and a commitment to society manifested in charitable behavior toward others. Although a Christological interpretation fits neatly into the Western tradition, it is a temptation better forgone because it is achieved at the cost of denying Jesus Ortiz's rich and complex ambiguity and by overlooking the dominant relationship established between the antagonists throughout the novel. Despite the descriptive parallels between Ortiz and Christ, such as their common rejection by establishment powers, their membership in an oppressed minority, their insistence on their own way, and their sacrificial deaths—all provocative analogies—the Ortiz of pre-sacrificial, unrecanted, anti-Semitic conviction is an unsatisfactory redeemer, especially for a survivor of the Holocaust. Similarly, Wallant's proclivity for the Christ-like suffering model in other fiction, need not impose a Christian messianic interpretation on the Jesus character. Distinction between the historic figure's intentional sacrifice and the fictional character's accidental altruism, an in-

stinctive act that foils his own criminal design against the pawnbroker, is crucial. Jesus Ortiz is, at best, a complex "sinner-saint,"[4] a
man whose single heroic act on Nazerman's behalf was consistently
preceded by prejudice, deceit, and a conspiratorial crime at Nazerman's expense.

The characters' provocative emblematic names, Sol Nazerman and Jesus Ortiz, posit Wallant's brilliant, ironic inversion of
the Jesus-Judas myth and simultaneously correlate Christian and
Nazi anti-Semitism. Just as Saul Bellow boldly implied the link
between historic Christian anti-Semitism and the Holocaust with
the relationship between Jew and anti-Semite in *The Victim,* so Edward Wallant dramatizes the connection in his compelling antagonism between the survivor pawnbroker and his apprentice.

The Jesus-Nazerman business relationship may be read as an
inverse parody of the historic association of the Christian king and
his court Jew. Whereas European monarchs and noblemen welcomed mercantile Jews to enrich their personal and state coffers
and then expelled them, Wallant's poor Puerto-Rican black begs to
be initiated into the mythic business expertise of the Jew so that he
may improve his own economic position. In a scornful rejection
scene, Nazerman objects to Jesus' stereotypical insistence on the
Jew's natural affinity for business. The Holocaust survivor's unan-
ticipated response is a bitter summation of economic manifestations of historic Christian anti-Semitism, rather than the pure
business lecture:

> You begin with several thousand years during which you have noth-
> ing except a great, bearded legend, nothing else. You have no land
> to grow food on, no land on which to hunt, not enough time in one
> place to have a geography, or an army or a land myth. Only you have
> a little brain in your head and this bearded legend to sustain you and
> convince you that there is something special about you, even in your
> poverty. But this little brain, that is the real key. With it you obtain a
> small piece of cloth. . . . You take this cloth and you cut it in two and
> sell the two pieces for a penny or two more than you paid for the
> one. With this money, then, you buy a slightly larger piece of cloth,
> which perhaps may be cut into three pieces and sold for three pen-
> nies' profit. You must never succumb to buying an extra piece of
> bread at this point, a luxury like a toy for your child. Immediately
> you must go out and buy a still-larger cloth, or two large cloths, and
> repeat the process. And so you continue until there is no longer any
> temptation to dig in the earth and grow food, no longer any desire to

gaze at limitless land which is in your name. You repeat this process over and over for approximately twenty centuries. And then *viola*— you have a mercantile heritage, you are known as a merchant, a man with secret resources, usurer, pawnbroker, witch, and what have you. (*P*, 52)

Sol's tone is sardonic and accusatory, informed by Diaspora and Holocaust knowledge.

As the young shop assistant's efforts to ingratiate himself to his employer repeatedly fail, his anti-Semitic expression becomes increasingly shrill. Rather than a Christ-like figure offering compassionate love and sacrifice, Ortiz behaves as Christians have for twenty centuries, engaging in verbal and physical anti-Semitism. As he sits facing his church, the Tabernacle of Jesus Our Lord, he plots the pawnshop robbery, rationalizing his Judas-like betrayal of Nazerman with a classic anti-Semitic argument: "I don't owe that Sheeny nothin' really. What is he to me?" (*P*, 202). Like the Europeans of the past, who were philo-Semitic when it suited their national interests and anti-Semitic when it served internal political needs, who exploited Jews as convenient scapegoats, Jesus too determines to take advantage of the vulnerable Jew: "It occurred to him consciously . . . that opportunity could reside in other people's destruction" (*P*, 215). The downtrodden, impoverished American echoes Europe's envy of the propertied Jew that exaggerates Jewish economic power in order to justify subsequent anti-Jewish aggression, whether in religious pogrom or in a racial Final Solution. It is on the basis of such virulent anti-Semitism that Wallant ironically juxtaposes the conspiratorial Christian Judas with the betrayed Jewish Nazarene.

The novel's two crucifixion scenes parallel Christian anti-Semitism and the Nazi crime of genocide, clearly implying the development of the latter from the former. In both of these scenes, staged in Jesus' church, Ortiz links the agonized historic Jesus with the Jewish Holocaust victim. During prerobbery meditation, Ortiz moves from sympathetic contemplation of the crucified Jesus to sadistic contemplation of the twentieth-century Jew in similar agony. "He began to chuckle, harshly. Wouldn't everybody be shocked to see Sol Nazerman up there, his arm with the blue numbers stretched out to the transfixed hand?" (*P*, 238). The image is emphasized and underscored in a second vision: "the figure of a heavy man, awkwardly transfixed on a cross, a man with blue, cryptic numbers on his arm" (*P*, 247). Just as the baptized Jew was the martyr to Roman atrocity, so millions of non-baptized Jews through twenty centuries of Christian-ruled Europe have been martyred by Christians, whose anti-Semitic indulgences paved the way for and acquiesced to the German program of genocide. In his crucifixion contemplations, Ortiz manifests not the celebrated compassion of his namesake, but the historic persecutions against world Jewry carried out in his name by his followers. Furthermore, these scenes vividly intimate the correspondence of Ortiz's amused post-Holocaust meditation on Jewish suffering with Holocaust-era acquiescence to the plight of the Jewish people. These repeated visual parallels of the agonized Christ and Jew ironically imply the Christian source of anti-Semitism and genocide, since both the Nazis and their European collaborators were indoctrinated in Christian theology and culture that systematically presented the Jew as a pariah, an enemy of Christendom, and a vulnerable scapegoat for repeated massacres.

Ortiz's crucifixion meditation clearly demonstrates the correlation between religiously inspired anti-Semitism and racial and political manifestations of the same pathology. The young man's thoughts direct the reader to associate the suffering of the crucified Christ with that of the Holocaust victim. His desire to see the contemporary Jew on the cross and his indulgence in anti-Semitic persecution revery—matters oddly ignored in the critical literature which treats Ortiz as the saintly savior of the hard-hearted Jew—constitute instead Wallant's direct judgment of Christian Holocaust culpability, an indictment of Christian collusion in Nazi crimes against world Jewry. Thus, thematically and graphically, Wallant connects the agonized Christ not with his Christian follower, but with the Jew. "If in his consciousness Jesus conceives the Pawnbroker's power and wisdom to come from money, in his dreams he envisions Sol as Christ."[5]

The metaphoric parallel of Christian and Nazi anti-Semitism established in the crucifixion scenes is dramatically substantiated in the staged pawnshop robbery on the anniversary of the Nazi slaughter of the Nazerman family. On August 28, the followers of Jesus Ortiz appear, instrument of death in hand, to rob the pawnbroker. The new violence, coming as it does on the anniversary of the old, both echoes the past and heralds a new beginning. Because Jesus steps in the path of the bullet meant for the pawnbroker, Sol mourns the "one irreplaceable Negro who had been his assistant and who had tried to kill him but who had ended by saving him" (*P*, 278). Sol's purgative tears for Ortiz allow him to express the Holocaust grief he had hitherto repressed, allow him to weep for all his dead. This new ability to express his emotions is a significant release and a further stage, rather than the initial stage, of Sol's social rehabilitation. Having wept for those he lost, Nazerman is now able to reach out to others, to console Tessie Rubin for the recent loss of her father and to become more involved with Bertha's family, as foreshadowed by his invitation to his nephew to become his new assistant.

Although the Ortiz sacrifice does play an important role in Sol's emotional recognition scene, allegoric interpretation of that debt is unwarranted and is neither dramatically nor philosophically justified. To read the Ortiz sacrifice as the instigating force for Nazerman's social regeneration, as many do, is to forget Sol's compassionate equation of Mabel Wheatly's degradation with that of his wife and his consequent courageous denunciation of her oppressor; is to negate his entire period of suffering during the memorial month; and is to ignore the charity he has consistently given to other survivors. Sol's expressed concern for friends and family following Jesus' death is not a radical change of behavior, but merely a different means of articulating an established concern; it is not a sign of new spiritual discovery for a hitherto hardened alienated man, but the second or third stage of his return to the human community, further confirmation of a philosophic affirmation previously manifested in his dissociation from the Murillio partnership and his support of the Buchenwald survivors. Nazerman's response to the Ortiz sacrifice is consistent with his current social restoration, which is characterized by movement from self-willed isolation to engagement. Because Sol's self-imposed withdrawal is the result of Holocaust trauma, so too an instinctively generous act confirms his recommitment when he elects to risk his life by defying a Harlem gangster on behalf of an underclass prostitute. Estranged from humanity because of the wrongs he endured, Nazerman is also recommitted to his community because he realizes, primarily from the Wheatly-Murillio association, that one must take a stand against the exploiters of the powerless, the Nazis in our midst, and ally oneself with those who suffer.

The novel's conclusion—salvation of the spirit through a return to human community—is central to Judaic values and teaching. As such, Wallant's affirmative thesis is comparable to those of

Saul Bellow and Bernard Malamud. All are squarely in the Judaic affirmative mode and are rendered credible by Jewish historic experience, which has demonstrated that the hell people live through somehow enhances their capacity to live and love. Much as Malamud's complex Jewish-Christian encounter of Morris Bober and Frank Alpine in *The Assistant* is the precursor to the Nazerman-Ortiz relationship in *The Pawnbroker,* so is Nazerman the prototype for Saul Bellow's Holocaust survivor, Arthur Sammler. Both Nazerman and Sammler are contentious survivors; both weep for the enemies of their people—Nazerman for an anti-Semite who sought to harm him but saved his life instead, and Sammler for a fallen Egyptian soldier who died in the Six Day War trying to destroy the State of Israel and in the process effect the second genocide of the Jewish people. Nazerman follows the Jewish road to redemption in a commitment to life rather than a release from it. Had Wallant affirmed Christian salvation for a Jewish Holocaust victim, he would have betrayed both history and art. To cast Ortiz in the role of spiritual mentor and savior is too pat, too contrived to be aesthetically pleasing, philosophically convincing, or historically authentic. Instead, Wallant enhances the novel through the Jesus-Nazerman dichotomy, a brilliant, ironic inversion of the Jesus-Judas myth, which clearly rejects a simplistic, allegoric resolution in favor of a rich ambiguity and an insightful probe into the myriad possibilities of the human condition.

# CHAPTER THREE

*Seekers and Survivors: The Holocaust-Haunted Fiction*
*of Bernard Malamud*

The particularity of Jewish suffering as the metaphor for human suffering is central to Bernard Malamud's fictional universe. When asked whether he was a Jewish writer, Bernard Malamud replied:

> I'm an American, I'm a Jew, and I write for all men. . . . I write about Jews when I write about Jews, because they set my imagination going. I know something about their history, the quality of their experience and belief, and of their literature, though not as much as I would like. Like many writers, I'm influenced especially by the Bible, both Testaments. I respond in particular to the East European immigrants of my father's and mother's generation; many of them were Jews of the Pale as described by the classic Yiddish writers. And of course I've been deeply moved by the Jews of the concentration camps, and the refugees wandering from nowhere to nowhere.[1]

The Holocaust, in fact, was the catalyst for Malamud's studies in Jewish history, for his personal commitment to Jewish identity, and his certainty that "he had something to say as a writer."[2] Malamud himself attests to the significance of the Holocaust and historic Jewish suffering in his writing: "I for one believe that not enough has been made of the tragedy of the destruction of six million Jews. Somebody has to cry—even if it's a writer, twenty years later."[3]

Although Bernard Malamud does not confront the Holocaust experience directly, his fiction is clearly haunted by the Holocaust. His tales of postwar Jewish life are informed by Holocaust consciousness. The tragedy enters the Malamudian American universe variously through allusion, symbolic claustral and imprisoning imagery and metaphor, and physical and psychological survivor constructs. Survivors have populated Malamud's fictional world from his first collection of short stories, *The Magic Barrel* (1957), which received the National Book Award. The lover reenacting the Jacob-Rachel legend in "The First Seven Years" is a Polish refugee who "escaped Hitler's incinerators."[4] "Take Pity" relates the plight of Eva, a fiercely proud survivor who is so emotionally and ethically scarred by the losses she suffered in Hitler's demonic reign that she responds scornfully to a loving man's charitable efforts in her behalf. "The Loan" presents another emotional cripple, Bessie, who attributes her suspicions and militant self-protection to the calamities she experienced during Russian and German anti-Jewish campaigns. After her father was murdered by the Soviets, she found a home in Germany with a brother "who sacrificed his own chances to send her, before the war, to America, and himself ended, with wife and daughter, in one of Hitler's incinerators."[5] As Bessie enumerates this litany of twentieth-century Jewish suffering, her untended loaves of bread burn like "blackened bricks-charred corpses" (*TL*, 171), evoking the Jews who went to Hitler's ovens. The Malamud canon is populated by survivors who carry the terrible past near the conscious surface—ever ready to erupt and char the American hiatus of the transplanted European.

Among the most successful tales of *The Magic Barrel* and *Idiots First* are those that explore an American's encounter with a survivor or refugee-mentor who initiates the innocent to Jewish history. Whether they be survivors of European persecution or American psychological survivors, Malamud's Holocaust-formed characters lead radically altered lives. Adopting traditional Jewish literature's teacher-student character constructs, Malamud shows that the Old World Jew who steadfastly retains his Jewish identity offers valid instruction to acculturated American Jews. A pattern emerges in "Lady of the Lake," "The Last Mohican," and "The German Refugee," whereby the Holocaust escapee becomes the spiritual or historic mentor to an American Jew who had been either disinterested in Jewish history or openly hostile to Jewish identity. As in the case of immigrants who fled the czarist pogroms, Malamud's Holocaust survivor-mentors are inheritors and proponents of Jewish history and Jewish ethics; these survivor-mentors have something valid to teach American Jews, whose neglect of Judaism is at the root of their spiritual sterility. Despite the minor role of Holocaust survivors in Malamud's fiction, it is often through the influence of these figures that the American questers confront their pasts and achieve understanding, which initiates a cathartic reversal. Except in "The German Refugee," Malamud relegates the survivor's postwar accommodation to a minor chord and emphasizes instead the survivor's affect on self-denying or marginal American Jews.

"The Lady of the Lake" is an ironic, inverse recognition tale of a young American seeking romance in Europe. Henry Levin exchanges his mundane New York existence as floorwalker in Macy's book department for romance in Italy, where he seeks "what few got in the world and many dared not think of; to wit, love, adventure, freedom."[6] "For no reason he was sure of, except that he was tired of the past—tired of the limitations it had imposed upon him" (*LL*, 95), Levin, while en route to Italy and motivated only by inner doubt and ambivalence, casts off his Jewish identity and takes the name Freeman, suggestive of the freedom he wishes to attain. Levin's adoption of a new name in France, a country of established anti-Semitic fervor—played out in the late nineteenth-century Dreyfus case and twentieth-century Nazi collaboration of the Vichy government—signals the story's dominant ironic tone and underscores the discrepancy between appearance and reality.

Filled with expectancy and the conviction that travel is truly broadening, the American quester will come to terms with history through an encounter with a European in an episode of dual deception: the European is guilty of an indiscretion of omission, and the American of a blatant sin of commission. Freeman's preceptor, Isabella della Seta, is a beautiful young woman whom he meets while touring Isola del Dongo. She is an intelligent, sensitive foil to the pretentious, shallow Freeman. Her perceptive judgment, historic awareness, and spontaneous response counter his superficial knowledge of art, history, and culture.

Henry Freeman sets out to benefit culturally from his Euro-

pean experience, to live fully in the style of a Henry James protagonist. His failure to acknowledge his relationship to European
history and to feel its impact circumscribes his opportunities. As
Freeman approaches the island-garden, he observes the beautiful
woman from the water while meditating on a sad memory of his
own "unlived life" (*LL*, 98). Anticipating experience he believes
denied Jews in anti-Semitic social contexts, he denies his Jewish
identity. The second encounter between the two is rendered as a
visual inversion of the first. A naive Adam in the island's luxurient
garden, Freeman strays from his guide and fellow tourists to catch
a glimpse of the lady of the lake. This time he observes Isabella
rising from the sea—a Botticelli Venus: "Her dark, sharp Italian
face had that quality of beauty which holds the mark of history, the
beauty of a people and civilization" (*LL*, 102). The lady of the lake
is marked by history, but in ways Freeman does not expect.

Isabella's first words to Freeman, "Si e' perduto," are alle-
gorically suggestive. Articulated as an innocent inquiry of the tourist's direction, the question nevertheless penetrates the reality of
the American's spiritual condition. From the start, the European's
questions go right to the heart of the matter. "Are you, perhaps,
Jewish?" she wants to know (*LL*, 102). Freeman's denial of his
heritage reveals the core of his self-hate. His lie is the entrance cue
for an emblematically named comic scourge, "waving his cane like
a rapier . . . [Ernesto] whacked him across the seat of the pants"
(*LL*, 103). Reminiscent of a Jewish patriarch, Ernesto rebukes the
"Transgressor," and expels him from the paradisiacal garden.

Untruth and poor taste characterize Freeman's moral and
aesthetic failures. He rejects his hotel *padrona's* suggestion that he
tour a natural island rather than the commercial Isola del
Pestcatori. In a private palazzi tour, with Isabella as guide, Freeman is initially ecstatic about Titian, Tintoreto, and Bellini copies
and later dismayed at his inability to discern them from the real
thing. These events foreshadow the story's climax and establish
significant parallels between Freeman's failure to recognize the
copies and his analogous failure to recognize Isabella's Jewish identity. Malamud's juxtaposition of aesthetic and moral blindness foreshadows Freeman's final moral ineptitude.

Encouraged by Isabella's tenderness, Freeman seriously considers marriage and convinces himself that impoverished Italian
aristocrats would favor American opportunity for one of their own.
As Freeman contemplates a marriage proposal, the only difficulty

he perceives to the match is his Jewish background, for he is convinced that Isabella's initial inquiry signified traditional European anti-Semitism. Troubled, however, by his deception, Freeman rationalizes that he will let Isabella discover the truth after she has lived in America long enough to realize "it was no crime to be Jewish; that a man's past was, it could safely be said, expendable" (*LL*, 113). He also entertains the possibility of keeping the truth from her entirely, of changing his name legally and settling in an area where he is unknown in order to "forget he had ever been born Jewish" (*LL*, 114). Lying to his beloved disturbs Freeman more than denying his heritage, "what had it brought him but headaches, inferiorities, unhappy memories" (*LL*, 114).

Although the beloved lady of the lake is herself guilty of deception, her relatively minor indiscretion lies in pretense to economic grandeur and social position, play-acting as daughter of the manor rather than acknowledging that she is the caretaker's daughter. Her social aggrandizement is less significant than Freeman's self-renunciation, his denial of religious and cultural identity.

The lovers' next meeting is removed from the garden-island and set instead on a mountain summit overlooking Lake Maggiore. As the lovers survey the distant Alpine peaks, Freeman is about to propose marriage when Isabella asks whether he can visualize the seven peaks, "Like a seven-branched candelabrum holding white candles in the sky?" (*LL*, 116). Freeman hesitates and Isabella succumbs to her own fears and offers instead an analogy she believes would be more agreeable to a Christian, "Or do you see the Virgin's crown adorned with jewels?" (*LL*, 116). "'Maybe the crown.' he faltered. 'It all depends on how you look at it'" (*LL*, 116). In an ironic juxtaposition, the self-denying Jew remains true to his apostasy and the true Jew confesses her social deception. Love-sick and humiliated by his failure to observe the signs of poverty, Freeman contemplates leaving the area, but recalls that he came to Europe specifically to find love. He returns to the island to make a magnanimous marriage proposal.

In the climactic final meeting of the lovers, Freeman is once more given opportunity to declare his true identity. He offers marriage and once again she implores, "Are you a Jew?" (*LL*, 119). Freeman replies "How many no's make never?" (*LL*, 119) The ironic reversal is now complete; the self-deprecating American Jew who denies his association with collective Jewish history is summarily rejected by the woman he thought an Italian aristocrat, who is in fact a Jewish survivor of Buchenwald. Freeman's devalued prize is Isabella's treasured jewel. Unworthy of a Jewish wife, the apostate loses love precisely because he denied his Jewish identity. Just as he was deaf to Isabella's imploring question, so was he blind to her nakedness as she rushed into the lake during a previous encounter. The truth he failed to see then is painfully exposed in their final meeting when Isabella bares her breasts to reveal "tattooed on the soft tender flesh a bluish line of distorted numbers" (*LL*, 119). The Holocaust survivor renounces the lapsed American-Jew: "I can't marry you. We are Jews. My past is meaningful to me. I treasure what I suffered for" (*LL,* 120). The assimilated American Jew's cowardly plan to reveal his Jewish identity in the safety of America, is sharply juxtaposed to the survivor's wisdom and courage; his fraud is contrasted to her honesty. An authentic Jew, Isabella paid the penalty when it was a crime to be a Jew and remains steadfast to the heritage despite the world's contempt. Freeman, who has foresaken Jewish identity to gain love, impoverishes his life by dissociating himself from Jewish culture and history. "To embrace the fullness of life that Isabella here represents, he must embrace the particularity of his Jewish identity which is forevermore inseparable from the experience of the Holocaust."[7] Isabella remains a shadow figure, a dream figure in this story. Although as title character she is a persuasive force, the narrative focuses on Freeman. It is his character that is developed and explored. The Holocaust survivor remains a figure shrouded in mystery—a semiholy figure, one not to be approached with the ease and confidence of other characters. Isabella, rising out of the lake—a survivor phoenix, beautiful and silent—will be worshiped from afar.

Although Malamud elects not to probe the Holocaust experience, leaving the subject, like the lady of the lake, surrounded by mist, he attests to the impact of the Holocaust on Jewish consciousness. Isabella declares, "My past is meaningful to me. I treasure what I suffered for" (*LL,* 120). Her rejection of an inauthentic, self-denying Jew and her refusal to marry a non-Jew attests to the Holocaust as an orienting event in her life, one that influences her decision to choose affiliation with Jewish history and people rather than personal happiness apart from the collective identity.

Less elusive than "the lady of the lake" is Shimon Susskind, "the last mohican," another Holocaust survivor who is a spiritual mentor to an American art historian and critic traveling in Italy. In the role of *schnorrer*, traditional mendicant of Yiddish literature and folklife, Susskind intrudes more forcefully and influentially in the American's spiritual quest than did Isabella in Freeman's life. Like many *schnorrers* of East-European, popular Yiddish literature, Susskind is a comical, ethical guide, providing the Jew with the opportunity to fulfill his charitable obligations while mercilessly lecturing him. Reminiscent of the delightful comic hero of Israel Zangwill's *The King of the Schnorrers*, Malamud's Susskind is highly visible, agonizingly articulate when he chooses and vexingly evasive when it suits him to reverse the roles of pursuer and pursued. In addition to mendicant-instructor, the beggar gains spiritual stature from his correspondence to the *lamed vov tzaddik*, one of the thirty-six secret saints of Yiddish folklore. Paralleling the traditional hidden saint, Susskind is a common man, often boorish and verbally aggressive, an unconventional, often radical, spiritual advisor. Like his predecessors, Susskind materializes when a quester needs him, whether or not his presence is desired. He is persistent and relentless until success is achieved and then he disappears as mysteriously as he appeared.

As survivor-*tzaddik*, Susskind pursues where Isabella retreats. Having fled Germany, Hungary, Poland, and Israel, Susskind is a practiced survivor. He doggedly follows the American to strip him of selfish naiveté and to lead him to self-awareness, penance, and forgiveness. Like the clever beggars of Yiddish folklore, the *schnorrer*-mentor leads his initiate to spiritual health through fulfillment of the Commandments.

Susskind's protégé, Arthur Fidelman, is a failed painter and art critic/historian who has come to Italy to write a critical study of Giotto and search for aesthetic truth. From the moment of his arrival at a Roman railroad station, the young American is taken in hand by his comic guru, whom he will come to recognize as the paradigmatic Diaspora wanderer and refugee. Having ascertained that Fidelman is Jewish, Susskind approaches him with the brazen effrontery of the traditional comic *schnorrer* and offers to be his guide in exchange for Fidelman's second suit and a modest fee. Distressed that his first Roman encounter is with a *schnorrer*, Fidelman hopes a small cash donation will rid him of the beggar. Much to the American's consternation, Susskind resists dismissal. He appears, uninvited, at Fidelman's hotel and restaurant, repeatedly requesting the suit and money. Fidelman rejects Susskind's plea for a cash investment for a peddling venture, rejects his offer

of a partnership in a nonexistent business, and refuses the old man
his suit. Although Fidelman gives the beggar something, he does so
contrary to Jewish tradition, grudgingly, in a manner that humili-
ates rather than dignifies the recipient. Susskind then undertakes
Fidelman's education in the Maimonidean charitable code, that is
the gracious, free, willing, charitable act designed to sustain the
dignity of the recipient.

Repeatedly rebuffed by Fidelman, Susskind engages the
young man in moral debate in an effort to impress him with the
Jewish concept of communal responsibility. To Fidelman's outraged query suggesting that he is not responsible for the beggar,
Susskind replies directly: "Who else? . . . You are responsible because you are a man. Because you are a Jew, aren't you?"[8] Because
Fidelman resists Susskind's instruction, the beggar adopts a more
radical teaching style: he steals Fidelman's briefcase and Giotto
manuscript. The roles are reversed and Fidelman now anxiously
pursues Susskind.

The spiritual journey of the Bronx boy who expressed enthu-
siasm for "walking around in all this history" (*LM*, 144) takes an
unexpected turn from the pathways of the art world to the labyrinth of Jewish history—away from church, museum, and library
to synagogue, ghetto, and cemetery. On the night of the theft,
Fidelman has a nightmare that evokes his metaphysical plight and
foreshadows his pursuit of Susskind. He dreams of chasing the
refugee in Jewish catacombs under the ancient Appian Way while
threatening to strike him with "a seven flamed candelabrum."
Thus, with typical Malamudian irony, the transgressing American
transforms a religious artifact into a weapon. Because this happens
in Rome, it suggests the image of the seven-branched candelabrum
in the Arch of Titus, a symbol of Roman oppression of Jewry that
compounds the irony. In the dream, Susskind eludes the avenging
antagonist, fleeing among the crypts.

His manuscript gone, Fidelman is unable to work, he can
neither rewrite the missing chapter, nor create another. Plagued by
his loss, he is paralyzed, unable even to travel to Florence as originally planned. Eventually he devotes himself to searching for Susskind and the manuscript. The quest is fraught with difficulties, "his
heart was burdened, and in his blood raged a murderous hatred of
the bandy-legged refugee" (*LM*, 154–55). While tracking down his
prey on the banks of the Tiber, Fidelman enters a Sephardic synagogue whose congregants are celebrating a service. Untrue to his

surname, Fidelman imitates the devotional form of the ritually
purified worshipers, who "paused before a sink in an antechamber
to dip their hands under a flowing faucet, then in the house of
worship touched with loose fingers their brows, mouths, and
breasts as they bowed to the Ark" (*LM*, 155). He fails to encounter
Susskind, but his mentor has led him to another Holocaust sufferer, one still mourning his son who was killed by the Nazis in the
Ardeatine Caves and who directs Fidelman to the Jewish cemetery.
Stage two of his journey provides Fidelman another opportunity to
think of a fellow Jew's suffering and to express his sympathy before
resuming his search.

The artist-pilgrim who had felt elation as he experienced Italian history now wanders through the Jewish ghetto en route to the
cemetery where Susskind is occasionally employed to pray for the
dead. From the mazed streets of the old ghetto where "dark stone
tenements, built partly on centuries-old ghetto walls, inclined towards one another across narrow, cobblestoned streets" (*LM*, 156),
Fidelman wanders into the Jewish cemetery to discover yet another
Holocaust remembrance. Among the many burial places for those
slaughtered during the Holocaust, he stops before an empty
cenotaph whose marble slab is decorated with the traditional Star
of David and engraved with the bitter remonstrance of a Holocaust
orphan: "My beloved father / Betrayed by the damned Fascists /
Murdered at Auschwitz by the barbarous Nazis / *O Crime Orrible*"
(*LM*, 157).

Having come to Italy to study the work of a Christian painter,
Fidelman instead becomes immersed in the Jewish history recorded in the ghetto and the cemetery. Fidelman's character undergoes a metamorphosis, and when he finally catches up with
Susskind three months after their original meeting, their positions
are ironically reversed: Susskind is peddling rosaries on the porch
of St. Peter's, and Fidelman follows him home, spies on him, and
conducts a fruitless search that inspires another graveyard dream.
In this revery, the mentor rises from an empty grave to engage the
critic in a dialogue on the meaning and purpose of art. Fidelman is
left alone to ponder a Giotto fresco of St. Francis giving his gold
cloak to an old knight. The spiritual guide leads the novice to the
discovery of the meaning of art in the context of Judaic ethics—the
mother religion's insistence on human responsibility, on the sacred
duty of charity. The dream lesson, expressed in visual form, is the
moral lesson that the *schnorrer* had earlier sought to impart ver-

bally, attributing it to its Judaic sources: Torah, Talmud, and the writings of Maimonides.

The *tzaddik*-directed dream-vision provides successful resolution of the Fidelman-Susskind debate. Fidelman gives his suit to the *schnorrer*-survivor, performing a *mitzvah* (good deed), honoring the Commandments willingly, lovingly, with an accompanying wish that the old man wear the suit in good health.

> The survivor has taught the writer how to make human contact, the beauty of responsibility. Against his will, Fidelman learns what the ancient rabbis taught and what Susskind has always known: Jews— that is, human beings, *menschen,* in Malamud's terms—are responsible for each other. That is the essence of being human.[9]

Fidelman learns of the importance of the human bond from Susskind—the "last mohican," survivor of the near-extinct race of East-European Jews, survivor of man's ultimate inhumanity to man. From him, Fidelman learns the connection between aesthetics and ethics. Fidelman experiences epiphanal understanding in which he affirms the truth of Susskind's explanation that by destroying a chapter in which "the words were there but the spirit was missing" (*LM,* 162) he did the critic a favor.

The spiritual distance Fidelman has traveled in Rome, under the tutelage of a Holocaust victim, a paradigmatic suffering man, is enormous. The search for Susskind through synagogue, ghetto, and cemetery and in his dream to cemetery and synagogue led Fidelman to the realization that his understanding of art had been flawed. Only after the critic learns charity from Malamud's prototypical Jewish sufferer is he able to understand Giotto's interpretation of suffering humanity and achieve his pilgrim's quest. The Holocaust victim is well prepared to teach the shortcomings of passive acceptance of another human being's suffering. A victim of perpetual violence and disinterested acquiescence, he knows the historic lesson that the critic must learn.

In "The Lady of the Lake" and "The Last Mohican," the protagonists are American lapsed Jews, neglectful of Jewish history and ethical teaching. In each story an American is at the focus of the significant action and is instructed by a Holocaust survivor. The Holocaust experience of the mentors is essentially unexplored; it is brought to the forefront briefly and then only to suggest the antagonists' moral credentials. In each story the Old World sufferer insists on the usable Jewish past, the validity of Jewish culture, and the importance of ethical precepts to an assimilated American Jew floundering in a spiritual wasteland. With the appearance of "The German Refugee" in the 1963 collection of short stories, *Idiots First,* Malamud moves the Holocaust victim to center stage. Although the drama has an American narrator and we care about his impressions, it is the German Jew who is at the center of the tale. The narrative is focused on the debilitating experience of the refugee as perceived through an American lens.

"The German Refugee" is narrated by Martin Goldberg, English tutor to the German refugee Oskar Gassner. In addition to the professional relationship the men share as tutor and student, they also become friends. The narrator, unnamed until the last page of the story, is passionately moved by Gassner's plight. During their long walks, shared meals, and extended painful silences, the American charts the decline of a man deprived of the ability to communicate. This loss is the central metaphor defining the refugee's cultural and political disenfranchisement.

Unlike most of Malamud's immigrants, Oskar Gassner is well educated, an accomplished Berlin journalist and critic, a cultivated European intellectual suffering the discomforts of cultural displacement. Unlike the penniless Susskind wandering about Italy in search of charity, Gassner arrives in America with signs of his past well-being in tact, books and paintings, gifts of his Bauhaus associates. This refugee is employed to lecture on German literature, a position similar to the one he held in Germany; however, now he must lecture in English. Gassner's severe uneasiness with English renders this apparently safe position a precarious one. Certain that he will make a fool of himself, that he will fail to communicate intelligibly, the fifty-year-old emigre becomes depressed: "the thought of giving the lecture in English just about paralyzed him."[10] A German-Jewish intellectual, a man devoted to the transmission and exchange of ideas, Gassner believes he has been effectively silenced. The narrator confirms the validity of Gassner's psychological trauma by recalling the response of a refugee actor, who said of his loss of language: "I felt like a child, or worse, often like a moron. I am left with myself unexpressed. What I know, indeed, what I am, becomes to me a burden. My tongue hangs useless." (*GR,* 200) Thus, even though the story is set in the relative calm of America during 1939 rather than Germany or occupied Poland, the agony of the transplanted Jew, deprived of his citizenship and culture, evokes—albeit less intensely—the deprivations afflicting the Jews of his homeland. This becomes a powerful metaphor foreshadowing the imminent vulnerability of European Jewry. There are moments of relief from the story's morose mood when tutor and pupil experience a small measure of success with pronunciation exercises, but these are short-lived. As his maiden American lecture approaches, Gassner's melancholy blocks his productivity. Even the narrator's suggestion that the refugee compose his thoughts in German and delay translation is fruitless. Paralysis of will renders Gassner impotent. "No matter what language he tried, though he had been a professional writer for a generation and knew his subject cold, the lecture refused to move past page one" (*GR*, 201). Gassner alternates between frenzy and despair and in his worst moments transfers his hatred for the Nazis to hatred of the German language, "shouting he could no longer write in that filthy tongue" (*GR*, 202). The diction in which Gassner expresses his inability to write reflects *Kristallnacht* devastation. Just as the glass of hundreds of synagogues and Jewish-owned shops was shattered, so Gassner's life has been shattered beyond repair: "The whole legture is clear in my mind but the minute I write down a single word—or in English or in German—I have a terrible fear I will not be able to write the negst. As though someone has thrown a stone at a window and the whole house—the whole idea, zmashes" (*GR*, 206).

Still innocent of the magnitude of the Nazi crimes against the Jews, Gassner has already been victimized to debilitation. Despite his escape from the greater horror that will overtake those left behind, he is a defeated man and despises the Germans for what they have deprived him of, "for destroying his career, uprooting his life after half a century" (*GR*, 203). He now regards the German nation as "an inhuman, conscienceless, merciless people" (*GR*, 203). Completely demoralized, Gassner stops working but continues his friendship with his tutor.

It is through dialogue between the refugee and his language instructor that Malamud interjects Holocaust specificity and expository detail. We learn of Gassner's antipathy for his mother-in-law, who openly expressed anti-Semitic sentiments, and his insecurities about his wife, as he indiscriminately links the two, "Gentile is gentile, Germany is Germany" (*GR*, 197). Despite his wife's assurances of her loyalty, Gassner characterizes their twenty-seven-year marriage as a difficult one, citing her ambivalence about his

Jewish friends and relations as a source of frequent discord. Gassner's sensitivity to German anti-Semitism evidences itself in his
efforts to secure employment in America, "a month before
*Kristallnacht*, when the Nazis shattered the Jewish store windows
and burnt all the synagogues" (*GR*, 197).

Representative of the Fascist oppressor's capacity to degrade
its victim is Gassner's self-assessment: "I have lozt faith. I do not—
not longer possezz my former value of myself. In my life there has
been too much illusion" (*GR*, 206). He blames the Nazis for his loss
of confidence. Physically Gassner has escaped the Nazi regime, but
psychologically he remains chained to it. As Gassner forcefully
articulates his hatred for Germany, he threatens suicide should he
fail to present his lecture and confides that he already attempted to
kill himself during his first week in America. His rhetoric is a
reminder of the high suicide rate in the 1930s among assimilated
German Jews who were dismissed from their posts in the arts and
sciences and in the professional and business ranks. These Jews
were transformed into social pariahs, abject subjects of a government dedicated to their destruction, scapegoats vulnerable to the
whim of murderous hooligans.

Malamud objectifies the Holocaust atmosphere of this tale
through historic allusion and metaphoric suggestion. Like Wallant
and Bellow, Malamud symbolizes the demonic intensity of Nazi
repression through climatic conditions. News of the Polish mobili-
zation is presented in the context of a hellish summer heat wave.
Temporary relief from the heat is provided by a second-hand electric fan, but the relief comes to an abrupt end when the fan "coinci-
dentally" breaks down just as the Hitler-Stalin Non-Aggression
Pact is signed. As Poland rapidly succumbs to Germany's superior
military, Oskar walks haltingly, toys with his food, experiences eye
discomfort, and becomes increasingly sedentary. Suggestive of the
restraint suffered by German Jews in 1939 and foreshadowing the
death apparatus of the Final Solution is Gassner's labored
breathing—"breathing like a wounded animal" (*GR*, 207).

In addition to using weather conditions metaphorically, Malamud incorporates dreams and symbols endemic to Holocaust literature to convey the victim's subconscious anxieties. Gassner's
dream is more horrible than his experience, but it is prophetic of
what the Jews of Europe will endure. He dreams of "Nazis inflict-
ing tortures on him, sometimes forcing him to look upon the
corpses of those they had slain" (*GR*, 208). Malamud thus informs

the 1939 context with postHolocaust hindsight, anticipating episodes such as the *sonderkommando* gas chamber and crematoria work details. Stimulated by a letter from his wife declaring her fidelity, Gassner's next dream reveals his anxiety and foreshadows his wife's death and the mass graves that were to cover Nazi-occupied Europe. In the dream Gassner returns to Germany to visit his wife and is directed to a cemetery where he discovers blood seeping out of the earth above her shallow grave.

A change in Gassner's productivity occurs because he is so outraged by the narrator's assessment of German preference for Walt Whitman's poetry. Contrary to the American's impression that Whitman's appeal for Germans lies in his love of death, Gassner contends that Whitman's influence was his humanity, his celebration of *Brudermensch* and ironically laments the demise of transcendental spiritual unity in the Third Reich. He experiences a burst of creative energy and composes half his lecture in a single writing session. During an invigorating cool spell in the early fall, the refugee successfully delivers his lecture. Despite the siege of Warsaw, he convincingly recites Whitman's hopeful lines from "Song of Myself":

> And I know the spirit of God is the brother of my own,
> And that all the men ever born are also my brothers, and the
>     women my sisters and lovers,
> And that the kelson of creation is love . . . (*GR*, 211)

Two days later, the Holocaust becomes Gassner's personal tragedy. The American tutor, flushed with pride in his pupil's recent success, arrives for the English lesson and discovers that Oskar has killed himself. Hitler's poison has followed the refugee to America. He received an acrimonious letter from his mother-in-law informing him of his wife's final fidelity. "against her own mother's fervent pleas and anguish, [she was] . . . converted to Judaism by a vengeful rabbi" (*GR*, 212). For this crime against the Reich, Frau Gassner was taken, along with her new found co-religionists, by the Brownshirts to a Polish border town, "shot in the head and topple[d] into an open tank-ditch, with the naked Jewish men, their wives and children, some Polish soldiers, and a handful of gypsies" (*GR*, 212). Whether she converted as an expression of solidarity with her husband or because she believed it was better in the new order to die a Jew than live a German is unexplained. Whether out of guilt or sympathy for the Whitmanesque act of unity taken by his wife, Gassner too ends his life, as will millions of European Jews—either in the mobile gas vans of Chelmno or the more efficient gas chambers of Auschwitz and Treblinka. As his name portends, the German refugee dies by gas. Frau Gassner's death in a massacre and her husband's death by gas is the closest Malamud comes to treating the Holocaust directly in the fiction. By selecting as his protagonist a 1939 refugee, one of the talented fortunates who found employment in the arts and sciences in America, Malamud deals with a limited aspect of Holocaust reality and continues his preference for metaphoric rather than realistic Holocaust rendition.

Malamud's novels, too, are Holocaust haunted, not with survivors but with Holocaust references and metaphors. *The Assistant* (1957) and *God's Grace* (1982) contain Holocaust analogies and allusions evocative and emblematic of Jewry's oppression in Nazi-occupied Europe.[11] *The Fixer* (1966), based on the historic Mendel Beiliss blood libel trial, relates earlier anti-Semitic crimes with twentieth-century German atrocity. It is the Malamud novel most closely associated with the Holocaust. Just as I. B. Singer was mindful of Auschwitz when he wrote of the Chmielnicki Massacres of seventeenth-century Poland, so Bernard Malamud had the death camps in mind when he wrote of prerevolutionary, Russian anti-Semitism. In *The Fixer,* Malamud suggests similarities between the lies that support religiously inspired anti-Semitism and the secular canard of an international Jewish conspiracy and those that underpin the Nazis's racially inspired anti-Semitism. The historic perspective he provides documents Christian Europe's moral culpability in the Holocaust, clearly demonstrating that centuries of European, anti-Semitic violence prefigured acquiescence to and collaboration in Hitler's genocidal program. In an environment where Jews had for nineteen centuries been religious, political, and economic scapegoats, it was a relatively short step to passive acceptance of the Final Solution in the twentieth century. A government conspiracy of gross discrimination against the Jewish people characterized both czarist Russia and Nazi Germany. Czarist incarceration and pogrom in *The Fixer* may be read as a foreshadowing of and an objective correlative for Nazi concentration camps and crematoria.

While internal evidence provides adequate reason for read-

ing *The Fixer* from a Holocaust perspective, Malamud encourages
this view in an authorial comment indicating that he did not want
the book tied to the Beiliss case, because

> somewhere along the line, what had happened in Nazi Germany
> began to be important to me in terms of the book, and that is part of
> Yakov's story. The Dreyfus case is there, too . . . for me, the book has
> a mythological quality. It has to be treated as a myth, an endless
> story, more than a case study.[12]

The lens of mid-century, anti-Jewish atrocity and postHolocaust
consciousness facilitates Malamud's vision of Russia's anti-Jewish
policies. He attributes his ability to "relate feelingfully to the situation of the Jews in Czarist Russia partly because of what
[he] . . . knew about the fate of the Jews in Hitler's Germany."[13]
Conversely, the Beiliss case offers Malamud

> a way of approaching the European Holocaust on a scale that is
> imaginable, susceptible to fictional representation. For the Beiliss
> Case transparently holds within it the core of the cultural sickness
> around which the Nazi madness grew, representing as it does a
> symptomatic junction of the medieval demonological conception of
> the Jew as Satanic enemy to Christ and mankind, and the modern
> phobic vision of an international Jewish conspiracy, manipulated
> through commerce and politics and underworld activity by the sin-
> ister Elders of Zion.[14]

The Mendel Beiliss blood libel trial provides the historic context of *The Fixer*. The Russian-Jewish protagonist Yakov Bok (Mendel Beiliss) is a lapsed Jew, one eager to exchange the limitations of
*shtetl* life for the larger Russified world. Bok shed his religion as
easily as he shed its outer accoutrements, dropping a bag containing his phylacteries, his prayer shawl, and his prayer book into the
river in response to a boatman's anti-Semitic diatribe. He lives and
works clandestinely in Kiev, a city beyond the Pale of Settlement
designated for Jews. Like Mendel Beiliss, the brick factory overseer
is charged with the ritual murder of a Christian boy whose body is
discovered in a cave near the brickyard. The Russian police, accustomed to Easter blood libel charges, perceive the child's multiple stab wounds as conclusive evidence of ritual murder: a Jew
has shed the blood of a pure Christian child for use in Passover

ceremonial observances. The blood libel corresponds to the Nazi propaganda of excessive Jewish influence in German economic and political life, and Bok's two-year imprisonment while the Russian authorities fabricate a case against him parallels extended Jewish suffering in the Nazi era. That Yakov Bok is a scapegoat and precursor of the six million Jews who will lose their lives in the Holocaust is suggested in his emblematic name: Yakov (Israel) Shepsovitch (son of sheep) Bok (goat). Bok understands the lesson that Jews will learn in the Nazi era: "Being born a Jew meant being vulnerable to history, including its worst errors."[15]

That Malamud sees the Christian anti-Semitic pogrom as an antecedent facilitating Europe's acceptance of the Holocaust plainly emerges in a ferryman's genocidal fantasy. Unaware of his passenger's Jewish identity, the boatman ferries Bok across the Dneiper to restricted Kiev, all the while venting his hatred for the Jews in Nazi-style rhetoric:

> God save us all from the bloody Jews, . . . those long-nosed, pock-marked, cheating, blood-sucking, parasites. They'd rob us of daylight if they could. They foul up earth and air with their body stink and garlic breaths, and Russia will be done to death by the diseases they spread unless we make an end to it. A Jew's a devil—it's a known fact—and if you ever watch one peel off his stinking boot you'll see a split hoof. . . . Day after day they crap up the Motherland, . . . and the only way to save ourselves is to wipe them out. I don't mean kill a Zhid now and then with a blow of the fist or kick in the head, but wipe them all out, which we've sometimes tried but never done as it should be done. I say we ought to call our menfolk together, armed with guns, knives, pitchforks, clubs—anything that will kill a Jew—and when the church bells begin to ring we move on the Zhidy quarter, which you can tell by the stink, routing them out wherever they're hiding—in attics, cellars, or ratholes—bashing in their brains, stabbing their herring-filled guts, shooting off their snotty noses, no exception made for young or old, because if you spare any they breed like rats and then the job's to do all over again. (*F*, 28–29)

The ferryman speaks as progenitor for Julius Streicher, Joseph Goebbels, Adolf Hitler, and company. Through the boatman's frenzied diatribe, Malamud brilliantly evokes the chronological progression of the Holocaust from the early days of street hooliganism to the last murderous phase of the Final Solution.

> When we've slaughtered the whole cursed tribe of them . . . wherev-
> er we can smoke them out . . . we'll pile up the corpses and soak
> them with benzine and light fires that people will enjoy all over the
> world. Then when that's done we hose the stinking ashes away and
> divide the roubles and jewels and silver and furs and all the other
> loot they stole. (*F*, 29)

Confiscation of Jewish property prefigures a *Judenrein* Europe enriched by that property. The macabre pronouncement of the dis-
posal of mountains of Jewish corpses and worldwide pleasure in
the destruction of Jews calls to mind the lime pits and ovens of
Dachau, Buchenwald, and Auschwitz. Only the sequence of action
is inverted in the Russian proposal. Perhaps some Russian delicacy
dictated killing the Jews prior to robbing them.

Bok's prison hardships imply the atrocious conditions in the
Nazi ghettos and concentration camps. Yakov suffers a degrading,
dehumanizing incarceration. He endures extremities of weather
without proper clothing, sleeps on a vermin-infested mattress, and
eats foul food garnished with roaches. He is brutalized, beaten,
starved, poisoned, and subjected to daily body searches. Malamud's
delineation of the prison sequence is informed by the physical
conditions of the Nazi camps, and Bok suffers as the Jews did
under the Nazis, not for a crime committed, but for being born
Jewish. Bok's realization that "whenever he had been through the
worst, there was always worse" (*F*, 264), approximates the agony of
Holocaust victims' experiences. His tormentors seek to break his
spirit, as the Nazis strove to humiliate and degrade their Jewish
prisoners before killing them.

Like many of the six million, the prisoner of czarist oppression recognizes that he is subject to forces beyond reason.

> He had stopped thinking of relevancy, truth, or even proof. There
> was no 'reason', there was only their plot against a Jew, any Jew; he
> was the accidental choice for the sacrifice. He would be tried because
> the accusation had been made, there didn't have to be any other
> reason. Being born a Jew meant being vulnerable to history, includ-
> ing its worst errors. Accident and history had involved Yakov Bok as
> he had never dreamed he could be involved. The involvement was,
> in a way of speaking, impersonal, but the effect, his misery and
> suffering, were not. The suffering was personal, painful, and pos-
> sibly endless. (*F*, 141)

Bok accepts his place in history by refusing to save himself at the expense of his fellow Jews—a haunting foreshadowing of the attempts by Germans to get some Jews to betray others, and the steadfast decency of most to endure their plight rather than permit others to become victims of the Nazis prematurely.

Malamud's fictional world is Jobian, his "characters often cry out, defy, and accept."[16] Yakov's religious skepticism may be read as a parallel to Holocaust survivors' protests against divine injustice. Whereas Bok's father-in-law "subscribes to the position of Job. . . . For Yakov, on the other hand, God is guilty: . . . Yakov . . . concentrates upon God's injustice and Job's defiant reaction, his rebellion against God."[17] In an argument with his pious father-in-law, Bok bitterly refutes the old man's insistence on God's presence with his people: "He's with us till the Cossacks come galloping, then he's elsewhere. He's in the outhouse, that's where he is" (*F*, 14). Even when he reluctantly reads the New Testament given to him by his prison guard, Bok stresses God's culpability for allowing an innocent person to suffer crucifixion. If ambivalent about God, Bok is a devout believer in the right of Jewish people to live Jewishly, to honor the covenant, even when God fails. He remains defiant in his suffering to the end of his ordeal, choosing to suffer, not for God but for his fellow Jews. He chooses to endure a trial to support Jewish innocence and takes a stand for Jewish survival and the right of Jews to be terror free, pogrom free.

*The Fixer* is as much a novel of Jewish survival as are Holocaust novels. Like Holocaust writers who dramatize survivor regeneration through affirmation of Judaism and the Jewish people, Malamud casts Bok's spiritual survival in terms of political solidarity with the Jewish people. Bok's reaffirmation of his connection to Jewish interests coincides with his decision to reject Russian officialdom's offer to release him in exchange for his conversion to Christianity and his false testimony, which would endanger the entire Jewish population. He chooses self-sacrifice rather than betrayal of other Jews. His determination to prevent a pogrom that he knows would surely result from his false confession provides Bok the strength to withstand two-and-one-half years of sadism. His resistance to Russian brutality is reduced to the most elemental form, as it was in the Nazi camps: staying alive. Survival is resistance, for by staying alive Bok will force the government to bring him to trial. In the process he is transformed from self-denying to committed Jew. He discovers that his personal identity is more authentically related to his group identity than he had understood. Although Bok's transformation leads to political solution rather than orthodox religious observance, his new political awareness stems from his prison study of Jewish ethics, the Jewish moral imperative, and heightened loyalty to the Jewish people. Unlike Wiesel's and Singer's pious protestors who remain within the covenantal bond while contending with God, Bok's resolution is political rather than religious redemption.

Instead of concluding the novel with the historic acquittal, Malamud concludes the novel with Bok en route to his trial. To do otherwise

> would diminish a parable of universal relevance (the growth of a man) to an account of one a-typical historic moment (for the justice finally meted out to Mendel Beilis is not a justice one could rely on to recur in any repetition of the circumstances). And the inconclusiveness of the fable is surely its most important assertion of superiority over the conclusiveness of history. . . . The real trial is not a matter of sentence or acquittal but the imprisoned years which preceded it.[18]

As Holocaust parable, ending the novel prior to trial is most fitting. Its significance lies in the comparable injustice of Russian government sponsored anti-Semitic violence and the suffering of Jews in the Holocaust.

Malamud's use of Bok's dream parallels that of European Holocaust novelists' use of the device to delineate survivor anxieties. The dream vehicle of Russia's will to eliminate its Jews evokes Germany's Final Solution to the Jewish Problem. Czar Nicholas appears to reprimand Bok for being a Jew: "there are too many Jews—my how you procreate! Why should Russia be burdened with teeming millions of you? You yourselves are to blame for your troubles. . . . The ingestion of this tribe has poisoned Russia" (*F*, 225–26). The czar's anti-Semitism—although slightly less violent—recalls that of the ferryman, and his diction suggests Hitlerian jargon. The czar supported a program calling for the murder of one-third of Russia's Jewish population, exile of one-third, and Russification of the remaining third.

The government-sponsored pogrom in Russia parallels the

Final Solution of the Third Reich. The czar's genocidal intent of killing one-third of Russian Jewry parallels Hitler's annihilation of one-third of world Jewry. Calls by a mad priest for Bok's execution so as to expiate the death of Zhenia Golov anticipate the calls of Nazi Party members and their supporters to purge Europe of a poisonous racial influence. The official Russian investigation of the murder was nothing less than falsifying evidence to condemn a Jew for a crime that will affirm Christianity's religious prejudices. So too, the official German line constituted falsely blaming the Jews for Europe's economic and political ills and Germany's World War I defeat. Among many other Russian-Nazi analogies is the membership by Bok's employer in the Black Hundreds, an anti-Semitic league as dedicated to Jewish annihilation as Germany's *Schwarze Korps*, an organ of the SS. Bibikov, Bok's lawyer and the only Russian officer sympathetic to the Jew, is imprisoned and found hanging in his cell. Kogin, the only guard who showed Yakov compassion, is shot; both are grim parallels to the Nazi treatment of Europeans who sought to aid Jews during the Holocaust. Bok's tormentors know that a hostile populace will either remain silent and comply tacitly, or actively participate in the persecution of a Jew. Similarly, Hitler understood that an anti-Semitic world would either ignore his nation's barbarity against the Jews and thus perpetuate his goal, as did England and the United States, or contribute to the destruction of European Jewry as did Austria, France, the Ukraine, Russia, and Poland.

Addressing the subject of the "new novel," specifically the critical theory positing the subordination of content to the highest concerns of art—art as pure aesthetic—Malamud writes in support of fiction that values historic experience. Among the experiences he cites as crucial to his own art is "How Hitler, a fanatic with stench for a soul, came to power in Germany. A line of Jews more than a thousand miles long was gassed to death, their bodies plundered of shoes, teeth fillings, human fat for soap."[19]

Although Malamud appears reticent to treat the Holocaust directly, it is part of the informing consciousness of much of his fiction. The impact of the Holocaust on our time is forcefully rendered through his survivor-mentors initiating American innocents to Holocaust awareness through authorial commentary, metaphor, and allusion. That Malamud chose an indirect rather than direct method of coping with the most traumatic event of recent Jewish history offers powerful testimony to the American writer's difficulty in coming to terms with the literary transmission of the Holocaust and attests to the validity of Alvin Rosenfeld's thesis that

> all novels about Jewish suffering written in the post-Holocaust period must implicate the Holocaust, whether it is expressly named as such or not. An especially artful writer, . . . might succeed in oblique or indirect representation of this most horrific of all Jewish tragedies, but whatever the overt terms of their fictions, covertly the Holocaust will make itself strongly felt. . . . The phenomenology of Jewish suffering makes such identifications inevitable.[20]

# CHAPTER FOUR

*Chaim Rumkowski and the Lodz Ghetto in Leslie Epstein's*
King of the Jews

Leslie Epstein's Holocaust fiction is shaped by his preference for documentary testimony and by the Coleridgean principle of dissolving, diffusing, dissipating, in order to recreate.[1] In a *Partisan Review,* assessment of Terrence Des Pres' *The Survivor,* written three years before publication of *King of the Jews* (1979), Epstein observed:

> I have come, finally and reluctantly, to the conclusion that almost any honest eye-witness testimony of the Holocaust is more moving and more successful at creating a sense of what it must have been like in the ghettos and the camps than almost any fictional account of the same events.[2]

The commonplace quality of Holocaust horror —"the way in which it fit unobtrusively into our world"[3]—is powerfully conveyed in Epstein's appropriation and fidelity to the accounts and evaluations of historians Gerald Reitlinger, Leonard Tushnet, Isaiah Trunk, and Hannah Arendt and thus constitutes a significant con-

103

tribution to American evidenciary Holocaust literature. True to his belief that Holocaust fiction commands insufficient authority in its own right, Epstein has, like John Hershey in *The Wall,* appropriated the Ringelblum *Notes from the Warsaw Ghetto* and, like William Styron in *Sophie's Choice,* incorporated historic figures in his Baluty Suburb, which is modeled on the Lodz Ghetto. With greater artistic invention than Hershey and greater breadth and depth of historic matter than Styron, Epstein has sustained a provocative synthesis of historic analysis and creative imagination. *King of the Jews* is generally faithful to fact and to the tone of chroniclers and critics of the Lodz Ghetto Jewish elder. Like Rolf Hochhuth's *The Deputy,* Leslie Epstein's *King of the Jews* has caused controversy and contradictory critical reaction. Each work is situated between documentation and art, and each offers peculiar difficulties to the critic who must weigh the claims of history and art in evaluating the artist's interpretation of history. The authors adhere to the facts while allowing their imaginations free play as they transform their raw historic matter into art. Part of the fascination of reading Epstein's novel is the process of discerning the fusion of documentary and imaginative material. Often, when Epstein adds inventive material, he enhances the thematic import of his novel.

Reading Gerald Reitlinger's *The Final Solution,* Epstein became intrigued by the artistic potential of the Lodz Ghetto elder, Mordechai Chaim Rumkowski; it was an opportunity to recreate "a fabulous character and a wonderful story."[4] According to Reitlinger:

> In Lodz, . . . the Germans chose a president in October, 1939, who suited their purposes for nearly five years. Mordechai Chaim Rumkowski, the manager of a Jewish orphanage, was known for his skill in raising subscriptions. Besides this gift, which had such obvious appeal for the Germans, Rumkowski possessed resiliency. He was ordered to appoint a Jewish Council, who were then imprisoned as hostages. Badly beaten up while trying to obtain their release, Rumkowski was forced to appoint another council, but thereafter was not physically molested. He was treated like a dog outside the ghetto, but allowed to be a king within the barbed wire. He issued currency notes bearing his signature, and postage stamps engraved with his portrait, a genial elderly philanthropist with a cloak and a flowing mane of white hair, who moved about the ghetto in a respectable broken-down carriage. Rumkowski believed that the position the Germans had accorded him could be used to save Jewish

lives during the resettlements. Thus, in September, 1942, he marched to the station with the children whom the Germans had demanded—for had not the Germans spared his own orphanage? Even in August, 1944, when close on 100,000 Lodz Jews had been "resettled," he sponsored the treacherous appeal of the ghetto administrator, Hans Biebow. Then, perceiving the trap he had baited, Rumkowski voluntarily boarded the train for Auschwitz, where he was seen going into the gas chamber.[5]

In addition to providing Epstein the Rumkowski character, Reitlinger's book is most likely his source for several incidents, character relationships, and names.[6]

Although Reitlinger's basic description is the kernel for *King of the Jews,* Epstein gleaned extensive detail for his portrait of I. C. Trumpelman from Leonard Tushnet's *Pavement of Hell,* a study of the ghetto leaders of Lodz and Vilna, and Isaiah Trunk's *Judenrat: The Jewish Councils in Eastern Europe Under Nazi Occupation.* The Coleridgean theory of fusion is applied in Epstein's pastiche of the Lodz, Warsaw, and Vilna Ghetto experiences and in the skillful amalgam of Rumkowski and Jacob Gens (the Vilna Ghetto leader) with fictional invention. The inclusion and superimposition of speeches by Gens and Rumkowski invests the fictional Trumpelman with an authentic aura, while the invented material heightens his megalomania. Like all the scholars, diarists, and novelists who try to comprehend and delineate the Rumkowski figure,[7] Epstein is caught between sharply polarized feelings. Acknowledging the unprecedented evil under which the elder had to function, the novelist dramatizes the dilemma of balancing loyalty to one's people with obedience to the enemy who sustains one's position and authority. Lucjan Dobroszycki, editor of *The Chronicle of the Lodz Ghetto 1941–1944,* which appeared five years after *King of the Jews,* presents a contemporary's impression of Rumkowski as "a man divided into two extreme mutually contradictory parts: a well mannered man, tidy, peaceful, good, religious, a traditional Jew on the one hand and, on the other, sordid, ridiculous, ironic, slovenly, insideous, unpredictable, treacherous, murderous."[8] Italian survivor-novelist Primo Levi writes that Rumkowski "was or appeared to be a fool with a very respectable air; . . . an ideal puppet."[9] Levi judges Rumkowski's four-year presidency as "an amazing tangled megalomaniacal dream of barbaric vitality and real diplomatic and organizational ability."[10] Saul Bellow characterizes the Rumkowski reign as a parody of kingship, installed for Nazi amusement; the elder, "a mad Jewish king presiding over the death of half a million people,"[11] was forced to play the role of mock king to relieve the horror of the ghetto for the occupying Germans, who saw in his role further degradation of the Jews. In contrast to the brief portraits of Rumkowski in the works of Bellow and Levi, Epstein's characterization benefits from a thorough exploration of motivation and physical context.

Epstein's portrayal of Trumpelman, balanced by sympathy and condemnation, reflects the debate regarding the men whose Holocaust tragedy was compounded by the morally ambiguous role Germans thrust upon them. Epstein sympathetically dramatizes Trumpelman's dilemma—the virtually impossible task of saving Jews in an environment designed to annihilate them. Epstein's Trumpelman is a complex and contradictory figure: a sinner-saviour, a charismatic healer, an antipogrom activist, a persuasive speaker, a charlatan, a dictator, and a gullible victim. He is less evil than the Nazis he obeys and less good than the Jews he tries to serve. Trumpelman is at once a pathetic victim of a potent malevolent force, the epitome of vulnerability, a despot whose arbitrary vengeance represents the brutality and irrationality of the Reich's evil course. His noble effort to save Jews through their slave labor is balanced by his autocratic dispersal and deportation of smugglers, strikers, and sabateurs. Epstein's judgment against Trumpelman lies in three major areas: his self-delusion; his exultation in dictatorial power (illustrated in the issuing of ghetto currency and postage bearing his likeness); and, most tragically, in his betrayal of Jews through compliance with Nazi "resettlement" orders.

Unlike the ensuing chapters that faithfully adhere to the tragic events of the Lodz Ghetto and the career of its elder, the novel's first chapter, aptly titled "The Golden Age" and set in the two decades preceding the German occupation of Poland, relies heavily on literary invention to establish character motivation. Biographical detail in this chapter exaggerates Trumpelman's egocentricism at the expense of the complexity of his model's social and communal role. I. C. Trumpelman, a Lithuanian Jew from Vilna, arrives in the Polish manufacturing city of Lodz to make his fortune and rise in the sociopolitical hierarchy of the Jewish community. Trumpelman shares Rumkowski's mercurial business career, especially its failures—and his reputation for inappropriate conduct with female charges. However, Epstein supplants Rumkowski's decision to forgo a lucrative insurance contract in order to avoid a conflict of interest with Trumpelman's insurance fraud,[12] thereby rendering the fictional character immoral prior to his assumption of power. Similarly, although Rumkowski managed a famous orphanage whose reputation was among the best in Poland, Trumpelman is a self-aggrandizing, opportunistic buffoon who attains the directorship of the Hatters' Assylum by chance and administers it by whim. The Trumpelman of Chapter One shares neither his model's community-service record nor his political activism. Whereas Rumkowski was vice-president of the *Kehillah* (a Jewish community council elected by the populace to administer philanthropic institutions, organize Jewish schools, and license ritual officials) and fought Polish anti-Semitism through accommodation, and when that failed turned to Zionism,[13] Trumpelman is apolitical prior to ghettoization. Trumpelman occasionally engages in spontaneous heroism rather than disciplined political action and is motivated by genuine love of children and a hero complex. Epstein also takes liberty with Rumkowski's personal life to further demean the Trumpelman character. Rumkowski's courtship and marriage to a respected young lawyer becomes a tawdry liaison between Trumpelman and a singer, who is unaccountably transformed from victim-waif to scheming Lady Macbeth. The only similarity between the real and fictive elders' courtships and marriages is the union of an old man and a young woman.

Because the introductory chapter dramatizes Trumpelman in the role of buffoon sinner-saint, the burlesque ghetto-god of the remainder of the novel is more convincing. The invented biographic detail is consistent with Epstein's satiric tone and artistic purpose and meticulously establishes authenticity for the self-aggrandizing megalomaniac that Trumpelman will become under Nazi auspices. The perpetrator of a prewar insurance fraud is a credible wartime collaborator. A pre-Holocaust, mythic healer-hero who saves orphans from an epidemic and confronts anti-Semitic looters and hooligans during a pogrom is a believable Holocaust-era negotiator with the occupying military force. Charlatan physician begets charlatan ghetto-savior. It is important to note the discrepancies between invention and documentation, precisely because Epstein's characteristic adherence to and fusion of historic material is so impressive.

Although Epstein's work began in fascination with the most eccentric and controversial of the *Judenrat* elders, *King of the Jews* is a full scale study of a wide range of Holocaust events and subjects: the vicissitudes of a slave-labor ghetto with its overlords, police, bureaucrats, political factions, heroes, rebels, and victims. Far more than a realistic rendering of the hardships endured, the novel fuses history and art to convey the essential evil of the Nazi universe, particularly the insidious way it compromised its Jewish victims and led them to do its bidding.

Some artists have argued that traditional literary forms and vocabularies are unequal to Holocaust treatment, but Epstein has succeeded aesthetically in demonstrating how conventional forms can be adapted to Holocaust subject matter and has succeeded philosophically by using classical forms to elucidate Western civilization's role in the creation of a social and political atmosphere that fostered and supported the Holocaust. Unlike most Holocaust fiction that centers around a family and its associates, *King of the Jews* presents a panoramic grouping of public voices speaking in Greek choral dialogues representing social and political factions—voices unified by the interpretive presence of a survivor who attained maturity in the ghetto world. Characteristic of the novel's imaginative heights is the superb fusion of art and history that concludes Chapter 1, a morality play that is a prologue and transition from the "golden age" to the iron age of Nazism.

Christian and Nazi anti-Semitism are linked by evoking traditional medieval morality drama with a Nazi-sponsored street play whose literary and polemical source is church endorsement of the blood-libel canard periodically invoked to incite violence against Jewish populations. Adhering to medieval form, actors perform an anti-Semitic diatribe upon a wagon in the town square for an audience of soldiers, *Volksdeutschers* (ethnic Germans), Poles, and reluctant Jews. The narrator advises the audience that it will see an accurate historic event; he then verbally sets the scene: the Jewish cemetery in Prague where the alleged Elders of Zion met to conspire against Christian Europe and to further Jewish domination of the world. A Rothschild stereotype speaks predictably of financial control, and other tribal leaders address disruptive methods such as pestilence, famine, and economic upheavals. While the actors perform the ritual blood-libel charge of Jews draining the blood of an innocent Christian youth, the audience is encouraged to take vengeance against local Jews. Having stimulated the audience to violence, the stage manager detains it just long enough to watch the play's conclusion—the Nazis's gallant rescue of Christian Europe from the Jewish menace. From the wagon's heaven,

> a cloud descended with soldiers on it, the Others, the Lords and Masters. They shot bullets from their guns and the Elders of Zion fell into the pit. Then the top part of the wall shut up and the bottom third of the wagon opened. You could see that the Jews had fallen into the mouth of hell. There were flames there, real flames, among which the Jews danced.[14]

The cheering audience provides the play's epilogue, which has been carefully orchestrated throughout the performance. The audience is dismissed with the blessings of the occupying army to institute a spontaneous anti-Jewish action, to beat local Jews and plunder their property with impunity, a *Kristallnacht* writ small. Pagent cart bells and peeling church bells reverberate the thematic juxtaposition of Christian and Nazi anti-Semitism. The street play not only coalesces pernicious medieval blood libel and modern *Protocols of the Elders of Zion* propaganda, it introduces images of flame, smoke, and grave to foreshadow the crematoria and smoke-stacks of the death camps and the mass graves of Europe. Epstein's delineation of parallels between Christian and Nazi anti-Semitism recalls Rolf Hochhuth's in *The Deputy*. The play's "spiritual architect of Auschwitz [is] not Heinrich Himmler, but Ignatius Loyola, whose *Spiritual Exercises* are cited in act five as prototype of the extermination camps."[15] The church is linked to the Holocaust through Pope Pius XII and through one of its great saints, whose powerful imaginings of auto-da-fé foreshadow the crimes of the Nazis.[16]

Demonstrating the relationship of propagandistic art and its consequences, the apres-theatre hooliganism clearly and dramatically links medieval, church-orchestrated pogrom with the Nazi-orchestrated campaign of terror and stands as Epstein's indictment of Christian culpability in laying the foundation for the genocide of European Jewry. Juxtaposed with the play is a demonstration in an adjacent square where a prominent Jew is publicly humiliated. A financier, dressed in a fur coat that his tormentors have turned backwards and buttoned up the spine, is tossed like a ball between two German soldiers, one of whom beats him for daring to salute as the other rains blows on him for failing to salute an officer of the

Reich. The effect of this juxtaposition is Shakespearean, one scene echoes the other and enlarges its implications.

The morality drama's insistence on the canard of a destructive, secret Council of Jewish Elders provides an ironic transition to the actual German establishment of its *Judenrat*, the Jewish Council of Elders forced to administer German law in the ghetto. Although Epstein takes literary license with the details of the historic Lodz *Judenrat* creation, he does so to present an impressionistic scene of absurdist drama and to reinforce the causal connection between Christian and Nazi anti-Semitism.

The Nazi-appointed Jewish Councils were neither answerable to nor legitimated by the Jewish community. Although the Jews assumed that the Councils would represent and protect their interests, the Councils were imposed by the Germans to control Jewish populations and to be responsible to Nazi authorities for the implementation of their orders. The Council offered the illusion of Jewish autonomy and security within the legal order of the ghetto, while it was, in fact, an illusion expressly manipulated by the Nazis to facilitate orderly genocide. *Judenrat* officials suffered the strain of contradictory objectives, serving Jewish interests while complying with Nazi orders. Beyond the historic basis of the elder's portrait, much of the novel's authenticity stems from Epstein's recreation of the *Judenrat's* management of ghetto employment assignments, food and housing distribution, police operations; its prevention of sabotage; its compliance with German orders; and, most tragically, its role in implementing selections for deportations to concentration and death camps.

The *Judenrat* formation scene dramatically juxtaposes the dynamics of Nazi deceit and abuse of power with Jewish confusion and impotence. At the Cafe Astoria, a gathering place of influential Lodz Jews, *Obergruppenfuhrer* Grundtripp briskly defines the *Judenrat* operations to the Jewish patrons:

> This Council will be an instrument of our will among the Jews. It shall raise taxes and control its own police. It will run all religious organizations, all cultural affairs, all charitable institutions. It appoints the judges, the teachers, the hospital heads. . . . Your first task will be to draw up a census with the name of each able-bodied Jew. All men between the ages of fifteen and sixty must work on the river dike. The only exceptions are those too sick even to lift a shovel, and of course the sixteen members of the Council itself. The rest will work, work! (*KJ*, 41)

F. X. Wohltat feigns having the Jews' best interests at heart and warmly advises the Astoria group to choose from "The most intelligent, the most resourceful among you" (*KJ*, 42), knowing full well that the best and brightest will be killed to induce the submission of the remainder. While most of the Jews hope to outwit the Nazis by electing the dissolved *Kehillah* to the *Judenrat*, Trumpelman balks and convinces them to cooperate with the Germans in an effort to retain a small measure of control and responsibility for the Jewish community. Because he believes he is destined to play an important role in Jewish history, Trumpelman volunteers to serve on the Council and proclaims his code of survival through labor:

> You heard the news that the Conquerers set up labor brigades. But they don't care about damming the rivers or blasting tunnels for mountain roads. No! The Jews dig holes and then fill them in. They carry rocks from one side of the road to the other and then drag them back again. Jews working! That's what the Others want. (*KJ*,45)

Reacting to the group's counterproductive proposals, Trumpelman suggests that they accept the burden of leadership to save Jews from arbitrary German selection for hard labor, a foreshadowing of the argument for Jewish cooperation in the preparation of "resettlement" quotas.

> At least if there's a Judenrat to make a list, there will be exemptions. . . . To let children work in the river, to let sick people carry stones—it's the same thing as murder. . . . Either we have the courage to make this census or it will be made for us, according to whim, to passion, to chance! We have to do what we can! (*KJ*, 46)

The council members are forced to disrobe and entertain the Germans with a game of leapfrog and then they are shot. Although the fictional election and execution of the Council is condensed into one day and is, therefore, a departure from the historic Council's imprisonment prior to its murder,[17] the scene functions as another foreshadowing of later "selections." In an invented scene that suggests the precarious nature of Jewish life in Nazi-occupied Poland, I. C. Trumpelman survives the massacre because he dallied with the cafe singer when the others departed. With equal arbitrariness, he is elevated by the Germans to the position of chairman and ordered to appoint another Council.

Despite the critical charge that Epstein fails to present the true villainy of Germany at the expense of his attention to Jewish collaboration, making the Holocaust appear "an internal Jewish matter,"[18] Epstein does dramatize the Germans in a manner that suggests both their duplicity and their barbarism in debilitating, exploiting, brutalizing, and murdering six million European Jews. Although he uses euphemistic designations that work ironically, Epstein has done more than most American novelists to treat the Nazis in a way that dramatizes their corruption and evil. The novel's euphemistic designations for the Germans—"Brave Ones," "Warriors," "Others"—are a source of considerable critical ire;[19] however, these may be read as an allusive reference to *Nazideutsch*, the perversion of language to conceal criminal behavior—that is, to conceal the Nazi mission until they were certain that the nations of the world supported or acquiesced in their genocidal purpose. Rather than absolve the Germans of guilt, Epstein's parody of *Nazideutsch* echoes George Steiner's thesis that there is a straight line from corruption of language to corruption of power, from designating people as vermin to the extermination process; this parody is Orwellian in emphasizing Nazi criminality.

Just as the Jewish elder is modeled on Rumkowski, so, too, is the German administrator based on the Lodz chief officer, Hans Biebow. Beyond the influence of Gerald Reitlinger's presentation of Biebow, Epstein draws on the work of Hannah Arendt, particularly her assessment of Nazis as bourgeois businessmen, ordinary job holders and family men.[20] F. X. Wohltat, like Biebow, saw in a productive ghetto an opportunity for personal financial gain and consequently tried to stall its liquidation. Epstein creates Wohltat as an ethnic German who had been living in Lodz and knew the Jews prior to the invasion. An opportunist who rises to power by virtue of his German ethnicity, he deceives the Jews by appealing to them as a neighbor who shares their interest in their beloved city. In contrast to the novel's highest ranking German, Grundtripp, who remains the stereotypical arrogant, aggressive shadowy Nazi of American fiction, Wohltat is a believable, three-dimensional minor character.

Typical of Epstein's fusion and compression of historic sequence and duration of events is his linkage of a second Jewish Council and announcement of the establishment of the Baluty ghetto. In fact, the events were quite separate. The second Council was formed on November 11, 1939, and preparations for the ghetto had begun early in the winter of 1939. On February, 8, 1940, the Lodz chief of police ordered the establishment of the ghetto, and on April 30 ordered the Jewish quarter definitively closed.[21] Pretending ignorance of Grundtripp's intent to murder the first Council, Wohltat solicitously offers the Jews a ready solution to the haphazard beatings and killings: the organization of a protective "special quarter, just for the Jews" (*KJ*, 56) to which they must move within seventy-two hours.

The Germans offered several pretexts for the establishment of ghettos. They rationalized isolation of the Jews as a safety precaution for the Polish and ethnic German population, freeing them of the "criminal element," "bearers of contagious diseases," and from "economic parasites." In fact, the ghetto eliminated the economic presence of the Jews in the manufacturing center, dividing them from the local population by placing them in the decrepit Baluty slum district (the geographic region whose name Epstein takes for that of the fictional ghetto). The ghetto enabled the Nazis to curtail the food supply and hasten their death through starvation, a first step in the long range genocidal objective, and it offered the distinct advantage of conveniently assembling them for projected resettlement to concentration and death camps. Although the death centers had not yet been established at the time of Council and ghetto formation, ghettos were established by the Germans to process Jews toward the ultimate goal of annihilation.[22]

Like their historic counterparts, Trumpelman and the novel's Jews initially welcome the ghetto as a haven from oppressive mobs and sporadic, government-sponsored anti-Semitic violence. Like Rumkowski, Trumpelman envisioned the ghetto as an autonomous Jewish enclave, a miniature state with a large measure of self-rule, directing its own administrative bureaucracy, police force, fire brigade, postal service, currency exchange, school system, and health care. And, like Rumkowski, Trumpelman aspired to be the Moses of the ghetto, keeping his people alive until the defeat of Germany and Jewish liberation from slavery. Like Rumkowski, who ruled as a virtual dictator and led the longest surviving ghetto in occupied Europe, Trumpelman argues that the only means the Jews have to achieve *lebensrecht* is to make the ghetto indispensable to German needs. To that end, he transforms the ghetto into a major manufacturing unit.

Although most Jews objected to the elder's dictatorial rule

and bombastic style,[23] many believed he was acting on their behalf, welcomed his efforts, and praised him lavishly in the early years of the ghetto.[24] Two invented ghetto scenes early in the novel foster the image of a man consumed by both genuine desire to save Jews and illusions of grandeur. When Trumpelman enters a burning building during a ghetto fire and emerges unscathed half-an-hour later with a child the fire brigade could not reach, his reputation soars and the Jews transfer their faith in his apparent indom-inability to themselves—seeing the survival of many linked to this chosen one. Striving to reinforce his heroic image and the commu-nity's dependence on him, Trumpelman succumbs to deceit. In collusion with the German administrator, he orchestrates the res-cue of Jewish girls commandeered for German whoredom. Just as the Germans arrive at the grand opening of a "House of Pleasure," Trumpelman appears and sends the girls home to their families. He smashes furniture and announces that the *Judenrat* will trans-form the "House of Pleasure" into a "House of Culture" to serve Jewish needs. Later, Trumpelman is beaten by Wohltat for over-playing his part and destroying valuable property. That the elder sustained a beating is historically accurate; its cause was Rumkowski's plea for the release of the incarcerated Council mem-bers—not his unplanned destruction of furniture, which occurred as a result of his collaboration with Germans in a plan to elevate his standing in the Jewish community.

The Trumpelman/Wohltat alliance, far-fetched as it seems, is based on the Rumkowski/Biebow association.[25] Because the ghetto could not rely on help from the outside and would have to become self-supporting to survive, Rumkowski sought to prove to Hans Biebow that the Jewish workers were indespensible to the German war effort. Biebow, a former merchant from Bremen with a degree in business administration, saw an opportunity in a productive ghetto to improve himself financially and to rise in the Nazi ranks.[26] He "encouraged Rumkowski in his design to set up facto-ries. . . . he got orders from the armaments industry for Rumkowski; he prevailed on higher officials to permit checks from abroad to be used as working capital to start ghetto industry; he even argued that the Jews should get more food so that they could produce more."[27] The Germans supplied the raw materials for the Jewish laborers (often from confiscated Jewish property) at an arbi-trary price and paid the ghetto for its finished products in food, the cost of which was 20 percent higher than in the city.[28] Since the ghetto was sealed off from the outside world, it was through German agencies that the products of the factories were exchanged for food rations.

The Trumpelman/Rievesaltes rivalry is also founded on documentary evidence rooted in the Lodz Ghetto. Central to understanding the tone and detail of the Trumpelman/Rievesaltes relationship is a comparison of the fictional rendition with the historic analyses in Leonard Tushnet's *Pavement of Hell* and Emanuel Ringelblum's *Notes*. Rievesaltes is a composite of David Gertler, head of the Lodz Special Division, and the typical corrupt ghetto police official, the sharp dealer who made a profit by exploiting desperate human beings. Rather than Gertler's prewar Secret Police credentials,[29] Rievesalte's background involves ruthless criminality. He is a man void of moral scrupples—a characteristic common to Nazi lackies. David Gertler's police unit was "to inform Rumkowski of activities subversive of him and of the German rulers, to abort resistance efforts, and to uncover for confiscation any hidden Jewish assets in the ghetto."[30] Epstein's police chief is the elder's major personal and political rival. Although Trumpelman and Rievesaltes are drammatic foils, they lack clear moral distinction. Both are villains and victims of a great evil force that empowers them, even as it exploits, manipulates, and eventually destroys them. However, the ghetto rivalry is murky, a blurred confusion of fair and foul in each character. Epstein would have served history and art more faithfully had he restricted their contest to the political realm rather than demeaning tragedy with the farcical intrusion of the rivalry for Madame Trumpelman's affections.

Despite the Nazi pretexts for establishment of ghettos, their real intent is manifested in the creation of extreme conditions of deprivation and defenselessness. Through starvation, substandard housing, inadequate fuel and medication, and excessive hard labor, the Germans believed they would achieve the physical, mental, and social destruction of Jewish communities. Because the Jews were cut off from the general economy, their sources of income seized or prohibited, their businesses expropriated, their personal property stolen or confiscated, and because they were pressed into labor for which they received no payment, save insufficient food rations, hunger was a focal point of ghetto suffering. Epstein's just emphasis on the debilitating process of relentless starvation charts the terrible deprivation Lodz Jews suffered. Authenticity of ghetto conditions is also achieved by incorporation of the administrative establishment of soup kitchens, disbursement of rations, and the creation of garden plots. In contrast to the successful Vilna and Warsaw smuggling networks of adults and children, organized to bring contraband food into the ghettos to supplement the inadequate rations, Lodz Ghetto was effectively sealed prohibiting smuggling.

Among the methods Rumkowski used to solidify his power was the control of the ghetto food supply. To frustrate smuggling, which he perceived as a threat to his economic control, he instituted use of ghetto currency (Rumkies) to curtail the power and corruption of the ghetto police, who would then no longer find it profitable to deal with smugglers. In a scene that begins with rare comic relief, but develops as the turning point in the narrator's attitude toward Trumpelman, orphans conduct a madcap internal smuggling mission attempting to transfer a cow from the elder's estate to a clandestine nursery. When Lipiczany and his accomplices botch the job, the culprits (aside from Lipiczany) must pull the ghetto fecal wagon while wearing signs identifying them as smugglers.[31] The punishment is the catalyst for Lipiczany's reassessment of Trumpelman. Whereas Lipiczany had worshiped Trumpelman as his personal savior for delivering him from a coma and as ghetto savior for keeping Jews alive with welfare and work programs, he now condemns him. Epstein underscores Trumpelman's immorality by having him deny ghetto starvation: "Everybody in my Ghetto has enough to eat! Only they have to work! . . . The Elder won't allow Jewish loafers in the Balut!"(*KJ*, 80). Similarly, he demeans himself further by invoking Fascists as role models: "Someday an important official from Berlin—the Hunter, the Schoolmaster, maybe even the Big Man himself—will come to inspect our streets. He doesn't want to see merchants and middlemen: . . . when he sees workers . . . he will say, *Live! Live!*" (*KJ*, 80–81).

Complementing his fuller treatment of ghetto and *Judenrat* is Epstein's thorough and varied treatment of Jewish resistance to Nazi oppression. In addition to smuggling, the Hatters' Asylum orphans, soon distinguished from the others as "the fat orphans who lived inside the asylum," resist segregation from the underprivileged, and throw bags of sugar and wool over the walls that separate them from the less fortunate who earn a living by spinning sugar into flower-shaped treats and wool into patches and six-pointed stars. Their generosity and bravery is sharply contrasted to the corrupt, self-serving officials. The youngsters' assertiveness reflects the activities of Jewish children throughout Europe who slipped through sewers and ghetto walls, risking death to bring food into the ghettos.

Jewish resistance is also delineated in the ghettoites' defiance of a German ban on Jewish births. As production quotas increase and food supplies sent into the ghetto are reduced, the elder announces a German decree forbidding new Jewish life and the role Jewish police must play in enforcing the law. Some ghettoites interpret the order as a confirmation of the efficacy of Trumpelman's survival work policy—that ghetto labor has indeed become indispensable to the German war effort. Others register their defiance by aiding and abetting the delivery and care of Jewish infants. Epstein stages a dramatic vingette in which Trumpelman responds to a night scream to discover a clandestine maternity ward and nursery, evidence of resistance by the weaponless, starved, and enslaved. Torn between support for the Jews and fear of German detection, Trumpelman expresses his ambivalence by describing the nursery as an unregistered "factory," a challenge to his authority that he is willing to overlook. Trumpelman's prewar foil, the playboy socialite, Dr. Zam, whom he replaced at the Hatters' Asylum, has been transformed in the Holocaust crucible and now risks his life to assist Jewish births. In a scene prefiguring Dr. Zam's final sacrifice in the ghetto fighters' collaboration with Russian commandos, the prewar physician *manqué* is redeemed as a resistance worker who negotiates amnesty for the nursery patrons and workers. Unlike the punishment assigned the boy smugglers that testifies to Trumpelman's administrative paranoia, the nursery scene illustrates his compassion.

Holocaust literature amply records Jewish impotence in the face of Nazi atrocity. Only recently has there been recognition and documentation of Jewish resistance efforts in the ghettos and concentration camps. With the exception of the explorations of the Warsaw Ghetto uprising based on the Ringelblum diary in *The Wall* and *Mila 18*, American fiction has been essentially mute on the topic of Jewish resistance to Nazism. In the nursery, cow smuggling, and food transfer scenes, Epstein poignantly captures the tenacious, individual heroic acts of resistance. His accounts of the Lodz Ghetto's large-scale work stoppages and sabotage operations constitute a significant contribution to American literary treatment of the Holocaust. Guided by the same Coleridgean principles of

fusion that governed his character constructs, Epstein supplements
the historic strikes and leftist opposition that took place in Lodz
with events borrowed from the Jewish resistance movements in the
Vilna and Warsaw ghettos,[32] events that could not have been dupli-
cated in the sealed Lodz Ghetto.

"The Five Day Strike," in which the textile workers are emblematic of all the ghetto laborers, represents Epstein's careful incorporation of Lodz evidenciary material. Resistance mounts with
the rising death toll from starvation and disease, the ever higher
production demands, the demonic work taxes and needle taxes,
and rumors of a chair tax. Like Rumkowski, Trumpelman initially
responds to labor unrest with an appeasement policy, capitulating
to "the strong ones"—the butchers, porters, and draymen, who
demonstrate noisily, and the striking textile and shoe workers—by
allowing them to have shop stewards in the factories. He agrees to
increase relief allotments, supplementing the wages of workers
with families, allows the operation of independent soup kitchens,
and offers rent remittals.[33] He responds to the success of these
measures as did Rumkowski: by characterizing the strikers as a
threat to ghetto security; withdrawing all concessions; replacing
shop stewards with foremen to drive the workers to increased productivity; transforming food rations to weapons; closing independent soup kitchens; creating dissension by locking nonstrikers out
of their factories to deprive them of food; removing from the relief
roles those welfare recipients who refused to work; dismissing dis-
senters from their jobs, and adding their names to the "resettlement" lists in the event of further labor unrest.[34] When Trumpelman rejects a worker's explanation that inferior labor is the
result of starvation and exhaustion and countercharges that the
workers are committing sabotage by producing inferior uniforms,
a Bundist urges the workers to revolt, to refrain from sewing uniforms for the oppressor, to resist collaboration. The elder counters
by demanding that the ghettoites produce every uniform the con-
querer wears and that Lodz become the foremost clothing manufacturing center in Europe to insure their survival. He punctuates
his order by slapping the offending Bundist and overturning the
soup cauldron in front of the starving men. Thus, Trumpelman
defeats his own purpose and provokes a general strike.

Trumpelman is physically absent from the following forty
pages as Epstein concentrates on the plight of the striking workers

and the machinations of their Nazi antagonists. Here, the novelist abandons the ironic tone and adopts an objective, reportorial voice similar to that of the Ringelblum diary entries and the *The Chonicle of the Lodz Ghetto: 1941 to 1944*. Despite Trumpelman's absence from the scene, his influence is felt in the oppressive measures taken against the workers.

Political meetings are banned as are street gatherings of more than five Jews and indoor gatherings of more than ten unrelated Jews in one room. Solidarity within the Jewish community is undermined by officialdom's exploitation of internal political divisiveness. While the *Judenrat* tries to protect its power base, unjustly penalized nonstrikers turn against strikers; an orthodox rabbi resentful of Communist influence plots against the leftists; and nonleftists, Bundists, and others have difficulty coordinating resistance strategy.

The Nazis contribute to strikebreaking by instituting terrorist actions against individual rebels to dissuade others. They display the broken body of a tortured artist-resister and publicly murder him as an object lesson to obstinate Jews. On this occasion the German administrator advises the assembled witnesses: "All those who violate the laws of the Occupying Power will be crushed the way lice are crushed. Do not make trouble but return now to your work. . . . If you refuse, you will end up the same as this garbage" (*KJ*, 124). Wohltat despairs only of lost profits: "if the strike is not quickly ended, everything will be lost. Our investments. Our profits. A fortune in reichs-marks" (*KJ*, 139). He describes himself as a Chinaman and the Jews as his silk worms: "As long as they spin silk, I supply them with mulberry leaves. But if the spinning should stop, when there's no more thread—then off you go to the east" (*KJ*, 140).

Although successes such as the Communist liberation of fellow Jews from the ghetto jail are short-lived, other actions clearly demonstrate the heroic determination of large numbers against formidable odds. Massive resistance on the fifth day of the strike takes shape as a protest march of Jewish war veterans. To his chagrin, the German administrator discovers that he has gatling guns trained on people displaying the Kaiser's World War I flag and a banner bearing the black Austro-Hungarian eagle. Despite Grundtripp's momentary spark of German sentiment, he orders eighty hunger marchers and their leader gunned down. Further, he threatens collective reprisals should a house-to-house search for a Communist strike leader fail and finally debilitates the Jews by instituting a new food blocade. The strike is broken.

A chapter entitled "The Wedding" juxtaposes the normalcy and absurdity that characterized German rule, which was designed to deceive, degrade, and destroy European Jewry. Juxtaposed with joyous anticipation of an extra food ration in celebration of the elder's wedding is the first deportation action. Just as the earlier Jewish hope that the ghetto be a safe haven from sporadic violence contrasted with the German intent that it be a deportation assembly zone, so the initial response to "resettlement" reflected the Jews' inclination to hope for deliverance and the Nazi will to commit genocide.

> When the patients were suddenly removed from the hospital, when the prisoners disappeared from the Tsarnecka Street jail, everyone accepted the explanation that the former were being transported to rest homes, the latter to work on the unfinished dikes. Then all the clothes came back, but not the people inside them. Suits and shoes and dresses piled up inside the Virgin Mary Church. Here was a difficult moment, a time for unthinkable thoughts. But before the Baluters could give way to despair, a big batch of postcards came through the Jewish mail. Each one . . . said much the same thing. *Life goes on. We grow stronger. Here there is marmalade.* (*KJ*, 101–2)

From this early "action," it is but a short step to the more ominous and grotesque announcement of Hitler's wedding gift to his Jewish king and queen: "a magnificent gift. . . . All Jews of Poland, and later all Jews everywhere, are to be resettled on the island of Madagascar" (*KJ*, 109).[35] In a grotesque parody of the German dream of a thousand-year Reich, the bridegroom proclaims his enthusiastic acceptance of the sanctuary on behalf of his people: "We shall build a kingdom there to last a thousand years!" (*KJ*, 101). From this point in the novel, deportations and mass killings become commonplace. First, ghettoites from the hospitals and jails are "resettled"; then volunteers, political opponents, and nonproductive workers are assigned to "farm labor" to purge the ghetto of undesirables.

Nothing better demonstrates the moral dilemma of the *Judenrat* than the demand imposed on its members to provide the Nazis with lists of "resettlement" candidates, and no section of the novel better illustrates the strengths and weaknesses of the Coleridgean fusion strategy that Epstein uses as his principal creative method. In "A Decision for the Judenrat," the Council confronts the task of compiling "resettlement" lists. Starvation and mounting death tolls associated with normal ghetto food rationing, productivity schedules, and police actions had tried the Council members sorely. The new "resettlement" order devastates them. Their impotence to cope with radical evil or to resist German orders is manifest as they weigh alternatives including mass resignation, stalling, disobedience, and mass suicide. Try as they may to believe the German labor rationale, the *Judenrat* members suspect a ruse because they have been ordered to choose young or old, sick or healthy people. Some balk, suspecting that the "resettlement" conditions will be harsher than advertised. When the Council considers refusing to supply names, German military aggression is threatened:

> It's either you or the Death's-Head troops. . . . Do you want them to make up the quota? Do you know what that will be like? They grab the first person they see. No matter who. The more important, the better. It could even be a Judenrat official—or a member's wife, or a member's child. They do the job with rifles and fists. And no one's counting either! Take everyone you can! By the neck! By the throat! Get a good grip on their hair! Take two hundred, or three hundred! Watch them squirm! (*KJ*, 155)

Through choral voices raising every option and its objection, Epstein articulates the capitulation of the Judenrat and dramatizes not only the members' personal anguish and despair, but their utter lack of choice. Like the mother forced to decide which of her children will go to the gas chamber and which will live, the Council must choose among tragic options. Efforts to apply logic, reason, and ethics to the killing program are doomed. Members express outrage and fear: "It's a scandal for Jews to put down the names of Jews!" (*KJ*, 154); "To send citizens out of their own country in time of war is a violation of international law!" (*KJ*, 154); "How do we know they're going to a farm? Maybe they'll have to dig dikes, or ditches" (*KJ*, 154). As the dilemma becomes more painful for the *Judenrat*, there is a decided shift in tone from Jewish compassion to Nazi diction advocating the expendability of "anti-social elements"—jail inmates, like those taken previously, rather than productive workers. In a *Nazideutsch*, self-deceptive parody, an unnamed victim argues: "we look at things this way. Not who should go but who should stay. The biologically sound material. The socially valuable elements" (*KJ*, 161). Perhaps because the diction sounds too Germanic, another figure substitutes a bearable fantasy: "It is not a question of life and death. We are simply deciding who is to continue to live in the Suburb and who shall live on a farm. It's not as if we were condemning people to prison" (*KJ*, 161). One member dares to intimate the previously unthinkable and unuttered truth:

> Why does the Conquerer wish us to become his accomplices in this matter? Why doesn't he simply take the farmers himself? It can only be because he is going to commit a crime so big that even he dares not do it alone. What could such a crime be? I have not thought so far. I only know if I were one of the Others the thing I would want most is for the Jews to do it for me. (*KJ*, 163)

An ambitious chapter in an ambitious novel, this section illustrates the strengths and pitfalls of Epstein's design strategy. The fusion of historic matter and invention is somewhat uneven here. Rumkowski was in fact asked to list 20,000 Jews and was able to bargain with Biebow to save 10,000; Epstein reduces the "resettlement" order to 100, but he retains the 50 percent salvation rate.[36] In a scene representative of the selection dilemma imposed on many Jewish Councils, Epstein incorporates details and lines from Reitlinger's and Tushnet's reports of an exchange between Vilna's Jacob Gens and a rabbinic council that sought to advise him. However, he so embellishes the exchange that much of its tragic tone is reduced to posturing. In *King of the Jews* a beaten and tortured group of rabbis is delivered to assist the Council in its selections. The Talmudic passages begin and progress effectively until Epstein incorporates unrelated sexual matters and diminishes through farce what would otherwise have been a sustained, solemn scene of moral significance. Both because of the futility of the rabbinic mission and Epstein's satiric tone, this scene fails to sustain its early tragic dimension. Epstein renders a dignified portrait of the secular opponents of the *Judenrat,* but the rabbinic portrait alternates injudiciously between tragedy and farce. The artistic failure of the debate lies in the author's unfortunate fusion of the Talmudic arguments that the Vilna Ghetto rabbis used to dissuade Jacob Gens from collaborating on deportation with arguments irrelevant to the issue and tonally inappropriate to the discussion.[37] It may be that the scene's problem lies with Epstein's failure to control his ingenuity and invention, leading to one critic's despair that the debates read like "snappy one-liners" of the "hyperactive Jewish moral imagination."[38] Historians like Steinberg, Reitlinger, and Tushnet make it quite clear that the rabbis told Gens that his reasoning was wrong, "that a Jew could be given up to the governing authority only if he were personally guilty of a crime and not merely because he was a Jew"[39]; they advised him of religious law by quoting the response given seven centuries earlier by Maimonides: "If the Pagans ask you [Jews] to deliver up one of your numbers so that he might be killed, for otherwise they would kill you all, you must have everyone killed and not deliver up a single Jewish soul." The tonal problem results from the introduction of a set of extraneous arguments, which cloud and detract from the selection issue by drawing attention to their own facile ingenuity. Even the pertinent contentions raised that retain the character of Talmudic dispute—that is, the examination of alternatives and exceptions to a given proposition—loose their force when juxtaposed with irrelevant discussions of sexual conduct. Although Epstein defends these inclusions by arguing they were raised in other ghettos, they seriously diminish his deliberation scene. Pertinent rejoinders—such as, if "the whole may be saved by the loss of the part, then the lesser evil must be done" (*KJ*, 166), and another about exceptions to the Maimonides' ruling consisting of compliance to a demand for a particular person in order to avoid greater bloodshed, the invocation of *kiddush ha-shem*, choosing death to sanctify God's Holy Name, and the Masada solution—work successfully. Their significance is compromised by debate regarding sexual indiscretion. Perhaps Epstein succumbs to farce in this sequence because he is more sympathetic to secular rather than religious Jewish leaders, and by his regard for Hannah Arendt's thesis that the vastness of Jewish losses is attributable to the cooperation of the Jewish leadership.[40]

The Council members determine to commit suicide en masse rather than turn over Jews to the Nazis, and here, too, Epstein resorts inappropriately to buffoonery. A desperate act reads like a comedy of errors when the group awakens from the sleeping pills it believed to be cyanide. Trumpelman has tricked them. He denounces their cowardice, reasserts his autocratic rule, and insists the Jews select their own for "resettlement" and thereby try to save as many as possible.

Trumpelman responds to Council disapproval by offering himself for postwar trial, as Jacob Gens did. Although Trumpelman's speech includes much of the same content as the Vilna leader's oratory, it exaggerates the oratorical style and content to fit the Rumkowski personality. Jacob Gens admitted his part in selections and recognized his low standing among his detractors in simple diction:

> Many Jews regard me as a traitor . . . I, Gens, lead you to death and I, Gens, want to rescue Jews from death. . . . If they ask me for a thousand Jews, I give them because if the Germans themselves came, they would take with violence not a thousand but thousands and thousands and the whole ghetto would be finished. With a hundred I save a thousand; with a thousand I save ten thousand. You're people of spirituality and letters. You keep away from such dirty doings in our ghetto. You'll go out clean. . . . but . . . if I survive, I'll go out covered with filth and blood will run from my hands. Nevertheless, I'd be willing to stand at the bar of judgment before Jews. I'd say I did everything to rescue as many Jews as I could and I tried to lead them to freedom. And in order to save even a small part of the Jewish people, I alone had to lead others to their deaths. And in order to insure that you go out with your clear consciences I have to forget mine and wallow in filth.[41]

In addition to reiterating the increased number and ferocity of a German selection, Trumpelman also invites judgment, but much more flamboyantly and in a manner some critics disparage as too theatrical:[42]

> I invite you to put me on trial when the war is over. Get a jury. A judge. I'll explain before the Jewish people, before history, what I had to do. And what if they find me guilty? Let them put me inside a cage, like an animal! Yes, I'm guilty! Because I did not sit and wring my hands! I dipped them in ink, the same as blood. (*KJ*, 176)

The Gens's source speech was delivered when the mass killings of Ponary Forest, outside Vilna, were widely known. It should be noted that in January 1942, Rumkowski/Trumpelman would not have known of the mass killings at Chelmno. Rumkowski believed the German explanation that deportations were necessary to rid the ghetto of "unemployables."[43] Whereas suspicions would develop later with the failure of resettled workers to return, at this stage people simply refused to "volunteer" for transfer, expecting more primitive work sites than in the ghetto, and took what precautions they could to remove their names from the lists.

Just as Rumkowski thought his work policy would preempt his ghetto from liquidation, so Trumpelman initially hopes for exemption from the extremes other ghettos suffer. When the Germans told Rumkowski that the deportations were necessary to rid the ghetto of "unemployables," it must have seemed plausible since it conformed to his work policy.[44] Similarly, Trumpelman and the others believe they are providing laborers for agricultural and other work sites and prefer that fellow Jews make the selection. Whereas Epstein had portrayed Trumpelman as autocratic and despotic in earlier sequences, he generally indicates the old man's overriding ambition to serve Jewish needs through his German-created position. Until this point in the novel, Trumpelman has been portrayed as a concerned, benevolent dictator, an efficient manager of the ghetto work force. When deportation enters the ghetto equation, Trumpelman weakens and consents more readily than the others, justifying himself by selecting the least productive of the ghetto in order to save the most valuable, the workers and the children. To disobey German orders was to put one's own life, one's family, and the community in jeopardy. Obedience facilitated temporary stays of execution and saved a remnant. The chapter concludes with further evidence of Trumpelman's unconscious rejection of the mass destruction of the Jews, a dream of a postwar paradisiacal Jewish homeland in Madagascar where Stalin, Roosevelt, Churchill, and the Pope come to pay a state visit and watch Jews strolling, conversing, and studying the holy books.

"A Decision for the Judenrat" suggests the deliberative rhetorical style of Talmudic debate and discourse. Its sequel, "The Yellow Bus," filters through the tormented consciousness of an adolescent eyewitness to mass murder. Tormented by the ominous accusations of ghetto leftists that Trumpelman is knowingly sending Jews to slaughter, Lipiczany secretly boards a "resettlement" transport to discover the deportees' true destination. After a perilous journey, the youngster arrives at a mobile killing unit, which preceded the technologically advanced gas chambers. "The forest itself seemed enchanted," a fairy tale scene in which "a child, with a kindly, befuddled father, and a mother who wishes to kill him, is left in just such an unnamed wood" (199). As the ghetto orphan watches from his hilltop hiding place, he soon realizes that this is not a tale from the brothers Grimm, but an evil hitherto unimagined. In Hemingwayesque, reportorial prose, Epstein renders the slaughter with German precision rather than Jewish emotion. Trains full of Jews arrive.

> the deportees put down their sacks and valises and began to take off their clothes. They took all their things off, in spite of the winter's cold. The men and the women tied their shoes together by the laces. Then they stood up, approximately in a line. . . . Then the back door of the bus swung open and the thirty-odd Jews from the Suburb climbed inside.
>
> Nothing happened except that the door was shut. The Blond Ones stood in various places, with their arms crossed or with their fingers in their belts. Finally, the mechanic slid off the fender, clapped his hands together, evidently to warm them, and turned the crank. The motor started. The bus body shook. It rattled. . . . But it did not move from the spot. . . . It was like dreaming. A coach without wheels, with no one to drive it: yet the engine roared, the body shook and swayed for all the world as if it were speeding along on a journey.
>
> When the Jews came out of the bus, all of them. . . were dead. . . . A team of matched horses came from the direction of the mill, hitched to a rubber-wheeled cart. It was they who pulled the Ghettoites to the ravine. The clothing, the luggage, the shoes—that remained behind.
>
> And the pile grew larger as each new batch of Jews—always in groups of thirty—added its share. (*KJ*, 201–2)

Advancing from initial incredulity suggested by the fairytale analogy, Lipiczany's Nazi rite of passage transforms him from innocent victim to knowledgeable antagonist. His ebullient, ironic voice yields first to a traumatized whisper and then a mad shriek of outrage. Auditor to the victims' futile screaming, observer of the gassing, mass burial, and preparation for subsequent extermination contingents, the boy is paralyzed with fear. Unlike Tadeusz Borowski's experienced Gentile-Polish crematorium worker who adjusts to Jewish slaughter as long as it signifies his survival, Lipiczany is devastated. Borowski's protagonist becomes

> totally familiar with the inexplicable and the abnormal; having learned to live on intimate terms with the crematoria, the itch and

the tuberculosis; having understood the true meaning of wind, rain and sun, of bread and turnip soup, of work to survive, of slavery and power; having, so to say, daily broken bread with the beast.[45]

Lipiczany suffers the shock of first encounter. He walks at night, like a blind man, to the ravine where the bodies were dumped. He moves among them, touching them. Crazed into willing disbelief, he tries to wake them and lead them back to the ghetto. In a brief scene recalling King Lear, the youngster retreats into the past, calling on the corpses to remember with him, a childhood of flower gardens and raspberry drops. He imagines the deceased remembering Trumpelman's successes in saving them from the Nazis and finally dreams of a great bird spreading its protective wings over the Jews. With daybreak, the Nazi nightmare intrudes. A Jewish slave-labor corps works among the bloody corpses removing their hair and other items of value. In this company, Lipiczany recognizes a former Balut resident. Maddened by his corpse-stripping job, the ghost figure stares at Lipiczany without recognition, failing even to comprehend Lipiczany's urgency about returning to the ghetto to inform the elder about the mass murders.

Epstein judiciously breaks the continuum between the ravine scene and Lipiczany's return to the ghetto to introduce another ghetto population group and to reemphasize the causal link between Christian anti-Semitism and its culmination in the Final Solution. Although Epstein demonstrates that a long heritage of Christian anti-Semitism prepared fertile ground for European acquiescence and support of genocide, he also dramatizes the distinction between the two pathological forms of anti-Semitism. He discriminates between the Christian form of persecution, which manifests its hostility toward the Jewish religion in its goal of conversion, and the Nazi form, which finds biological existence of the Jews unacceptable, regardless of religious status. The third and final section of "The Yellow Bus" chapter depicts a Christmas Mass in the Church of the Virgin Mary, which the Nazis left intact for Christian converts despite destroying all the ghetto synagogues. The celebrants, descendants of baptized Jews and recent converts, who like many of their predecessors converted to insure temporal salvation of their first-class citizenship, harbor delusions of survival despite having been reclassified as Jews under Hitler's racial laws. Although they expect isolation from the general population and mistreatment, they also anticipate escape from the death sentence that unbaptized Jews suffer. The elder quickly disabuses them of false hope: "A Jew is whoever Horowitz says is a Jew. That's why we're all here together" (208). Addressing the life and death of Jesus, with appropriate analogies drawn to the plight of contemporary Jews, Trumpelman reiterates traditional anti-Jewish church teachings concerning Jewish refusal to accept the divinity of Jesus. Accepting the deicide canard and its persecution rationale, the converts respond hysterically and ecstatically, fully embracing the prejudices of their adopted faith:

> "That's why the Jews suffer now! Because they wouldn't believe!"
>
> "It's because they killed him!"
>
> "Even the Elder admits the blood is on their heads!"
>
> "And on the heads of their children!" (*KJ*, 210)

One of the novel's rare scenes in which Trumpelman is void of self-interest, the exchange is a good example of sociological and philosophical authenticity, especially in the elder's rebuke of the converts, "It's not because the Jews killed Christ that they have to suffer, but because they gave Christ to the world" (*KJ*, 210). Structurally, the sermon unites the preghetto morality play and its ensuing violence with the Mass, foreshadows the deportations, and provides an effective transition to Lipiczany's report of the forest gassing.

The youngster returns to the ghetto a transformed creature. His physical appearance reflects the psychological trauma of witnessing the murder of the Baluty ghettoites: "He did not look like a boy any longer. Scratched, crooked, filthy, he looked like a beast" (*KJ*, 206). Bewilderment, denial, crazed paralysis have by now given way to anger and the will to thwart the genocide program. The child apprises the elder of the mass murders and begs him to stop the roundups. Revealing his impotence in the face of German power, Trumpelman asks: "'What if it's true? What do you want the Elder to do? To announce it? What suffering then! What a massacre! It's better if they think they're going to a farm'" (*KJ*, 211). The reply, derived from remarks attributed to Jacob Gens and the distinguished German-Jewish leader, Leo Baeck,[46] suggests the elder's likely prior knowledge of the transport destination and reaffirms Lipiczany's earlier shift from Trumpelman proponent to antagonist. The child's news confirms the suspicions of the *Judenrat*; however, others reject the news as the rantings of a child who either misunderstood what he saw or invented the scene. Still others, who grant the probability of the mobile gas units, despair over the lack of weapons and support from Christian partisans to combat the atrocity.

While Lipiczany bears witness openly and seeks to effect change through sabotage, others bear witness indirectly and covertly through graphic or written testimony. Evocative of the secret work of historians and archivists in Vilna, Warsaw, and Lodz, who recorded ghetto history at grave risk to their own safety, Epstein introduces performing and visual artists who document and comment on the Holocaust in satiric monologues at the Cafe Astoria, in the ghetto *Makbet* performance, and in painting and photography. Three minor characters, a mature painter and two youthful photographers, knowingly risk torture and death to record the grim suffering of the Baluty residents. The painter, Klapholtz, upon receiving a commission to paint the ceiling of the Church of the Virgin Mary, uses the opportunity to document ghetto suffering. For this offense to the German occupation, the artist is arrested, tortured, his broken body displayed to the Jews, held up against a wall by one Death Header while another shoots him as an object lesson for other protestors. The orphans Krystal and Lifshits chronicle Grundtripp and his *Totenkopfers* at work by photographing Jews hanging upside down, Jews being humiliated, the street assaults accompanying the morality play, the killing of the painter-witness, and other ghetto degradation. Trumpelman discovers their darkroom and warns them that they are committing an offense punishable by torture and death, yet they persist in the value of testifying: "We have to remember! . . . so people will know!" (*KJ*, 59). Through these three portraits Epstein honors those ghetto and concentration camp witnesses who recorded Holocaust history in diaries, histories, and drawings, and he testifies to the power of art to respond to the human condition.

Epstein's model for the boy photographers is probably the Lodz Ghetto photographer/artist Mendel Grossman, whose book *With a Camera in the Ghetto*[47] was published two years prior to *King of the Jews* and appears to be the source of several descriptive passages in the novel.[48] Grossman took thousands of photographs of the Lodz Jews, their illnesses, their hunger, their degradation. He recorded the distribution of food rations, workshop industries, domestic life, human beasts of burden pulling excrement wagons, deportations, public executions—all scenes similarly documented by Krystal and Lifshits. To deceive the Gestapo and ghetto police, Grossman carried his camera under his coat. He kept his hands in his pockets to manipulate the camera, and turned his body to direct the lens, slightly parted his coat, and clicked the shutter.[49] Similarly, Krystal is described as wearing a long raincoat that came past his knees, even in the summer sunshine, and secretly operating a Kodak left in the orphanage by an American visitor during a prewar inspection. The boy photographers' record of the central square execution of Klapholtz closely approximates Mendel Grossman's photography of the execution of a Viennese Jew.[50] His climb of an electric power pole to photograph a convoy of deportees, and his ascension of the church steeple to capture a change of guard at a barbed-wire fence are reflected in the boys' climb up the chimney of an industrial plant, and their precarious perch to document the Klopholtz assassination.[51] Just as Grossman had "a job in the photographic laboratory of the department of statistics in the ghetto,"[52] and kept his unofficial record with the knowledge and cooperation of Lodz Jews who believed in the historic value of his work,[53] the team of Krystal and Lifshits display their camera openly to photograph "official" ghetto events such as the arrival of German personnel and other dignitaries at the opening of the House of Pleasure and the Trumpelman wedding.

Throughout the ghettos of Europe, art was a significant means of spiritually transcending Holocaust reality and an expression of resistance to Nazi dehumanization efforts. Ghetto residents simultaneously resisted the Nazi effort to dehumanize them and covertly criticized their oppressors through participating in musical concerts, literary readings, and plays. Like the Vilna Ghetto's mock trial of Josephus Flavius as a Roman collaborator—with its obvious comparison of the former soldier turned court historian,[54] and Jacob Gens, former career officer turned ghetto commandant—Epstein's *Makbet* performance dramatizes contemporary evil and draws an intriguing analogy to the Shakespearean study of political corruption. Throughout the ghettoites' *Makbet* performance, its prologue, and aftermath, Epstein emphasizes the role external evil plays in the moral decline of the ambitious monarchs. The play is introduced by a Shakespearean prologue, delivered by a jester, the Cafe Astoria comedian. Recalling Elizabethan fools free to speak the truth, the comedian narrates the tale of a distant city's "resettlements" to mock the Baluty *Judenrat* and the elder for their compliance with deportation orders.

> The Others ordered the Judenrat to make a list of one hundred Jews. If the Council refused to do it, the Lords and Masters would snatch up a thousand on their own. Of course there was a big discussion. Some members would not put down even a single name. But a different faction won out. They said, *We are rescuing nine hundred Jews.* The problem was, the Others were not satisfied. They kept asking for more. Every time was supposed to be the last time, but it never was. Pretty soon only half the town of Stok was left, and then only a quarter. And so on. . . . In the entire town there were only two people left, both members of the Judenrat. Then the train pulled in once more. The one Minister says to the other, "You go. Otherwise it will be harder on the rest of us!" (*KJ*, 215–16)

*Judenrat* collaboration so deftly suggested in the satiric prologue is amply enlarged in the play. Madame Trumpelman recognizes herself in the guilty Scottish queen and prophetically warns her husband that they will be judged. Similarly, the Baluters' sympathy for Macbeth's victims reflects their own suffering and impending tragedy. A terrible dramatic irony prevails as the ghettoites weep for the legendary Scots while their own police force gathers outside to herd them into waiting transports. As the ghettoites respond to the theatrical tragedy, the authorial voice addresses the reader directly in a passage fraught with graphic detail of ghetto degradation:

> Everyday they saw things more frightening than witches and fogbanks and hooting owls. Was there a man or a woman in the House of Culture who had not lost, one way or another, a person he loved? Could any spectator know for sure that he, himself, would not be deported before the week was out? No! No! Not likely. Here people walked around thin as sticks, with their bones practically showing. In the winter the Baluters froze. They choked from the smell in the summer. You could always hear some mad person shouting, *an English tailor!,* or some other meaningless phrase. It was as if hell had been moved to the surface of the earth. And the worst thing, the horror of horrors, was that the citizens of the Suburb had got used to their lives. Sometimes the newspapers would blow off the corpses: there would be the green face or the blue face or even the healthy-looking pink face of a person you knew. (*KJ*, 223–24)

Tucked into the heart of this realistic rendering of ghetto death is the *Macbeth* hellgate allusion, which not only returns the reader to the theatrical parallel but strikes at the core of evil underlying the Scottish and Nazi murderous realms—deception and dissembling.

The "Makbet" chapter expresses Epstein's belief in the power of art to influence and interpret human behavior. The Baluters, themselves victims of unprecedented persecution, empathize with bleeding Scotland. Ironically, though they need only look at the starved, diseased, maimed, and dead in their own ranks, they appear numb to their own plight, yet responsive to dramatic tragedy. Implicit in the audience reaction is Epstein's criticism of an unresponsive, uncharitable international audience that watched knowingly and idly as the Nazis and their collaborators performed their drama and the Jews suffered their tragedy.

As the play comes to its inevitable conclusion and Malcolm's army approaches Dunnsinane to end the usurper's corrupt and murderous reign, the ghetto police fill the aisles, rubber clubs poised to drive the audience to a deportation roundup. When one *Judenrat* member tries to calm the crowd with lies about it being a special agricultural contingent and therefore safe, a man in the crowd exposes the equivocator, speculating that the destiny of the transport is to serve agriculture as "fertilizer." The roundup is directed by Rievesaltes, and it is to him that the terrified ghettoites appeal rather than to Trumpelman. Like Dr. Mengele at Auschwitz, Rievesaltes directs the people to move in one of two directions, one leading to temporary ghetto reprieve, the other to the trains and certain death: "crooking his finger at some cards, turning his thumbs down at all others—[he] . . . had become the god of life and death" (*KJ,* 234).

Thus, the theater scene concludes with an historic usurpation drama. While Macbeth is replaced by the rightful heir to the Scottish throne, Trumpelman, who came to power by Nazi whim, is just as arbitrarily displaced by his rival Rievesaltes. Paralleling the threat Chaim Rumkowski felt from David Gertler when Hans Biebow manifested his displeasure with Rumkowski by elevating his police chief,[55] the roundup scene ends with Trumpelman's recognition of Rievesaltes' ascension. Just as Madame Trumpelman had recognized her parallel to Lady Macbeth and the Trumpelman/Macbeth correspondence during the course of the play, Trumpelman now recognizes in the roundup epilogue that his favored position with the Germans, and therefore his ghetto powerbase, has been usurped by Rievesaltes. While the ghettoites petition the new power broker, Trumpelman blusters an ironic, self-aggrandizing speech reminiscent of Macbeth's guilty ravings that conclusively demonstrates his impotence. Whereas the content of the speech is derived from the Vilna Ghetto elder's reference to his bloody hands, which facilitate others' purity, its rhetorical emphasis echoes Rumkowski's preference for hyperbole.

> I, Trumpelman, came like a robber to rob you of your dearest ones. I, Trumpelman, took you by the hand and led you to death. It's Trumpelman who made you work until your hearts explode. No wonder you turn from him now! Abandon him! What a monster he is! Lock him up in a cage! . . . We are in the same cage together! . . . In this same cage with us there is a hungry lion! He wants to devour us all! . . . I am the lion tamer. I stuff his mouth with meat. It's the flesh of my own brothers and sisters! The lion eats and eats! . . . Thus, with ten Jews, I save a hundred. With a hundred, I save a thousand. . . . My hands are bloody. . . . If your hands are clean, it's because mine are dirty! (*KJ*, 234–35)

This recognition theme that concludes Part I of the "Makbet" chapter is further developed in the chapter's second section conceived in the classical pattern of a Greek satyr play, and thus functions as commentary on the main tragedy. The steambath, where Trumpelman confronts the Nazi hierarchy, works both as a visual and verbal echo of Macbeth's encounter with the witches on the foggy heath and as an allusion to a steambath meeting in which Himmler and his colleagues conspired to destroy the Jews.[56] The steambath conference in which *Obergruppenfuhrer* Grundtripp and Wohltat plot to deceive, confuse, and destroy the Jewish king recalls the witches' conclave as they plotted to destroy the Scottish king. As the witches deceived Macbeth with visions of false security, Wohltat dissembles with Trumpelman, first by playing on his ambition and then through illusions of safety. As Macbeth was led to believe he would survive Malcolm's attack, Trumpelman was led to believe his ghetto would escape the liquidation that the nonproductive ghettoes suffered. As the disillusioned Macbeth cursed the witches, so Trumpelman confronts Wohltat with his lie, citing Lipiczany's eyewitness account of the forest gassings as evidence of the German program of genocide.

Maintaining the relationship to the satyr play's chorus of half-human beasts, representing an indecent view of life, Epstein shows

Trumpelman in the company of beastial creatures who goad the old Jew by confirming Germany's genocidal program. Grundtripp interrupts Wohltat's attempt to prolong the resettlement deception and taunts Trumpelman with news of the Warsaw Ghetto liquidation. He exudes pleasure in the destruction of Polish Jewry:

> Tell him about the roundup in Warsaw. One-third of the Jews! And Czerniakow swallowed poison. The Elder of Warsaw is dead! Why keep these things a secret? We should announce it to the world! Do you think anyone will object? They'll thank us. They'll applaud. A thousand years from now people will remember us precisely for this, the way they remember Pasteur. (*KJ*, 237)

This proud assessment, composed in language evocative of *Nazideutsch* extermination rhetoric, accurately attests to the Holocaust-wrought reduction of the Jewish global population by one-third, international complicity in Nazi crimes, and further suggests an inverse, ironic prophecy of future judgment of Nazi criminality. Finally, a voice invoking Heinrich Himmler lauds German courage: "The hard part is to perform the task, without reward, without recognition, and still remain good human beings. That takes toughness!" (*KJ*, 237). This self-congratulatory speech is, of course, self-damning and yet another instance of the novel's dramatic indictment of Nazi criminality. The scene also alludes to the self-incriminating official German documentation of the Final Solution.

The classical recognition pattern of the "Makbet" chapter is now complete with Trumpelman's understanding that his work policy will not save even a remnant of his Jews, that, in fact, he was deluded by the Nazis whose real intent was to murder the Jews of his ghetto and all Europe as a prelude to the destruction of American Jewry. Further, he realizes that genocide of the Jews is Germany's preamble to the final solution of the Polish problem, the Slavic problem, and the Negro problem until the "earth's population would be turned into Jews" (*KJ*, 238).

The deportation schedule accelerates and three rival groups vie for ghetto power and loyalty. After placing Trumpelman under house arrest, Rievesaltes' forces assume key ghetto operations. Although the Jewish Council continues to run the soup kitchens, ghettoites perceive the police force under Rievesaltes' leadership as the Jewish governing power. The accelerated resettlement deportations spark organized leftist resistance, just as the untenable work conditions had earlier provoked the five-day strike. The leftist coalition aims to disrupt Jewish cooperation with resettlement transports and to pose a viable threat to the *Judenrat* and the Jewish Police. Bold actions are openly taken. Resistance fighters remove the mandatory yellow stars, execute a policeman and a *Judenrat* member, and sentence Trumpelman to death for crimes against the Jewish people.

In contrast to extended scenes of starvation, labor exploitation, and mass killings, Epstein introduces rapid, staccato sections to dramatize the armed rebellion. The Trilling Brigade's death sentence against Trumpelman fails when the appointed executioner, Lipiczany, is tricked by the wiley old man and delivers the group's leader, Lipsky, to the elder's house believing that Trumpelman now will help arm the resistance. Then, using Lipsky as bait, Trumpelman entices Rievesaltes to his home with the ploy that he will be able to arrest a Communist in the act of smuggling guns. In an effort to rid himself of both enemies in a single coup, Trumpelman informs Grundtripp that the men will be found at his home in a conspiratorial meeting. At the appointed time the elder goads the Jews into a duel, with the agreement that the winner execute the elder. Trumpelman gives the signal to fire precisely as Grundtripp enters the room and the German is felled by Rievesaltes' bullet. During the ensuing capture and beating of Rievesaltes, Lipsky escapes, allowing Epstein to incorporate yet another portion of documentary evidence from Vilna Ghetto history.

The fictional manhunt is based on the historic evidence of the Gestapo pursuit of Commander Itzik Wittenberg and the internal struggle of the Vilna Ghetto United Partisans Organization.[57] Through incorporation of this event, Epstein is able to explore the moral dilemma of handing Jews over to Germans once again, but this time the problem (which had been the exclusive province of the *Judenrat*) is faced by a radically different political organization. Like the members of the United Partisans Organization, the Trilling Brigaders must decide whether to turn over their leader or to jeopardize the entire ghetto population. Echoing the earlier Council deliberations, opinions vary and passions grow intense. Some advise Lipsky to surrender, positing the individual's despensibility and the larger Communist agenda. Others argue that the German ultimatum is but a pretext to destroy the ghetto, and they counsel armed rebellion. Lipsky parallels this acquiescent stance to *Judenrat* capitulation that the leftists had so vehemently denounced: "Hand one over, we'll save many. For that we sentenced the ministers to death" (*KJ*, 268). "For the first time" another partisan admits, "I feel sympathy for the Jews on the *Judenrat*" (*KJ*, 268). Like Wittenberg, Lipsky had a secure hiding place and a gun. And, like Wittenberg's colleagues, Lipsky's colleagues consider it impossible to launch an attack against the Germans to protect him. Neither group was prepared to defend one leader at the expense of the entire ghetto and each urges the resistance leader to surrender for the larger good. Lipsky, like Wittenberg, saw in the German plan an intention to seize a resistance leader and, in so doing, divide the ghetto against itself. In both the Vilna case and the fictional version, the Germans insisted that the resistance leader be taken alive, and in each instance the fugitives sought to escape disguised as females. Consistent with Trumpelman's tendency toward self-delusion, he tells the Jews witnessing the public hanging of Lipsky and Rievesaltes that the execution of these traitors will spare the ghetto, unlike Vilna, which had been liquidated the previous day. Just as the Wittenberg case did not save the Vilna Jews, so the Lipsky manhunt and execution is immaterial to the deportations and mass murder of the Jews of Lodz.

By 1944, time is measured in deaths. A year has passed since the double execution of Rievesaltes and Lipsky, and "Tens of thousands of lifetimes. Hundreds and hundreds of trains" (*KJ*, 272) have taken the Baluty Jews to their slaughter. When the Germans delay their retreat from the approaching Soviet Army to honor their primary commitment to genocide, a Jewish Red Army commando parachutes into the ghetto and joins forces with the Trilling Brigade to pave the way for Soviet entry into the city and for ghetto liberation. The Trilling Brigade is to join forces with a group of Jewish partisans who had escaped from Poland in order to fight with the Russians. Together they must secure the city bridge, which the retreating Germans are expected to destroy to impede Russian access to Lodz. Against enormous odds, the starving, weakened brigade unit escapes from the ghetto, works its way through the Aryan sector of the city, kills several armed German soldiers, and makes off with their weapons. The brigaders wait in vain to be relieved by the conquering Red Army. They witness instead a German massacre of the Jewish commandos. As they open fire from their hiding place, they notice that the ghetto is burning. Once again, they are faced with bitter choices, whether to rescue the Jews in the ghetto or to continue as they are—securing the bridge for the Red Army. Choosing the latter, they are betrayed by the Russians who ignore their signals to enter the city. All but three perish in a tank engagement with the Germans.

The surviving Trilling Brigaders are captured and present at the ghetto's liquidation, a resettlement so vast that boxcars, tenders, flatcars, and even first-class passenger coaches are pressed into service. Trumpelman climbs into the coal car that contains his beloved children from the Hatters' Asylum and tries to comfort them with lies about sharing his immunity and survival in Madagascar, but he is interrupted by Lipiczany who exposes the elder's lie: "There is no Madagascar. The train stops at Oswiecim. That's where they burn. They burn! . . . Oswiecim is the homeland of the Jews" (*KJ*, 301). As Trumpelman feebly disputes Lipiczany, he catches sight of the ghetto lights burning, and in a mad frenzy swings himself out of the car onto the ghetto street, where he dashes from house to house to turn off the lights because the *Judenrat* cannot afford to waste electricity. The train moves forward to Auschwitz with thousands of Jews, including Lipiczany and his Trilling compatriot Nachman Kippnis, but without Trumpelman.

Using the framing device of the survivors' sea journey to America, Epstein delineates the last days of the ghetto and the Auschwitz experience from Lipiczany's point of view. Lipiczany and Kippnis outlived the Holocaust because the Baluters had the good fortune to arrive at Auschwitz when "the death house was already full" (*KJ*, 304); they were spared the customary platform selection and "got safely in." Too sick to take part in the death march after the Germans blow up the killing apparatus, they are presumed close enough to death and left in their bunks where they are rescued by the Red Army. Faithful to the mystery surrounding Rumkowski's death,[58] Epstein incorporates various reports of Trumpelman's end. Lipiczany indicates that of the two hundred Baluty Auschwitz survivors, a minority contend that Trumpelman remained hidden in the ghetto, but a majority said he was in the last transport to Auschwitz and died there. Among the contradictory stories of Trumpelman's arrival and treatment at Auschwitz, one version contends that he was driven up in a special command car with a letter "from Wohltat or some other high official, that supposedly guaranteed him all sorts of favors inside the camp. However, as soon as the letter was opened, Trumpelman was led to a wall, where he was shot" (*KJ*, 305). Another version insists that "to amuse the Kapos and guards, the Elder was allowed to carry on as if he were still in the Ghetto, strutting about, giving orders" (*KJ*, 305) another, that he watched the Baluters march into the death house and joined the end of the line. In yet another version, he is reported to have sought anonymity, but was recognized by Baluters and beaten to death. Finally, months after the war's end, a rumor that Trumpelman managed to survive in the ghetto and is still hiding there brings the boys back to their home where they conduct an unsuccessful search for the elder.

In the seventeenth century, an age of belief, John Milton called on his muse, Urania, in *Paradise Lost* to explain the ways of God to man; Epstein invokes in the coda's title and ship's name the same poetic muse to explain the ways of man to man. Here the novelist directly addresses the theme of bearing witness, of recording human history, and of becoming engaged in the meaning of that history. Writing in the 1970s, when revisionist historians and Eastern bloc politicians are trying to deny the full measure of Jewish losses in the Holocaust by universalizing rather than particularizing Germany's genocidal plan against Jewry, Epstein confronts the deception and warns us against Holocaust amnesia. Dramatic presentation of this theme appears in the coda recollection of a postwar, Holocaust memorial intended to honor the ghetto dead. Instead, the dead are dishonored in the speech by the town's Polish mayor, who, having served the Nazis faithfully during their occupation, now faithfully serves the Russian occupiers. To win a bet with a Russian dignitary, the Pole delivers his entire Holocaust oration without a single reference to the Jewish victims. The historic source for this scene explains Epstein's decision to write a book about the Holocaust without once using the words *German* or *Nazi*, an exercise in rueful vengeance and a mocking indictment of those who deny Germany's designation of Jewry for annihilation in the Holocaust.[59] Like Saul Bellow's Arthur Sammler, Lipiczany too depicts a Poland joyous at the prospect of a *Judenrein* country, and postwar Polish anti-Semitism is the decisive factor in the boys' decision to start a new life in America.

Rhetorical reenforcement of the admonition to refrain from Holocaust amnesia and to bear witness is suggested in the novel's refrain, "Ladies and Gentlemen, you decide." The witnessing survivor-narrator repeatedly involves the reader in his moral judgments, warning one to be constantly vigilant to the failure of the retrospective imagination to find meaning in history. In addition, the refrain recalls Tadeusz Borowski's "This Way for the Gas,

Ladies and Gentleman," a devastating account of a man adapting to genocide. Epstein's refrain reminds us that we must reject the silence of the Holocaust generation and bear witness.

Beyond its literary allusions to Milton and Borowski, the coda is resonant with the voice of Samuel Beckett. Just as Beckett's play ends with the two world-weary tramps Vladamir and Estragon waiting for Godot, hoping to be saved, to find peace, to end their homelessness and wandering, so *King of the Jews* ends with Kippnis and Lipiczany arriving in the New World hoping for a better life. Lipiczany, something of the existential, zany clown, as his name suggests, allows the blind Kippnis his illusions and affirms, despite his own doubts, that America, unlike post-Enlightenment Europe, will be the land of promise fulfilled—a place to live in dignity. Although Beckett implies the uncertainty of an eventual meeting with the unreliable Godot and repeatedly dramatizes the futility of pinning one's hopes on him, showing the essential absurdity of waiting for Godot, the tramps' waiting signifies their steadfast faith and hope. So, too, Kippnis and Lipiczany, who have played Lucky to Trumpelman's Pozzo, who have known terrible suffering and anguish, who have known the worst of the human condition, remain hopeful. Lipiczany chooses to kindle his blind friend's hope in a better future. Like the *Makbet* ghetto audience and Beckett characters, the Epstein survivors need something to believe in to sustain life. But as the "Urania" approaches New York Harbor, "the smoke and steam from thousands of chimneys spread like a lid on the air" (*KJ*, 309). Thus, Epstein juxtaposes purging water imagery with the imagery of the gas chambers, suggesting a new beginning for the survivors, but a beginning that is forever seared in the Holocaust crucible.

Epstein's work stands alone in American Holocaust fiction as an exploration of the *Judenrat*. Forgoing the characteristic American pattern of the exploration of sympathetic Jewish victims coping with survivor syndrome, Epstein examines the morally dubious among the victims, the police lackies and the compromised ghetto administrator. He shares with Hannah Arendt, whom he greatly admires, the mixed critical response to the negative assessment of Jewish leadership during the Holocaust. Just as Arendt's banality of evil thesis is disputed, so, too, Epstein is perceived by some as neglecting Nazi criminality while unjustly indicting the Jewish victims.[60] Critical assessment of *King of the Jews* has been sharply divided between those who condemn Epstein for belittling tragedy with farce and those who commend the work as a serious historical narrative. *King of the Jews* has been attacked most severely for a tone critics perceive as inappropriate to Holocaust material.[61] Yet Epstein thinks the tone is the chief virtue of the book.[62] He explains:

> It's not the first time in my life that I wanted to write an essentially serious . . . philosophical treatment of something only to have . . . the book speak in its own language, its own tone. And although I tried many ways of avoiding that tone, I found myself stuck with it. . . . About thirty pages into it, I began to realize who in fact the speaker of the book really was; that it had to be one of the children. It had to be one of the few who survived. It had to be someone who made his way to America. It had to be a kind of mixture of the European and American in tone and that's why the book is written the way it is.[63]

Epstein rejects the notion that the tone is bitter or composed of black or gallow's humor and instead describes the book's dominant voice, Lipiczany's voice, as "open-hearted."[64] He defends his ironic tone by citing its similarity to that he found years later in the Oscar Rosenfeld entries[65] in *The Chronicle of the Lodz Ghetto*.[66] Additional support for the authenticity of the ironic tone appears in Holocaust-era compositions, such as the Yankev Herszkowicz street ballad, which "deflated Rumkowski's largesse by comparing it to the manna of the desert,"[67] and in the increasingly ironic treatment of traditional Yiddish literary sources responding to the unprecedented horror of Nazism.[68]

    Epstein argues that because the material is so painful, he would have been unable to approach it without being ironic, rueful, and wry.[69] Dismayed by what he perceives to be vicious attacks and an incomplete reading of his book, Epstein recounts his personal and professional development, specifically his deliberate emotional control at the time of his YIVO Institute research and his writing of *King of the Jews*.

> I think I must have sensed soon after I arrived at the library that if I were to get through such material at all, to say nothing of being able to think about it and shape it, I would have to draw a psychic shutter, thick as iron, between myself and these accounts of the fate of the Jews. Thus I sat through the winter, . . . calmly and callously reading.[70]

Tonal comparison of the narrative voices of Lipiczany with Tadeusz Borowski's Auschwitz kapo suggests the significant distinction between Lipiczany's "open-hearted" morality and Borowski's cynic. The Polish kapo can live well by Auschwitz standards, as long as he herds the Jews into the gas chamber. Lipiczany retains his prewar purity because he allied himself with the ghetto resistance fighters and judges the collaborators by prewar moral standards. In Borowski's story one sees that the essence of the Nazi universe is the systematic collapse of ethical and moral distinctions. In Epstein's book, narrated from a Jewish survivor's point of view, moral distinctions are fervent and a crucial component of spiritual resistance to Nazism. Epstein, like Richard Elman in the Yagodah trilogy, argues uneqivocably that it is the Nazi system that transformed ordinary people into villains. Elman and Epstein clearly distinguish between free choice and the choice between unacceptable alternatives that characterized the Jewish plight. In the Nazi ghetto and concentrationary environments, the Nazis enjoyed freedom of choice, and they chose to render another people extinct; the free world had a choice, and it chose, in large measure, to acquiesce to the genocide program; the *Judenrat* had a choice, whether to offer up to slaughter some or all, and consistently chose to save as many as they could.

Most writers acknowledge the extraordinary difficulty of writing Holocaust fiction. Epstein has adapted one of the most controversial and painful aspects of the Holocaust universe and has developed a narrative mode that generally copes successfully with the intrinsic difficulty of dealing "imaginatively with genocide" and "the morally ambiguous politics of survival."[71] Robert Alter observes that "no work of fiction has opened up so fully the unbearable moral dilemma in which the *Judenrat* members found themselves, governing with a pistol at their heads, administering the processes of death, corrupted of course by their awful power, yet trying to preserve life when there was no real way to preserve it."[72] Similarly, Terrence Des Pres, author of *The Survivors*, judges *King of the Jews* "the best novel yet written about the Holocaust."[73] Epstein's is a moral voice that does not spare the Nazis. It is one that recreates the hellish system they devised, dramatizes its physical and moral victims as well as its spiritual and moral victors, and in that process confronts the twentieth century's calamity through a superb fusion of documentary and creative imagination.

# CHAPTER FIVE

*The Trial of the Damned: Richard Elman's*
*Holocaust Trilogy*

The subject of Richard Elman's Holocaust trilogy is the tragic plight of Hungarian Jewry in 1944.[1] Hungary was the sole country in which the Nazis knew they were losing the war when they initiated their genocide operation, and it is the only place where the Jews had irrefutable knowledge about the extermination program while they were still free. The Hungarian mass deportations were not carried out secretly, as the previous transports had been, but openly executed in full view of the world. The trilogy focuses on the period when the Hungarian government was responsible to the Germans for carrying out their racial policy, the period when Eichmann and his team of deportation specialists applied the expertise of several years of European deportations in order to maneuver the Jewish community into complete submission and to mobilize the Hungarian government for expeditious destruction of its hitherto protected, native Jewish population. Because Elman's setting is Hungary, he incorporates some of the more distasteful and controversial aspects of the Jewish failure to act decisively during the Holocaust. There are brief references to

142

Hungarian-Jewish disinterest in the persecution of German and Polish Jews and the passive role of the Jewish leadership. Although Hungarian Jews were quite powerless to act against their nation's Axis ally, and the narrator distinguishes between their impotence and the West's purposeful neglect of Jewry's plight despite its power, he nevertheless condemns Hungarian-Jewish passivity in the face of the systematic slaughter of fellow Jews.

Richard Elman's chronicle of a family's ordeal traces the oscilation from hope to despair that characterized the destruction process in Hungary, "an erratic development in which periods of near tranquility alternated with outbursts of destructive activity."[2] He probes Holocaust profundities and examines characters who react differently to injustice based on their diverse social and psychological backgrounds, which he renders with distinctive voices and sensibilities. The first volume, *The 28th Day of Elul* (1967), relates the Yagodah family's destruction from the perspective of its surviving son, Alexander Yagodah. The second, *Lilo's Diary* (1968), is the 1944 journal of a young female ward of the family, the quintessential victim. The third, *The Reckoning* (1969), is a moral and historic accounting, a fusion of a subjective moral assessment and an objective analysis of the economic and political forces contributing to the Holocaust, narrated from the perspective of a mature Holocaust victim, the paterfamilias Newman Yagodah. Although Elman's original design called only for the first volume, Elie Wiesel convinced him to write Lilo's story, and then Elman himself decided to add *The Reckoning* to tell the father's story since the topic of patriarchy and problematical family relationships interested him.[3] After several attempts to write a fourth volume dealing with the perpetrator's point of view, Elman abandoned the project.[4]

Throughout the trilogy, authorial judgment looms against man and God for grave crimes against humanity and the covenant. Elman's work is an early example of fiction's Holocaust-wrought theological and philosophic redefinitions. He asks whether we need to revise our ideas about human nature in light of Holocaust truth and whether the covenantal relation of the divine and human continues in the postHolocaust era—questions that reflect the crises of faith and human understanding in our time. The survivor probes the meaning of God's absence in the Holocaust and asks whether a God of mercy and love would countenance extermination of the innocent and whether conventional wisdom about human nature requires reexamination.

To pursue these theological and philosophic concerns, *The 28th Day of Elul* is structured as a Holocaust memoir, the response of an Israeli survivor to an American lawyer regarding the codicil of a will stipulating that his inheritance of an uncle's estate is dependent upon his allegiance to Judaism.[5] Alex Yagodah's reply to the proviso is the vehicle for dramatizing the problem of religious faith in the post-Holocaust age. Initially Yagodah glibly offers the lawyer an orthodox legal response, "According to Jewish law the son of a Jewish mother is a Jew forever."[6] Ignoring the advice of his mistress, who cynically argues that Yagodah simply tell the American what he wants to hear, he attempts a truthful response, which develops as a treatise on religious faith in the era following an unprecedented threat to covenantal belief.

Catalyst for the protagonist's Holocaust recollection is the legal term *liquidation*. Enraged, Yagodah explosively juxtaposes the language of estate liquidation and that of *Nazideutsch*, charging international acquiescence to the German intention to "liquidate" European Jewry as the first step in the genocide of the Jewish people.

> Liquidated! In German *liquidiert!* Which can also be described as *ausgemerzt!* or *erledigt!* . . . Many now use the polite vocabulary. They speak of the *holocaust* as some regrettable lapse in manners, or, if they are fund-raisers, as if to refer to some heroic event in the Bible or Greek Epic. Although I much prefer the bluntest words for what happened, by now all words are traps. Let us simply say those who were are not any longer; and it wasn't their fault. (*E*, 12)

Maintaining the legal diction, Yagodah moves quickly to Holocaust judgment. "It will give me as great a joy to help in the liquidation of what remains of Uncle Bela as he . . . was instrumental in helping our enemies *register* and *account for* and *liquidate* us" (*E*, 15). Alex offers in evidence a brief summary of the destruction of his family and others, including a report of putting people in a "special barracks . . . . which was deliberately placed alongside the railroad ties . . . because the Germans hoped to save on Zyklon gas by having the allied bombers do their executions for them" (*E*, 13). Thus, he explicitly attacks his American uncle and implicitly attacks the West for acquiescing to Germany's grand design to obliterate Jewry. Changing places with the interrogating attorney, witness turns prosecutor putting his benefactor in the dock to investigate his wartime knowledge of the camps. Alex is contemptuous of his assimilationist uncle who had the timerity to betray Jewish identity for economic mobility, yet now seeks to dictate the religious affiliation of a Holocaust survivor who paid the price of Jewish identity. Continuing his verbal attack, Alex cites complicity in Germany's genocide program exemplified by British and American rejection in 1942 of Jewish pleas for assistance, despite knowledge of the death camps. Similarly, Elman indicts East-European governments that negated their rhetorical condemnation of Nazism through active support of the Nazi genocidal objective. Alex cites specific examples of non-German complicity in Holocaust crimes.

> The Slovakian government actually paid Germany a fixed sum for every Jewish soul who was made to leave the mother country on condition that he or she would never be allowed to return . . . every fourth one of Hungary's leaders vacillated between being Jew-killing zealots and cowardly equivocators. . . . There may have been a few nice people among the gentiles but we never saw any of them after 1942. (*E*, 163–64)

Clig's gentiles watched as the Jews were herded out, "shedding crocodile tears for us, but these we knew would be the first to see what could be looted once we were, in fact, deported" (*E*, 166).

Alex puts man and God on trial in a bitter response to his uncle's request. Paralleling and surpassing the failure of governments to aid Jewry, looms enigmatic divine failure. God stands accused of dishonoring the covenant by failing His devoted servants, by allowing His people to be shot or bludgeoned into mass graves, to be burned, sometimes while still alive, in crematorium ovens and lime pits. A self-hating Jew who has internalized the anti-Semitic stereotype in order to compensate for his inability to direct his aggression against the logical enemy, Alex directs his criticism against himself and the Jewish community. An acculturated Jew—neither a Wieselian nor Singerian Jew "of faith questioning God because of his faith, the faith of Abraham in God that cannot tolerate injustice on the part of God"[7]—Alex nevertheless raises theological questions of import. Denying neither the authenticity of rebellion nor the authenticity of faith, Alex begins his struggle in denunciation and ends it in acceptance. Although he cannot explain the inexplicable, he concludes, "I believe" (*E*, 24), echoing the traditional affirmation of faith many victims recited as they entered the gas chambers. Simultaneously accepting God and protesting His neglect of the suffering, Yagodah, like the believers of Singer and Wiesel, holds God accountable for Holocaust injustices. He wrestles with the terrifying realization of the coexistence of a just and merciful God and an evil creation:

> But the Supreme One—does He not stand condemned as the Supreme Murderer in our scheme of things? Perhaps that is why people here say they are "Jews without God." To be so secularized is to be unforgiving . . . whereas to accept God now one must forgive a Murderer, a Mass Extermination Expert, and if one doesn't believe, it becomes much easier to pin down blame, to sort and in turn be sorted. (*E*, 162)

In order that the protagonist's theological position be understood and the survivor's post-Holocaust purpose—to "bear witness . . . to the facts of Their death" (*E*, 25)—be fulfilled, Elman focuses the major portion of the novel on the survivor's Holocaust memories, cast as flashbacks to his youth. Yagodah's is a terrible tale of the dehumanization of persecutor and persecuted. As Alex sits under a fig tree in an Israeli settlement, striving to define the precise nature of his Judaic identity, his thoughts turn to Clig, a name closely resembling the Hungarian city of Cluj, but reformulated as an ironic pun on the Yiddish word for smart, *clig*.[8] His consciousness is flooded with memories of his Hungarian past, memories that reflect Jewish impotence in the face of an anti-Semitic power structure. Elman parallels the Yagodah-Skirzeny economic and social feud with the betrayal and murder European Jews suffered at the hands of their countrymen. Corresponding to Hungarian-Jewish history, the Yagodah family's withdrawal from political reality parallels national self-deception: "Our press told us what we wanted to know. Our press lied, knowing this would please our prejudices" (*E*, 62). Although Hungary deported stateless Jews from its newly acquired territories (that is, Slovakian, Romanian, and Yugoslavian territories acquired as Hungary's prize for becoming Hitler's ally in 1941), until 1944 Hungary protected its native "Magyarized" Jews. Hungary's sovereignty was respected by the Nazis, "with the result that for Jews the country became an island of safety in 'an ocean of destruction.'"[9] Hungarian Jews lived in relative security among their countrymen until March 1944. It is true that the young Jews were in labor battalions and generally suffered maltreatment, execution, and high losses, and all Hungarian Jews endured restrictions; however, compared to the Jews of Poland and Germany, they enjoyed a haven of well being, living among the general population rather than being herded into ghettos and concentration camps. The result was self-delusion. After Adolf Eichmann and his staff arrived in Budapest, plans for the deportation of remaining Hungarian Jews were developed and expedited with unprecedented rapidity and intensity.[10]

Alex tempers his initial criticism of middle class Jews, noting that they "never knew all the horrors of the emigrations and deportations, and some of us lived like the last Acadians" (*E*, 63), but he condemns them, reporting that when they did learn about "crystal night," they callously dismissed it, rationalizing that the German-Jews had brought disaster upon themselves by intermarriage and assimilation. Alex's father, himself a parvenu, preferred to look the other way, to ignore German brutality while anticipating the return of German high culture. According to Alex, the family members distanced themselves emotionally from the unpleasant events of Poland and Germany, since "what was happening . . . was quite remote from our town" (*E*, 40). Since Hungary and Germany were allies, business as usual and normal domesticity were the means by which the Yagodahs rationalized and exempted themselves from the real threat Germany posed to Hungarian Jews.[11] The fictional patriarch, Newman Yagodah, like his historic counterparts in the Hungarian-Jewish leadership, tried desperately to be counted as an Hungarian national. The elder Yagodah was convinced "that the politicians and the 'responsible classes' would not allow Hitler to have his way for much longer . . . convinced—in fact—that Nazism was a temporary aberration of the German personality" (*E*, 32). Describing the delusive process, Alex recalls the following:

> In Transylvania there was no war until 1942. Hungary was left autonomous. No German administrators were appointed. We Jews went about conscious that something somewhere was dreadfully amiss but never absolutely convinced that it would or could affect us. The local authorities from the Ministry of the Interior continued to treat us with the same historic mixture of envy, contempt, and civility. (*E*, 31)

Alex explains that Hungarian Jews of his class were callous because they wanted to believe they were different from Polish Jews, safe in a country that actually accepted them and would regard them as full citizens. They were optimistic that Hungarian nationalists would protect them and gullible enough to believe that if matters became worse even members of the notoriously anti-Semitic Arrow Cross would make exceptions for their favored Jews. They held these foolish dreams until the mail stopped, shortly after America declared war on Germany.

The weakness in human character that allows one man to take comfort in his safety while another suffers is manifest in Alex's observation that while working-class, Jewish youths and young women departed in the early transports, he was relieved not to be among them, grateful that his father, a member of the Jewish Council, "pulled strings" allowing him to remain with the family, to spend his time painting his mistress in the French Impressionist style, and to study French and English. Similarly, the self-delusive belief in the safety of Hungarian Jews is evidenced in their faith that they would survive through work. "When the deportations began we were told that people were only going to work in Germany for the war effort, that they would be treated as workers" (*E*, 68). Those who remained in Hungary accepted the official explanation and concentrated their efforts on survival and accommodating the ever-shifting regulations under Nazi occupation. Writing from the vantage point of postHolocaust hindsight and guilt, Alex distinguishes between his limited wartime knowledge and the information that surfaced from the Joel Brand case[12]— namely, that some Jewish leaders knew about gas chambers as early as 1942, although most of the Hungarian-Jewish leadership did not.

Holocaust reality, ignored because it was happening to German and Polish Jews, eventually becomes the existential condition of Hungarian Jews. With painstaking detail, Elman recreates the "Aryanization" of Hungary and the dehumanization of a subject people that preceded the indignities to be suffered in the concentration camps. Elman's delineation of the Yagodah fall closely follows the historic account of the demise of Hungarian Jewry documented by Raul Hilberg in *The Destruction of the European Jews*.[13] Paralleling the historic patterns, Elman introduces the creeping incursions that eventually strip the family of its delusions. He charts a pattern of economic and civic harassment to convey the ever increasing abuses. Local functionaries who had agreeable relations with Jews were replaced by Nazi sympathizers from outlying districts, who willingly implemented ordinances designed to curtail Jewish civil rights.[14] Ukrainian lackies and German soldiers pursued anti-Semitic measures aggressively, instituting a curfew, placing "defensive guards" in front of Jewish businesses and forcing Jews to register as aliens. As the erosion of Jewish citizenship got underway, the Nazification of Hungary began to take on a momentum of its own and Jews suffered accordingly. Local authorities advised the Jews of Clig to remain indoors for their own safety and to refrain from making the work of public servants more difficult. The Jews obeyed and the anti-Semites went about their business with ease. The police expropriated Jewish property, forced Jews to pay ransom on their homes and special taxes. The government encouraged Hungarian gentiles to benefit from these discriminatory regulations and to renege their debts to Jews. Further, gentiles were required to leave the employ of Jews or suffer Nazi reprisals. Following the German model, it was a short step from economic harassment to physical abuse. Yagodah's automobile is expropriated, the household help resigns, his debtors refuse to repay their loans, and eventually hoodlums stone him. The family experiences economic, civil, and criminal harassment replicating the national turmoil, oppression calculated to render the victim populace docile prior to its deportation to the killing centers.

Like other Holocaust chroniclers (Susan Schaeffer, Hana Demetz, Ilona Karmel), Richard Elman depicts the physical losses of middle-class European Jewry through careful and lengthy descriptions of their pre-Holocaust material opulence, their pleasure in a handsome four-story brick house with a large, extensively landscaped garden. The fragility of Yagodah's claim is evidenced in the rancor harbored against him by the estate's former owner, a bankrupt wine merchant who had to forfeit the house to cover a bad debt. Skirzeny manipulates the dangerous political situation to his advantage in order to cheat the Yagodahs of their home. The microcosm of the Yagodah-Skirzeny feud is analogous to macrocosmic Jewish/pro-Nazi Hungarian antipathies.

The parental economic antagonism is extended by the psychosexual rivalry of the younger generation, and both are conveyed in the context of historic European anti-Semitism. Jewish vulnerability is emblematically implied in a homosexual reference to the male rivals and dramatically staged in Lilo's rape. After spying on the cousin lovers, young Miklos, Skirzeny's stepson, torments Alex and rapes Lilo. He taunts the lovers, daring them to report the attack to the police, whose job and inclination it is to protect the Christian rapist and condemn the Jewish victim for seduction and race mixing. Elman's Miklos, a compendium of Hungary's anti-Semitic sentiments, a man who clearly enjoys the Nazi inversion of justice, may be an allusive evocation of his name-sake, Admiral Miklos (Nicholas) Horthy, whose authoritarian, aristocratic regime reflected his sympathy for Italian Fascism and German Nazism.[15] The villain's last name closely approximates that of the pro-Nazi who overthrew the Horthy government to install an even more pro-Nazi force, the RSHA man in charge of special tasks, *Oberstrumbannfuhrer* Skorzeny.[16]

Analogous to the stripping of Jewish property by Hungarian police and officials prior to deportation, is the elder Skirzeny's systematic attempt to have the Yagodahs legally transfer their wealth to him. Skirzeny and his alleged accomplice demand real property (household goods, personal jewelry) on the pretext of securing papers for the Yagodah's escape. He deceitfully promises escape, as Eichmann promised the Jewish Councils that Hungarian Jews had nothing to fear if all German requisitions for goods and services were met. To the post-Holocaust consciousness, the Skirzeny/Yagodah bartering session evokes the larger political negotiations between Germany and Rudolf Kastner and Joel Brand— the exchange of Hungarian Jews for massive supplies and money for the war effort.

Whereas the elder Skirzeny's extortion is analogous to the Nazi confiscation of Jewish property, the younger's rape of Lilo foreshadows the violence Hungarian Jewry will endure. On the morning following Miklos' attack, the Jewish families of Clig are assembled in the town square to play the prologue to their tragic drama. Were their fate not so horrible, the scene of the self-aggrandizing bourgeois paterfamilias presenting his family to the nation's ruler would be comic. Instead, it is a pathetic demonstration of a deluded assimilated Jew presenting his family for Nazi mayhem. Yagodah wears ceremonial dress, a formal frock coat, striped pants, gray silk four-in-hand tie, and prominently displays his war decorations.[17] He tries to impress the Nazis with his appreciation of German culture and bureaucracy. The scene is a deft delineation of one man's folly, impotence, and desperation, evoking one people's helplessness and another's criminal abuse of power.

The assembly scene is the strongest in the novel, amalgamating the trilogy themes, benefitting both from documentary authenticity and dramatic presentation. It combines the immediacy of contemporary terror with post-Holocaust knowledge. It is at this stage that the survivor argues that some "should have known by then" what was in store for them; "others—like my father—more than half suspected" (*E*, 111). Because this is the first time the entire Jewish population is brought together in a public square, ominous speculations arise, but are evaded, for in June 1944 "there were already so many rumors that they became confused with one another" (*E*, 111). Incorporated in the assembly scene are historic references to the expressed hope of some that Hitler would allow the Jews to emigrate to Turkey and Madagascar in exchange for the ransom needed for the German war effort, which was by then in deep trouble. With the Russian army quickly closing in, survival seemed plausible. "Miracles may not have seemed possible, but our history had taught us to respect the unpredictable" (*E*, 112). Alex attributes Jewish acquiescence to fear of collective retribution and general confusion. Elman skillfully distinguishes here between the Holocaust-era anger and the fuller understanding of the survivor, as Alex calls upon the American lawyer to avoid judging victims from the perspective of postwar hindsight, implying a condemnation of those who denounce Jews for going to slaughter like sheep. Alex poignantly explains the human predilection for life and hope, even in the face of disaster, taking great pains to outline the unusual circumstances of the victims: "Do not question our beliefs. . . . They grew out of the very life we were leading. Unarmed and ill-prepared, beset by murderers too, we saw and heard many different things. . . . Understand: the condemned man usually thinks there's another appeal" (*E*, 112).

The assembly scene is a metaphoric foreshadowing of the concentrationary experience that awaits those who survive the initial selections. As in the concentration camp orientations, the Jews of Clig are stripped of their watches, rings, and coins for the German war effort, kept standing in the sun for hours while German soldiers with bayonets encircle them in the square and other soldiers take positions on balconies with their rifles pointed at the crowd. Just as the duped Jews were herded toward the gas chambers believing they were going to delousing showers, so the Jews of Clig are convinced they are being deported to pay for the sabotage of neighboring Jews. This ruse is used to redirect Jewish hostility from the German enemies toward their coreligionists and to imply

that there is a legitimate reason for the current "action." According
to the Nazi rationale, the Germans are simultaneously protecting
the Jews of Clig from the temptation to commit sabotage and allowing them advance opportunity for "special atonement." This specious explanation is articulated in Nazi extermination rhetoric, attesting to the real reason for the roundup: "Clig will be cleansed.
The infestations will not be allowed to spread" (*E*, 131).

Although Alex remembers these Jews at their weakest, falling
into the Nazi trap and blaming other Jews rather than the real
enemy for bringing this punishment on them, he admonishes the
American lawyer not to condemn the victims because the American
"code of ethics [is] for free men in a free society" (*E*, 133). Alex
testifies to the impossibility of resistance: "Resistance? . . . They are
an army and we are a bunch of school children" (*E*, 122). He rejects
the notion that Jews could have organized an effective resistance
on the basis that they were unarmed and unassisted, the victims
both of anti-Semitic governments and national resistance groups
actively working for Jewish annihilation and for German defeat.
The bitter survivor informs the self-righteous lawyer that to condemn the hopeless victims for their own degradation is the ultimate
obscenity. To accuse unarmed Jews of failure to resist when armed
nations like France capitulated and collaborated with the Nazis is
outrageous. He argues instead that the free world, which ignored
Jewish cries for help, is a guilty partner in genocide.

Returning to Alex's Holocaust-era anger, frustration, and bitterness, Elman dramatizes the son's disgust with the elder's failure
to arrange the family's escape when it was possible to leave Hungary. His anger is extended to the Jewish Council of Elders and he
mistakenly equates their responsibility with that of the local Germans and those in control in Budapest. Thus, Elman skillfully uses
this scene to examine the allegations of some postwar historians
who accuse the Jewish Councils of Holocaust complicity. Later,
Alex rejects this thesis on the grounds that "it confuses victims with
victimizers" (*E*, 157), arguing that the council members are not
deserving of contempt simply because they took responsibility for
the welfare of others, and he implies that only an anti-Semite
would make such an accusation.

Although Elman does not include the concentration and
death camp environments in his trilogy, Alex notes that they were
aware of Theresienstadt, the model camp, and he alludes to Auschwitz in the officer's assembly announcement that the able-bodied

will work and the "unfit can expect special treatment at camps so designated" (*E*, 132). The justification speech is followed by dispersal orders reminiscent of concentration camp "selections"—the able-bodied were separated from mothers, Jewish elders, children, and those too weak to work. The first male group is sent for physical examinations and the second group to return home and await further instructions. All are told that within forty-eight hours they will be "resettled, given special treatment" (*E*, 132). They are warned against rebellion, and told that failure to follow orders will "lead to a savage justice" (*E*, 132). The prophetic diction clearly establishes the narrator's dual perspective. In line with Hannah Arendt's assessment of Nazis as bourgeois family men, Elman characterizes the German officer who addressed the assembled Jews in the square as

> never more than a petty functionary in the German machine who, . . . had placed highly in the civil service examinations. . . . Such men persist in all bourgeois societies. They are cold, ruthless, methodical, not cruel themselves but always to be found near the scene of cruelty. (*E*, 129)

Following the concentrationary experience suggested by the officer's remarks, father and son undergo a dramatic evocation of the concentrationary induction ceremonies. In a predeportation physical examination they encounter the dehumanizing process camp inmates routinely suffered. Medical examination and tattoo identification initiates the transformation from person to object—from citizen to slave—prodded and processed for the enhancement of the Third Reich. The protagonist painfully observes his father's vain attempt to maintain his dignity by impressing an inattentive German medical officer with his fluent Viennese German and his familiarity with German values. The elder Yagodah's efforts to distinguish himself from the others whose plight he shares are useless. He is just one of the mass; his wrist is sprayed with a freezing-cold solution, until "the flesh stings, and then turns numb." Before he can object,

> motors whir like the sound of a dentist's drill. Your arm is a piece of lead. In just three or four movements of the thing against your flesh the mark is made; and you don't have time to feel the pain. . . . Only now you have a number on your wrist. (*E*, 169–70)

Inured by the experience, the Germans view the blue-tattooed Jews "like beef on the hook" (*E*, 177). For the victim, involuntary tattooing is a realization of his vulnerability. Alex had naively thought of his skin as his personal property and "resented the intrusion." Elman uses gallows humor to strip the scene of pathos, citing Alex's bitter self-recrimination:

> Like a good little *chedarist*, I thought I must memorize my new numerals, as if some great teacher had set out an exercise, until it occurred to me: How absurd. When one is in possession of the urtext, memorizing is a foolish waste of time. (*E*, 178)

Although Elman departs from historic accuracy by staging a tattooing session prior to deportation,[18] the scene offers effective foreshadowing and metaphoric commentary. The tattooing is as integral to the evocation of a concentration camp scene as are the German officer's "selection" speech and the physical examination.

Elman stages the examination scene in the railroad terminal to evoke the boxcars carrying Jews across Europe to extermination centers. Thus, while the scene has dramatic immediacy, it is informed by post-Holocaust awareness. Contributing to this interpretation are the survivor's short, lyrical passage about cranes fleeing the roof of the terminus building to escape the suffering of earthbound Jews—earthbound, that is, until they go "up in smoke" (*E*, 161) and his association of Mark Chagall's floating Hasidim with the Jews who "went up in flames alive" (*E*, 161).

Under the terrible pressure of the forty-eight hour deportation notice, Yagodah desperately tries to barter with Skirzeny for his family's escape, offering his estate and furnishings for safe passage from Clig. To insure his gains in the unlikely survival and suit for redress for their losses, Skirzeny has prepared a document stating that the property will pass to him and to his heirs in perpetuity. Furthermore, Yagodah must sign a statement agreeing that the "transaction is being made without duress or *force majeur*" (*E*, 203) as a safeguard against criminal accusation should the victorious powers charge him with illegal expropriation. Making the apt postwar analogy with Dr. Kastner's negotiation with the Allies for supplies for the German war effort in exchange for Jewish lives,[19] Skirzeny offers to facilitate the Yagodah escape from Clig for their property. He agrees to secure papers identifying the Yagodah family as Christians of Jewish descent and arrange their transportation to safety. Frustrated by his father's delusion that they can pass as Christians and by the consumate uselessness of the ruse, since baptized Jews with four or five generations between them and their Jewishness were being deported, Alex succumbs to an orgy of self and group hatred, blaming his father and Jewish leaders rather than Nazi and Hungarian assassins for their plight. Once the estate exchange is negotiated, Skirzeny betrays the family claiming that there are only papers for eight and Lilo must remain behind, a ruse to provide his stepson with the woman he wants. Yagodah accepts Skirzeny's explanation of limited papers and Lilo concurs that she is the obvious choice to remain because she has the best chance to pass as a gentile maid in the Skirzeny household. Although Lilo understands her uncle's decision, she detests it. Vexed to be left behind at the mercy of her rapist, she rages at Alex, the only person who knows of Miklos' indecent intentions. Alex's half-hearted offer to remain in her stead is ineffective. The family must comply with Skirzeny's demands. To save eight, Newman Yagodah sacrifices one, a clear analogy to the decisions Jewish Councils had to render. The survivor claims to have no use for guilt, but it is clear that he is guilt-ridden. Forever vivid in his imagination is a "cameo of betrayal," an image of Lilo clawing at her face as he and his father are driven away in the last wagon.

Just as the Jews who were sent to the gas chambers were told they were going to "showers," so are the Yagodahs deceived and led into a trap. The memoir concludes with the survivor's summation of Skirzeny's betrayal. He meets father and son at their hiding place to say he has sent the women ahead, a departure from the agreed plan, and instructs the men to remain in a barn where he will send a car for them the following day. When a car arrives, it is bearing soldiers, but because Alex sees its arrival, he is able to escape, only by leaving his sleeping and weakened father behind and running into the woods. Alex Yagodah's remaining war experience is quickly summarized. He wanders in the woods for weeks, living on leaves and tree bark. Eventually he is found by peasants, soundly beaten, and taken in as a servant and sexual slave for a crippled peasant girl. Later, partisans turn him over to the Soviets who initially threaten to kill him as a spy, but spare him that he may serve as an orderly for a political commissar. After recuperation near the Black Sea, he is allowed to go to Turkey where a Jewish rescue service, the Joint Defense Appeal, arranges to transport him to Palestine where he volunteers for military service with the Pal-

estine Brigade and returns to fight in Europe. Following demobi-
lization, Alex visits Clig for a few hours, but he is unable to return
to the family home. In Israel, he eventually learns from Jewish
agencies of his father's forced labor and death from typhus in
Auschwitz, his mother's arrest and transport to a detention camp at
Mauthausen and then to Auschwitz. In addition, he learns that Lilo
perished in the bombing raid that began as his "escape" wagon
pulled out of Clig.

Many reviewers have echoed Alex Yagodah's condemnation
of Newman Yagodah for leaving Lilo at the mercy of the
Skirzenys.[20] Implicit in this criticism is the assumption that
Yagodah exercised freedom of choice. In doing so, they blame the
victim. The Jew was without free choice; his dilemma was whether
to accept Skirzeny's conditions and save eight or sacrifice all nine
people. The negotiations had included passage for the whole family. It was only at the last moment that Skirzeny presented his ultimatum and that the Jew capitulated. When William Styron's character, Polish-Catholic Sophie, has to choose which of her children
will live and which will be gassed, readers respond sympathetically—never condemning her for assigning one child to imminent
death and the other to temporary salvation. Yet when Elman's
Hungarian Jew, who is unaware of the younger Skirzeny's lust for
Lilo, must choose between survival of eight people and the possible
sacrifice of one against the certain destruction of nine, he is vilified.
Whereas Sophie knew one of her children would die and it was
entirely her choice which might survive, Yagodah is given no options. He is told Lilo will stay. While Skirzeny is spared moral
judgment, the impotent Jew is damned by his son and by literary
critics, who ignore the protagonist's warnings against fallacious
judgments of victims, thus demonstrating the ease of maligning
victims rather than condemning anti-Semitic criminals. The novel's
moral dilemma turns not only on the German crime against Jewry,
not only on Christian Europe's ready acquiescence to Germany's
genocidal goal and its betrayal of Jews into the hands of their
persecutors, but also on post-Holocaust injustice toward Jewry.
That Elman condemns the tendency to blame the victim is evident
in his protagonist's warning to his American correspondent to distinguish between the criminals and their victims. Although Alex
finds fault with everyone, he recognizes degrees of guilt, raises
critical distinctions between sins of commission and sins of omission. Skirzeny and his sort are guilty of exploiting the victims; the

Hungarians are guilty of surrendering the Jews to the Nazis; the Nazis are guilty of genocide; and Newman Yagodah, the Jews, and God are guilty of sins of omission: Yagodah and his counterparts for their failure to emigrate when they could have and for having good faith in their countrymen's decency, and God for being false to the covenant.

Although he condemned his father in 1944 for misjudging the Hungarian situation and leaving Lilo to Skirzeny, Alex judges differently in 1961, explaining that his father was neither so foolish to believe all Skirzeny told him nor so callous as to trust him with one of their own. Instead, Yagodah interprets his father's behavior as a sign of "his powerlessness and impotence and not some truth about his character *per se*" (*E*, 256). Similarly, he sympathetically quotes his father's defense of the Jewish elders forced to cooperate with the Nazis in compiling lists for deportation: "It was better for our own people to make the choices than to allow the Arrow Cross to do so because . . . We can at least be more gentle and helpful than they are and consequently make our friends' ordeals a little easier" (*E*, 257).

Like Singer in *Enemies* and Wallant in *The Pawnbroker*, Elman is starkly convincing in his rejection of easy and painless survivor regeneration. The world's insistence on Holocaust amnesia or recovery is pathological, as was its acquiescence to the Holocaust. Denuding the subject of sentimentality, Elman often brings new insight to the topic of victimization through dramatizing postwar bitterness and revealing the absurdity of hope for complete recovery from Holocaust ravages. Authentically angry about an injustice that never should have occurred, Alex is justifiably outraged by the atrocities the world tolerated and probably would tolerate again. Yagodah's resentment mirrors that expressed by the French resistance fighter, Jean Amery, who resents facile reconciliation with the architects of the concentrationary universe. A survivor of Nazi torture, Amery writes contemptuously of "so-called reeducators from America, England, or France" eager to forgive Germany.[21] The Frenchman's distaste for philosophers and psychiatrists who denounce victim bitterness provides an interpretive touchstone for Yagodah's rancor. Amery argues that to internalize his past suffering and bear it in emotional asceticism would make him the accomplice of his torturers. Like the Auschwitz survivor, Yagodah remembers the evil perpetrated against Jewry, is wary of easy reconciliation, and will not join the criminals in their efforts to forget or to rewrite history. Writing in the Vietnam era and deeply moved by the moral crisis in American society, Elman indicts failing humankind, indicts the free world for contributing to Hitler's crime, and implies that the world's acquiescence to and complicity in genocide taints its legitimacy to judge the victims.

Few American novelists draw any connection between events of the Holocaust and contemporary Israeli politics. Elman does. Just as Alex expresses religious ambivalence and affirmation, so he vacillates between castigating and championing Zionism.[22] In each instance he is motivated by a history of anti-Semitism and the Holocaust. Just as he vacillates from expressions of positive group identification to self-hate, Alex has become an Israeli citizen, yet occasionally utters anti-Semitic/anti-Zionist propaganda that equals the slander of Israel's worst enemies. One critic describes Yagodah as "a psychological first; an Israeli suffering from Jewish self-hate."[23] Most offensive in this regard is Yagodah's comparison of Israel and Israelis to Nazi Germany and Nazis:

> If, therefore, I speak only of those atrocities which made a madhouse out of Europe (and not about what has happened since), perhaps it is because I am forced to believe that it was such events which conditioned all of Israel to the murder of innocent fellahin, the slaughter at Port Said of Egyptian families, the continual border sniping, yes, and the growing militarism, racism, and chauvinism of this place. . . . But since we were the first great modern multitude of Victims of the State, is it surprising that we should have created a modern state of our own in which victimizing others became a way of life? (161–62)

Elman, who supports a Jewish homeland, claims this speech is an illustration of Yagodah's intemperance.[24] In its failure to distinguish between Nazi Germany's genocidal policy toward the Jews and the violence and injustice committed against relatively small numbers of a population, in the context of belligerence between two hostile factions in an ongoing war—a state of perpetual warfare initiated by five Arab states upon Israel's birth as a modern state—lies the same sort of political ignorance that contributed to the Hungarian debacle. Although Yagodah is outrageous here, on other occasions he endorses Israel's right to self-defense, in light of Holocaust history and concerted Arab efforts to destroy Israel. According to Elman: "Yagodah is not quite an Israeli. He still lives in temporary quarters. . . . He accepts shelter with bitterness because there is no place else he can go. No place to return to."[25]

Although Elman does not share the psychological, restorative visions of Bruno Bettelheim and Victor Frankl, he does affirm Jewish collective survival and support a Jewish homeland. Unlike the psychiatrist-survivors, Alex did not rise above the Holocaust, he was and will always remain its victim, describing himself as a "survivor surviving—selfconsciously wish[ing] to affirm . . . kinship with dung heaps and ashes" (*E*, 277). Gone are his prewar assimilationist illusions. He can look back at his past for the terror it was and be certain only that cultivated Europeans "inhabited a house of the blind in a country called death" (*E*, 277). *The 28th Day of Elul* concludes, as it started, with the subject of a post-Holocaust Jew's self-identity. Alex observes that if Jewry exists, he is a part of that collective: "I am one of them for sure. What other meaning would my life have? I am a Jew. What else should I call myself save *victim?*" (*E*, 276). His experience has taught him the void and left him with terrible awareness. Although Yagodah's response contains none of the religious erudition of Emil Fackenheim and Eliezer Berkovits, it insists on association with Jewry as the works of these scholars do.

In striving to come to terms with the problem of faith in the post-Holocaust period, Elman explores traditional thematic and stylistic Jewish literary responses to catastrophe: providential interpretation of history; acceptance of a silent, hidden God who remains aloof from human evil to honor the principle of free will; and biblical allusion and countercommentary. That there has been undeserved suffering has been evident to Jews since the biblical period. The history of persecution accounts for modification of the theological concept of retributive justice with the principle of *hester panim*, God hiding His face:

> Awake, why sleepest Thou, O Lord?
> Arise Thyself, cast us not off forever.
> Wherefore hidest Thou Thy face
> And forgettest our affliction and our oppression?
> . . . . . . . . . . . . . . . . . . . . . . . . . . . . . . . . . . . . . . . . . .
> Arise for our help,
> And redeem us for Thy mercies' sake. (Psalm 44)

The psalmist's construction of God's hiddenness is frequently appropriated in Jewish Holocaust literature to explain divine inaction in time of tribulation and as indication of human evil entirely separate and distinct from divine judgment. Although Elman's prose echoes biblical cadence and parallelism, Yagodah's post-Holocaust denunciation of God for crimes against the covenant parodies the psalmist's mournful, supplicating tone.

> Only He betrayed us. He profaned us. He took our prayers in vain. He mocked us. He rewarded us with cruelty. He listened but did not hear. He was there and He was not there when we needed Him. He led us into injustice. (*E*, 24)

By parodying and reformulating the psalmist, the survivor's protest against the Almighty conforms to Jewish literary tradition. This time-honored device consists of radical reinterpretation by means of reformulation or inversion of a text of the canon, which may be interpreted as a means of articulating faith despite the terror of separation from God. In this instance the sacred text is put to irreverent use to issue a protest. In his analysis of classical Yiddish writers' use of liturgical parody—putting the sacred text to irreverent use—David Roskies claims they are motivated by "their desire to imitate the sacrilege, to disrupt the received order of the text in the same way as the enemy, . . . disrupted the order of the world."[26] This analysis seems appropriate to Yagodah's reformulation of the traditional celebration of divine attributes. "This technique of imitating the breach of God's promise in the parody of Scripture . . . [using] 'symbolic inversion' and 'countercommentary'" is a basic form of Jewish response to catastrophe, for "to mimic the sacrilege allows the individual to keep faith even as the promise is subverted."[27]

Yagodah caustically concludes that Chosenness of the Jewish people consists of being chosen to bear the burden of God's long silences and absences from history, being chosen to suffer guiltlessly.

> Whoever may have thought he was responsible, whichever way the thing was eventually carried out, in the end only He was responsible. We placed ourselves in His hands and He did not disappoint us. I tell you there is a straight road from the Ark of the Covenant to the ovens at Ravensbruck, Treblinka, Auschwitz, Statlo, and the other places, and it is lined on both sides with the bleached bones of my fellow Jews. I believe in those Jews as the work of the Jewish God. Only They will never fail me. I believe in Them far more than I believe in the State. The bony sockets of Their eyes stare blankly past all of us toward the Disaster to which They bear witness as God's

Chosen People. And we, the living, cursed with our lives, bear witness again and again to the facts of Their death. That is why we are here. (*E*, 25)

The expectation of the righteous to receive God's protection for consistent observance of His commandments is thus ironically and tragically reversed. They are chosen not for earthly salvation, but destruction. In this manner Elman echoes Elie Wiesel's dictum that the purpose of survival is bearing witness to atrocity in order to prevent its repetition. Elman speaks first and foremost as a moralist, affirming the victims and rejecting implications of a providential interpretation of Holocaust history. Since God has granted mankind freedom, He tolerates the sinner and abandons the victim. If man is to act on his own responsibility, God must absent Himself from history or be present without being manifest. Thus, perhaps without intention, Alex Yagodah affirms God by bearing witness to his silence. In a caustic illustration of the peculiar nature of the covenantal relationship that coalesces polarities, man must observe the commandments and God may abandon His agreement.

The volume's title, *The 28th Day of Elul,* and its epigrams from the book of Jeremiah provide interpretive guidelines.[28] Elul, the sixth month of the Jewish calendar, is the period of preparation for repentance.[29] During the last week of Elul, prayers for forgiveness and mercy are recited. Spiritual reckoning is set specifically in the sacred period when God's thirteen attributes were revealed,[30] suggesting that faith is rewarded and that the sinner will be pardoned and accepted back to God. Elul then is the time when a Jew, as he is, even one as spiritually wanting as Yagodah, can come close to God. All that is necessary is that he desire to do so. The Hebrew letters for the word *Elul* suggest a phrase from the Song of Songs referring to the love between God and his people.[31] Since the Holocaust brought that relationship into question and occasioned the examination of the covenantal bond, the combined Elul allusion and Jeremiah epigraphs of Jewish defeat followed by redemption and the novel's Israeli setting insist that despite the severe strain put on the covenant by the Holocaust, the relationship remains intact.

> Did not your father eat and drink?
> He did what was right and just,
> And it went well with him.

Because he dispensed justice to the weak and the poor,
  It went well with him.
Is this not true knowledge of me? says the Lord. (Jer. 22:15–
  16)

The burden of Elman's Book One epigraph from Jeremiah, chapter 22, is the foretelling of the wages of disobedience to the covenant, a warning to those who break the commandments, and a
promise of regeneration contingent upon honoring the Mosaic
covenant. Jeremiah addresses the need to restore religious ideals of
justice and piety. Jeremiah knew disaster was imminent, and in
trying to cope with its implications, he pointed the way to preservation of the remnant. Book One deals with Yagodah's Israeli period,
signifying the return of the remnant to Israel through flashback to
the European period leading up to the devastation of Hungarian
Jewry. The biblical lesson of the epigraph, the righteous model of
the ancestral way, is an ironic critique of Yagodah's way of accommodation and yet implies the promise of redemption even for this
sinner.

   Similarly, the Jeremiah epigraph to Book Two corresponds to
the Jewish period of exilic suffering under Babylonian captivity
and the novel's treatment of invasion, occupation, deportation, and
death. At the same time, the passage includes an intimation of
redemption in its concluding line, "in the peace thereof ye shall
have peace." This passage foreshadows the promise in Jeremiah,
chapter 30, foretelling the destruction of the nations in which the
Jews were scattered and the return and rebuilding of Jerusalem:
"The city shall be rebuilt" (30:10), "and they shall come back from
the land of the enemy" (31:10). Jeremiah's polar functions, threatening judgment and promising restoration, suits Elman's treatment of the spiritual return of the individual sinner and the Elul
implications of spiritual restoration, as well as the historic manifestations of collective diasporan suffering and regeneration in the
Israeli homeland.

   *Lilo's Diary* complements the analytical, historic perspective of
the survivor in *The 28th Day of Elul* and the contemporary so-
cioeconomic assessment of the victim in *The Reckoning*, which fuses
personal and documentary perspectives. Whereas the first and
third volumes address the collective Hungarian-Jewish Holocaust
experience, from anticipatory and retrospective analytical points of
view, the second volume shifts from predominantly theological,

political, and social themes to chart the psychological trauma induced by dependence and Holocaust anxieties. In accord with this shift of perspective, Elman emphasizes psychosexual imagery and metaphor to convey Nazi violation of Jewish life. Writing at a time when the feminist movement was becoming vocal, Elman decided to "take the liberty of a fiction writer," and opted to construct the second volume not only from a feminine perspective but in Lilo's voice.[32] *Lilo's Diary* is a young woman's assessment of female and Jewish vulnerability, dramatized first in her role as ward in the Yagodah family and second as fugitive/captive in the Skirzeny household. Through parallels to her own sexual exploitation and social/psychic indignities in both households, Lilo begins to understand Holocaust suffering.

Reminiscent of F. Scott Fitzgerald's self-indulgent, beautiful, spoiled rich girls, so taken with self that they have no love left for others, Lilo is self-serving and narcissistic. But Lilo is not Judy Jones, and the Holocaust is not the American Jazz Age. Lilo is more cerebral, more analytic than Fitzgerald's women; her suffering is more intense and tragic. Orphan in a threatened sanctuary, Jew in Nazi-occupied Hungary, fugitive among enemies, Lilo suffers multiple perils. The young, beautiful woman is a complex, paradoxical creature: suspicious and trusting, passionate and cold, aggressive and meek; more profoundly complex in her self-portrait than she was in her fiancé-cousin's guilt-induced memoir. A major theme in *Lilo's Diary* "is the impingement of reality on a consciousness trained to abide by self-contained illusions, trained to maintain at all costs the façade of business as usual."[33] The diary entries reveal Lilo's brutally frank assessment of her own contradictions, the hopeless ennui of a liaison with her artist *manque* cousin, dependence on a scheming bourgeois guardian who controls her fortune, and ambivalence toward her rapist, whose blond beauty and vivacity Elman modeled on a high-school and college friend who "had the Aryan good looks of a Hitler *Jugend* and a becoming softness of smile and expression."[34]

Interpreting her life through the prism of Shakespearean tragedy, she writes:

> Prince Hamlet chose an antic disposition. It so happens it went poorly with him. My deceit is my apparent simplicity. If I were ever honest and open to a fault it would not go well with me. So I shall never let on what I know to be true. Never shall I declare myself. Never shall I forgive. Never completely give in.[35]

Using the diary as an extended soliloquy, Lilo reveals her own
motives, flaws, and foibles; her suspicions about her guardian,
whom she suspects has stolen her birthright and embezzled her
family's property; her impatience with Alex and her ambivalent
feelings toward Miklos. Secretly contemptuous of her uncle, she
nevertheless plays the role of admiring, dependent female to his
patronizing paterfamilias—counterfeit Ophelia to Yagodah's obliging Polonius. Although Yagodah is self-impressed with his political acumen, he is a mere prattler of political and social platitudes.
Lilo's analysis of her uncle seems more objective than Alex's account and is consistent with Hannah Arendt's political and social
analyses of assimilated Western European Jewry and as such foreshadows Newman Yagodah's self-assessment in the third volume.
Lilo's perception of the elder Yagodah's Holocaust reactions coincides with reported acculturated, middle-class Austrian and German-Jewish sensibilities. Yagodah indulged "his dream—to have
the respect of others, to be a man of substance" (*LD*, 65). And, like
self-beguiling German Jews, Yagodah expected his World War I
military record to stand him in good stead with the Nazis. Convinced that the war could not last more than another year, that the
Hungarians were making secret contacts almost daily with the Allies through the Vatican, Newman Yagodah deceived himself as
others did in early 1944 that Hungarian Jewry would escape the
fate of Polish Jewry. He believed that Hungarian Jews would enjoy
Vatican protection, despite evidence that the Vatican's interests
were limited to saving only baptized Jews—hence not Jews, but
Christians.[36]

With a sharper eye and more caustic tongue, Lilo observes
and comments on the trilogy's major players, on the disintegrating
family, and on the corruption of public institutions. She recognizes
that all the inhabitants of the Yagodah household live as prisoners,
"each imprisoned within himself, each a victim of his own crass
appetites and vanities" (*LD*, 12). Furthermore, Lilo confronts her
own duplicity, confesses to being calculating in personal relations,
but rationalizes that her social machinations are necessary for survival. Aware of an orphaned schoolmate who was taken away with
the first labor drafts in 1942, Lilo seeks to assure her uncle's protection and, therefore, tolerates his son's sexual advances, thereby
placating and manipulating the father. In fact, she measures her
strength and will power by her capacity to feign submission to
Alex.[37] It is for her "a joyous assertion of the will to surrender

to . . . [Alex] so *willingly"* (*LD,* 45). Submission to seduction equals survival. Hence, Lilo considers herself in control of the liaison. Just as Lilo's position in the Yagodah household anticipates her role in the Skirzeny household, her rape by Miklos Skirzeny foreshadows his stepfather's violation and betrayal of the Yagodah family, which is, in turn, emblematic of the betrayal and destruction awaiting Hungarian Jewry.

In addition to displaying varied interpretations of the same historic event, the trilogy structure permits Elman to enlarge the Holocaust panorama. Thus, an event minimized in one volume is magnified in another and vice versa. In the accounts of the Yagodah males, the dominant mood is impotence—helplessness of the Jewish community leaders to protect loved ones from Nazi violence. In *The 28th Day of Elul,* the Holocaust survivor claims that the Yagodahs suppressed what they knew of the destruction of Polish Jewry by 1944 to evade facing their own danger, yet the contemporary diarist emphasizes their awareness and fear. In *Lilo's Diary,* the victim writes graphically about known horrors: "Rumors of every kind now exist: Of huge camps where the dead are thrown into cauldrons of lye to make fat while the dying work until they have no more strength. . . . Terrible rumors! Of fusillades, mass executions, epidemics" (*LD,* 32). Contrary to expectations of despair, a surprising voice of resistance emerges in the orphan's revelation of her own strategy for domestic survival and the trilogy's single report of a Jewish resistance movement. Lilo writes of a young cousin determined to join a resistance unit in Croatia. The young man's report of the refusal of the elders in his town to allow the young to burn the local ghetto for fear of mass reprisals parallels Clig's Jewish hierarchy's caution and failure to support violent rebellion—cut off as they were from external support; however, it does add the dimension of resistance—a topic generally overlooked in American Holocaust fiction.

The contrast between volumes one and two is particularly striking in the portrayal of the deportation assembly. Elman detailed the scene in the first volume, engaging the reader in the agonizing wait for information and the victims' anxiety and humiliation. In *Lilo's Diary,* he begins the scene with a reference to its conclusion, "We have no more than forty-eight hours left in Clig" (*LD,* 128). Faced with the reality of deportation, Lilo's sophistication disintegrates into bewilderment and innocent exclamations regarding the injustice of undeserved punishment:

> It is so cruel. The wicked are not punished. We are punished. *Everyone of us. Mothers. Little children. Old people. Our friends, our neighbors.* . . . *"There will be no 'exceptions.'"* The entire city and its suburbs— "Judenrein." We are herded together like cattle in the principal square. . . . We listen, and then we are sent home again to pack our belongings, told we have no more than forty-eight hours left to us in Clig. Our destinies have been decided. We shall be sent to work elsewhere, those of us who are lucky. (*LD*, 129–30)

Despite knowledge of Nazi methodology in Poland and her earlier ennumeration of death camp rumors, Lilo is dumbfounded, amazed by Hungarian deportations because the war seems so close to its end. Truth gives way to disbelief and self-delusion.

> Can it be that they will uproot even the aged? Are none to be spared? It is brutal and senseless. Why now, when our liberators must be so close at hand? How do they expect to profit from any of this? We have been irrevocably betrayed, but by whom? (*LD*, 130)

Although the shock of a personal encounter with the Nazi apparatus temporarily dulls Lilo's perception, once she regains composure, she assesses the government's agreement to the deportation order and the popular response realistically: "Our neighbors shall be the accomplices to all this. Before we say adieu to them, the looters will be among us" (*LD*, 131). Yet she notes that Jews cannot expect the gentiles to protect them when men like her uncle do little. As she ponders their inevitable doom, she daydreams of finding some brave soul among the Jews of Clig to commit the sabotage allegedly executed by neighboring Jews, which was only a pretext for Clig's punishment. Again, insight corrects wishful thinking and she realizes that the Plevinitz story is "just another lie, told to lull us into not taking up arms" (*LD*, 131). In a bitter inverse parody of Shylock's "Hath not a Jew eyes" soliloquy, Lilo asks why the Jews are selected for such calumny. And, finally, she asks the same question that occurs to Alex in his post-Holocaust torment, "What is human after all?" (*LD*, 134). Her answer has all the marks of Holocaust metamorphosis: "To be human is to be abject" (*LD*, 134).

The Jeremiah epigraph to *Lilo's Diary* provides an interpretive reading to Lilo's generally clear-sighted explication of personal and public events, her capacity to see through German deceit and Jewish delusion:

An appalling and horrible thing
is come to pass in the land:
the prophets prophesy in the service of falsehood,
and the priests bear rule at their beck;
and my people love to have it so;
what then will ye do in the end thereof? (Jeremiah 5:30–31)

Among "the prophets [who knowingly] prophesy in the service of falsehood" are the Hungarian officials and German officers who willingly deceived the Jews. Germans appropriately play a minor role in the trilogy, since few were needed in Hungary to implement the Final Solution, because the native government, an Axis ally, was willing to implement the German genocide plan. In addition to the officials administering the deportation in the first volume, the second book adds an officer who is similar to Hannah Arendt's banal bureaucrat, an otherwise "decent" bourgeois gentlemen caught up in events beyond his control. He is a homesick, war-weary grandfather, who believes he is simply doing his duty. The billeting officer "visits" the Yagodah home, behaving as though he is making a civilized social call. Yet he "talks of arrangements, resettlements, redistribution," adding "nothing personal against 'the Israelites' as a race" (*LD*, 113). Unlike the wishful thinkers, "people [who] love to have it so," like the Jewish Councils and Lilo's aunt who writes a household inventory in expectation of postwar reclamation, Lilo generally acknowledges the full implications of the "appalling and horrible thing [that] is come to pass in the land."

Whereas Lilo is generally correct in her public assessments, she seriously misjudges when she blames fellow victims rather than the criminal perpetrators for her suffering. Resentful that she is to be left with the family whose son raped her, yet convinced Yagodah tried to include her in the escape group, Lilo determines to make the Yagodahs suffer, to look at her, as they depart to imagined safety. Expressing no rancor toward the gentile who sealed her fate, she blames only her fellow victims, as she had in the earlier rape scene blamed her cousin rather than Miklos. As Alex is inclined to blame his father and the Jewish Council for the predicament of the Jews, so Lilo temporarily condemns father and son. Her misplaced scorn thus echoes the German's successful transfer of Clig Jews' wrath from the Nazis and Hungarians to the Plevinitz Jews, the alleged authors of their fate.

With Lilo left behind to be Miklos Skirzeny's whore, Elman

introduces yet a further perspective to the trilogy—that of a
*Judenrein* Hungary. The elder Skirzeny's observation that he expects the Yagodahs are "packed in goods trains, and racing to
heaven-knows-what destination" (*LD*, 138) testifies to his betrayal
of the Jews and is emblematic of gentile Europe's knowledge of
Germany's treatment of "resettled" Jews. Lilo understands that the
family is destined for death and wonders whether it is proper for
her to pray the mourner's *Kaddish* for them. This assimilated girl,
who doesn't know the Hebrew prayers, prays "for all of them like a
crazy hermit because I miss them all so and, angry as I am, I do not
hate them" (*LD*, 139). She "prays with perfect cynicism, and rage
and pity" (*LD*, 139).

The remainder of the volume deals with Lilo's rapid physical
deterioration. She suffers from dysentery, cramps, hunger, and
painful skin irritations. Corresponding to her failing health is
Miklos' diminished interest in her, marked by erratic fluctuations
from tenderness to abuse. Finally, her beauty marred, Miklos abandons her. In an ironic turn of events, Lilo's potential for survival
improves as she undergoes a Holocaust metamorphosis from the
younger gentile's whore to the elder's pawn. Although she has lost
favor with Miklos, his stepfather sees her value as his "safe-con-
duct" when the liberators enter Hungary. Should the Nazi collaborator be pressed to demonstrate his innocence in a war trial, he
will have Lilo as evidence of his generosity in saving Jews from the
Nazi net.

Although Elman has concentrated his theological theme in
the survivor's memoir, he concludes *Lilo's Diary* with a prayer-
parody addressing similar issues raised in *The 28th Day of Elul*,
which effectively unites the two volumes. In anger and confusion
Lilo prays a perverted pastiche taken from "Hear O Israel," the
central prayer of the Jewish liturgy; *Avinu Malkenu,* the hauntingly
beautiful supplication recited in synagogue services during the ten-
day period of the High Holidays, the Days of Judgment; Psalm 23
attesting to God's goodness and mercy; and the mourner's *Kaddish*.

> Dear God, Dear Murderer, thy will be done
> Thy Kingdom come
> Our Father, Our King
> Give us this day our Daily Hunger
> Our Father which art in Heaven
> Curse us, despise us, murder us, betray us

O Lord Our God Thou hast set up a table before us
In the presence of our enemies
My cup runneth over . . .
*Yisgadal . . . V'Yisgadal . . . V'yisroman. (LD,* 153–54)

Thus, Elman concludes the volume with a brilliant allusion evoking the traditional prayers; at the same time, he suggests through brutal fragmentation and invented diction the disruption of Jewish life wrought by the Holocaust and through their unseemly fusion, an echo of Alex's biblical countertext. Furthermore, in an appropriate addendum, Elman reminds us of the instigator of the calamity necessitating the parody by shifting to German, a language Lilo believes appropriate to sentimental poetry and carnage and, therefore, appropriate for praying to God, the murderer. Lilo's prayer-parody echoes the survivor's indictment of God for his Holocaust passivity, its poetics of sacrilege that echo Andre Schwarz-Bart's *The Last of the Just* parodic concluding prayer, linking God with the horror of the Holocaust in a roll call of the death camps:

And praised. Auschwitz. Be. Maidenek. The
    Lord. Treblinka.
And praised. Buchenwald. Be. Mauthausen. The
    Lord. Belzec.[38]

The final volume of the trilogy, *The Reckoning: The Daily Ledgers of Newman Yagodah, Advokat and Factor* (1969), parallels the moral accounting of a bourgeoise parvenu and the society that shaped him with an account of the destruction of Hungarian Jewry in the larger context of the forces leading to and including the Holocaust. Elman's use of the ledger complements the first-person narrative introduced in the "letters" of *The 28th Day of Elul* and the journal structure of *Lilo's Diary*. Like the first two, *The Reckoning* is set in Clig, Hungary, in 1944, but substitutes a prewar and Holocaust vantage point for the hindsight of the first survivor's account; it also adds the economic and sociological analyses of a chronicler educated in the twin crucibles of World War I and the Depression to the second victim's psychological emphasis.

*The Reckoning* is an assessment of private and public corruption by "a sinner in search of meaning, disclosing . . . the decay of a value system."[39] Newman reveals himself in this volume as a smug, pompous, venal, calculating, bourgeois business man, a self-centered and dependent lover, a demanding and deceitful husband, and a loving but ineffectual father. Adept at analysis of social and economic problems, he fails to act on the most pressing political issue of his time. Deception is an integral part of Yagodah's daily existence: he deceives his Jewish wife, Ilona, to keep her from discovering his gentile mistress, Ileana; he deceives others with his business practices; and he deceives himself by believing the Enlightenment myth—that he is a European among Europeans—and disbelieving the significance of European anti-Semitism. Yagodah's most tragic failures—limited vision and courage—account for his decision to remain silent about German intentions for Hungarian Jewry.

To pass the time while banned from productive work under the pro-Nazi Hungarian regime, Newman Yagodah, manufacturer, financier, and economic consultant, ponders and parallels his personal history to Jewish-Hungarian history and writes a monograph entitled *The Abolition of Poverty*. According to Yagodah's assessment, in the 1930s Europe had

> more food, more money, more clothing than ever before, yet—at the same time—hundreds of thousands, perhaps millions, . . . were without, lacking, underemployed or unemployed, so undernourished and so discouraged and despondent that some of them, particularly among the gentiles, reached for any straws, in anger, concupiscence, violence.[40]

Ironically, while Yagodah ponders the European economic failures of the 1930s that contributed to the Holocaust, he fails to assess the current dangers to Hungarian Jews and fails to act in time to save his family. Although he knows the Polish Jews are being incinerated, he works on his manuscript and passively waits for the Allies to eliminate the Nazi stranglehold on Europe in time to save Hungarian Jews from a similar fate.

Yagodah's ledger is the self-assessment of a man who finally understands that he is and has always been the duped subject of Christian caprice, a second-class citizen of the body politic—a social and economic pariah, an alien among countrymen he would embrace, a Jew estranged from coreligionists who would embrace him. Newman Yagodah is, as his first name implies, the new man, the post-Enlightenment Jew, a representative of a failed social experiment. The experiment failed because Europe dishonored its promise to accept Jews as full-fledged citizens sharing in the political, cultural, and economic lives of their respective countries. In practice, the Jew's acceptance was always limited. He was free to disassociate himself from Jewish groups and causes, free to fight in Hungary's wars, free to work in a restricted capacity in its economy, but never free to enjoy social relationships with gentile neighbors. To achieve the status of tolerated European, the Jew was free to become a nominal Jew, never free to be a devout Jew and a Hungarian, or Frenchman, or German.

Newman Yagodah is the dramatic embodiment of historian Hannah Arendt's composit of the Jewish pariah—the Jewish social outcast whose political emancipation was incomplete. According to Arendt, "During the 150 years when Jews truly lived amidst, and not just in the neighborhood of Western European peoples, they always had to pay with political misery for social glory and with social insult for political success."[41] Such is Newman Yagodah's situation. Although academic success yielded a positive self-image and admission to the University of Vienna, he was socially ostracized, and he soon realized that cultivated Europeans are also anti-Semites.

> The others would not have me. I loved the same things they loved, yet to them I was to be distrusted, an exotic, a figure of scorn. How wrong I was to think that it could have been any different, to think that through my talents and intelligence I might escape the judgments of knaves and viscious scoundrels. At our lectures, which I attended one might almost say religiously, our professors made anti-Semitic remarks religiously, as if hate, too, was the stuff of the curriculum of law, history, philosophy, and physics, and those who did not hate, those who were decent and amiable and opposed such behavior, were regarded by students and authorities as Bohemians, or scoundrels, or dangerous radicals; they too were renegades to the student body I so much envied and admired. (*R*, 127)

Yagodah's capacity for clear thinking was short-lived. He believed he enjoyed the acceptance of his World War I comrades, with whom he pretended to laugh as they defied death. Still unable to accept the full extent of his exclusion, he reveals himself again as the outsider, remembering being "so thrilled, so vibrant, that they were willing to accept me as one of them, that I was not their Jew; but their comrade" (*R*, 113). Unlike Hannah Arendt's noble, conscious pariah, who "tried to make of the emancipation of the Jews the ideal it should have been—an admission of Jews as Jews to the ranks of humanity,"[42] Yagodah, like most assimilated European Jews, was content with limited acceptance; he was content with permission "to ape the gentiles or an opportunity to play the *parvenu*.[43] So grateful was he for a crumb of toleration, that he was satisfied to have his Jewishness forgotten, negated. He was, in essence, content with deception, content to be tolerated at the expense of his real identity. Thus, Elman makes evident that the anti-Semitism that was rife in Viennese society between 1910–1914 was part of the established European tradition, and he implies that this foundation was instrumental in Germany's successful management of its genocide program—an implication underscored by references elsewhere to the Vatican's efforts to save baptized Jews in utter disregard for the lives of observant Jews.

*The Reckoning*, more documentary in tone and detail than the first two volumes, includes data that appear in standard Holocaust histories. Newman Yagodah's reflections on public events and his personal experiences during the 1930s and early 1940s offer the reader a condensed account of early twentieth-century Hungarian history. Just as Hungarian territorial ambitions are cited as the motivation for the Hungarian-German alliance, Hungarian disenchantment with Germany follows expansionist achievements and the subsequent inability to disentangle itself from Nazi policies. Elman's treatment of the German invasion emphasizes its dual imperatives: maintaining Hungary in the Nazi orbit by installing pro-Nazi officials and annihilating Hungarian Jewry. Through the vehicle of Yagodah's recollections, Elman demonstrates the historic progression of Nazi influence in Hungary, an erratic political climate marked by periods of relative Jewish safety and peril corresponding with Hungary's reluctant and erratic cooperation with the Axis powers—the successive cycles of hope and disappointment, from relaxation of restrictions to aggressive persecution, that preceded the final slaughter.

In marked contrast to the survivor's diatribe based on full Holocaust knowledge, Newman Yagodah's ledger is written in the voice of a bourgeoise sentimentalist who coveted full European citizenship, but now suffers disenfranchisement, a victim caught up in events he can neither fathom nor control. Relatively trivial moral transgressions disturb him because he suppresses his larger outrage—mass murder of Polish and German Jews. Hence, he laments financial corruption in Hungary.

The most singularly dreadful effect of this war, . . . is that terrible moral reprobacy afflicting all of civil and official life, . . . it is now common practice to bribe, seduce, and corrupt officialdom whereas before it was always something that one resorted to with some hesitation. (*R*, 36)

Whereas this early observation reflects the relative safety of Hungarian Jews under the Kallay government, his later notes reflect the harsher more repressive measures of the Horthy regime designed to ameliorate Germany's fears that Hungary would desert the Axis and conclude a separate peace with the Allies. Given the choice between German military occupation and a German approved government, Horthy chose the latter and, therefore, pursued an aggressive accommodation to Germany's destructive goals: increased Jewish labor batallions, increased requisition of Jewish goods and wealth, promotion of ever more severe anti-Jewish biases in the professions and economy, and after March 19, 1944, prohibition of gentiles working in Jewish households, sharp restrictions on Jewish freedom of movement, establishment of curfews, and finally, ghettoization in designated areas prior to deportation.

Elman establishes documentary authenticity in his careful correspondence of Yagodah's personal defeat and the public humiliation of Hungary submitting to Nazification. The collapse of the bourgeois paterfamilias parallels the destruction of Hungarian Jewry that began with anti-Semitic press attacks and progressed to "aryanizations" of labor unions and businesses, imposed Jewish "contributions" to the war effort, the institution of discriminatory legislation requiring Jews to add a middle name of Isaac or Sara, systematic separation of Hungarians and Jews, government encouragement of gentiles blaming Jews for the nation's problems and exploiting them. Even non-Jews who were disinclined to cooperate with government anti-Semitic policies were vulnerable:

The new government is using brass-knuckles tactics for the first time against those who would even pretend to be on friendly terms with us: dismissals without notice; accusations of disloyalty; house arrests and, in some cases, transportations and incarcerations. . . . Now employers are held "Judaistic" or "pro-Yid"; to remain on friendly terms with us is considered a "culpable breach of loyalty," and a "defamation of political leadership." (*R*, 61)

Yagodah's unsettled economic status illustrates the precarious existence of Hungarian Jews. His commercial and professional work is severely limited and finally stopped altogether by government decree. Yet substantial payments to Nazi causes are imposed on him. He must make financial contributions to the German-Hungarian war effort, to the Arrow Cross, the League for Widows of the Fuhrer Legionaires of the Eastern Front, and pay a constant flow of bribes to the director of Public Services, to the Factory Guards Association, and to former friends and neighbors who extort exorbitant payment for services. Since his income is negligible, he is forced to deplete his savings and to barter his home.

It is not inconceivable that Yagodah had some basis for hope that Hungarian Jews would escape the fate of Polish Jewry. While the Kallay government of 1942–1944 expanded the expropriatory process and the Jewish labor forces, it resisted deportations to the Eastern concentration and death camps. Characteristic of Elman's historic accuracy is Yagodah's expectation of special dispensation for military service. Hungarian regulations in force between 1938–1941 allowed exemptions for wounded and decorated military veterans from various discriminatory laws. Yagodah's 1930s wishful thinking regarding the ability of Jews to be Hungarian in public and Jewish in private is paralleled by his 1944 expectation that military service will exempt him from the fate of Jewish non-veterans. Like the German Jews who deluded themselves into thinking the Nazis would spare Jewish veterans, Yagodah, too, thinks his distinguished military record will guarantee exclusion from the fate of Polish Jewry. He discovers instead the reality of being a disposable Jew. His was the delusion of the post-Enlightenment assimilated Jew who mistakenly expected his loyalty to his nation to be reciprocal. Like a cuckolded husband, Yagodah is bewildered by his country's betrayal of its Jewish citizenry.

The reader gains new understanding of the plight of Hungarian Jews from Newman Yagodah's statements about his work on the Jewish Council. The Council references convey German terror and Jewish impotence caused by intragroup animosity, each vying to save his own family from disaster while simultaneously trying to serve the community. The victims' moral dilemma is poignantly dramatized in the elders' realization that to save oneself or one's own family meant another would be lost to fill the deportation quota. Although Yagodah is able to save his son from an early deportation, he must face the wrath of an angry father whose son was deported. Another irate Jew advises Yagodah: "They are preparing this stew for all of us. Whether you like it or not we are all going to boil inside the very same pot" (*R*, 87).

The deportation assembly scene, the most heartrending of the first volume, is reconstructed at length in the third, but with significant differences, primarily in the areas of economic and historic analysis and a thorough expository rendering of Newman Yagodah's earlier life. These details shed light on his contemporary confusion and anxiety. In *The 28th Day of Elul* the assembly scene simultaneously benefits from dramatic immediacy and post-Holocaust insight. It is rendered in great detail to inform the innocent American lawyer of Holocaust history and to convey the progressive humiliation and degradation of a people. As a survivor memoir and reflection, the account is coherently delivered and benefits from a twenty-year historic perspective that parallels it to the concentrationary universe. Conversely, *The Reckoning's* presentation is fragmentary and diffuse, evoking the confusion and terror of the victims who must make judgments based on Nazi deceptions, Hungarian duplicity, and world wide disinterest. Newman's assembly rendition dramatizes the victims' frustration, impotence, confusion, and fear. Unlike the survivor's diction and gallows humor, which reflect Holocaust irrationality, Newman's questions suggest prewar concepts of rational behavior and consequence: *"What is happening to all of us?"* and *"How have we deserved any of this?"* convey his moral indignation. "To be herded like so many cattle, to be branded like so much scorched and writhing flesh—*why us?* For what purpose?" (*R*, 111).

In place of the survivor's analytic account is the victim's silent petition:

> *No No No not yet please because we are helpless and weak and we really don't wish to harm anybody,* but the world is, . . . indifferent to our protestations. . . . If we are to be sacrificed, it is a matter of inevitability, declares this indifferent world. But why? For what? What might we have done to make an indifferent world compassionate? (*R*, 129)

In sharp contrast to the survivor's bitter understanding of world indifference to Jewry's slaughter is the victim's desperate hope for deliverance. In accord with the third volume's larger sociological and historic approach, its assembly scene becomes a memorial tableau of those to be lost in the Holocaust, a prefunerary elegy for lives about to be vanquished. Stopping the deportation process in *medias res,* Elman freezes time—as the Jew's wrist is frozen prior to tattooing—to incorporate a flashback detailing Newman Yagodah's checkered history, a childhood scarred by economic and emotional insecurity, an adolescence mixed with the pain of social ostracism and poverty relieved by academic achievement, a courtship beginning in passion and deteriorating into a marriage of social and economic convenience. Alternating retrospective revery with contemporary interruptions, Elman boldly contrasts the promise and vigor of a civilized and productive European life with intimations of approaching debasement and death. The assembly scene provides expository detail on how the crass materialist was forged in the crucible of poverty and social ostracism. The son of a selfish philanderer who deserted his family, Newman Yagodah was raised in his grandfather's household, and after the old man's death, he suffered loneliness as the neglected child of an overworked mother forced to give all her attention to earning a living. Yagodah was a sensitive but troubled adolescent alienated from his boorish brother and his mother's equally boorish lover. Academic success and hard work were the vehicles of his escape from squalor to a profession and marriage above his social class. Although Newman remains an unattractive person even in his own narration, he is more richly drawn, a complex amalgam of the contradictory forces of the early twentieth-century patterns of alternate integration and segregation of European Jews. This portrayal engages the reader's sympathy for Newman Yagodah much more fervently than does his son's account in *The 28th Day of Elul.* The satiric treatment in *Elul* of the elder's preening in the assembly scene gives way in *The Reckoning* to the pathic collapse of a carefully and painstakingly constructed social demeanor in the decades prior to the Nazi madness.

The assembly digression is further enriched by Yagodah's speculation on how his fate might have differed had he chosen socialism, Zionism, or emigration to America after World War I rather than supporting Hungarian nationalism and joining the ranks of industrial-capitalists. Elman is one of a small company of writers who link the subject of Zionism and an independent state of Israel to their treatment of the Holocaust. Like I. B. Singer's secular Jews, who realize that the only salvation for Jewry is an independent state, Elman's Hungarian nationalist becomes pro-Zionist, writing of the need for a Jewish nation and homeland. However, since he is so attuned to European life and unwilling in advanced years to emigrate, Yagodah remains a philosophical Zionist and tries to convince his children to leave Europe, stipulating in his last will and testament that they "use the means I have given them to emigrate to Palestine to live out their lives as Jews in a Jewish Nation" (*R*, 80). The Jewish parvenu, who vainly sought entry to the "respectable" gentile world through professional and business associations and was rewarded with betrayal and rejection, wants a more substantive citizenship for his children. He has neither a significant position in Hungarian society, which is itself in the process of moral collapse, nor an alternative Judaic tradition. As Yagodah prepares for deportation, he rejects his earlier optimism for a tolerant post-Enlightenment Europe and recognizes that the Holocaust is the culmination of centuries of Christian anti-Semitism: "all the martyred dead of our history, the mounds of dust and ashes, the blasted hillochs of graveyards. . . . Before our eyes swirls the future, more clouds of ash and dust" (*R*, 114).

Yagodah's assembly square revery ends with an abrupt return to contemporary reality—the urgent need to negotiate his family's escape. He turns for assistance to Skirzeny, the person who will benefit most from his departure. The extortionist, a representative European gentile, profits from the genocide of the Jews. He agrees to arrange a family escape on the condition that he gains the estate, and a bonus of the estate furnishings, that Yagodah won from him in a business transaction. Accustomed to providing for his family and having others beseech him for assistance, Yagodah is now reduced to dependence on Skirzeny's mercy.

Significant among the strengths of the trilogy is the recreation of the Jewish-Hungarian plight as an analogue to the death camp experience, without setting the fiction in the camps. Through the assembly roundup and subsequent escape strategy, Elman evokes camp despair and desperation—the bitter loss of control over one's destiny and the process of becoming subject to malignant whim. Yagodah is neither a tragic hero nor a martyr in the traditional literary or religious patterns because he has no freedom to choose, no freedom to act and bear the consequences. Skirzeny, like Dr. Mengele of Auschwitz, determines who will live and who will die, selects which Yagodah family members will be included in the fraudulent escape plan and which will not. Despite the appearance of Yagodah as a negotiator, he is simply a pawn is Skirzeny's system of capital gains, as the Jewish elders were pawns of the Germans.

Just as options were severely restricted in the camp universe, so, too, are Yagodah's. The only real choice Yagodah has is whether to cooperate with Skirzeny and try to save eight of nine family members, or refuse Skirzeny's demand for Lilo and condemn his entire family to death. His "choice" is within the Holocaust framework of alternate evils and is not comparable to the moral challenges of free men in ordinary circumstances. Because Yagodah is operating as a victim of Nazism, his behavior must be judged in the same way we would the inmates of the concentration and death camps, as the behavior of persons suffering atrocity. Yagodah's "choice" is similar to that of Tadeusz Borowski's mother in *This Way For the Gas, Ladies and Gentlemen,* a mother whose will to live is so strong that she tries to distance herself from her child during the Auschwitz selections because she instinctively senses that she has an opportunity to survive as an unencumbered worker, but is destined for immediate gassing if she remains with her young child; it is also similar to that described by Olga Lengyel, a physician-survivor of Auschwitz, who writes of physicians killing the newborn infants and pretending they were stillborn in order to save the mothers who would otherwise have been sent to death with their infants.[44] Yagodah's pre-camp selection is an evocation of camp brutality, where families were arbitrarily separated for slave labor or slaughter, where parents sometimes had to choose which child should go to the gas chamber first. Yagodah's family selection may also be read as the private analogue to his public position as Jewish Council member. On the private level, he is forced to choose, as he did in the public sphere when ordered to measure one life against another, who will go into a labor or death transport and who will remain behind.

Lawrence Langer, whose observations of Holocaust literature are among the most salient, isolates an important truth of Holocaust reality as it applies to victims and survivors: "the Holocaust has little to do with playing the hero, for victim or survivor. . . . Imposing heroic expectations misinterprets the moment; no triumphant gesture exists";[45] suffering does not automatically lead to moral growth. "Staying alive in the camps sometimes required the practice of being less then human."[46] One may say the same of those destined for the camps, already tattooed and listed for the transports. From the safety of a reader's armchair, some demand that Yagodah be more than human, save all nine, despite his powerlessness. Rather than the victim, it is the destructive experience that is to be condemned. Rather than the victim, forced to operate within a system he did not create, perpetrators of the crimes are to be condemned. Yagodah is neither hero nor villain, just an ordinary man caught in extraordinary circumstances. Yagodah's moral dilemma is a projection of camp existence, which often required prisoners to prey upon each other in order to survive. It is not the Jew who barbarized the moral premises by which civilized people live but the Nazis and their willing collaborators. To shift the blame for moral laxity to the Jewish victim is intellectually absurd and morally reprehensible. And Elman has shown us that it is still possible, despite all we know, to fall into the trap of blaming the Jews for every abomination, including Holocaust misconduct. "Heroic defiance, growing into tragic insight, needs a vision of moral order to nourish it, and this is precisely what the Holocaust universe lacks."[47] Richard Elman understood this. 'Tis a pity some of his critics have not.

The trilogy gains substance from the manifold ways in which the three volumes intertwine. Elman advances the cause of American Holocaust literature in his explicit inclusions of Holocaust history. Moving past mere delineation of the existential Holocaust experience, he explores the Holocaust's implications for Jewish religious and political survival, employing theoretical discussion, dramatic treatment, and epigraphical allusion to Judaism and Zionism. Further, since he has created characters suffering from self-hatred, hatred predicated on internalizing anti-Semitic prejudices within a culture that postulated polarity between European Jews and non-Jews, the trilogy demonstrates the danger of Jews succumbing to out-group anti-Semitic identification of the sort Jean Paul Sartre describes in *Jew and Anti-Semite*. Furthermore, both Newman and Bela argue against the false lures of assimilation and urge post-Holocaust Jews to live as Jews in the Diaspora if necessary, but preferably in a Jewish nation. Each incorporates variations of this attitude in his last will and testament, and the family's Holocaust survivors transform the vision into reality.

Like Elie Wiesel, Elman is concerned with the central issue of the Holocaust: how it came to be that one people decided to annihilate another; how it came to be that world opinion condoned this crime; and how, in the light of our post-Holocaust knowledge, we must rethink man and God. Like Wiesel, Elman isolates the inversion of values whereby the innocent are called upon to justify their survival. Elman's survivor-protagonist also shares with Wiesel's survivor in *Dawn* the vital connection between the violence of the Holocaust and the new Israeli consciousness, one fashioned by Holocaust awareness and fused with the lingering presence of the Holocaust dead. Although Elman's survivor did not experience the concentration camp, he shares with Wiesel's characters the notion that post-Holocaust man cannot live by the same values that served him in the pre-Holocaust era. Alex Yagodah shares with the narrators of Wiesel's *The Accident* and Singer's *Enemies* the knowledge that the disintegration rather than the reintegration of the survivor is the primary post-Holocaust existential truth. "Anyone who has seen what they have seen cannot be like the others, cannot laugh, love, pray, bargain, suffer, have fun, or forget."[48] The Elman survivor, like the Wiesel survivor and the Singer survivor, is different, maimed and trapped by what he has survived.

Elman's significant contribution to Holocaust literature is noted by Elie Wiesel who wrote, his "ideas are provocative, his outcry uncompromising, . . . [he] touches on the most important human and philosophical questions of our time."[49] The trilogy's epigraph, taken from Miguel De Unamono's *The Life of Don Quixote and Sancho*, accurately mirrors Elman's narrative purpose:

> I would open up your breast and in your heart's core, I would make a wound into it I would rub vinegar and salt, so that you might never again know peace, but would live in continual anguish and endless longing.

Unamuno's words provide an apt prologue to Elman's moral scrutiny, his sensitivity to the atrocities in which his fellows were transformed to smoke and ash, and his concern that their suffering may be forgotten, as their pleas for help were unanswered. The author of the trilogy, like the writer of the epigraph, uses the moral imperative of the creative artist to address the elemental anguish of the human heart so that his readers will be touched and moved to think and feel and remember and ask, as the survivor does, "What was it that perished in the camps—Man or the idea of Man" (*E*, 15)?

# CHAPTER SIX

*Kaddish and Resurrection: Isaac Bashevis Singer's*
*Holocaust Memorial*

Isaac Bashevis Singer did not experience the Holocaust directly, as did his family left behind in Poland. Yet the *Shoah* has strongly influenced his thought and is a recurrent theme in his fiction. Singer chronicles events heralding the catastrophe and explores the psychological and theological burdens of survival in Yiddish, the language of emigré-survivors and of Polish Jews who vanished in the Holocaust. Writing from the perspective of psychological rather than physical survival, Singer commemorates a way of life destroyed in the twelve-year Nazi reign of terror. Although he refrains from setting the fiction in the concentrationary universe, he memorializes the Jews who perished in the ghettos and camps; he reminds the world of their suffering, and keeps their Yiddish language vibrant, their traditions and customs accessible. In his realistic outline of the onslaught and effects of Germany's Final Solution to the "Jewish Problem" and in his metaphoric treatment of the Chmielnicki Massacre, a seventeenth-century Holocaust analogue, Singer's sensitivity to the *Shoah* is at the core of his fiction and emerges as a major component of character

181

development. For the survivors particularly, "the Holocaust has imposed itself as the paradigm of all history . . . in the aftermath of the Holocaust, . . . [one exists] in a new epoch, whose essential conditions are defined by what happened in the Holocaust itself."[1] Singer's writing lacks the immediacy of Holocaust-era documentation and the dramatic tension of realistic flashback. Nonetheless, his work adds important historic and theological dimensions to American Holocaust fiction through its focus on the causal relationship of traditional Christian anti-Semitism to Nazism, its delineation of the major catastrophes of the Jewish Diaspora as "so many announcements of the Holocaust, of which they are prototypes,"[2] and its exploration of the theological implications of the Holocaust.

An early work, *The Family Moskat* (1950), which correlates family events with Jewish history, traces Polish-Jewry's internal fragmentation resulting from the *Haskalah*, the Jewish Enlightenment, and the early stages of Jewry's demise in the Final Solution. The narrative concludes with an unusually graphic rendition of the German bombardment of Warsaw. The protagonist, Asa Heshel awakes to the "roar of planes," "the clatter of machine guns," "the rattling of anti-aircraft guns," and "the crash of bombs." Powerful visual images reinforce the sounds of war. Homes, shops, and factories are ablaze; their contents are strewn wildly about the streets. Singer simultaneously suggests the cosmic and historic significance of the Holocaust by juxtaposing Asa's thoughts of cataclysm—"of an eclipse of the sun, of Messianic expectation"[3]—with another character's realistic description of the sky, "filled with sulphur-yellow fumes" (*FM*, 603). The lengthier Yiddish language edition of the novel extends the graphic presentation and contains a visceral description of a dead family, including a child, whose "intestines poured out of his body as out of a pot."[4] The imagery emphasizes the abrupt shift from ordinary domestic life to the horrors of war. The burden of the description shifts from the loss of individuals to massive, collective losses in the city: "There had been so many deaths . . . that the corpses could not all be removed" (*FM*, 604).

Among the themes that will recur in Singer's later Holocaust fiction are comparison of Hitler to historic enemies of the Jews and philosophic speculation on the nature of Hitler's villainy, the nature of evil in God's universe, and the nature of God in an evil universe. In a theological meditation accompanying his decision to remain in Poland with his family rather than escape, Asa attributes malevolence to God:

> according to Spinoza, Hitler was part of the Godhead, a mode of the Eternal Substance. Every act of his had been predetermined by eternal laws. . . . Every murderous act of Hitler's was a functional part of the cosmos. If one was logically consistent, then one had to concede that God was evil, or else that suffering and evil were good. (*FM*, 594)

The English version of the novel ends with a nihilistic pronouncement—"Death is the Messiah. That's the real truth" (*FM*, 608).

Contrary to the despairing conclusion of the English edition, the Yiddish edition's ending, which emphasizes the incongruity of the invasion coinciding with the holy Rosh Hashanah–Yom Kippur New Year season, represents the diversity of Jewish Holocaust responses. It includes protest against God's failure to uphold the covenant and petitions for Messianic deliverance. As Warsaw is beseiged by the Nazis, the High Holy Day worshipers attend services, chant the traditional prayers, praise God, and weep for their dead. One worshiper, who had put his hopes in the Enlightenment's new ideas, realizes "Darwin could not help him, nor Spencer" (*YFM*, 108). Another responds to a prayer about God's gifts to the world with a bitter observation, "Everything was a deception: religion, evolution, progress, mankind itself" (*YFM*, 108). Throughout the second day of Rosh Hashanah, the Nazi airplanes continue to bomb the city's Jewish sections and the prayer house is full again. In a speech focused on the holiday themes of judgment and mercy, the rabbi comments on contemporary events and the nature of good and evil, explaining God's withdrawal from human affairs: "For the sake of free choice the Infinite made himself Finite. For the sake of free choice, the evil powers were created" (*YFM*, 110). As the worshipers listen to the sounding of the ram's horn, some think of the *shofar* of the Messiah, hoping that the end of Jewish suffering is at hand. Hopeful in the opening stages of the war that God will intervene and deliver the Jews from destruction as He had in the past, Singer's Jews recite the benediction over the wine and include the phrase, "Who hast chosen us among all the peoples." Although the Yiddish edition amply addresses the impending disaster, it also dramatizes in the dialogue of two Hasidim the religious hope that sustained Jews despite a history of persecution: "There is no such thing as despair. . . . Of course, things are bitter. Jews are in danger. . . . Heaven forbid, surrender before the Redemption. . . . If the devil wants sadness, then let him burst with frustration. We will be hopeful" (*YFM,* 112). Conversely, Asa sees the world as a murderous realm where might triumphs. He picks up the Bible to scorn the prophets, deriding their vision of grace and righteousness in light of current events. His initial impulse to hurl the Bible to the ground gives way to kissing it in recognition of the majesty of Jewish morality. He reads a lengthy passage that addresses the commandments to be holy and God's promise to set the Jews apart as His chosen people, "to be a nation consecrated to the Lord." As the bombs continue to explode, the Jew who sought non-Jewish wisdom returns to that of the fathers, reading the words that "the eternal Jew has flung at eternal evil" (*YFM,* 114). Singer then shifts the scene to a distant forest where Zionists are gathering to escape to Israel, and he implies that some will succeed. This glimpse of hope is substantiated by a Messianic pronounce-ment contradicting the English edition's nihilistic ending. Rather than proclaiming Death as the Messiah, the Yiddish version is re-demptive. Responding to the taunting citations of God's silence and withdrawal in Israel's time of trouble, the promise of Moses rings forth: "Rise up and fear not. Yours is the final victory. Unto you will come the Messiah" (*YFM,* 116).

In *Enemies, A Love Story* (1972), Singer's first novel set in America, he guides the reader through the Holocaust labyrinth from geographic—if not psychological—sanctuary. Because he "did not have the privilege of going through the Hitler Holo-caust,"[5] Singer approaches the catastrophe indirectly. In this drama he sharply schematizes characters according to their sur-vival traumas. Unlike Edward Wallant's survivor-protagonist in *The Pawnbroker* and Susan Fromberg Schaeffer's Anya who experi-enced the concentrationary condition directly, or Leslie Epstein's characters who endure the hardships of the ghetto before resettle-ment in Auschwitz, Singer's Herman Broder is a protected fugitive suffering deprivations and anxieties but avoiding the extremities of ghettos, camps, and crematoria that marked the fate of his fellow Polish Jews. Broder's references, allusions, and summations come from public information and reports from acquaintances who suf-fered Nazi brutality first hand. Herman Broder, his wives, and a supporting emigré cast convey diverse philosophic, social, and psy-chological versions of survival, "as if they were now the central bearers of Jewish fate, and as if the definition and resolution of the ultimate questions of philosophy, politics, and religion can never again be made without reference to their experience."[6]

That the Holocaust influences and complicates survivors' postwar public and private lives is axiomatic in Holocaust fiction. Holocaust knowledge sets the survivors apart from uninitiated American Jews. Broder's private life is complicated by the Holocaust; his public life haunted by it. Believing that his wife and children were killed by the Nazis, Broder expresses his gratitude to his wartime benefactor by marrying her. Herman alternately envisages their American home as a prewar paradise and a wartime shelter, and Yadwiga shares her husband's postwar obsession, re-enacting her role as protector. When Broder leaves on a simple business trip, Yadwiga bids him farewell "as if the Nazis were ruling America and his life were in danger" (*E*, 16). They endure a childless marriage because Herman believes it is irrational to have children in a world where innocents are subject to Nazi brutality. Because Broder has nothing in common with this peasant who had been his family's servant, he becomes embroiled in an extramarital affair with Masha, a woman with whom he shared a romantic liaison in a displaced-persons camp. Broder's marriage is complicated by entrapment in a bigamous union with Masha, who feigns pregnancy, and the unexpected appearance of Tamara, his first wife, who escaped from a mass grave where she and her children were left for dead.

Herman Broder lives in New York, but remains psychologically trapped in his Polish hayloft, his survival marred by memories of suffering. "A ghost who writes,"[7] Broder earns his living preparing scholarly articles and sermons for an American rabbi, but he is religiously ambivalent. The paradigmatic, disoriented refugee awakens in the morning confused about his whereabouts, uncertain whether he is hiding in the hayloft, is in a displaced persons camp, or is free and safe in America. He suffers recurrent bouts of terror approximating those he experienced evading Nazi bayonets as they pierced his haystack and he suffers the anxieties associated with fear of detection. Recollections of hunger and thirst, numbness in his hands and feet, high fevers induced by insect and rodent bites, and lengthy deprivation of daylight—elements that characterized his three-year confinement in the hayloft—still haunt the survivor. Guilty for escaping the degradation and brutalization fellow Jews suffered in the ghettos and concentration

camps, Broder designs a postwar lifestyle that is "a moral equivalent for the war: he creates situations so absurdly painful, so anx-
iety-ridden, so oppressive, that vicariously he experiences in New
York what he has missed in Europe."[8]

Wartime fugitive tensions generate postwar apprehension
manifested as fear of capture by Nazis and perpetual search for
sanctuary. Broder studies urban streets "as if America were destined for the same destruction as Poland" (*E*, 133), even though he
understands "Jews were allowed to live freely here!" (*E*, 17). Despite rational evidence of Jewish safety and vitality in American
society, Broder plots a survival strategy in the event of a Nazi
invasion. He concludes that his Coney Island bathroom would be a
superior hideout to his Polish hayloft because the toilet will double
as chair and bathtub as bed. Here he will enjoy light and air, keep
writing paper and books. Reflective of the enormity of Broder's
Holocaust-wrought insecurity and loss is his observation that even
the "stars gleamed like memorial candles in some cosmic synagogue" (*E*, 133).

Among the writers who explore the emotional trauma of survivors, Singer is one of the very few whose protagonists indulge in
revenge fantasies. Broder, a former Talmudist, has been so transformed by the Holocaust that his concealment fantasies coalesce
with those of violent resistance. In the eventuality of a Nazi invasion, he plans to have a loaded revolver or machine gun in his
hiding place to kill the tyrants, to "welcome them with a volley of
bullets and leave one bullet for himself" (*E*, 10). He "often thought
of positions from which it would be possible to shoot" (*E*, 17), and
"discovered methods of destroying whole armies, for ruining industries" (*E*, 132). Unlike Wallant's Sol Nazerman who dreads
sleep with its persecution nightmares, Herman Broder enjoys pre-
sleep revery in which he "waged his usual war with the Nazis,
bombed them with atomic bombs, blasted their armies with mysterious missiles, lifted their fleet out of the ocean and placed it on
land near Hitler's villa in Berchtesgaden" (*E*, 123). By expressing
the victims' resentment, writers like Singer, Wallant, and Elman
articulate the psychic condition that self-righteous moralists without Holocaust experience often condemn. Innocent Americans,
like Elman's lawyer and Wallant's social worker, deny the right of
victims to harbor resentment against their oppressors. In Broder's
world no such opposition arises. Although Broder and Masha acknowledge the practical inefficacy of bitterness, they accept it as an

integral part of postwar existence. In his less violent imaginary vagaries, Broder brings "to trial all those who had been involved in the annihilation of the Jews" (*E*, 132).

When memories of personal loss subside, external influences, such as a newspaper description of a survivor's recollection of German concentration and Russian slave-labor camps, catapult Broder back to the Holocaust universe. According to Broder, the Holocaust is a continuation and culmination of an historic persecution pattern: "The pogrom of Kishinev never ceases. Jews are forever being burned in Auschwitz" (*E*, 30). Furthermore, as a detainee in a displaced persons camp, Broder was privy to news of postwar anti-Jewish actions. That the crimes of the Holocaust did not deter postwar violent anti-Semitism is clear from the murderous reception Jewish survivors received from their Polish countrymen when they tried to return to their homes. No sooner had the surviving remnant tried to reclaim life than their countrymen became their new persecutors. Compounding the violent postwar European anti-Semitism was the political anti-Semitism responsible for detaining Jews in European and Cyprus detention camps to prevent their emigration to Palestine. Finally, Broder's postwar rehabilitation is marred by Germany's resurrection as a postwar industrial power, the rise of neo-Nazism and concomitant whitewash of past atrocities. Holocaust agony intensifies with the realization that "in the Munich taverns, murderers who had played with the skulls of children, sipped beer from tall steins and sang hymns in church" (*E*, 248). Broder rages against a world that fails to bring Nazi war criminals to justice, awarding amnesty to "three-quarters of a million 'small Nazis'" (*E*, 19), a world impervious to Jewish pain while generously rebuilding Germany and rewarding its war criminals. He condemns short-lived, international post-Holocaust sympathy for Jewish victims coupled with weakening Holocaust remembrance; he bitterly rejects reconciliation with Germany, convinced that German reparations cannot compensate for Nazi crimes. In Broder's voice one hears Singer's lament that the surviving remnant continues to suffer, ignored by the nations that acquiesced to earlier persecution, while the architects and technicians of the gas chambers and the industrialists who worked millions of slave laborers to death continue to profit from their crimes. Broder's anguish stems not only from Holocaust-era outrage but from evidence that mankind has adopted rather than repudiated the Nazi model. Beyond personal and particular Jewish loss,

Broder laments the tragedy Nazism has unleashed on the world as the primer for twentieth-century, politically motivated mass murder; Nazism was the training ground for Uganda, Biafra, Vietnam, and Cambodia. He laments that violence has become an acceptable tool of governments. That Nazi genocide was not an aberration but a model others have emulated is a source of grave concern to Singer and "blasphemy on the ashes of the tormented" (*E*, 19).

Like Bellow, Schaeffer, and Wallant, Singer broadens the novel's Holocaust exposition and the spectrum of Holocaust response by reinforcing his protagonist's views with those of a survivor chorus. The choral message of Singer's perpetual victims and mourners is "that the Holocaust will affect the Jews more, rather than less, with the passage of time."[9] Masha, Broder's Holocaust soulmate, is among the most severely psychologically damaged survivors. Enduring years in ghetto and concentration camps, she weighted only seventy-two pounds at liberation. Her bayonet inflicted facial scar is emblematic of her battered psyche. Emotionally incapacitated and existentially directed by Holocaust experience, Masha attributes her postwar physical lethargy and psychological paralysis to concentration camp conditioning, claiming that since the Nazis forced her to do things for so long, she is unable to act on her own volition. Even her love-making with Broder is Holocaust besmirched. Masha plays Scheherazade, enhancing their erotic trysts with stories from ghetto, camp, and postwar Polish ruins to satiate Herman's psychotic need for vicarious Holocaust suffering.

Singer uses the character of Broder's first wife to introduce the peculiar horror Jewish parents suffered witnessing their children's deaths prior to their own. Just as her husband's trauma is marked by daydreams reflecting his wartime hiding, so Tamara's postwar hallucinations of communing with her dead parents and children reflect her agony of separation from her loved ones. Left for dead herself with a bullet lodged in her body, she escaped and found sanctuary in a gentile household. Whereas Broder worries about international indifference to Jewish suffering and Allied failure to punish war criminals, Tamara addresses victimization and diversity of Holocaust behavior. She cites instances of degradation and benevolence, contrasting Nazi transformation of Jews into police functionaries, who cleared Jewish homes, dragged victims from hiding places, and herded them into the death transports, with the altruism of starving Jews offering food rations to victims they consider more needy than themselves. Despite all her own efforts to bear witness, Tamara Broder believes that histories, memoirs, and documentaries are inadequate to Holocaust enormity, because the victims themselves have repressed or forgotten all but a fraction of their suffering.

With the cameo portrait of Shifrah Puah, Singer contrasts Holocaust-induced negative behavior and psychic trauma with Holocaust-wrought piety and reverence for life. Masha's mother, Shifrah Puah, perpetually dresses in mourning for her relatives exterminated in ghettos and camps and responds to life's burden with religious fervor. Unlike Broder who is excited by abundant food, Shifrah Puah is abstemious in honor of those who starved in the camps, where one "would have risked his life for a piece of bread, a potato" (*E*, 49). In addition to reading the Yiddish press for survivor notices, she uses food money for books about Maidanek, Treblinka, and Auschwitz.

In addition to physical and psychological trauma of survivors, Singer explores the varieties of religious Jewish Holocaust responses. His survivors echo the theological reactions promulgated by Richard Rubenstein, Emil Fackenheim, and Eliezar Berkovits. Like the theologians, the fictional survivors categorically reject any attempt to explain the Holocaust as just retribution for sin. In their various stages of despair and hope, Singer's characters express the gamut of emotions: from Rubenstein's judgment that the only response to the death camps is rejection of God,[10] to Emil Fackenheim's insistence on reaffirming God and Judaism,[11] to Eliezar Berkovits' acceptance of the *hester panim* thesis (hiding of the face of God)[12] and his assertion that the Holocaust is unique in the magnitude of its destruction, but not unique in the theological dilemma it presents to religious faith.[13]

Masha and Broder occasionally echo Rubenstein's recognition of the meaninglessness of existence in a universe where there is neither a divine plan nor divine concern and the recognition that the human condition reflects no transcendental purpose. Neither, however, seems to follow Rubenstein's path of "the death of God" thesis nor his concomitant call to replace devotion to God with devotion to the community of Israel in order to create meaning. Masha, who shares none of the compunctions of the orthodox, bluntly indicts God as a Nazi collaborator, a butcher God. Rejecting theories of retributive and regenerative powers of suffering, she argues that even if it had been God's purpose to strengthen Jewish devotion through suffering, the Nazi scourge was immoral and ineffective, for "the religious Jews had been practically wiped out. The worldly Jews who managed to escape had, with few exceptions, learned nothing from all the terror" (*E*, 45). Like Broder, Masha believes that history is a cycle of persecution, but unlike Broder, she denounces God for normalizing such history. Consequently, she blasphemes by desecrating a *mezuzah*, the oblong container placed on the doorposts of Jewish homes containing a roll of parchment on which is written the *Shema*, the Judaic prayer proclaiming the oneness of God, and two biblical passages about love for God and His precepts (Deuteronomy 6:4–9; 11:13–21).

Orthodox foil characters who round out Singer's multifaceted treatment of survivors' religious responses reject both Masha's contemptuous censure and Broder's protest against God. Masha's mother, Shifrah Puah, and Tamara's uncle, Reb Nissen, remain religiously observant and community directed, escaping the isolation and purposelessness that drive Broder to despair and Masha to suicide. These pious Jews, cling even more tenaciously to Orthodox Judaism after Holocaust devastation. Reb Nissen, who traveled to America just before Hitler's troops invaded Poland, observes ritual mourning one day a week for the family and other martyrs he left behind. He fasts and diligently performs the rites governing mourning ritual. Unlike the protestors who condemn God or question His judgment, Nissen struggles to find meaning in the Holocaust. He responds to Tamara's catalogue of Nazi and Russian outrages with a line from Isaiah, "'And man is bowed down and man is humbled.' When people stop believing in the Creator, anarchy prevails" (*E*, 79). Thus, he adheres to his belief in a just and merciful God because the alternative is unbearable. Shifrah Puah's character illustrates the Berkovits resignation to God's willful absence from history. Like Berkovits, Shifrah Puah does not exonerate God for the suffering of righteous and innocent Jews, but she derives some solace from the belief in their ultimate redemption; she prays for the martyrs and follows Fackenheim's and Berkovits' prescriptions to strengthen her faith through observance of the commandments. She observes Jewish law and ritual to honor Holocaust martyrs and to preserve their memories; her actions contrast vividly with her daughter's similarly motivated sacrilege. To sanctify the Holocaust martyrs, the mother lights memorial candles for the dead, prays three times a day, and obeys the religious commandments more zealously than she had in the prewar period. Believing that God had taken the blessed souls, the pious Jews to Himself, and allowed the others to exist, Shifrah Puah conducts her survival as an act of contrition, an apology for having "remained alive when so many men and women had been martyred" (*E*, 44). The pious old woman's name is an appropriate fusion of the names of two biblical women renowned for their resistance to tyranny, tyranny specifically designed—as was the Nazi plan—to effect the destruction of Jewry. Shifrah and Puah were midwives who thwarted Pharaoh's genocidal order to kill all male children born to Israelite women. Their moral courage, which extended beyond saving the children from assassination to nurturing and sustaining them with food and drink, is the ethical and emblematic lesson of Exodus 1:14–17 and the model for Singer's fictional, virtuous mother figure.

Whereas Shifrah Puah and Reb Nissen reflect the unshaken faith of the older generation of Orthodox Jews, Tamara . . . begins in the Rubenstein camp and by novel's end shows Fackenheimian resistance to Nazism by a commitment to the essential survival of Jewry through a commitment to the Jewish religion. Tamara represents the younger, assimilated Polish Jews whose Holocaust metamorphosis began in apostasy and secular assimilation and ended in spiritual return and religious regeneration. In her pre-Holocaust youth, Tamara sought to supplant Orthodox Judaism with secular social reform, to replace religious Messianism with Marxist Messianism. Disillusioned by Soviet anti-Semitism, Tamara returned to Judaism and embraced Zionism as the only practical political movement supportive of Jewry. Tamara's metamorphosis parallels public events:

> In the late thirties, when the Nazi leaders had visited Poland and nationalist students beat up Jews and forced Jewish students to stand during the lectures at the university, Tamara . . . turned to religion. She began to light candles on Friday night and to keep a *kosher* household. (*E*, 64)

As the Holocaust progressed in its murderous path, she adopts a Rubenstein-like radical denial of God, "If God was able to watch all this horror and remain silent, then He's no God. . . . Souls exist; it's God who doesn't" (*E*, 82–83). Through Tamara's religious metamorphosis, Singer notes the two extremes of Jewish theological Holocaust response: the Rubenstein assertion of the death of God

and the Fackenheim return to Judaism. Her post-Holocaust return
and commitment to Orthodox Judaism is derived from the failure
of Communism and Socialism to value, protect, and preserve their
Jewish adherents, and a Fackenheimian conviction that only
through the practice of Judaism will Jews deny Hitler a
posthumous victory. Tamara's Jewish regeneration foreshadows
the spiritual return of Singer's protagonist in *The Penitent* (1983),
who renounces Western secularism for Judaism.

Despite his character's accommodations, divine silence in the
face of the Holocaust slaughter gives Singer no rest. In authorial
voice, he admits:

> I feel a deep resentment against the Almighty. My religion goes
> hand in hand with a profound feeling of protest. Once in a while, the
> old Jewish hope for the coming of the Messiah awakens in me. There
> must come an end to our blindness. There must come the time for
> some revelation! My feeling of religion is a feeling of rebellion. . . . I
> often say to myself that God wants us to protest. He has had enough
> of those who praise Him all the time and bless Him for all his cruel-
> ties to man and animals.[14]

This anguished cry appears in an unpublished, and as yet untrans-
lated, book, *Rebellion and Prayer or the True Protestor,* that Singer
wrote at the time of the Holocaust.[15]

Like many Jewish writers who protest God's Holocaust-era
silence, Singer's rebellion has its roots in the prophets and the
biblical patriarchs. Abraham, Job, Moses, and Jeremiah articulate
their anguish with God's passivity in the face of injustice. Singer's
protest echoes Jeremiah's complaint:

> Wherefore doth the way of the wicked prosper?
> Thou hast planted them, yea, they have taken root;
> They grow, yea, they bring forth fruit;
> Thou art near in their mouths,
> And far from their reins. (Jeremiah 12:1–2)

Hasidic literature, too, which is a vital part of Singer's heritage, is
replete with tales in which God is accused of trangressing His covenantal obligation toward the Jewish people. Like Elie Wiesel,
Singer does not pronounce the death of God as has the American
radical theologian Richard Rubenstein. Wiesel and Singer acknowledge God's sovereignty, while denouncing His failure to save the

Jewish people from slaughter. Neither God nor humankind are
absolved of Holocaust guilt. Like Elie Wiesel's young autobiographical protagonist in *Night* who cries out "How I sym-
pathized with Job! I did not deny God's existence, but I doubted
His absolute justice,"[16] Singer's survivors cannot reconcile the just
and merciful God with the Holocaust. Wiesel resolves the problem
by acknowledging the presence of evil in God.[17] Although Singer
explores, through Broder's voice, the thesis that God is in league
with the devil and with Hitler, he rejects it in the authorial voice
and contends that a human being will say this only in moments of
great despair.[18] He argues that God is unjust and that man has the
moral obligation to protest God's injustice. Because he believes,
with Eliezer Berkovits, that God tolerates human evil to insure the
principle of free will, he argues that man must protest human and
divine injustice. Just as Elie Wiesel's criticism is in accord with
Kabbalistic philosophy,[19] so Singer's protest reflects traditional
Jewish thinking. Both writers refrain from repudiating God, but
assert that God has sinned against humanity. In spite of God's
Holocaust shortcoming, Wiesel and Singer maintain that the Jew
must continue to honor Israel's covenant with God. God has
faltered, but it remains the duty of the observant Jew to faithfully
honor Torahic law.

The paradox of the protesting believer is manifested most
dramatically in Broder's character. Both in the Holocaust and its
aftermath, Broder lost faith in the human race and its religious and
political systems. He believed: "Religions lied. Philosophy was
bankrupt from the beginning. The idle promises of progress were
no more than a spit in the face of the martyrs of all generations"
(*E*, 30). Although he stops short of Masha's denunciation of God as
a Nazi collaborator, Broder correlates divine impotence with
human impotence, "if a God of mercy did exist in the heavenly
hierarchy, then He was only a helpless godlet, a kind of heavenly
Jew among the heavenly Nazis" (*E*, 123). Singer explains that his
rebellious characters believe in God and although they know that
His wisdom is great and His mercy may be great, they also protest
His injustice when they witness the suffering of the righteous.
Since Singer believes that protest is a part of religion,[20] his charac-
ters' remonstrances are not evidence of irreconcilable conflict with
God, but ongoing protest and petition. Thus, Broder expresses his
protest by modifying his conformity to Orthodox practice. On Yom
Kippur he fasts, but he refrains from communal synagogue prayer

and on other occasions desists from uttering prescribed prayers of praise.

Although Broder faults God's Holocaust silence, he remains steadfast to the ethical values of Judaism. Like Asa Heshel, the lapsed Jew in *The Family Moskat* who recanted his apostasy, Broder, too, concludes that apostasy from Judaism is a dismal error: "If a Jew departed so much as one step from the *Shulcan Aruch*, he found himself spiritually in the sphere of everything base—Fascism, Bolshevism, murder, adultery, drunkenness" (*E*, 170). Broder considers the modern alternatives to Judaism ineffectual and rejects the secular philosophers on the grounds that one could simultaneously be a devotee of their thought and a Nazi; one could be a paragon of European culture and perpetrate or implement atrocities. He condemns Christianity on the same basis, as "a faith which had, in the name of God, organized inquisitions, crusades, bloody wars" (*E*, 170).

Anticipating the redeemed protagonist in *The Penitent*, Broder attributes his moral fall to his departure from Judaic law and plans to free himself from the "licentiousness into which he had sunk when he had strayed from God, the Torah, and Judaism" (*E*, 169). Because the civilized and cultured West spawned and tolerated Nazism, Broder and other outspoken Singerian survivors condemn the moral failure of the religious and secular West. In his final analysis, Broder finds the only real antithesis to Nazism is Judaism. He argues, "If we don't want to become like the Nazis, we must be Jews!" (*E*, 171). He concludes that there is only one appropriate path for him, "to go back to the Torah, the Germara, the Jewish books. . . . Since he was suffocating without God and the Torah, he must serve God and study the Torah" (*E*, 170–71). Emblematic of Broder's spiritual return to God through Judaism is his decision to live by the commandments, to father a child, to abandon ghost writing, and to teach. In America, a land he believes barren of the once vibrant Judaism that flourished in Eastern Europe before the faithful were murdered by Hitler and Stalin, Broder's resolution weakens. In contrast to the successful repentance and redemption quests of Singer's Old-World, Orthodox Jews, which succeeded because they "lived in a world where Jews still had a culture and a language and an inner world of their own, one which could sustain waverers,"[21] Broder's "spiritual aspirations [may] die for want of a nourishing atmosphere."[22] Because the ghetto Jew's identity was a coherent, organic whole, because he belonged to a people and to God, his spiritual return was potentially successful, whereas the assimilated Jew is lost, afloat in a spiritual wasteland. Singer implies Broder will attain spiritual renewal if he translates intellectual conviction into action and leads an integrated Jewish life. Unlike the Christian presentation of Jew as archetypal outsider and symbol of contemporary alienation,[23] I. B. Singer "sees the true experience of alienation and exile not in the ghetto Jew, but in the emancipated and enlightened Jew."[24] Although the ending is ambivalent, Tamara's speculation that Broder has found his hayloft, strongly suggests the possibility of spiritual return. Although withdrawal from community is not the conventional Jewish approach to redemption, Singer's Jews frequently stray from traditional Jewish means and values to arrive at similar ends. Just as Yasha Mazur, an earlier reformed apostate with whom Broder shares many sins, repented alone in a brick cell, so Broder may have withdrawn from assimilated society to a figurative hayloft, free of distracting temptation, to work out his return to God and Jewish law.

Because Singer believes that non-Jewish civilization is a slaughterhouse, a culture that laid the foundation for the Final Solution in its own religiously inspired pogroms, a culture whose adherents often willingly acquiesced to or openly supported the genocide of Jewry, he affirms the achievement of Holocaust restoration in Judaic civilization, in its religion, ethics, literature, and community. Thus, Singer entrusts the rearing of the next Jewish generation to Yadwiga, a righteous gentile who risked her own life to save a Jewish life during the Holocaust and then converted to Judaism, and Tamara, the Jewish mother whose children were murdered by the Nazis. He suggests Holocaust restoration is possible in the nuturing of the next Jewish generation according to Jewish law. Tamara sustains Yadwiga and Broder by acting as Jewish guardian to their child, establishing a Jewish home for Yadwiga and her baby in an apartment attached to the Jewish bookstore she operates. Singer thus implies that survival will flourish in the essential contexts that have sustained Jews through the centuries, Jewish home and study. The novel concludes with symbols of hope, birth, and regeneration, an apostate's probable return to Judaism, and the birth of a new Jewish life to affirm and rebuild the people that lost so much in Germany's crime.

The motifs of God's Holocaust-era injustice coupled with human obligation to honor the covenant, and the Jew's post-Holocaust obligation to sustain Judaism, found in *Enemies* will be echoed in *Shosha* and *The Penitent.* In each instance Singer presents this view in a way that honors the covenantal bond between God and the Jews. Singer's protest—like those of Abraham, Job, Moses, and Jeremiah—acknowledges the self-concealing and the self-revealing Divinity and thus bears witness to his faith.

*Shosha* (1978) is Singer's transition Holocaust novel, reiterating the Holocaust-eve themes of *The Family Moskat,* extending the theological questions raised in *Enemies,* and incorporating an autobiographical narrator to transmit Holocaust history given him by survivors. *Shosha* is a projection of Singer's fate had he remained in Europe and is a memorial for the Jewish millions who perished there. Designed as a loosely structured memoir, *Shosha* records representative Jewish reactions to the outbreak of the Holocaust. Aaron Griedinger, a struggling writer, returns to Warsaw from a brief teaching stint in the rural provinces to sustain his beloved Shosha as the conflagration advances.[25] Aaron's career resembles Singer's early period in Warsaw. While earning his meagre living as a Yiddish translator and journalist, he works on a novel about a false Messiah that will attain the critical recognition Singer received for *Satan in Goray.* Aaron's Warsaw circle consists of representative Jewish figures: orthodox pietists, secular intellectuals and litterati, all living "in a quiet despair, . . . just waiting and trying to forget, by making love, reading books, speaking about some non-existent hope,"[26] but doomed for the crematoria and lime pits of Poland.

Set in Poland during the late 1930s and early 1940s, *Shosha* captures the suffering of a beleaguered people, "people . . . on the edge of a volcano that has not yet erupted but may do so at any moment,"[27] people enduring the tripartite force of Polish, Russian, and German anti-Semitism. Singer debunks the thesis that a few madmen are alone guilty of genocide and posits the view that "a large part of the masses want to kill, plunder, rape, and do what Hitler, Stalin, and tyrants like them have always done."[28] Whether the war had been won by the Nazis or the Communists, the author-narrator notes that their common goal was the annihilation of European Jewry. Whereas native American Jewish writers generally offer muted reference to Christian Holocaust culpability, the Polish immigrant writer forcefully and repeatedly articulates the congruent anti-Semitic goals of Christian and Nazi Europeans. In contrast to Edward Lewis Wallant's symbolic crucifixion scene linking Catholic and Nazi anti-Semitism, Singer boldly asserts the connection: "The Poles meant to get rid of us. They consider us a nation

within a nation, a strange and malignant body. They lack the courage to finish us off themselves, but they wouldn't shed tears if
Hitler did it for them" (131). In a poignant Yom Kippur scene, the
narrator, presumed by a barber to be a fellow Catholic, becomes
the captive audience for a venomous anti-Jewish diatribe. With
the razor at his throat, Aaron listens to the barber's harangue, dramatizing the commonalities of Christian and Nazi anti-Jewish
prejudice.

> They've taken over all Poland.... The cities are lousy with
> them.... they swarm like vermin everywhere.... There's one con-
> solation—Hitler will smoke them out like bedbugs.
>
> I'll tell you something, dear sir. The modern Jews, those who shave,
> who speak a proper Polish, and who try to ape real Poles, are even
> worse than the old-fashioned Hebes with their long gaberdines, wild
> beards, and earlocks. They, at least, don't go where they aren't
> wanted. They sit in their stores in their long capotes and shake over
> their Talmud like bedouins. They babble away in their jargon, and
> when a Christian falls into their clutches, they swindle a few
> groschen out of him. But at least they don't go to the theater, the
> cafes, the opera. Those that shave and dress modern are the real
> danger. They sit in our Sejm and make treaties with our worst en-
> emies, the Ruthenians, the White Russians, the Lithuanians. Every
> one of them is a secret Communist and a Soviet spy. They have one
> aim—to root out us Christians and hand over the power to the
> Bolsheviks, the Masons, and the radicals. You might find it hard to
> believe this, dear sir, but their millionaires have a secret pact with
> Hitler. The Rothschilds finance him and Roosevelt is the mid-
> dleman. His real name isn't Roosevelt but Rosenfeld, a converted
> Jew. They supposedly assume the Jewish faith, but with one goal in
> mind—to bore from within and infect everything and everybody. (*S*,
> 162–63).
>
> But Hitler will clean them out! He promises their millionaires that
> he'll protect their capital, but once the Nazis are armed he'll fix them
> all—ha, ha, ha! It's too bad that he'll attack our country, but since we
> haven't had the guts to sweep away this filth ourselves, we have to let
> the enemy do it for us. What will happen later, no one can know.
> The fault for it all lies with those traitors, the Protestants, who sold
> their souls to the devil. They're the Pope's deadliest enemies. Did
> you know, dear sir, that Luther was a secret Jew? (*S*, 163–64).

The speech reeks of canard and fallacy that characterize Christian
anti-Semitism. Further, Singer's attribution of Nazi extermination

rhetoric to a preconcentrationary-era Pole, reared in Roman Catholic anti-Semitism, demonstrates the ease with which Europeans progressed from one mode of anti-Semitism to another. Singer parallels the barber's monologue, Polish press reports postulating Jewry as Poland's greatest enemy, and government reception of Hitler's representatives to show the similarity of individual and collective Polish anti-Semitism.

The mystery of faith in an age of atrocity is another recurrent Holocaust theme appearing in *Shosha*. The novel's Spinozan, Morris Feitelzohn, adamantly decries faith in a benevolent diety. In 1939, Feitelzohn argues that Jews deluded themselves and others by creating the illusion of a just and merciful God responsive to the human condition. In the epilogue, we learn that this debunker of Jewish illusions recanted during the darkest period of the Holocaust. While in hiding, he reconsiders the heritage of generations and supplants ridicule of the faithful with rage against the Deity—rage religiously expressed. Despite the unorthodox diction, Feitelzohn echoes the nonfictional authorial voice in his rebuke of the Almighty and in his advocacy of the kabbalistic belief in man's need to complete God's work in the world:

> for all His sins since the Creation. He still maintained that the whole universe was a game, but he elevated this game until it became divine. . . . The essence of his words was that since God is eternally silent, we owe Him nothing. . . . True religion, Morris argued, was not to serve God but to spite Him. If He wanted evil, we had to aspire to the opposite. If He wanted wars, inquisitions, crucifixions, Hitlers, we must want righteousness, Hasidism, our own version of grace. (*S*, 171)

The protagonist's brother, Rabbi Moishe—modeled on and named for I. B. Singer's younger brother who perished—is Feitelzohn's theological foil. Faithful to his biblical namesake, the rabbi loyally discharges the laws and rituals of Orthodox Judaism. Like Moses, he trusts God's purpose and anticipates divine deliverance from the contemporary Pharaoh. While the world begins to crumble around him, he finds solace in God and in Judaism, convinced that religious observance signifies the continuation of the Jewish people. As the Moskats invoked the Passover theme of Jewish deliverance from Egyptian bondage, noting the contemporary relevance of the *Haggadah* history, so, too, does Rabbi Moishe draw

an appropriate analogy to Hitlerean oppression and its awaited
end as he lights the Hannukah candles to commemorate Jewish
victory over the Syrian despot and worshipers of Baal. The language of the Moskat Passover celebrants—"And it is this same
promise which has been the support of our ancestors and of us, for
in every generation our enemies have arisen to annihilate us, but
the Most Holy, blessed be He, has delivered us out of their hands"
(*FM*, 577)—is repeated by Rabbi Moishe almost verbatim: "In each
generation our enemies rise up to destroy us, and the Holy One,
blessed be He, is saving us from their hands" (*S*, 192). In each
instance the worshipers remember historic examples of Jewish
liberation from tyranny hoping that God will again intercede on
their behalf. For the Orthodox, the oppression and slavery suffered under Syrian and Egyptian despots provides a model for
facing the Hitler onslaught. No matter how bleak history is, Singer's Holocaust-era religious devotees are sustained by their faith in
an interceding Deity. A pious Jew who believes the Messiah will
come either when the world merits him because of its goodness or
because of its terrible evil, the young rabbi accepts Hitler's war
against the Jews as the possible "birth pains of the Messiah" and is
ready to die *kiddush ha-Shem,* a martyr's death, sanctifying God's
Holy Name. Singer's early Holocaust-era believers are often distinguished from their survivor counterparts by their single-minded
belief in divine intercession. History has taught Moishe that "there
have been many Hamans and they will all come to a bad end" (*S*,
188). As early Holocaust victims, it is natural that Moishe and the
Moskats anticipate heroic human endeavor in the mode of the
Maccabean Revolt or divine intercession as in the Passover exodus
from Egyptian slavery. Their belief in the God of revelation is as
convincing as is survivor knowledge of the hidden and silent God.
Innocent of the technological implementation of genocide, the religious regarded Hitler as another in the catalogue of historic anti-
Jewish tyrants—a Pharaoh, a Czar, a Chmielnicki, a Petluria. Thus,
the Feitelzohn-Moishe juxtaposition dramatizes diverse Jewish theological responses to the Holocaust, from covenantal protest, to
resignation, to divine mystery, matters that will receive increasing
attention in the fiction of Jewishly educated American novelists—
Cynthia Ozick, Arthur Cohen, and Chaim Potok.

Singer generally approaches and transcends the Holocaust
abyss to avoid direct dramatization. Between the main body of the
novel, which concludes as the Nazis are about to invade Poland,

and the epilogue, set thirteen years later in Israel, is Holocaust silence. Singer relies on the reader's knowledge of the Holocaust to supply an essential part of the reading experience. In the epilogue, during a chance meeting in Israel, the narrator and another survivor ennunciate the Holocaust fate of their group—Shosha's death in flight from Warsaw, and the deaths of Aaron's aged mother and Rabbi Moishe, who survived transit by cattle car only to succumb under the strain of hard labor and severe weather in Russia.

The social and political failure of the European Enlightenment, a minor theme in *Shosha,* is significant in the canon and attains dominance in *The Penitent.* The Holocaust exposed the moral failure of the Enlightenment's political panaceas. Non-Jewish followers of the Enlightenment had no love for Jews, no desire to save them from genocide. In Singer's world, among the greatest ironies of the Holocaust is the lapsed Jew's discovery that the Judaism he abandoned is morally superior to the philosophies adopted in its stead. Similarly, Aaron castigates himself for having "thrown away four thousand years of Jewishness and exchanged it for meaningless literature, Yiddishism, Feitelzohnism" (*S,* 256). In the darkness of the Holocaust, even Feitelzohn saw that "The heritage of generations had wakened within him, and he hurled sulphur and brimstone against the Almighty; at the same time the words themselves blazed with a religious fire" (*S,* 271).

Singer does not presume to answer the Holocaust enigma. In the epilogue's encounter between the narrator and the surviving Haiml in Israel, both express continued bafflement at the radical evil unleashed by Nazism. In their concluding discussion, Haiml compares himself to a "squashed fly," alluding to Gloucester's famous comment at the end of *King Lear,* "As flies to wanton boys are we to the gods" (*King Lear,* IV. i). Although Aaron rejects the view that malicious gods make us suffer for their sport, he offers no explanation for Holocaust suffering. There is no satisfactory explanation—not for the sufferer, not for the survivor, not for Singer. Jews will struggle to survive and wait for answers. While they wait they are obliged to uphold the covenant. Singer's emphasis on covenantal responsibility is evident in the near verbatim repetition of Feitelzohn's declaration: If God allows evil to flourish in His creation, the Jew's job is to combat it. "If He wants war, inquisitions, crucifixions, Hitlers, we should desire honesty, Hasidism, our own version of grace" (*S,* 271).

Another innovative aspect of this traditional Holocaust work is Singer's introduction of an Israeli theme. Although Singer suggests no direct connection between the Holocaust and political establishment of the State of Israel, he sets the novel's epilogue in Israel to contrast Diasporan and Israeli attitudes toward Jewish self-defense in a hostile environment. As the cycle of violence and reprieve of Jewish history takes a new turn, with Arab states dedicated to Israel's destruction, Aaron and Haiml speak of post-Holocaust Jewish assertiveness. Haiml attributes the change to the Holocaust and to the acceptance of the Zionist call for Jews to abandon their historic military passivity in favor of armed resistance to force. Haiml proudly contrasts Israeli independence and power with historic Diasporan impotence: "here no one went like a sheep to the slaughter. Our lads from Warsaw, Lodz, Rawa Ruska, and Minsk suddenly turned into heroes like the fighters in the time of Masada" (*S*, 265). Haiml's jubilation in the Jewish state is tempered by recognition that its survival in the midst of five enemy states is highly dependent upon a world largely hostile or indifferent to its existence. Thus, Singer notes the importance of Israel to post-Holocaust regeneration and to Jewish confidence as a sign that the historic pattern of passive resistance to anti-Semitism is over and a new epoch in Jewish history has begun.

Singer's Israel is a land of survivors. Like the American survivors in *Enemies*, the Israeli survivors in *Shosha* continue to suffer physical and psychological Holocaust wounds. Haiml is certain that the souls of the perished have come to rest in Israel, and like Singer's other survivors, he lives with memories of those killed in the Holocaust. Haiml doubts that the generation of victims and its children will recover without scars and puts his hope in future generations: "Perhaps their grandchildren will be normal if the Almighty doesn't send a new castastrophe down upon us" (*S*, 274). A true Singerian, Haiml concludes that if the most violent collective disaster of the Jewish people was followed by rebirth of a Jewish nation, the Messianic dream may still be possible, one may hope "the dead will be resurrected" (*S*, 269). Hamil's position is not unlike those of Eliezar Berkovits and Emil Fackenheim who hold that if one may take the Holocaust as evidence of God's hiddenness, one may also interpret the ingathering of the Jews in Israel as evidence of God's presence in history and as an affirmation of the redemptive promise.[29]

In two short stories, "The Mentor," set in Israel in 1955, and

"Hanka," Singer continues to use the author-narrator to explore the Holocaust survivor trauma. The stories dramatize the reunion of Polish Holocaust survivors and the narrator, an internationally celebrated author on a lecture tour in Israel and Argentina respectively. The reunion offers a backdrop for recollection and transmittal of Holocaust experiences. The scribal narrator, whose personal and professional similarity to Singer establishes an authentic voice, records the experiences of Holocaust survivors revealed to him directly or indirectly through a Jamesian confidant. As the author exchanges news with compatriots whom he hasn't seen either since leaving his village in 1922 or since emigrating from Poland in 1935, they lament neighbors and families who "had perished in the ghettos and concentration camps or had died in Russia of hunger, typhoid fever, and scurvy."[30]

In "The Mentor," Singer dramatizes the theme of Holocaust-induced loss of religious faith in an internal tale told by the narrator's former student, Friedl, now an accomplished physician, writer, and Zionist. The Holocaust crucible has transformed her from faithful Jewish scholar to bitter agnostic. Friedl (meaning Joy), whose name ironically negates her existential despair, cites the Holocaust as the cause for rejecting her father's belief in the "miracles God performed for the Jews" (*TM*, 102). Friedl's protest against God's Holocaust betrayal recalls Broder's and Masha's bitter accusations and echoes Richard Rubenstein's death of God thesis. "After what happened to them," Friedl argues, "one must be absolutely stupid and insensitive to believe in God and all that drivel. What's more, to believe in a compassionate God is the worst betrayal of the victims" (*TM*, 102–103). That Singer holds Friedl's view suspect is evident both in his narrator's philosophic challenge and the *Nazideutsch* rhetoric he uses for her speech: "Nazis are enemies of the human race, and people must be allowed to exterminate them like bedbugs" (*TM*, 103). As Jew and physician, Friedl should revere life, but the Holocaust experience evoked such a bizarre metamorphosis that she appropriates Nazi rhetoric to express her contempt for the Nazi system. Deprived of family, faith, and language, Friedl is left with the Nazi legacy of hatred.

In another inversion, Friedl changes places with her mentor and offers to be his guide. She becomes mentor to the uninitiated narrator, who in turn will become the transmitter of her tale. Reversing the mentor-student relationship, she poses rhetorical questions, philosophical questions that have been implied throughout the Holocaust *oeuvre* of Singer: "where shall we go from here?" (*TM,* 112) Where does the Holocaust road lead? What path shall mankind take from the Holocaust abyss? The story offers no resolution; it simply articulates the central questions.

In "Hanka," which shares both theme and narrative method with "The Mentor," the narrator encounters his cousin who is the lone survivor of her immediate family. Cast in the role of tour guide, Hanka operates as Holocaust mentor, charting the troubled course of her misguided parents, who reared their children "to be one-hundred-percent Poles" believing assimilation was the remedy for traditional Polish anti-Semitism.[31] Just as Friedl remains psychologically and spiritually unhealed in the aftermath of the Holocaust, so Hanka, who was psychically and physically wounded by the Holocaust, remains a perpetual Holocaust victim, a member of an exterminated tribe. An ambulatory corpse, she argues against facile expectations of postwar rehabilitation. Acutely cognizant of Jewish history as a chronicle of suffering, her Argentinian sojourn is a reminder of fifteenth-century Spanish crimes against Jewry: "The men still dream of inquisitions and autos-da-fé" (*H,* 18). Singer returns to the Israeli theme of *Shosha's* epilogue in Hanka's concern about the Arab promise of a second Holocaust. However, unlike Hamil, she even doubts Israeli dreams of regeneration: "We are surrounded there by hords of enemies whose aim is the same as Hitler's—to exterminate us" (*H,* 14). Perhaps because Hanka emigrated to Argentina—home and haven to both escaped Nazi criminals and their victims—rather than to Israel, she shares none of Hamil's confidence in the Israeli capacity to withstand Arab promises of genocide. Hanka remains incomprehensible to the narrator whose Holocaust innocence precludes thorough understanding of his cousin's encounter with absolute evil. Both "Hanka" and "The Mentor" provide Singer's strongest pronouncement on the inability of nonwitnesses, however well-intentioned, to comprehend Holocaust history completely.

Departing from unadulterated realism, Singer introduces in "A Wedding in Brownsville" and "The Cafeteria" a supernatural element to render Holocaust sensibility and experience. Like Edgar Allan Poe's tales of the grotesque and arabesque, these stories fuse the real and surreal to create "the displacements of consciousness and sensibility . . . which more than anything else provide the distinctive literary and personal qualities defining him as a writer."[32] Singer seduces the reader into the supernatural realm through an extended sojourn in a realistic urban environment, which in turn solidifies the fantasy realm. In "A Wedding in Brownsville," the passage from the real to the surreal is so carefully wrought that one is scarcely aware of the transition until the tale's conclusion. In "The Cafeteria," Singer fashions a grotesque imp— Hitler's ghost who presides at a meeting of his henchmen.

"A Wedding in Brownsville," one of the first Singer fictions set in America, combines Holocaust memoir with an elegy for Orthodox Judaism that has been severely diminished in its American metamorphosis. Dr. Margolin, the protagonist, is a pre-Holocaust immigrant who has successfully assimilated to American society. He maintains association with a fraternal society whose membership consists of his village countrymen; he provides free medical treatment for needy Jews and works for a Jewish publication. An Old World Jewish prodigy able to recite long passages from Bible, Talmud, and the commentaries, Margolin disdains deracinated American Jewishness and Anglicized Yiddish. Although he remains theologically apart from American Judaism, he feels ethnically and emotionally connected to the Jewish people.

Like Singer, despite leaving Europe before the Holocaust, Margolin's life was nevertheless fundamentally changed by the catastrophe. "His family there had been tortured, burned, gassed,"[33] and his sweetheart killed. His wife, a German gentile, was caught between a Nazi brother who died in a Russian prison camp and a Communist brother who was shot by the Nazis. Perpetually lamenting the Nazi outrage, Mrs. Margolin, like Yadwiga of *Enemies*, "had become almost Jewish in New York" (*WB*, 230), befriending Jewish women and joining Hadassah, a Jewish women's philantrophic organization.

Prompted by elegaic feelings for his murdered countrymen, Dr. Margolin sets out alone in inclement weather to attend the wedding of Senciminer descendants. During the journey, his taxi is involved in an accident; this incident provides the transition to his wedding fantasy. He is alternately actor and observer at a reception in which his deceased relatives and friends remember those who died, and they ponder God's Holocaust passivity: "why did God . . . create a Hitler. . . . Why did He need world wars? . . . What had they been thinking of, those pious uncles of his, when they were digging their own graves?" (*WB*, 233–34). Eschewing the theological debates of the novels, Singer condenses the matter in an inversion of attributes, with Margolin assigning sins of commission

to God and virtue to humanity, thereby condemning God's failure
to honor His covenantal obligation to the faithful guardians of His
commandments.

The meditation is a thematic prologue to the wedding drama.
Reflecting the ritual breaking of a glass at weddings to commemorate the destruction of the ancient Temple—characteristic of traditional Jewish remembrance of sorrow during times of joy—Singer
deftly fuses marriage celebration and memorial service, wedding
joy and Holocaust grief. Since most of the guests were inmates of
Hitler's camps, when they greet each other, they mourn the lost six
million, their unborn progeny, and their loved ones:

> "My father? He was killed. I'm the only one left of the entire family."
> . . . "Sorele? Shot. Together with her children." . . . Zilberstein?
> They burned him in the synagogue with twenty others. A mound of
> charcoal was all that was left, coal and ash" . . . They killed everyone,
> everyone. They took a whole people and wiped them out with Ger-
> man efficiency." (*WB*, 237)

Throughout the wedding ceremony and reception conversations
are Holocaust-directed: "How close we came ourselves! All of us
are really dead, . . . We were exterminated, wiped out. Even the
survivors carry death in their hearts" (*WB*, 238). Paradoxically, as
the wedding guests recite the death toll, they conclude with the
Hebrew toast, *Lechayim* (to life).

The sociologically and culturally authentic immigrant wedding reception provides an appropriate background for the joyous
reunion of Margolin with Raizel, his first love whom he thought
had perished in the Holocaust. So moved by his love for Raizel is
Margolin that he intends to divorce his wife and marry the girl. In
the midst of his marriage proposal to Raizel, Margolin realizes that
he is recovering his lost love in death. Having died in the taxi
accident; Margolin is reunited with all the Sencimin Holocaust victims. The story concludes in Singerian fusion of natural and supernatural, suggesting that "time and space seem to be no more than
categories of the mind. Dr. Margolin is killed, but he does not cease
to exist; nor does Raizel and, by implication, neither does anyone
else, including the six million victims."[34]

In "The Cafeteria" Singer adds a supernatural referent
through the impressions a confidant offers the writer-narrator. He
strengthens the narrator by transforming him from the detached

observer-recorder of "The Mentor" to participant. The narrator is a writer, like Singer, who frequents a New York City cafeteria to visit with Polish-Jewish countrymen who "talk about Yiddish literature, the Holocaust, the State of Israel."[35] The Broadway cafeteria is a meeting place for retired teachers, rabbis, translators, writers, and Holocaust survivors, including an Auschwitz entrepreneur who is reported to have kept a store in his straw mattress: "a rotten potato, sometimes a piece of soap, a tin spoon, a little fat" (*C*, 87). Among the cafeteria regulars is Esther, a woman who looks much younger than the others and speaks of having read the narrator's work in prewar Poland, in Russian prison camps, and finally in German displaced persons camps. She prophetically declares the narrator to be her writer, and as the tale progresses, he does become the transmitter of her Holocaust history. In the Jamesian manner, Esther is the informing intelligence and the narrator the transmitting agent.

Survival trauma, a major theme in *Enemies*, emerges dramatically in the physical and emotional struggles of Esther and her invalid father. In conversations with the narrator-scribe, Boris Merkin reveals that he and Esther escaped to Russia in 1939, while his wife and the remaining children were trapped in Nazi-occupied Warsaw. Sharing the fate of many of Singer's Jewish Communists, Merkin was denounced as a Trotskyite and sent to Siberia where he was soon politically disillusioned and physically maimed. He tells an awesome tale of life in death, of the strategies prisoners devised to gain an extra portion of watery soup or an extra piece of bread, of their lice picking techniques, and their general degradation that paralleled the Nazi concentration camp environment.

While Merkin informs the narrator of his physical suffering, Esther's life illustrates survivors' psychological torment. She is a bereft and broken human being, robbed by the Holocaust of her family and husband, struggling to care for her ailing father, despite his death wish. Esther is another of Singer's walking corpses—alive only to psychic grief and physical pain resulting from wartime deprivation. For this survivor, the absurdities of peace parallel the horrors of war. Because Esther sustained her Holocaust injuries in Russian camps, she is ineligible for reparation payments unless she can convince German physicians of her emotional trauma, an indignity she rejects.

As in "A Wedding in Brownsville," Singer develops a densely patterned, realistic tableau in an urban American Jewish milieu to substantiate the supernatural. Esther tells an incredulous narrator about witnessing a Poe-like imp of the perverse directing a meeting of men clad in white robes with swastika-inscribed sleeves. When she learns that the cafeteria has burned, she recants her original estimate of the improbability of this event and believes that the vision was real and the fire a direct result of her discovery. Following reports of Esther's holocaustal suicide by gas, the narrator sees her walking on Broadway with a man known to have died many years before. Just as Hitler's ghost haunted Esther's consciousness, so Esther's ghost now haunts the narrator, and he concludes that "If time and space are nothing more than forms of perception, as Kant argues, and quality, quantity, causality are only categories of thinking, why shouldn't Hitler confer with his Nazis in a cafeteria on Broadway?" (*C*, 95) Transformed by the experience into accepting the irrational as an omnipresent, if limited, component of the universe,[36] the narrator finally believes Esther's report. The bond that links survivor and narrator is that forged by "mutual appreciation of the irrational way the universe conducts itself."[37]

In his most recent Holocaust dominated work, *The Penitent* (1983), Singer resurrects and develops the sacred passion previously reserved for minor characters who held fast to the values of traditional rabbinic and Hasidic Judaism, despite Holocaust history. The title character of the *The Penitent* is Joseph Shapiro, a lapsed Jew who attains Holocaust restoration by asserting his Jewish identity and returning to Torah Judaism. Hand-in-hand with commitment to Judaism in *The Penitent* is commitment to the State of Israel. The penitent's spiritual return culminates in his emigration to Israel. Although Singer has set several works in Israel, implicitly suggesting a connection between his treatment of the Holocaust and its antithetical historic expression, it is not until *The Penitent* that he moves from the tentative suggestion of *Shosha*'s epilogue that the survival of Israel is a negation of Hitler's plan to destroy Jewry to forthright assertion that commitment to the Jewish state is as central to Holocaust repair and restoration as is renewed commitment to Judaism.

Just as Coleridge's ancient mariner feels compelled to narrate his spiritual fall and resurrection to the wedding guest, so Singer's penitent recounts his spiritual redemption to an autobiographical narrator whom he meets at Judaism's sacred shrine, Jerusalem's Wailing Wall. At the remnant of the ancient Temple, Shapiro, a remnant of European Jewry, whose illustrious ancestors included

Rashi and King David, speaks of Holocaust motivated apostasy and spiritual return to Judaism. By fleeing to Russia when the Nazis invaded Poland, Joseph Shapiro escaped the fate of three million Polish Jews. At war's end, he smuggled himself out of Stalin's hell, married his prewar love in a German displaced persons camp, and emigrated in 1947 from Europe to begin life anew in America. Unlike many Singerian survivors who live in refugee enclaves where they suffer Holocaust-wrought insecurities, the Shapiros enjoy American society and postwar prosperity. Worldly success, however, leads to Shapiro's spiritual decline, and he soon regrets the corruption and contritely returns to Jewishness, "and not merely to some modern arbitrary Jewishness, but to the Jewishness of . . . [his] grandfathers and great-grandfathers."[38] Singer adapts a classical journey motif to dramatize the penitent's spiritual quest, mapping each step from self-recognition to painful testing and eventual attainment of *t'shuvah*, spiritual return to God, law, and membership in a religiously observant community in the Jewish state.

Since the Holocaust was the pivotal event of Shapiro's life, his categorical imperative, he measures morality and spiritual lapses by Holocaust standards. Thus, he views his ethical failure as betrayal of "the Jews who had donned prayer shawls and phylacteries and gone off to the cemeteries to die martyrs' deaths" (*P*, 27). To be a descendant of observant Jews, to have studied and lived according to Judaic law, and to have exchanged that vision for a gentile life style, he reasons, is to betray "the whole of Jewish history" (*P*, 27). His guilt is manifest in troubled sleep, in nightmares about hiding from the Nazis in a cellar with his parents and other Jews and discovering that he is a Nazi among Jews "dressed . . . in a brown uniform and a swastika" (*P*, 27).

Although Singer's books are replete with characters who abandon orthodoxy for secularism, a concomitant disillusionment-spiritual return pattern emerges. Whereas the shift to secularism dominated the dramatic tension in the earlier fiction, with the spiritual return treated in a brief concluding coda, in *The Penitent* return to Judaism is the central theme and provides both the drama and resolution to the Jew's problem in the modern age. With *The Penitent*, Singer's work comes full circle. He has repeatedly told the story of the Jew who abandons orthodoxy of Torah and Talmud for Enlightenment freedom and found it a bitter disappointment. Like Asa Heschel, Yasha Mazur, and Herman Broder, Shapiro abandons assimilation for a return to God and

Judaism. Whereas Singer concluded *The Magician of Lublin* and *The Family Moskat* with protagonists arriving at this decision, it is only in Shapiro's case that recognition is achieved early in the story and dramatic tension given to the attainment of spiritual restoration. To withstand the moral anarchy of modern secular life, Shapiro willingly accepts the yoke of the Torah.

A repentant sinner, Shapiro echoes Singer's disillusioned secularists who denounce both Eastern and Western utopian schemes that attracted assimilated and lapsed Jews. Disenchantment with Western philosophies, noted in *Shosha*'s epilogue, dominates *The Penitent*. Shapiro contends that the Jew's assimilation to Western Enlightenment catapulted him from Jewish piety to a quagmire of secular debauchery. He repudiates post-Enlightenment Europe and its German paradigm of high culture, seething with barbarism, licentiousness, and injustice, on the grounds that one "could be versed in all their philosophies and still be a Nazi" (*P*, 37). Contrasting the Jew with the practicing Christian who could simultaneously be a Nazi, Shapiro argues:

> The Talmud Jew doesn't kill. He doesn't take part in wild orgies. You don't have to fear him in the woods or on a lonely road. He doesn't carry a gun. He doesn't scheme to come to your house when you are away and sleep with your wife. He has no wish to dishonor your daughter. Although he didn't adopt Christianity, he's been turning his other cheek for two thousand years, while those who profess Christian love often plucked out his beard, along with a piece of the cheek. This Talmud Jew doesn't deal violently with any race, class, or group . . . even the worst among them don't murder, don't hunt, don't rape, don't justify killing, don't scheme to liquidate whole classes and races, don't transform family life into a joke. (*P*, 44–45)

Similarly, in agreement with *Shosha*'s Aaron, and Haiml, Shapiro judges the political and social panaceas that European secular Jews adopted as "inadequate to the moral life." He repudiates both the nineteenth-century Jewish revolutionaries, who justified the pogroms in Russia as an expression of popular rebellion against the Czar, and their twentieth-century Communist counterparts, who were duped by the illusions of modernity, social revolution, and atheism.

The moral failure of characters who have abandoned the religious laws of Moses and Maimonides for European and American secularism has been a recurrent theme of Singer's fiction. The novels repeatedly dramatize the shortcomings of secular messianism and a Diasporan experience fraught with inquisition, massacre, religious martyrdom, and genocide. For Singer, the Holocaust, more than any other atrocity, reflects the moral inefficacy of the political, social, and religious systems that willingly coexisted with Hitlerism. In the face of such moral bankruptcy, the penitent returns to the ethics and teachings of the fathers. Shapiro achieves redemption through dedication to Torah and integration in a Hasidic Israeli community.

To critics who have followed Singer's prolific career, *The Penitent's* criticism of Enlightenment secularism comes as no surprise, although for many the stridency of its orthodox polemics is unwelcome. From the beginning of his career, Singer parted company from mainstream modern Yiddish literature's celebration of the *Haskalah,* the Jewish Enlightenment that reached its full force in East-European Jewish life in the late nineteenth and early twentieth centuries. Many intellectuals applauded the *Haskalah* as a liberating, vitalizing force, delivering Jews out of the ghettos into modernity. It replaced Jewish pietism with secular Jewish intellectualism, promulgating a doctrine of separation of religion and culture. However, from his early days among the Warsaw litterati, Singer saw the danger of spiritual destruction in modern Yiddishists' adoption of "secular, rationalist, humanist, libertarian, meliorist" directions.[39] Conversely, Singer's central theme has been the confrontation of God and man. Singer returns Shapiro to an enclave of pious Jews because he believes "the truth is that what the great religions preached, the Yiddish-speaking people of the ghettos practiced day in and day out."[40] He affirms the moral life, because it is the answer to the slaughterhouse of history.

The penitent's return to orthodoxy is neither easy and direct nor free of the same nagging reservations related to Enlightenment failures. Just as Holocaust memory dissuades the penitent from Western civilization, so it is also the source of and challenge to his religious resolution. An inner voice mocks the spiritual quester ridiculing his worship of a callous diety: "Where was He when the Jews of Poland dug their own graves? Where was He when the Nazis played with the skulls of Jewish children? If He does exist and He kept silent, He is as much a murderer as Hitler" (*P,* 47). This internal inquisitor echoes Shapiro's own prepenitent challenge to Jewish charity solicitors. Although he dutifully supported the charities, he censored God's impotence in the face of Hitler's rule, asking "where was God when they burned His Torah and ordered those who studied it to dig their own graves?" (*P*, 20). The paradox of God's silent witness to the Holocaust remains the Jew's torment and Singer's recurrent theme.

Although Singer is anguished by God's enigmatic Holocaust passivity, he nevertheless creates protagonists who are pious Jews faithful to the silent and hidden God, despite, or because of, suffering in the Holocaust crucible. In *The Penitent*, one such Jew, a Hasidic rabbi who remained pious despite hard labor and beatings at the Maidanek concentration camp, enacts the role of Shapiro's spiritual mentor and leads the quester back to orthodoxy. Performance of a *mitzvah*, honoring the commandment to help fill a prayer quorum for public worship, constitutes Shapiro's first step toward redemption and is the occasion for his meeting with his survivor-mentor. An American Hasidic study house, reminiscent of that in his Warsaw past, is the setting for the penitent's transformation. While watching the rabbi pray fervently, "the soul just barely reposed in this saintly body" (*P*, 51), Shapiro prays wholeheartedly for the first time since the war. Shapiro is convinced by his new capacity for devotion that God has delivered him to this synagogue and to this rabbi for spiritual renewal. Having started the day in observance of the commandments and holy prayer, "with words about justice, sanctity, a God who had granted men understanding and who will revive the dead and reward the just" (*P*, 53), Shapiro easily undertakes a second redemptive act— *tsedakah* (charity), graciously giving his money to those who need it. Rejuvenated by sincere and ardent prayer in the company of pious, learned Jews, the penitent is ready to pursue traditional Judaism through intense study of the holy books to find "not the 'wisdom' dispensed by psychoanalysts, with their wild, unfounded theories and farfetched conclusions" (*P*, 59), but a plan for righteous living in reverence for God and His creation.

Whereas the first stage of Shapiro's repentance leads the quester from American business to Jewish synagogue and study hall, the second stage involves a journey from New York to Jerusalem. He flees moral abomination, escapes "from a civilization that is a slaughterhouse and a brothel" (*P*, 63) and embarks instead upon a journey to Israel, Judaism's spiritual center. On the airplane Shapiro is repeatedly buffeted between the forces of good and evil, embodied in an observant Hasid and an archetypal Lilith. The penitent struggles against the seductive converters that succeed where auto-da-fé and inquisition failed, the assimilationist forces advocated by the Jewish temptress who occupies the seat beside him. Priscilla, an allegoric configuration, tries to confound Shapiro by raising questions about Existential rationalism during the flight and later in Israel. A lapsed American Jew whose immorality Singer attributes to apostasy, Priscilla echoes the disembodied "evil spirit," challenging God's existence and beneficence. As the daughter of an assimilated Jewish American family, she was sent to Sunday school "only because it was considered fashionable to be connected, no matter how superficially, with religion" (*P*, 77); she is ignorant of religious law and ethics and uninterested in cultural and ethnic Jewish identity. Despite recognizing this woman as an "Evil Spirit," the narrator succumbs to her sexual wiles and mentally defiles his repentance. Because the post-Holocaust world is deprived of the richly textured religious/cultural/social fabric of East-European Jewry, Shapiro fears that he will be unable to live purely and contemplates abandoning the quest and returning to New York. Ironically, Priscilla's contempt for the Hasid's ritual dress strengthens Shapiro's fidelity. Her mockery affords Shapiro the recognition that his failure to acknowledge his own piety openly and directly exposes him to temptation.

Against secular corruption, easy virtue, and lapsed faith, Singer posits the virtues of Orthodox Judaism. Book One ends with the pentitent's arrival in Israel; he concludes that the Orthodox are Jewry's greatest asset because

> they have isolated themselves from worldliness more than any other Jews in our history. They were exactly that which Moses demanded: a holy people, guarded by a thousand restraints, a people which "shall dwell alone and shall not be reckoned among the nations." True, they are no more than a small minority, but great ideals have never become mass movements. (*P*, 93–4)

Book Two is Singer's most insistent dramatization of Emil Fackenheim's thesis that post-Holocaust Jews must lead Jewish lives or grant Hitler a posthumous victory. Shapiro's nightmares illuminate the correspondence of Holocaust destruction and Jewish self-inflicted diminishment through assimilation. In a tone of righteous indignation reminicent of Amos and Jeremiah, Shapiro rebukes Israeli secularists for failing to honor Torah and Talmud, for embracing and installing non-Jewish culture in Israel. Secularism in Tel Aviv—mirroring that in New York, Paris, Madrid, or Rome—suggests that "the Enlightened have attained their goal. We are a people like all other peoples. We feed our souls the same dung as they do" (*P*, 99). Thus, Shapiro condemns worldly Israeli Jews as he had earlier condemned lapsed Diasporan Jews, Jewish Freudians, and Jewish leftists.[41]

Despite his pronouncements in favor of Orthodox discipline and ritual, the quester suffers Holocaust-induced religious doubt. His sleep is plagued by nightmares of Jews driven by whips as they dig their own graves, nightmares of Nazis torturing Jews or leading them to the ovens. Unable to pray wholeheartedly as he had in the New York Hasidic study house, Shapiro now prays mechanically and ineffectually, thoroughly disheartened by God's Holocaust-era silence and contemporary failure to intercede in the face of an Arab threat of a second Holocaust. He despairs that

> each benediction seemed a lie. Not even the slightest proof existed that God would resurrect the dead, heal the sick, punish the wicked, reward the just. Six million Jews had been burned, tortured, obliterated. Tens of millions of enemies lurked over the State of Israel ready to lay waste that which Hitler had left untouched. Former Nazis in Germany drank beer and spoke openly about new massacres. (*P*, 104–5)

In another instance, while Shapiro is in the midst of prayer, the evil spirit tries to dissuade him with accusations of God's Holocaust complicity: "What did God do for us Jews that we should love Him so? Where is His love for us? Where was His love when the Nazis tortured Jewish children?" (*P*, 132). The only convincing argument the "voice of evil" presents opposing Orthodox Judaism is its faith in God, who abandoned the pious during the Holocaust. When this technique fails, the "voice of evil" adopts a Zionist guise urging Shapiro to put his idealism to national rather than theological service. Israel needs soldiers, engineers, and technicians to keep the country going, patriots rather than pietists who will simply pray while the Arabs slaughter them. Shapiro remains undaunted. Just as Singer emphasized the causal connections between Christian and Nazi anti-Semitism in *Shosha*'s epilogue, so he focuses in *The Penitent* more insistently on the example set by Nazi Germany for the Arab genocidal intent toward the Jews of Israel. Just as

Haiml worries about an Arab devised Holocaust, so Shapiro is concerned for Israeli survival in a land mass surrounded by five nations as fanatically dedicated to its destruction as Hitler was to the Final Solution.

That the Holocaust has crystallized Shapiro's commitment to Judaism is unequivocally stated in his final dispute with Priscilla, who condemns Holocaust-motivated rejection of Germany as a Jewish self-indulgent grudge. Conversely, Shapiro interprets the catastrophe as the logical culmination of historic Christian anti-Semitism. Because he sees an intimate connection between Christian and Nazi anti-Semitism, he believes that Western religion and philosophy are morally bankrupt and so he justifies his rejection of those systems in favor of a spiritual return to Orthodox Judaism in Hebraic rather than contemporary Western terms. Reiterating his Jewish affirmation that concluded Book One and the first day's narration, he seeks redemption in his commitment to Jewish law. With greater knowledge of the implications of his decision than Philip Roth's Eli Peck, Shapiro, too, dons the Hasidic gabardine as a shield against worldly temptation. As a person who understands the Jewish emphasis on righteous deeds, Shapiro knows he "must act in a Jewish way" (*P*, 161) to achieve the restoration he seeks. Although the God of the Exodus and of Sinai failed at Auschwitz and Bergen-Belsen, Singer's Jews are not absolved of their part in the covenant; they must honor Mosaic law through righteous living. Shapiro affirms the hidden, silent God and accepts the Torah and the Talmud as the primary ethical codes for human decency.

In his zealous effort to counter Priscilla's facile dismissal of Jewish grief and her pardon of German crime, the penitent offers the most pessimistic interpretation of the Holocaust as retribution for Jewish assimilationist lapses:

> God chose us out of all the peoples and wanted us to avoid their abominations, but we often do the same as our persecutors. He keeps punishing and we keep sinning. . . . Within our time we were dealt the worst blow a people can receive, yet we learned nothing from it. (*P*, 153)

*Mi penei hata'einu* ("because of our sins we were punished") was the classical Jewish theological doctrine developed as an explanation for earlier national calamities, but one that Jews generally dismiss as an explanation for the Holocaust. Recognizing that the punishment dictum is an unacceptable Holocaust thesis, Shapiro abandons searching for a reason and posits the Fackenheim thesis for a Jewish return to religion and dedication to community as an appropriate response to the *Shoah*. Like most Jewish Holocaust thinkers, Singer rejects outright the possibility that the purpose of the death camps and crematoria was for divine instruction. The Holocaust remains, finally, an absolute evil and injustice with no acceptable explanation.

Shapiro's quest for the antithesis of Hitlerism and Stalinism repeatedly leads to Orthodox Judaism and to Jerusalem, where he discovers peace at the prayer house of Sandzer Hasidim, because here he finds precisely what Hitler tried to destroy in Europe and the element he believes absent from modern American Jewry—*Yiddishkayt* ("love for Jewishness, love for a fellow Jew") [*P*, 115]. Here Shapiro is able to study and pray fervently among the pious, who shun the Enlightenment dictum of being a man in town and a Jew at home and living integrated public and private Jewish lives.

Among the Hasidim, Shapiro's despairing retribution utterance gives way to the dominant affirmative position in Jewish thought. His Holocaust regeneration is cast in the mode of Jewish mysticism's Lurianic kabbalists.[42] These mystics respond to God's withdrawal from history by exerting even greater effort to usher in the messianic age. Within the kabbalist's cosmological system, there is an unbroken interconnection between the metaphysical world and the material world. Evil may be obliterated by the triumph of human morality. Kabbalists regard prayer as the medium that unites people with God, and they advocate *tikkun*, a continuous act of repair and restoration, to hasten the advent of the Messiah. Jewish mysticism stresses both God's manifestation and hiddenness and man's obligation to honor the Sinai convenant regardless of God's self-restrictions. Messianic and mystical interpretation of historic disaster as a demonstration of increasing divine withdrawal from history in turn demands greater human effort in the restorative process—that is, undertaking a holy mission to usher in the messianic age. Shapiro shares the kabbalist's belief that through the study of the Torah and observance of its precepts in conjuction with fervent prayer Israel will make its contribution to cosmic fulfillment. The classical orthodox and the mystical paths to redemption both involve the triad of God, Torah, and *ahavat Yisrael,* commitment to and love of the Jewish people. Shapiro's return to Torah Judaism within a Hasidic Israeli community is a viable means of achieving Holocaust restoration through renewal of Judaism and Jewry. Had he remained in America, he might have achieved piety; in Israel, however, he is part of a larger movement of collective regeneration that gives testimony to the failure of collective destruction that the Holocaust was designed to achieve. Shapiro achieves that which his fellow Holocaust survivor, Herman Broder, sought—"to go back to the Torah, the Gemara, the Jewish books" (*E*,56).

Lest the reader assume that I. B. Singer has abandoned his protest against God's Holocaust-era passivity, the author explains that while Joseph Shapiro may have made peace with man's inhumanity to man and a hidden God, he has not; he continues to be shocked by life's miseries and brutalities.[43] In an authorial note to *The Penitent,* Singer argues "there is no basic difference between rebellion and prayer."[44] Singer believes in the morality of protesting divine and human injustice. He explains:

> I had even related my philosophy of protest to Jewishness. The Jew personified the protest against the injustices of nature and even those of the Creator. Nature wanted death, but the Jew opted for life; nature wanted licentiousness, but the Jew asked for restraint; nature wanted war, but the Jew, . . . sought peace.[45]

That the Holocaust cloud covers much of I.B. Singer's fiction is clearly evident from the early commemorative works to the later narratives set in America and Israel. He consistently avoids realistic descriptions of ghettos and death camps in favor of focusing on the lives destroyed in those camps, the living lost and the maimed. Like Elie Wiesel, Singer has brought to the forefront of Holocaust literature the theological and metaphysical implications of the catastrophe. In the short stories, *Enemies, Shosha,* and *The Penitent,* believers and skeptics alike decry God's passive acceptance of radical evil. The Holocaust-wrought religious crises and restorations of Singer's protagonists parallel those of Eli Wiesel's characters. At the conclusion of the autobiographical *Night,* Wiesel sees himself as a corpse, and by the end of *Dawn,* Elisha has been transformed from victim to executioner and is caught in his own reflection. *The Accident* ends with Eliezer engrossed in self-assessment. By the end of *The Town Beyond the Wall,* Wiesel's protagonist is looking into the face of another person, prepared to recommit to the human bond and begin the Holocaust healing process. Similarly, Holocaust trauma is most damaging in Broder's obsessive fears—social withdrawal, and self-condemnation—and Holocaust regeneration is achieved in Tamara, Haiml, and Shapiro's rejection of secular movements and their affirmation of Jewish religious and political activism, manifested in their contribution to Jewish learning and the State of Israel. In Wiesel's progression toward reconfirmation of God and Judaism despite Holocaust injustice, Gavriel of *The Gates of the Forest,* who has found his way back to Hasidism, recites the *Kaddish* for his dead friend. Similarly, Shapiro is a spiritual quester whose odyssey has taken him from the gates of Holocaust hell to a spirituality found with the guidance of Hasidic Holocaust survivors. Holocaust restoration according to Wiesel and Singer, both sons of Hasidic rabbis, lies in a return to God, a revival of Judaism, and a reestablishment of a safe Jewish homeland in Israel.

# CHAPTER SEVEN

*The Dybbuk of All the Lost Dead: Cynthia Ozick's*
*Holocaust Fiction*

Cynthia Ozick writes about Jewish history
and the Holocaust with extraordinary literary grace and a level of
erudition unprecedented in American literature. Unlike Saul Bellow who resists the label "Jewish writer" as restrictive and con-
straining, but whose work is nevertheless permeated with Jewish
values and literary and linguistic influences, Ozick embraces the
designation and seeks to express her artistic vision in Jewish terms,
overtly illuminating her fiction with the wisdom of Jewish sources.
She announced this intent at the Weizmann Institute in Israel in
1970, as a participant in a cultural dialogue between Jewish Americans and Israelis. In these remarks—later published as an essay,
"Toward a New Yiddish," with a preface that modifies her original
optimism—Ozick speaks of the creation of an indigenous American Jewish literature in English. She characterized this writing as
"[A] liturgical literature [which] has the configuration of the ram's
horn: you give your strength to the inch-hole and the splendor
spreads wide."[1] This writing is "centrally Jewish in its concerns"
and "liturgical in nature." By "liturgical," Ozick does not mean

"didactic or prescriptive" but "aggadic" in style, "utterly freed to invention, discourse, parable, experiment, enlightenment, profundity, humanity."[2] In Ozick's view, Jewish writing is distinguished not by sociological observation and delineation, but by the incorporation of Jewish religious and historic matter; it is a fiction "impregnated with the values of Judaism."[3] Unlike many American Jewish writers who create Jewish ambiance through sociological realism and a mere hint of Jewish theology, Ozick is deeply knowledgeable of Jewish religious sources, languages, and history and imaginatively integrates them into her fictional universe. Pertinent to Ozick's commitment to a literature that she characterizes as "centrally Jewish in its concerns" is the treatment of the Holocaust as the orienting event of the century. Although Ozick claims that she would prefer not to write about the Holocaust in fiction because documentary work should be enough, the subject enters her work "unbidden, unsummoned."[4] Holocaust allusion, experience, and thought are manifest in much of Ozick's fiction. Indeed, it would be unthinkable for a writer as deeply moved by Jewish history as Ozick is to create fiction that is Holocaust free.

Cynthia Ozick's first novel, *Trust* (1966), a favorite of the author's,[5] is a huge work that addresses many of the concerns that will continue to absorb Ozick throughout her career and introduces the exquisite style of the later critically acclaimed books. Western civilization's Greek/Hebrew dichotomy, identified by Matthew Arnold, constitutes the central thematic and stylistic tension of the Ozick canon and is the dominant theme of *Trust*. Ozick's characters struggle with the artistic and sensual lures of Pan and the moral imperatives of Moses. Characterizing her own literary metamorphosis while writing *Trust* as an evolution from secular to sacred, Ozick asserts "I began as an American novelist and ended as a Jewish novelist. I Judaized myself as I wrote it."[6] In *Trust* it is through Holocaust subject matter and the character of Enoch Vand, the only Jew in the novel and the only character who undergoes a major intellectual and moral transformation, that Cynthia Ozick emerges as a Jewish writer.

*Trust* concerns a young woman searching for her identity. The unnamed narrator, the daughter of Allegra Vand and Gustave Nicholas Tilbeck, bears the last name of her mother's first husband, William; she is reared by her second husband, Enoch Vand, but seeks the natural father she has never met. She rejects the influence of her mother, a dilettante in politics and art, and of

William, a hypocritical Calvinist who exercises the power of the purse and exhibits Christian anti-Semitic prejudice rather than the Christian virtues of compassion and mercy. The antithetical forces that actively engage the imagination of the protagonist are the Hellenic and Hebraic values of her natural and legal fathers. Tilbeck, "a male muse," an elusive quintessential pagan, lives free of divine and human law. Enoch Vand, the Mosaic foil to Tilbeck's Pan, is ever responsive to human and communal need and rededicates himself to divine law.

The novel's structure is contrapuntal, juxtaposing Greek and Hebrew models as they impinge on the narrator's consciousness. As Ozick testified, *Trust* was started with an American perspective. The imprint of Henry James is evident in the narrative technique and the American-European exchange. The ten-year-old child is brought to Europe in 1945 by her mother who plans to join her second husband. Allegra's Jamesian intent is to expose her daughter to European culture, but like other young Jamesian American girls, the narrator instead discovers Europe's evil. Rather than cloister, cathedral, and castle, the narrator discovers concentration camp, death camp, and crematorium. Each of the novel's four sections takes its title from a place suggesting the controlling influence on the narrator of the character associated with that place. "America" introduces the contradictory social and political influences in the narrator's life; "Europe" develops Enoch's Jewish historicism; "Brighton" develops William's Christian morality and Mamonism; and "Duneacres," Tilbeck's sensual paganism. The drama is set in the mid 1950s, following the narrator's college graduation and the commencement of her identity quest. Although the time frame suggests the culmination of Vand's influence and the initiation of Tilbeck's sway, the narrative and thematic development of each force remains constant, even when presented from William's Christian point of view. Just as the Hellenic quest is about to begin at the end of "America," it is postponed in the pivotal second section, "Europe," for an extended Holocaust flashback. Jewish values reappear in a substantive political-moral dispute in "Brighton." "Duneacres," devoted to Tilbeck's paganism, ends with an Hebraic coda, which implies that, though the Hellenic force enjoys strong seductive appeal, the Hebraic view will be an omnipresent, dissenting, analytic influence. The Hebraic view remains vital throughout the work in antithetical scenes that emphasize either the dramatic presence of Enoch Vand or authorial

Hebraic commentary. Through Vand, who becomes the novel's central moral register and authorial voice, Jewish history serves as a point of reference and Jewish values function as the novel's enduring touchstone.

In *Trust,* Holocaust reaction is a criterion by which Ozick assesses characters. She charts the Holocaust responses of the narrator and her parents from 1938 to the defeat of Nazism in 1945 and into the postwar decade—responses that range from indifference to engagement. We learn that while Vand demonstrated his opposition to the Mosley Fascists and was jailed for it in England, Tilbeck lived comfortably in Germany in 1938 and shared none of the dismay with Hitlerism that Vand exhibited. Furthermore, although Tilbeck was ejected from Germany because he was suspected of being a Communist spy, he was later deported from Prague because he was thought to be a Nazi spy. He was neither. His antics were motivated by exhibitionism, a desire to outrage authority, rather than by political philosophy. Tilbeck describes himself as apolitical, earning his living playing piano for either side during the war. "Pleasure-seekers among the displaced,"[7] Allegra and the narrator remain aloof from holocaustal tragedy while Enoch becomes obsessed with the catastrophe. Deeply impressed by the Holocaust, Vand has "something in him of the refugee, which was absurd, because he was born in Chicago" (*T,* 52). The Holocaust crucible accounts for his refugee psyche and his metamorphosis from political to religious activism, from pre-Holocaust Communist to post-Holocaust observant Jew. During World War II, Vand was assigned to the Office of Strategic Services, and with war's end he remained "a liaison between the dead and the living, and between the dead and the dead, and between the soon-dead and the too-soon dead" (*T,* 66). Recording the Holocaust toll, he views himself as

> an adviser to corpses, an amicus curiae with respect to corpses, a judge, jury, witness, committeeman, representative, and confidante of corpses. He had no office, but went wandering from boundary to boundary sorting out corpses, collecting new sources of more corpses, overseeing and administering armies of corpses. (*T,* 66)

In an unremitting litany, Enoch and his associates chant the names of the dead and the names of the horrid places where Nazis murdered European Jewry:

"Lev Ben-zion Preiserowicz," intoned the first assistant.
"Auschwitz," answered the other.
"Wladzia Bazanowska."
"Belsen."
"Schmul Noach Pincus."
"Buchenwald," came the echo, slow as a thorn.
"Velvel Kupperschmid."
"Dachau," the voice fell like an axe.
"Wolfgang Edmund Landau-Weber."
"Buchenwald," the reader yawned.
"Roza Itte Gottfried."
"Belsen," said Enoch's young assistant, picking at his teeth with
an ivory thumbnail. (*T*, 75)

Weary and devastated by the task of registering the mounting
death tolls, the Jew despairs and rages. It is in Vand's passion for
Jewish history that he most convincingly echoes Ozick's polemical
voice. Ozick has asserted: "I am in thrall to the history of the Jews.
It is the history of the Jews that seizes me ultimately, and with the
obligation of *kavanah*."[8] Vand's transformation is the dramatic enactment of Ozick's pronouncement.

The burden of Holocaust shame and indifference is carried
by the novel's non-Jewish characters, Allegra and the narrator.
Allegra believes her husband is engaged in futile labor, and her
daughter is bored by the "sad redundant madrigal, . . . all those
queer repugnant foreign names, cluttering the air without mercy,
. . . pushy, offensive, aggressive, thrusting themselves unreasona-
bly up for notice" (*T*, 75). To the girl's naive question regarding the
purpose of keeping the names of the dead, Enoch responds,
"Smoke leaves no record and cinders don't have funerals" (*T*, 76).
The juxtaposition of Enoch's lament with the girl's shameless apa-
thy and immoral disdain for the dead clearly indicts the gentile
world, which greeted the slaughter of European Jewry with either
passive toleration or active administration of the death factories.
Misguided by her mother, an artist manqué, the narrator responds
to the rhythms of the catalogue rather than its meaning.

Dachau, Belsen, Auschwitz, Buchenwald, the order varying, Auschwitz, Buchenwald, Belsen, Dachau, now and then an alteration in the
tick and swing, Belsen, Maidenek, Auschwitz, Chelmno, Dachau,
Treblinka, Buchenwald, Mauthausen, Sovibar—tollings like chorus
of some unidentifiable opera of which I could remember the music
but not the import. (*T*, 75–76)

The degree and intensity of Holocaust encounters, as well as Jewish/non-Jewish affiliation, explain, but do not justify, the sharply divergent Holocaust responses of Enoch and his family. Enoch has seen death first-hand; the women know it intellectually. Enoch has been to the concentration and death camps; the women have witnessed a border suicide. Enoch is a Jew who feels the loss of a third of world Jewry; the women are Christians reared in a religion that has historically chosen the Jews as scapegoats for expulsion, inquisition, pogrom, and decimation. Whereas Enoch's major contact has been with the Jewish dead, Allegra and the narrator are more often in the company of European refugees, whose chances for survival were enhanced simply because they were not Jewish. The reactions of Americans to the Holocaust are measured against the reactions of Europeans. Anneke, the narrator's Dutch governess plays foil to Allegra. She refuses to enter Germany, whereas Allegra has no such revulsion, despite her marriage to a Jew who deals daily with the Holocaust dead. Allegra is indifferent to refugee suffering; she rages against "the unsanitary survivors of a war not yet three months dissolved into history" (*T*, 63); she disapproves of refugees because "they have no sense of responsibility" (*T*, 63). These attitudes characterize Allegra's selfishness and presage her daughter's boredom with Enoch's commemoration of the six million. Although the child remains inarticulate about Nazi barbarism, the author metaphorically evokes revulsion to German crime. Sickened by bad milk as they cross the German border, she retches over a German tank. The vomit forms an outline of Europe, suggesting its putrid history, the Enlightenment promise gone sour.

> The map had begun to drip off the tread, hung with nuggets of mud. And then Africa succumbed, and then the shadow of Asia, and then the vague Americas, and lastly Europe gave way, split open by sudden rivers; the yellow Mediterranean of milk overran them all, sucking up mass after mass and sending out those reeking fetid familiar airs. (*T*, 64)

Soon after this incident, they witness the retrieval of the corpse of an Italian mutilated by the war who has committed suicide on his journey home. Again Allegra's response is callous, an articulation of personal inconvenience, she "didn't come to Europe for this" (*T*, 65). Insensitive to the war-wrought catastrophes, Allegra expresses her discomfort at the odor of her child's vomit-stained blouse, and the Dutchwoman bitterly rebukes her, "when you are so near Germany there are worse things to smell" (*T*, 65). Undaunted, the American continues to miss the point, arrogantly charges the victim with exaggeration, and underlines her separation from the suffering by use of the pronoun *you:* "you people like to turn every stink into a moral issue" (*T*, 65). Even the child is more sensitive to the reality of Europe and recognizes her mother's retreat into the myth, fantasy, and romance of a royal and religious Europe, "all spectacle, dominion, energy, and honor. And all the while she never smelled death there" (*T*, 78). The innocent child condemns the unfeeling woman, whom she says "saw nothing and knew nothing" (*T*, 102).

The narrator contrasts her mother's failure with her stepfather's sensitivity to the "deathcamp gas, . . . [that] swarmed from his nostrils to touch those unshrouded tattooed carcasses of his, moving in freight cars over the gassed and blighted continent" (*T*, 78). Enoch and his ledgers have ruined Allegra's Europe—"and not the noble ruin of a burned-into-rust-and-filigree abbey, the sort of ruin that time has brought to its knees not cruelly, but in the manner of a sacerdotal genuflection, and graces, and eventually condones" (*T*, 104). Dejected by Enoch's gloom, Allegra reprimands him for his failure to acknowledge human progress since Cain and Abel. She, on the other hand, adds insult to ignorance by blaming the victims for their own misfortunes, uttering *absurdia* such as: "there must be something wrong with a person in the first place, . . . to make him end up a refugee. There's logic in that, isn't there? And morality too, . . . there is no such thing as gratuitous harm. I mean who would chase or murder someone for no reason at all?" (*T*, 101). The acquiescent by-stander thus joins the Nazi criminal perpetrator in blaming the victim. Although the narrator shows greater sensitivity than does Allegra, her Holocaust impressions are but temporary and sporadic. Her assertion of enduring Holocaust sensitivity, "the cadenced psalmings of the deathcamps which did not leave our ears, were for me then a hieroglyph of Europe, and have since so remained" (*T*, 89), is dramatically negated. To the contrary, the narrator later joins Allegra to advocate Holocaust amnesia rather than Holocaust memory. Grief remains Enoch's province.

Ozick's presentation of uncaring gentiles may be historically more realistic than the American gentile women in Norma Rosen's fine Holocaust novel *Touching Evil*, who are ardently responsive to

Jewish suffering. When Rosen's women listen to the names of the death camps, they commiserate with the women who suffered unjustly, express emotional solidarity with the murdered Jewish women and children, and change their lives accordingly. Conversely, Allegra Vand listens to her husband and his associates catalogue the names of the dead and the camps in which they were starved, enslaved, tortured, and murdered, and she denigrates commemoration as futile, "As though all that meant anything anymore, except to the relatives" (*T*, 88)

Sharing Saul Bellow's belief in the writer as moral voice and believing "that stories ought to judge and interpret the world,"[9] Ozick repeatedly juxtaposes the Jewish character's moral indignation with the gentile characters' indifference to genocide, a pattern of character and theme that recurs in the later fiction. To delineate the sharp distinction between Vand and the non-Jews, Ozick elaborates the Hellenic/Hebraic and Christian/Jewish polarities: the non-Jews romanticize killing; the Jew condemns murder. "He was well past Lethe, and well past Nepenthe, and far past the Styx or Paradise. He took it all as simple butchery" (*T*, 76). The narrator speculates that Enoch may think of himself as a scholar-saint, "maybe Maimonides, feeding data to . . . History . . . cursed her for the smoke and the cinders and the corpses, and pleaded for the Evil Inclination and the Angel of Death" (*T*, 76–77). Just as the words and images of Greek culture suggest Holocaust forgetfulness, so the Hebraic diction and allusions demand accountability and commemoration. Europe is Allegra's cultural wonderland; Enoch's graveyard. The bright promises of Western civilization, particularly of the European Enlightenment, had failed dismally. Europe became a charnel house.

The polarity of Holocaust sensitivity/insensitivity evident in the dichotomy of Enoch and Allegra is charged also with the Jewish/Christian polarity that will emerge as one of Ozick's recurrent themes. Ozick dramatizes these distinctions through prose redolent with Hebraic and Christian images and diction. Enoch's grief and moral outrage are conveyed in biblical and liturgical language and allusion and Jewish folkloric references; Allegra's indifference is depicted through Christian anti-Semitic rhetoric and later embellished by William's anti-Semitic remarks. Enoch reverently holds his ledger of the dead against his chest: "as though it contained life. . . . He clung to it in the fancy . . . to dare . . . call out the *Shechina* in a blazing presence too terrible to remember afterward, . . . he wore on his body that book of woe as he might have worn Urim and Thummim, to deliver up manifestations and to court the unmanifestable and dazzle it into disclosing its faceless face" (*T*, 101). Beginning with language suggestive of Jewish veneration of life, Ozick sustains the reverent tone through Hebrew diction. *Urim* and *Thummim* signify light and perfection; they were mysterious objects thought to have been contained in the breastplate of the high priest when he entered the presence of the Lord to ascertain God's will in matters of national import.[10] Enoch's prayer for the *Shechina*, the majestic and omnipresent God, solidifies Ozick's liturgical tone. This portion concludes with the narrator's speculation that Enoch may view himself as "a failed Ezekiel. Thigh-deep in all those names and designations—crumbled, . . . into ash, and the ash of ash—he could not recall them into flesh and sinew" (*T*, 105). Because Enoch seems mired in gloom, the narrator limits her allusion to Ezekiel to the prophet's initial vision of doom and omits the accompanying prediction of restoration. Three months after World War II, it was still too early for revival visions. Whereas the narrator seems sympathetic to Enoch's dismay in the immediate aftermath of the Holocaust, ten years after war's end she voices impatience, charging that Enoch's continued Holocaust focus is abnormal, a sign that he is possessed by an evil spirit and rendered irrational.

> For what could it have been other than a dybbuk which had entered him and taken hold of his escaped Babylonian intellect and his infidel compassion?—the dybbuk of all the lost dead, the dybbuk of the martyrs, the dybbuk of the slaughtered millions, the dybbuk of cinder and smoke, . . . I comprehended him at last. I saw what he waited for, the extraordinary sign, the consecrated demonstration, which he did not dare to name Messiah. He was waiting for the deliverance of history. . . . He awaited justice for the wicked and mercy for the destroyed. He awaited the oblivion of devouring Europe . . . even at the price of sublime civilization. (*T*, 200–201)

Thus, in one splendid epiphany, the narrator advances from slandering Enoch as an obsessive possessed by an evil spirit to recognition of his Messianic and apocalyptic longing. Further, she associates his devotion to Holocaust witness in this lengthy vision with that of the high priest of the Temple "in the moment of utterance of the Name of Names within the Holy of Holies" (*T*, 201).

To include Holocaust material beyond Enoch's experience, Ozick introduces cameo portraits of a refugee, Siegfried, and a survivor, Anneke, who enter the narrative for brief scenes and whose dramatic importance is based on their Holocaust experiences and attitudes. Siegfried escaped Austria prior to its Nazification, and Anneke survived the Nazi occupation of Holland.

Representative of many assimilated Jews who converted to Christianity to enjoy first-class citizenship in countries that had open anti-Jewish policies is Siegfried, a baptized Jew who found safe haven in England where he worked as a cook and general handyman for Allegra in 1939. The irony of his conversion lies in its failure to spare him. The poor man is bewildered to discover that under Reich law, even as a second-generation Lutheran who had repudiated Moses as a "worldly legalist," he is reclassified as a Jew and subjected to public beatings and "forced naked to play underwater like a whale" (*T*, 372). Betrayed and estranged from his Viennese compatriots, he is astonished to discover that "a country is a traitor to a man! A whole nation turned seditionist. A government betraying its own citizen!" (*T*, 372). Describing Siegfried's flight in summary fashion, Ozick incorporates Holocaust events in her flashbacks, "escapes, bribes, Switzerland, Italy, a filthy boat, Portugal, England, the man, the woman, three sons, alive, alive, survival!" (*T*, 372), which are consistent with the pattern of ironic allusions to the novel's title. Ozick concludes the Siegfried cameo with his Holocaust-informed perception: "Never trust. Trust is a word for the firing squad" (*T*, 372).

Discrimination between Jewish and non-Jewish victims of Nazi terror, including the betrayal of Jews by their fellow sufferers, finds expression in the portrait of Anneke, the narrator's governess. Like Europeans who were distressed to be under Nazi occupation, but willing to denounce Jewish countrymen either for self-preservation or to turn a profit on the transaction, Anneke uses her position with the Vands to exploit Enoch's political influence, to advance her brother's interests, and to steal from the family. Although she detests Germany for the indignities she and her family suffered, she is without qualms about terrifying her young charge. She maliciously alarms the child—whom she erroneously believes to be part Jewish—with tales of misfortune should Allegra dismiss her. As a lost child, the narrator will be mistaken for a refugee and interred in a camp, "contract a disease among all the sick little Jewesses" (*T*, 67), and then be sent to Palestine where she will die of thirst in the dessert. In another variation on the persecution theme, the governess asserts that the child will "be shot before the Wailing Wall by a firing-squad from Arabia" (*T*, 68). Ozick's Holocaust canvas is enlarged by Anneke's behavior. The terror she inflicts on the narrator in order to assure her silence, regarding misappropriation of family funds and neglect of her costodial obligations, recalls the systematic deceptions perpetrated on the Jews by both Nazi and anti-Nazi antagonists.

In addition to offering an understanding of themes and character models, the study of *Trust* provides a key to Ozick's later stylistic treatment of the Holocaust. Without developing the concentrationary universe of camp and crematoria through the plotline, Ozick implies its immediacy through an historic recorder with direct access to the camps and their few survivors and through metaphor, allusion, and diction graphically illustrating Holocaust reality—methods that will reappear in *Bloodshed, Levitation,* and *Cannibal Galaxy.* She achieves a critical balance between the immediacy of the European setting and the distance necessary to probe the long-term implications of the event that forever changed perceptions of humanity and deity. Because Vand is a psychological survivor who saw the camps but did not have to survive them, his characterization permits the author to summon the moral indignation of the survivor, but frees her from the added burden of developing survival syndrome. Vand's camp litany graphically addresses the magnitude of the catastrophe:

> And all the while freight-trains scratching on bomb-twisted tracks howled out of the east with a cargo of tattooed corpses . . . and in the privacy of his intellect he lit centuries and burned history to hallow his intemperate goddess. (*T*, 80)

Enoch is a man "annointed in agony," confronting the aftermath of the Final Solution. In another instance, the deliberations of Enoch and his coworkers appear in a fusion of business and holocaustal diction, suggesting the disposition of superfluous material, diction that transports the reader into the reality of the camp universe.

> They complained that the market was reluctant; that there were no reputable outlets; that facilities for distribution were a tangle of contradictions; that the supply of the products exceeded . . . the demand for it; that it was consequently impossible to dump even what-

ever portion was already released from the wholesalers and the
chains. This was their language, although I knew it was corpses they
meant, and mass graves, and exhumations, and freight cars lurching
westward, and names lost forever, and the blind tongues of the dead,
and cinders and smoke. (*T*, 123–24)

In contrast to the commercial jargon of supply and demand connoting the profit quotient of the Nazi slaughter of the Jews, Ozick
combines biblical and mythic diction to suggest epical Jewish suffering. Enoch perceives himself a scholar-saint,

feeding data to his goddess . . . the grim faced nymph Geopolitica,
wearing a girdle of human skin and sandals sinewed and thonged by
the sighs of dead philosophers. . . . He cursed her for the smoke and
the cinders and the corpses, and pleaded for the Evil Inclination and
the Angel of Death jointly to carry her off; but she remained. . . .
Enoch leaned brooding among the paper remnants of the damned:
the lists and questionnaires, the numbers and their nemeses; every
table spread with the worms' feast; the room a registry and bursary
for smoke and cinders. . . . she formed herself out of the slaughter;
the scarves and winds of smoke met to make her hair, the cinders
clustered to make her thighs; she was war, death, blood, and. . . . She
came up Europa. (*T*, 76–77)

Vand spends his time and energy agonizing over the human loss.
And Ozick suggests the moral and historic implications of Germany's technological capacity to kill millions expeditiously; its sadistic conversion of human skin to lampshades, bone to ash, and
flesh to smoke; its instrumental contribution to the collapse of
Western civilization through the creation of a bureaucracy based
on genocide. The moral indignation and graphic diction of this
passage most closely resembles the author's Holocaust indictment
in "The Biological Premises of Our Sad Earth-Speck." The essay,
anthologized in *Art and Ardor,* documents the ultimate failure of
German racists and their accomplices in transforming "living
bodies into corpses, corpse into bone meal, and all in the course of
less than an hour."[11] Ozick is as passionate in her denunciation as
Enoch is in his:

It is a monstrosity—an abnormality, a deformity, a contortion and a
mutilation so stupendous and disordering that it must somehow
result in consequences for the ordinary regulation of the planet. . . .

> The German aberration murdered millions of human beings—
> among them some six million Jews, . . . according to an original de-
> sign of Spirit incarnated as "racial purity," as "the Aryan ideal":
> proof of that incarnation being those millions of corpses of Jews.

> The Holocaust—the burnt offering of the Jewish people in the fur-
> nace of the German Moloch—is an instance of aberration so gargan-
> tuan that it cannot leave wary nature . . . unshaken.[12]

Ten years after World War II, the two gentile women and the
Jewish Holocaust recorder are as far apart in consciousness as they
were in 1945. The women have learned little from history. For
Allegra, Enoch's record keeping remains inconsequential. Concerned with her husband's advancement to ambassadorial rank,
she is impatient with his Holocaust obsession and rebukes him: "it's
all over. . . . The concentration camps are all over!" Similarly, the
narrator who had claimed to be transformed by Holocaust consciousness also accuses Vand of Holocaust preoccupation and argues for the Holocaust amnesia so common in the non-Jewish
world. As a Jew and a Holocaust witness, Vand sees the world
crime-ladden, unclean, and unredeemed. "How do you clean
murder away?" he asks the college graduate. And she glibly replies,
"By forgetting it"; "It was long ago, all that" (*T*, 191). This heated
conflict between the narrator, who claimed to be permanently af-
fected by the death camps, and her stepfather reveals the self-
delusive cant of Christians who utter platitudes about the Holocaust and conceal Christian Holocaust culpability. The narrator,
reprimands Vand for being unforgiving, urges him to abandon
vengeance, to forgive, to be merciful, to be Christian. Vand deftly
dispels her façade of holiness, demonstrating the vacuity of her
words in the historic context of centuries of Christian anti-Semitic
violence, from the Inquisition to the Final Solution, mocking
"Christendom's idea of mercy, a tit for a tat—mercy granted in
exchange for guilt confessed. Guilt is what feeds mercy—. . . And if
there is no guilt to be given over as a unit of barter, then no mercy
at all, then the stake and the oven instead" (*T*, 193). Just as the
church and the third Reich did not absolve Jews from being Jews,
Vand does not forgive Nazis for being Nazis. In Vand's judgment,
and in Ozick's there is no expiation for Holocaust crimes.

> Nobody has a right to look at the ash and the bones and say: I am
> merciful, therefore I forgive this crime. So how much more per-

verted to look at the spared criminal nation and say: I am righteous, therefore vengeance on this seed is mine. No holy tit for tat permitted, nothing liturgical, no ministerial exemptions, no hope, no expiation! . . . Because the crime is too big for us, in our human littleness, to presume to forgive it or to avenge it. The crime is the crime of crimes! It's too huge! too heinous! too foul! too fiendish and monstrous!—Too big! . . . we're not God! It would be ourselves we would have to forgive or avenge. (*T*, 194)

Enoch and narrator argue the essential nature of history in a manner resembling the debate Ozick witnessed on the subject of Jewish history between Erwin Goodenough, a scholar and historian, and Maurice Samuel, essayist, historian, and novelist. The crux of the Samuel/Goodenough discourse, as Ozick reconstructs it from memory, is that Goodenough contends history is what a people has done and what has been done to them, only what has been. Samuels insists that history is the significance of data and more: "History is what has happened. And also a judgment on what has happened."[13] Ozick reiterates this thesis in her own voice as well. "History for the Jews, is not simply what has happened, it is a judgment on what has happened. History is to the continuum of events what the Sabbath is to the progression of days."[14] Enoch echoes Samuels and Ozick; he awaits history's judgment.

The judgment is conveyed in the novel's brief reference to the Nuremberg Trials during a shipboard conversation between the narrator and an American Army colonel, who explains that soldiers are to be absolved of criminal charges because they simply follow government orders: "What's done is done. We can't waste time going back, we've got to prepare for that kid over there" (*T*, 170). Like the American government he represents, the colonel is less interested in prosecution of Nazi war criminals than he is in the potential Communist threat. The scene thus effectively juxtaposes Nazi rationalization of crimes against humanity and the West's postwar harboring of Nazis to advance its Cold War objectives— one position against the other, each morally reprehensible.

The theme of Holocaust absolution introduced in the reference to the Nuremberg Trials reemerges in a confrontation between the narrator and Enoch when the narrator tries to convince Vand to abandon his insistence on vengeance against Nazi criminals. She cites God's promise to Noah after the flood that He would thereafter refrain from universal destruction regardless of the degree or extent of human evil. This citation once again demonstrates the narrator's insufficient understanding of Enoch's point of view. He did not call for universal punishment, but simply for retribution against war criminals. This scene also works as an effective transition from the theme of human Holocaust culpability to divine Holocaust culpability. Vand first exposes the narrator's faulty interpretation of the post-flood promise and then explores God's Holocaust-era failure. Rather than interpreting God's self-restrictive response as a sign of absolution to war criminals, Vand reads it as a sign of God's abdication from covenantal promise, which in turn requires more human responsibility for the administration of justice. At this stage in his holocaustal agony, Vand accuses God of atheism, betraying justice and delegating retribution to historic forces.

The theme of divine passivity in light of holocaustal horror, which is substantially developed in the fiction of Elie Wiesel and I. B. Singer, appears briefly, but provocatively, in *Trust*. Although Vand's diction is secular, he expresses ideas similar to those of the educated and observant Jewish characters of Wiesel and Singer who challenge God on moral grounds. Vand, too, explains divine silence in the face of crime and counterevidence to the covenantal redemptive claim, first by finding God guilty of breaking His own Law—hence calling Him an atheist—and then according to traditional Jewish Messianic and mystical interpretations of catastrophe, which contend that the meaning of historical disaster "requires greater human effort in the salvific process"[15] and that it demonstrates "increasing divine hiddenness or withdrawal from history."[16] History will have to sanctify itself to revalidate the covenantal, redemptive promise. Like the Jewish sages of earlier devastations who argued that God was not absent from history but self-concealed, thereby necessitating greater human effort in the redemptive process, Vand looks for redress in the public sphere and turns to the independent study of Jewish sources to effect renewed righteousness and holy mission. He tells Allegra

> First I was born, and found the world the way it is, and myself a Jew, and God the God of an unredeemed monstrosity, . . . so naive was I that I didn't despair or suspect. . . . and in my simplicity I thought that whatever you came upon that seems unredeemed exists in this state for the sake of permitting you the sacred opportunity to redeem it. I used to have a crooked idea that man finds the world

> unwell in order to heal it, I had the presumptuousness of thinking
> myself one of the miracle rabbis. (*T*, 397–98)

Enoch's speech is Hasidic in diction, tone, and attitude. As genocidal evil promoted covenantal revision, historic redress will en-
courage Messianic redemption, and justice will be served. Uncon-
vinced, Allegra challenges Enoch's position as being vindictive and,
therefore, typically Jewish. She admonishes him to desist speaking
like a Jew. Allegra's advice is the standard invitation of Christians
that Jews stop being Jews. Authentic Jews distinguish themselves
from others and Enoch's stubborn insistence on that distinction
constitutes his first step on the path to Judaic return.

Vand's religious evolution begins with his rejection of the
Communist Party, in which he served as a youth leader until the
formation of the Hitler-Stalin pact. Although Enoch faults God for
reneging on His covenantal obligations in His holocaustal passivity,
he asserts that he was never an atheist: "I've always been aware of
God. My complaint has been that he hasn't returned the favor . . .
It's God who's the real atheist, . . . He keeps denying himself by
lack of action; he's turned his back on being God" (*T*, 190). Despite
Enoch's dismay in God's covenantal betrayal, he feels solidarity
with the Jewish people, which, in turn, leads Enoch to the study of
their sacred books and back to Jewish belief. By novel's end, Enoch
Vand approaches the Lurianic Hasidic belief in man's restorative
task in history—that is, helping to free the hidden God by liberating divine sparks. He does so by committing himself, under the
guidance of a Holocaust survivor, to the traditional Jewish life of
prayer and study. By insisting on bearing witness and affirming his
commitment to Judaism, Enoch Vand and his literary descendants
resemble the Jew whom Arthur A. Cohen describes in his theological interpretation of the Holocaust: one who voluntarily assumes the task of attaining meaning and wresting instruction from
the historical event.[17] In addition to sharing the compulsion to
bear witness with many survivors, Vand seeks to reinvigorate the
Jewish people and rebuild Judaism as a viable Jewish response to
the catastrophe:

> He began taking lessons in Hebrew from a refugee. . . . The number
> tattooed on Enoch's teacher's forearm was daily covered by phylac-
> teries. He had a beard. . . . Under the refugee's tutelage, Enoch read
> the Bible all the way through in Hebrew. It took him three years. . . .

> At the end of that time Enoch began the study of the Ethics of the
> Fathers. . . . Then he asked for the whole Talmud. (*T*, 567)

Enoch Vand studies the classic Jewish texts as Ozick does to know
"what it is to *think* [Ozick's italics] as a Jew."[18] In his evolution
through the Holocaust crucible from apostate to affiliate, Vand is
the literary patriarch of later Ozick prodigal Jews, who return to
Judaism either through their own Holocaust witness or through
the guidance of a survivor, Bleilip of *Bloodshed* and Feingold of
*Levitation*. Both Bleilip and Feingold are acculturated Jews who
return to Judaism through the Holocaust witness of religious survivors, figures whose Holocaust sufferings are instrumental in the
returnees' religious transformations.

Biblical and apocryphal allusion are definitive components in
the development of Enoch's character and the novel's larger moral
and human Holocaust concerns. Although they are separate from
the recognized canon of the Scriptures, Apocalyptic and Pseudepigraphical writing were outgrowths of prophetic literature, sharing
many of its attributes. This literature responded to human despair.
It was written during a period of national crisis when the forces of
evil were apparently in the ascendency and it appeared that the
Jewish people were about to be suppressed or annihilated by their
enemies. The message of the apocalyptic writers is one of hope for
the persecuted, encouragement for the faithful to uphold their
tradition, anticipation of punishment for the wicked, and reward
for the righteous. The first section of the Book of Enoch opens
with an account of a vision given to the patriarch of a holy figure
who will execute judgment on the ungodly and spare the righteous.
The patriarch rejects the pleas of the wicked and pronounces their
doom. The second section of the Book of Enoch includes parables
reiterating impending judgment and a notice that God will send
the Messiah to execute His will. Similarly, the fourth section begins
with an account of dream visions of the history of the world, from
the time of the flood to the establishment of the messianic kingdom—punishment of the wicked and the rewards of the righteous.

Selection of the name *Enoch* for the novel's central Holocaust
witness provides metaphoric confirmation of the character's dramatic role. By using the name *Enoch*, Ozick indicates that she desires the reader to draw a parallel to the biblical figure and the
appropriate historic and religious correspondencies. From the beginning of the novel, which is set in the same time frame as the

conclusion, Ozick prepares the reader for Enoch's religious transformation by frequent references to his "prophetic" character. The
biblical Enoch is said to have been rewarded for his piety by escaping the death of ordinary mortals and instead, like Elijah, being
taken to Heaven without the agony of death.[19] In addition, he is
credited with the pseudepigraphical Book of Enoch, declaring
God's just punishment of the unrighteous.[20] The fictive, "prophetic" Enoch is also a writer, keeper of the Holocaust book of the
dead at war's end, essayist advocating the influence of Moses over
Pan, and author of prophetic aphorisms at novel's end. He echoes
his biblical namesake's rebuke of evildoers in his apocalyptic renunciation of communism and Nazism. He sees Europe as an open
trench and judges it with prophetic insight and wrath. "He saw not
Lucifer, but all of Paradise fallen. . . . He saw commissars and
storm troopers linked" (*T*, 374). Ozick uses this language to describe Enoch's political revelation, his understanding that he had
been duped by the idealistic goals of communism into an "idyll of
trust in heroic governments" (*T*, 374). Like many intellectuals of
the 1930s, Vand sought redress for the suffering of humanity in
the ideals proclaimed by the Communist Party, and like many
Western intellectuals, he understood the Nazi-Soviet alliance as
proof of communism's moral bankruptcy. Recognition of the
failure of European philosophic and political promise frees Enoch
Vand for religious realization. His vision, like that of the patriarch,
anticipates the coming of the Messiah and the vindication of the
Jews. His arguments with Allegra and the narrator regarding vindication of the Jews and the need to hold the Nazis accountable for
attempted genocide of European Jewry parallel the apocryphal
voice. Enoch Vand's final correspondence to the patriarch may be
seen in his postwar return to religious piety; he too "walks with
God." Ozick's decision to return the lapsed Jew to orthodoxy confirms his Jewish particularity. In Ozick's fiction the authentic Jew is
not the assimilationist, not the alienated archetype, not the universal victim, but the covenanted believer, the "transmitter of a
blazingly distinctive culture."[21] The name *Vand* symbolically confirms Ozick's thematic intent. The Yiddish word *vand* (meaning
wall) alludes to two major catastrophes of Jewish history: the destruction of the Temple and the Holocaust, as embodied in the
remaining western Wailing Wall of the Temple and the insidious
wall of the Warsaw Ghetto.[22] The religious and historic association
explain Enoch's final course and lend significance to his Holocaust

experience. The biblical parallel gives moral stature to the fictive character, and the affinity between the biblical and fictive Enochs substantiates the Hebraic as the enduring moral vision of the novel.

Paradoxically, Enoch's apocalyptic message regarding Holocaust culpability is delivered to unhearing Christians. Ozick underlines this irony with explicit reference to the fall of the Roman Empire and implicit reference to the Nazi Third Reich, which sought to emulate—albeit more efficiently—Rome's destruction of the Jews and was itself defeated:

> When Titus' monument to the sacking of Jerusalem, that great arch made for eternity, crashed among the plunderers of Rome, nothing remained to speak glory but those raised representations of the Scroll and the Seven-armed Candelabrum; as though not chance but the Temple had ruled, even for mere sculpture, what was to survive the boot of history. (*T*, 152)

As Titus, who thought he diminished Judaism when he destroyed the Temple, failed, so Ozick implies that Hitler's demented dream of an Aryan empire built on the bones and ashes of European Jewry was doomed to failure. The final message of the apocalyptic portion lies in Enoch's notice to his gentile wife and daughter that he rejects de-Judaization. When the narrator tries to transform his messianic vision from the Jewish to the Christological view, his rejection finally allows her to comprehend his Jewish rejection of Christian otherworldliness:

> Christ was one of Enoch's great villains. . . . He believed the divine ought to keep hands off, and not send messengers to meddle with affairs they know nothing of: he insisted God ought to stay what he is, a principle which it is blasphemy to visualize. And he chose Christ for enemy not merely for his cruelty in inventing and enforcing a policy of damnation, but more significantly for his removal of the Kingdom of Heaven to heaven, where, according to Enoch, it had no business being allowed to remain . . . and ought instead to be brought down again as rapidly as possible by the concerted aspiration and fraternal sweat of the immediate generation. (*T*, 375)

Making its first appearance in *Trust,* and reemerging in *Bloodshed, Levitation, Cannibal Galaxy,* and several shorter works, is Ozick's confirmation of the causal relationship between Holocaust transformation and authentic Jewish self-definition. A secularist at the start of his Holocaust discovery, Vand chooses to remember and honor the dead by committing himself to the Judaism that shaped their identities. Enoch Vand's role as redemptive quester heralds the spiritual rebirths of Bleilip in *Bloodshed* and Feingold in *Levitation*. Under the tutelage of a Holocaust survivor, Vand studies Torah, Talmud, and the Ethics of the Fathers. This pattern will be repeated by Bleilip under the guidance of a Hasidic *rebbe* who is also a Holocaust survivor. As Holocaust witness and catalyst for redemptive Judaic return, Ozick is in the theological camp of Emil Fackenheim and Eliezer Berkovits and in the literary company of Saul Bellow, Isaac Bashevis Singer, and Arthur Cohen.

The ramifications of the Holocaust grow ever wider in Ozick's short-story collections. She develops themes addressed in *Trust* and explores the distinctive influence of the Holocaust in the lives of American Jews and prewar immigrants who neither experienced the *Shoah* directly nor witnessed its impact directly as had Enoch Vand. *The Pagan Rabbi and Other Stories* (1971) includes two works with Holocaust concerns: "Envy; or, Yiddish in America" and "The Suitcase." In each Ozick emphasizes the moral burden of the Holocaust, its meaning in history, and its significance to nonwitnessing Jews.

Ozick conceived "Envy" as an elegy for Yiddish and its murdered speakers:

> a lamentation, a celebration, because six million Yiddish tongues were under the earth of Europe, and because here under American liberty and spaciousness my own generation, in its foolishness, stupidity and self disregard had, in an act tantamount to autolobotomy, disposed of the literature of its fathers. I thought of my own now middle-aged generation of American Jewish writers as unwitting collaborators in the Nazi extirpation of Yiddish. . . . It seemed to me . . . that if we did not come to the heart and bones of the language itself we would betray it and ourselves, becoming amnesiacs of history.[23]

The story's antagonists, an obscure Yiddish poet, Edelshtein, and a celebrated Yiddish storyteller, Yankel Ostrover, are based on recognizable historic models and represent the difficulties of writing in a language whose audience has been systematically exterminated. Ozick's treatment of the disgruntled Yiddish writer is both satiric and sympathetic. She mocks his foibles, particularly his hypocritical wish to be free of the "prison of Yiddish," to enjoy Ostrover's fame; however, she sympathizes with his genuine devotion to Yiddish. A complex character, Edelshtein is riddled with ambiguities. Echoing well-known Yiddishist criticism of I. B. Singer's fiction and its popularity with non-Jewish readers, Edelshtein ascribes Ostrover's success to translation and asserts that the writing fails to embody Jewish values, pandering instead to the gentile reading public with stories of sexual and supernatural fantasy.

Employing Holocaust diction, Edelshtein mourns the demise of Yiddish: "the language was lost, murdered. The language—a museum. Of what other language can it be said that it died a sudden and definite death, in a given decade, on a given piece of soil?"[24] Unlike Sylvia Plath's unfortunate use of Holocaust terminology to render psychic trauma, Ozick's use is integral to the Yiddishist's consciousness, not just rhetorical flourish. Edelshtein expresses both his jealousy of Ostrover's success and his self-criticism in holocaustal allusion. He wonders why Ostrover's work should be the only "survivor": "As if hidden in a Dutch attic like that child. His diary, so to speak, the only documentation of what was. Like Ringelblum of Warsaw. . . . And all the others lost? Lost! Drowned. Snuffed out. Under the earth. As if never" (*E*, 51). Conversely, he voices his self-contempt for using the Holocaust language to describe personal grievance: "He felt himself an obscenity. What did the death of Jews have to do with his own troubles? . . . He wanted someone to read his poems, no one could read his poems. Filth and exploitation to throw in history" (*E*, 75). Edelshtein's self-hate emanates from guilt, "for having survived the deathcamps—survived them drinking tea in New York!" (*E*, 74). He rages in frustration at the wife of another Yiddish writer, telling her that they are dead and associating his death as a writer with the Holocaust: "Your house is a gallows, mine is a gas chamber" (*E*, 67). "Whoever uses Yiddish to keep himself alive is already dead" (*E*, 67).

Like Enoch, Edelshtein feels connected to Jewish history—as all Jews were at Sinai so all Jews were at Auschwitz and Babi Yar. Illustrative of his tendency to think historically is his tale of a Russian poet's murder for composing in Yiddish and associating her secret endeavor to remain culturally Jewish with the suffering of Spain's secret Jews, the Marranos, who were killed for practicing Judaism. His grief is particular and personal, ranging from the death of a Kiev student with whom he studied Torah—"a golden head," who could be alive as a Soviet citizen but more certainly is "dead in the ravine in Babi Yar" (*E*, 42)—to the six million people lost between 1939 and 1945: "A little while ago there were twelve million people—not including babies—who lived inside this tongue, and now what is left?" (*E*, 74).

Although much of "Envy" is a lament for the dead Jews and their lost language, Ozick argues for revitalization of Jewish language and literature. As Enoch returned to the sacred books, Edelshtein urges regeneration through the revival of Yiddish, through the legacy of the language that nourished Jews for centuries: "If we fabricate with our own syllables an immortality passed from the spines of the old to the shoulders of the young, even God cannot spite it. If the prayer-load that spilled upward from the mass graves should somehow survive!" (*E*, 74) The language, he asserts, will transport the post-Holocaust generation beyond Western civilization's alienation and nihilism to Jewish affirmation. "*Mamaloshen* doesn't produce Wastelands. . . . With all the suffering no smashing! No INCOHERENCE!" (*E*, 82). The dignity and sanctity of this position is in its Talmudic analogy: "In Talmud if you save a single life it's as if you saved the world. And if you save a language? Worlds maybe. Galaxies. The whole universe" (*E*, 83). Just as Ozick calls for the spiritual survival of the Jewish people, for Jews to live as Jews through curtailment of Diasporan assimilation, the Yiddishist urges the use of Yiddish as the language true to Jewish thought, a language of Jewish ideational liberation and self-emancipation from the host culture.

In the collection's second Holocaust story, "The Suitcase," Ozick introduces a topic generally avoided in American fiction: direct confrontation between Jew and German, each stripping away the assimilated American veneer to respond passionately to Holocaust history. Against the backdrop of an artist's one-man show, Ozick stages a drama of Holocaust antagonism between the artist's German father and his Jewish mistress. Paralleling the Jew's Holocaust sensitivity is the German's Holocaust amnesia. Gottfried Hencke, a pilot for the Kaiser in World War I, "no longer thought of himself as a German."[25] Preferring to forget the Holocaust, he disdains people who persist in expressing their outrage about an event so long past. Like Hitler's chief architect, Albert Speer, Hencke prefers to perceive himself as an apolitical architect who merely built towers in that period. The Jew, Genevieve Levin, provokes him and will not permit him to indulge in escapism. Instead she takes every opportunity to address German Holocaust culpability. When the artist's innocent wife refers to Jung as "some famous Jewish psychiatrist," Genevieve directs her retort to the artist's father: "He isn't a Jew," . . . That's why he went on staying alive" (*S*, 108). Further, she appears to badger Hencke to confirm her analysis:

> You know perfectly well that Jung played footsie with the Nazis. It's public knowledge. He let all the Jewish doctors get thrown out of the psychological society after the Nazis took it over, and he stayed president all that while, and he never said a word against any of it. Then they were all murdered. (*S*, 110)

Although there is no reason for Genevieve to presume that Hencke is a Nazi ideologue, she persistently baits him. She compares the gallery crowd to a concentration camp. . . . Everybody staring through the barbed wire hoping for rescue and knowing it's no use" (*S*, 108). She likens the artist's precise brush strokes to "shredded swastikas" (*S*, 109). At this stage of the story, the Jew seems vindictive and abusive toward a harmless old man who has not only refrained from expressing Nazi sympathies but has made a concerted effort to mute his German interests. Thus, precisely at the point when reader sympathy veers to the German beleaguered by a shrill Jew, Ozick turns the tables and intimates that the old man's innocence in the Holocaust is the result of a geographical accident. We soon see that although this German was not a card-carrying Nazi Party member, he might well have been had he lived in Europe under Nazi rule. Genevieve's attack provokes him to respond in German, a language he normally avoids, thus indicating his emotional discomfort in facing Jewish charges of Nazi sympathy. As he bears his soul, we understand that he uses a double standard to measure wartime suffering. Whereas he seems to ignore or forget Jewish Holocaust losses, the R. A. F. bombing of Cologne in which his sister died remains an open wound: "A horrible tragedy. Even the great Cathedral had not been spared" (*S*, 109). Genevieve intrudes on his lamentation, counterattacking with questions about German war crimes, specifically the contents of the shampoo produced by his brother-in-law in Cologne during the war. Genevieve poses questions calculated to expose the discrepancy between Nazi atrocities such as those carried out in the concentration camps against an unarmed population and a military strike against an armed wartime belligerent; she demands to know, "What were its secret ingredients? Whose human fat? What Jewish lard?" (*S*, 119)

Hencke does nothing to dispel Genevieve's perception of him as a Nazi sympathizer. Although he rejects the Nazi label, Ozick strips his innocent veneer and reveals a man undisturbed by the slaughter of Jews. Philosophically inclined toward Schopenhauer, a well-known anti-Semite, Hencke harbors similar anti-Jewish prejudices. Refraining from openly insulting Genevieve, he instead offers a self-incriminating aside to his son: "A superior woman. . . . A superior race, I've always thought that. Imaginative. They say Corbusier is a secret Jew, descended from the Marranos. . . . These women have compulsions. When they turn up a blond type you can almost take them for our own" (*S*, 120). Hencke's speech reveals his embrace of Nazi racist ideology. Masking his professional jealousy of the celebrated architect Corbusier with a racial slur about his Jewish ancestry is characteristic of the Nazi method of disposing of undesireable business or professional competition. His speech is redolent with anti-Semitic allusions—from vulgar, blatant racism to sly innuendo. The Jew's early attack may have seemed a venomous diatribe against an innocent old man, but Hencke's speech which is festering with the poison of Nazi anti-Semitism, is self-damning. Despite Hencke feigning disapproval of Nazism, his speech exposes his basic racist attitudes. He tries to silently dismiss the Jew's Holocaust accusations, but when pressed relentlessly, he argues that "History was a Force-in-Itself, like Evolution" (*S*, 109), thereby absolving Germans of their crimes—but he shows no such inclination for the bombing of Cologne in which his sister perished. Typical of Ozick's historicity is her allusion to Marranos and its implied link to the Inquisition—the medieval, church-orchestrated genocidal program against Spanish Jewry—as a model for Nazi racial genocide. Similarly, Hencke's rationalizations evoke revisionist historians' denial of the magnitude of German war crimes.

With the holocaustal mood established through confrontational dialogue, allusive references to concentration camp and swastikas, Ozick enriches the holocaustal timbre of the scene with background music that is a vibrant reminder of Nazi duplicity. She describes the reception music in military diction: "a saxophone opened fire" (*S*, 120). "The saxophone machine-gunned him in the small intestine" (*S*, 121), a vivid reminder of the Nazi effort to lure Jews calmly into the gas chambers at Auschwitz with an orchestra playing at the "shower" entrance. Thus, as the Germans camouflaged murder with art, Ozick emphasizes the travesty by reversing it, superimposing the language of war on art.

In a brilliantly conceived final scene, Ozick transports the reader from the literal to the metaphysical implications of her subject. The music's cacophony is interrupted by "[A] scream . . . out of the bowl of apples (*S*, 121), as Genevieve discovers that her purse has been stolen. Hencke's response to the distant scream is a dreamlike, ecstatic image of Genevieve hurt, "In his heart she bled, she bled" (*S*, 121). He appears to will her pain and associates that wish with her Jewish identity—the Jew in exile, "He listened to her voice—such a coarse voice. . . . A Biblical yell, as by the waters of Babylon" (*S*, 121).

When he understands that Genevieve's purse has been stolen, he insists that his son reimburse Genevieve for her airline ticket home, an allusion to reparations payments. For a brief interval the antagonists speak to each other civilly, and Hencke confides to Genevieve that he is deceiving his son about being in New York solely for his show; the single suitcase he carries is a ruse and four other cases are in his hotel room as he prepares for a trip to Europe. Still distracted by the loss of her purse, Genevieve asks in a detached manner whether he is going to Germany. Hencke becomes defensive and emphatically denies that possibility, claiming "Not Germany. . . . Now only Scandinavia is the way I remember Germany from boyhood. Germany isn't the same. All factories, chimneys" (*S*, 126). His reference to manufacturing heralds an abrupt end to the civility, because for the Jew the word *chimneys* triggers images of death camp chimneys: "Don't speak to me about German chimneys. . . . I know what kind of smoke came out of those damn German chimneys" (*S*, 126). Hencke feels the full brunt of her attack and believes her merciless, but he masks his discomfort with continued talk of his paternal deception: "I have the one bag only to mislead. I confess it, purposely to mislead" (*S*, 126). Hencke's use of the word *confess* after her accusation, coupled with the references to the death factories of Germany, lead naturally to an interpretation of the suitcase deception as an evocation of the Nazis' deception of the Jews—telling them to bring one suitcase to the deportation trains for "resettlement" trips, when they were, in fact, bound for Auschwitz, Chelmno, Treblinka, and Buchenwald. As Genevieve indicates belief that he is not really traveling to Sweden, he responds to her implicit charges of Nazi sympathy by referring directly to the Holocaust victims and making one more pathetic attempt to separate himself from Nazi criminality: "Not Germany, Sweden. The Swedes were innocent in the war, they saved so many Jews. I swear it, not Germany. It was the truckman, I swear it" (*S*, 126). Through Hencke's fusion of Germany's guilt and the theft of Genevieve's purse and his insistence on his innocence in both counts, he is in fact confessing his guilt. Hencke's final Nazi characteristic is to place blame elsewhere—like Nazis who absolve themselves of crimes by using the lame excuse of following orders. So threatened is Hencke at this point that he insists on opening his suitcase for inspection, despite the fact that no one has accused him of the theft. Ironically he acts guilty for a crime he did not commit, but fails to acknowledge his real crimes.

All the Holocaust imagery of the final scene unites, revealing metaphoric implications of the names of the antagonists, the scream from the apple bowl, and Hencke's revelation of his deceptions; the final scene becomes a parodic inversion of the Garden of Eden expulsion. Genevieve (Eve) has lured Gottfried not into sin but into a symbolic admission of guilt. The story's last line is a mad midrash of Wieselian proportion, allowing the apparent fool to utter the truth. Commenting on the theft, the artist's wife, herself a victim of deception, sums up the evening's importance, "Tonight what criminals we've harbored unawares!" (*S*, 127).

In the next collection, *Bloodshed and Three Novellas,* Ozick returns to a major theme of her fiction and essays, Jewish identity. Two of the stories, "A Mercenary" (1974) and "Bloodshed" (1970), unite the topics of Jewish identity and Holocaust history. These novellas present diametrically opposed resolutions to the Jewish encounter with anti-Semitism and its most horrendous manifestation. In the first instance, the pathology of self-hatred is explored as a by-product of Nazi victimization. In the latter, strengthened self-definition and communal association emerge as viable reactions to the Holocaust.

In "A Mercenary" Ozick uses a series of surprising inversions and identity transformations to explore cultural identity. She juxtaposes the careers of two men who fabricate identities they think will make them diplomatically and socially acceptable as representatives of an African nation in the United Nations. Morris Ngambe is a native-born, Oxford-educated black man who is uncomfortable in New York, "a city of Jews." Stanislav Lushinski is a Polish Jew who survived the Nazis and the Russians and works as the P. M. (Paid Mouthpiece) for a small African country. Born into a European society that hated Jews, Lushinski tries to escape his heritage and is a patriot of a country where he lived for only fourteen months, twenty-seven years prior to the timeframe of the novella.

"A Mercenary" appropriately begins with an epigraph from

Joseph Goebbels: "Today we are all expressionists—men who want
to make the world outside themselves take the form of their life
within themselves."[26] The tragic Nazi success of that statement is
manifested in the mercenary's repression of his Jewishness. Living
for the first six years of his life under Polish anti-Semitism with
assimilated parents who took comfort in their blond Polish appearance, but despaired of their otherwise adored son's dark
"gypsy" look, he learns first-hand with the Nazi invasion of Poland
of the disadvantages of being Jewish. After paying Polish peasants
to care for their child until war's end, the Lushinskis try to escape
Poland but are discovered and shot. Modeled on Jerzy Kosinski's
Holocaust child-fugitive in *The Painted Bird*,[27] the helpless young
Lushinski is abandoned in the forest by the Poles who already have
their money and fear the consequences of German discovery.
Lushinski learns to think of himself as prey when the Poles regret
their earlier decision to send him away and decide instead to denounce him in anticipation that the Germans "might go easy on the
village, not come in and cart away all the grain without paying and
steal the milk" (*AM*, 28). In a series of violent episodes resembling
those of *The Painted Bird*, Ozick's protagonist reflects on the disadvantages of being Jewish as the peasants "baited and blistered and
beat and hunted him" (*AM*, 37) and finally hang him by his wrists
from the rafter of a shed where they detain him for the Germans.

"A Mercenary" is the portrait of a survivor who is

> so deeply frightened that he must hide forever. He survived through
> hiding and he can't imagine living the rest of his life without hiding.
> He hides so supremely, so grotesquely, that he becomes an African
> when he is not an African, but a white man and a Jew.[28]

Ozick's interest lies in dramatizing an extreme case of cultural displacement, one in which the victim forgets his own history and
culture and assumes the character traits formulated by his
oppressor.

Lushinski is the Jew described by Jean Paul Sartre in *Jew and
Anti-Semite*, the person whose identity is defined by the other who
bears him ill will, rather than the Jew whose self-image is based on
religion, culture, literature, and language. Lushinski's self-image is
so distorted by the anti-Semite's lens that he executes his diplomatic
role by turning his back on the Israeli ambassador in the United
Nations General Assembly. The role of United Nations diplomat is

a bitterly ironic twist to the Jew's character in light of the United Nations anti-Semitic bias, which is disguised as anti-Zionism.[29] In this international anti-Semitic forum, Lushinski seeks the unctuous role of safe and appreciated Jew—that is, the Jew who betrays his Jewishness.

Although a self-hating Jew, Lushinski insists his lover—whom "they spoke of as a German countess—her last name was prededed by a 'von'—but . . . seemed altogether American" (*AM*, 21)—read *The Destruction,* a documentary account of the suffering Jews endured in the Holocaust. He resents her reading Holocaust fiction because "Romance blurs" (*AM*, 38). He wants her to read the data, the tables and figures, the train schedules, the numbers of trains. Despite weeping over the camps and Eli Wiesel's memoir, *Night,* she challenges the significance of the Holocaust and, echoing Hencke's sentiments, expresses irritation with those who posit its extraordinary magnitude. Quibbling with the book's title, *The Destruction,* she charges hyperbole, "It isn't as if the whole world were wiped out. . . . It wasn't *mankind,* after all, it was only one population. The Jews aren't the whole world, they aren't mankind are they?" (*AM*, 38–39). Although Lushinski outwardly plays the Jew-hater, this response triggers a Jewish cord in him and he attacks her position, which is often used in the contemporary political arena to deny the particularity of Jewish suffering. "Whenever people remember mankind, . . . they don't fail to omit the Jews" (*AM*, 39). Lushinski contests her universalist argument denying the particularity of Jewish Holocaust loss by subsuming it with other national losses, such as the Russian denial of the magnitude and specificity of Jewish losses at Babi Yar by commemorating only Russian deaths. In an article entitled "All the World Wants the Jews Dead," published during the same year as "A Mercenary," Ozick deals with the Yom Kippur War and the Arab effort to effect an Israeli Holocaust. Part of her exposition of Arab, Russian, and Nazi anti-Jewish sentiment hinges on the distinctions between Jewish particularity and universalism.

> The Final Solution, some insist, was "a crime against all mankind," not "just against Jews: as if to say that if this were declared a crime only against Jews, then it could not be considered a crime against mankind.

> When the world wants Jews to start dying again, it begins to speak of mankind.[30]

Ozick's mysterious tale of submerged and emerging identities concludes with a letter to Lushinski from Morris Ngambe, who has been shedding his European veneer for his real African identity. The letter is about a Japanese terrorist jailed in Israel for complicity in a Tel Aviv airport massacre. Because the terrorist has been hospitalized for an incomplete self-circumcision, we learn that the man who wanted to destroy Israel has, since his incarceration, studied Hebrew and the Bible; he has become fascinated by the Jewish religion, grown a beard and earlocks, and has in fact tried to become the covenanted Jew he sought to destroy—similar to Bernard Malamud's Frank Alpine who began as an anti-Semite and by novel's end converts to Judaism. Whereas Lushinski's self-hate was reinforced by Holocaust incarceration, the Japanese terrorist learned respect for the people he hated and in an ironic reversal chooses to make himself one of them. Paradoxically, Lushinski, who describes himself as free because he is a Holocaust survivor and can suffer nothing worse than the Holocaust, is still bound to "the old terror in the Polish woods" (*AM,* 51) caught in another's limiting definition, while the jailed Japanese has redefined his own identity.

The drama of Jewish identity in "Bloodshed" is based not on antipathy between the Jewish world and its antitheses, as in most Ozick fiction, but on distinctions within the Jewish world. The protagonist is a professing Jew who will, in the course of a visit to a Hasidic community of Holocaust survivors and their children, shed his intolerance for Jews of another ilk and learn the meaning of *ahavat Yisroel* (love of Israel) preparatory to spiritual renewal. Bleilip is a *"mitnagid, . . . purist, skeptic, enemy of fresh revelation, enemy of the hasidim!"*[31] Like many Jewish critics of the Hasidic movement, especially its eighteenth and nineteenth-century versions, Bleilip objects vehemently to the mediatory role and personal authority of Hasidic charismatic leaders. Assimilated with only a smattering of Jewish education, Bleilip disdains Hasidic style and is afraid the faithful will try to impose their ways on him. Apprehensive that his host will "thrust a headcovering on him" (*B,* 50), or insist he utter the blessings associated with food, Blielip's diction reflects his combative attitude. Like the evil child of the Passover *Haggadah* who separates himself from the Jewish people by using the second person reference rather than the collective singular, Bleilip speaks disdainfully, addressing his hosts as "you people." Using speech calculated to insult, he asks his cousin how she likes her *shtetl,* implying a parochial, narrow existence, cut off from the world she enjoyed prior to adopting Hasidism. Despite his contempt for the sect, Bleilip has nevertheless come to this community of pious Jews, "lured by their constituents. Refugees, survivors. He supposed they had a certain knowledge the unscathed could not guess at (*B,* 59). Like the secular Jews who seek Sammler's advice and judgment because of his Holocaust experience, Bleilip also attributes special awareness to the Holocaust survivors.

Ozick turns the tale on the *mitnagid* and makes him the subject of a Hasidic exemplum; she employs traditional Hasidic characters and formulations and enchants the reader with a tale within a tale, whose commentary reveals the theological and human implications of the Holocaust. The skeptic, a potential suicide, will in the course of the tale, and despite himself, capitulate to a *rebbe* whose spiritual leadership he initially fails to recognize.

The first portion of the narrative not only establishes Bleilip's hostility toward the Hasidim but also structurally evokes the audience pattern of the great Hasidic courts of Europe. When a petitioner came to consult the spiritual leader, he first encountered the *gabai,* whose interview preceded the *zaddik's,* much as a nurse takes a patient's history prior to the physician's examination. Yussel, his cousin's husband, gives Bleilip a tour of the community, proudly guiding him past the *yeshivot,* patiently showing him a life devoted to prayer and sacred study while leading him to the spiritual master. Whereas Bleilip's cousin attacked him for judging the Hasidim fanatics and primitives, her husband believes that Bleilip is searching for something and attributes his arrogance to insecurity. He has come to the community precisely because he wants to see martyrs. This insight disturbs Bleilip who would prefer less accuracy and more nostalgia. No sooner does the guide inform the skeptic that Hasidim are not saints and that their *rebbe* is no performer of miracles, than the blood rushes to Bleilip's head in ecstasy that they have a *rebbe.*

The preliminary interview over, Bleilip is invited to evening prayers and an opportunity to hear the rebbe. Ill at ease because of his inferior knowledge of Hebrew and ritual, he searches the congregants for the *rebbe* and fails to recognize him. In the postprayer study session, Bleilip feels like a boy in a man's world; his alienation and limitation is evidenced in disparaging thoughts about the language of their discussion. "The noise of Yiddish in his ear enfeebled him still more, . . . it was not an everyday language with him, except to make cracks with, jokes, gags" (*B*, 62).

At the center of the story is the *rebbe's* explication of the ancient *Yom Kippur* Temple rite of *azazel*, whereby one goat is dedicated to God and another, a scapegoat, symbolic of the community's sin, is driven into the wilderness.

> This pair of identical goats was meant to remind the Jew of Jacob and Esau, who were identical twins. The goat that was dedicated to God was meant to recall Jacob who lived a life of godliness. The other goat, which was sent into the wilderness, represented Esau, who lived far away from his people. The casting of lots to decide which of the two goats was to be offered up to God and which allowed to go off into the desert was to remind the Jew of his opportunity to make his own choice between the two opposing ways of life represented by the two animals.[32]

When Bleilip confesses that he once killed a pigeon, the *rebbe* calls him Esau and rebukes him for denying his despair and atheism, "Esau! Beast! Lion!" In response to the rebbe's shocked reaction—"Then you are as bloody as anyone' (*B*, 72)—linking Bleilip with Esau the hunter, Bleilip introduces a self-incriminating parallel distancing himself from fellow Jews by referring to the Hasidim as "You Believers."

Through the *rebbe's* questioning of whether the goat atoned and the high priest purified and hallowed the people and his own answer, Ozick adapts the ancient *azazel* interpretation to Bleilip's spiritual crisis and the novella's Holocaust theme. "Only the Most High can cleanse, only we ourselves can atone" (*B*, 65) is the response of a people who reject the possibility of vicarious atonement for sin. Advising Bleilip that "despair must be earned," the *rebbe* demands he surrender the guns he is carrying and lectures him on the danger of his deceptive toy gun. Juxtaposing the ancient people's symbolic transference of sin to the scapegoat and modern man's more brutal transfer of the world's ills to the Jews, and consequential slaughter in European Zyklon-B shower room, the *rebbe* articulates the post-Holocaust despair that has brought Bleilip to the brink of suicide:

> You may say those were other days, the rituals are obsolete, we are purer now, better, we do not sprinkle blood so readily. But in truth you would not say so, you would not lie. For animals we in our day

substitute men. . . . we were in villages, they drove us into camps, we
were in trains, they drove us into showers of poison. (*B*, 65–66)

The *rebbe,* subject of a Buchenwald freezing experiment—which
cost him several fingers because he was immersed only up to his
elbows, unlike others who were wholly immersed in blocks of ice
and perished—reveals that the despairing vision he has just enunciated is, in fact, Bleilip's perception.

The *rebbe* is a believer in "influences," "turnings." He believes
that "a man can be turned from folly, error, wrong choices. From
misery, evil, private rage. From a mistaken life" (*B*, 69) The sur-
vivor-*rebbe* is prepared to lead Bleilip to redemption. Yom Kippur
atonement, leading to redemption, turns on the Hebrew word
*t'shuva* (meaning return), for sin is seen as turning away from God
and repentance as turning toward God. Recognizing that Bleilip
suffers the modern crisis of faith, the *rebbe* helps him to understand
that the believer and doubter are often one, "That it is characteristic of believers sometimes not to believe. And it is characteristic
of unbelievers sometimes to believe" (*B*, 72). When Bleilip assures
the *rebbe* that he intends harm to no one, the *rebbe* invites him to
*ma'ariv* prayer in Jacob's tent. In acknowledging his belief in God
despite Holocaust history, the skeptic does become what he had
earlier told the *rebbe* he was "a Jew. Like yourselves. One of you" (*B*,
67). At the time Bleilip uttered the statement, it was a lie and the
*rebbe* exposed it. The Hasidim believe in God and have joy and trust
despite their Holocaust experience. Bleilip had none of this faith
and joy. Having come in scorn, Bleilip concludes his visit in praise.
He is grateful that Yussel brought him to the *rebbe* and the story
concludes with his recognition that he had unconsciously come "for
a glimpse of the effect of the rebbe. Of influences" (*B*, 72). "The
day . . . felt full of miracles"(*B*, 72). Like I. B. Singer's penitent,
Bleilip finds spiritual return through a guide who is both survivor
and Hasid. In awe of their experience, Bleilip learned from the
survivor-Hasidim who knew the bloodshed of Buchenwald and the
deception of the toy showers of Auschwitz. Esau has indeed returned to Jacob's tent through the spiritual guidance of a wonder-
working Hasidic rebbe.

The title story of Ozick's 1982 collection, *Levitation: Five Fictions,* recalls the Holocaust themes and character constructs of *Trust*
and "Bloodshed." The husband and wife of "Levitation," Jim and
Lucy Feingold, are novelists who share a professional understand-

ing but are divided on the significance of historic Jewish martyrology and the Holocaust. Literary descendants of Enoch and
Allegra Vand, the Feingolds are partners in a mixed marriage, and
they differ sharply about the relevance of Jewish history. Like
"Bloodshed," "Levitation" treats the encounter of the survivor-
mentor and the American Holocaust initiate and the theme of
Holocaust sensitivity as touchstones of authentic Jewish identity.

The first section of "Levitation" introduces a seemingly close
marriage between two authors who admit their secondary literary
status, but "fancied themselves in love with what they called 'imagination'."[33] The wife reads only *Emma* and writes poetry. The husband reads widely, but concentrates on Jewish history, writes about
medieval persecutions of European Jewry, and works on a novel
about Menachem ben Zerach, a fourteenth-century survivor of a
Spanish massacre in which his relatives were among six thousand
Jews killed in one day. Since Jim's passion for Jewish history does
not extend to Jewish women, he married Lucy, a Protestant minis-
ter's daughter who developed an affinity for biblical Hebrews at
age twelve. Inspired by a psalm, she "hoped to marry out of her
tradition" (*L,* 3). With marriage, Lucy, who had regarded herself as
"an ancient Hebrew," converted to Judaism. She proves an inauthentic Jew since she remains unmoved by the most cataclysmic event
of twentieth-century Jewish history and appears impatient with
Jews whose Holocaust consciousness is strong.

The second part of the novella dramatizes the polarity of
husband and wife, destroying the façade of intimacy established in
the first section. At a party the Feingolds give to boost their status
in the literary community, they taste the disappointment of rejection when the luminaries they hoped would attend do not come.
Lucy's social disappointment increasingly manifests itself as disenchantment with her husband's Jewish interests and Jewish associates. Already uncomfortable with the presence of a seminary
friend of Feingold who examined her for her conversion, Lucy
evidences annoyance with Feingold's theological discussion that
evolves into a treatise on atrocities:

> to wit, the crime of the French nobleman Draconet, a proud
> Crusader, who in the spring of the year 1247 arrested all the Jews of
> the province of Vienne, castrated the men and tore off the breasts of
> the women; some he did not mutilate, and only cut in two. (*L,* 11)

The evening proceeds with Feingold's litany of anti-Jewish persecutions and his ironic observation that the same year witnessed the creation of the Magna Carta and the dishonor of Jews forced to wear the badge of shame, "and that less than a century afterward all the Jews were driven out of England, even families who had been settled there seven or eight generations" (*L*, 12). Later in the evening Lucy finds her husband regaling the guests with blood-libel slanders and the consequent massacres.

Like I. B. Singer telling the history of European anti-Semitism as so many prologues to the Holocaust, so Ozick prepares for her Holocaust narrative with a history lesson outlining centuries of persecution. Unmoved, Lucy listens to Feingold speak of the 1279 slaughter of Jews in London who were maliciously accused of crucifying a Christian child, of a mob burning a synagogue in Munich in 1285 on the same pretext, of three centuries of libel and murder. Among the Jewish guests listening to Feingold, the voice of a refugee emerges urging him to approach the modern period.

The husband's sympathy for medieval Jewish martyrs and the wife's disinterest sets the scene for their contrasting Holocaust reactions. As the refugee describes the sadism, horror, and mass murders he witnessed, the Jews in the room are intensely pained. Lucy, who has romantic notions about biblical Hebrews, has no particular empathy for post-Jesus Jews. Since her compassion is limited to Christian suffering, she superimposes a Christian framework on his testimony:

> She visualized a hillside with multitudes of crosses, and bodies dropping down from big bloody nails. Every Jew was Jesus. That was the only way Lucy could get hold of it: otherwise it was only a movie. She had seen all the movies, the truth was she could feel nothing. That same bulldozer shoveling those same sticks of skeletons, that same little boy in a cap with twisted mouth and his hands in the air—if there had been a camera at the Crucifixion Christianity would collapse, no one would ever feel anything about it. Cruelty came out of the imagination, and had to be witnessed by the imagination. (*L*, 14)

Here is a woman who is bored by exposure to history. Her romantic imaging of a crucifixion is more real to her and more painful than the documented murder of millions. Holocaust sensitivity, Ozick seems to say, remains a major gap between Christian and

Jew. Feingold is tormented by the memory of all the martyred Jews, whereas Lucy feels nothing for Jewish victims who have typically been persecuted by Christians. As she listens to the report of a mass killing, families falling like sacks into a ravine, limbs all tangled, she feels nothing. "Lucy decides it is possible to become jaded by atrocity. She is bored by the shootings, and the gas and the camps, she is not ashamed to admit this. They are as tiresome as prayer" (*L,* 19). Juxtaposed to Lucy's unashamed disinterest is the heightened engagement her husband and the Jews feel in response to the refugee's story. Soon "the room was levitating," the Jews floating upward like the figures of a Chagall painting, leaving behind the Holocaust-insensitive Christian. Lucy remains earthbound, admitting that only the suffering of Jesus could move her. As the Jews share their ecstasy, from which Lucy feels excluded, she experiences an epiphanal vision realizing her true affinity with the pagan nature gods and the essentially irreconcilible distinctions between Jewish and non-Jewish values, and she gives herself to nature. Just as Allegra was bored by Vand's Holocaust documentation and obsession, so Lucy finds her husband unreasonable. And just as Allegra's insensitivity grows in proportion to Vand's dedication to Jewish interests, so Lucy's imagination fails to respond Jewishly as Feingold's allegiance to Jewish history increases. Lucy converted to Judaism, but does not share the deep connections to Jewish history of other Jews. At heart Lucy remains a Christian, intensely feeling the torturous death one Jew suffered two thousand years ago, but oblivious to the prolonged torture that six million Jews suffered in her own time. Ozick joins the Yiddish poets who extend the traditional metaphor of all Jews being present at Sinai to receive the Torah to all Jews being present at Auschwitz to inhale the gas.

*The Cannibal Galaxy* (1983) explores varieties of responses by survivors more thoroughly than the earlier works. In contrast to the minor roles her survivors had enacted as witnesses and mentors to assimilated American Jews, survivors are now the novel's principal characters. Their ordeals and their Holocaust-wrought transformations take center stage in the fiction's universe. Ozick's second novel, *The Cannibal Galaxy,* shares *Trust's* realistic style and European setting and *Bloodshed's* theme of the Holocaust as a formative, philosophic, and practical influence. This work adds a new level of discourse to American Holocaust literature by elaborately interweaving crosscultural sacred and secular literary sources to enhance the Holocaust tapestry with significant new insight.

The tension between Greek and Hebrew values at the heart of Ozick's work prior to 1983 finds a measure of resolution in *The Cannibal Galaxy* and in "Bialik's Hint," an essay written the same year. Each intimates the possibility of fusing the central traditions of Western civilization. While the novel addresses the values of cultural synthesis, it does not evade the enduring difficulties inherent in the fusion of contradictory value systems. Reminiscent of other Ozick protagonists caught between the lures of Western and Jewish cultures, Joseph Brill devotes his career to teaching both traditions. Born of Russian-Jewish parents who have immigrated to France, the Sorbonne-educated, naturalized American is a fifty-eight-year-old bachelor administering a Jewish day school in an unidentified middle American city. A melancholic "counter of losses,"[34] Brill entered education with Talmudic zeal, recognizing that *"the world rests on the breath of the children in the schoolhouses"* (*CG*, 4). After three decades of school administration, he despairs. "He saw himself in the middle of an ashen America, heading a school of middling reputation (though he pretended it was better than that), beleaguered by middling parents and their middling offspring" (*CG*, 5–6). Once a visionary, he is now earthbound. A pre-Holocaust astronomy student, he is a post-Holocaust contemplator of the mundane. He now believes "in the prevalence of ash" (*CG*, 5). To explain Brill's transformation, Ozick composes a contrapuntal structure of interlocking European and American sequences dramatizing the effects of historic upheaval in Brill's life.

Shifting the narrative in alternate flashbacks and flashforwards from postwar America to prewar and Holocaust-era France, Ozick relates the survivor's attitudes to his formative Holocaust experiences and establishes sociological and historic authenticity for the novel's French-Jewish ambiance. In a beautifully written two-part European flashback, Ozick portrays the sensitive young French Jew adjusting to European cultural and religious anti-Semitism. Unlike the old-French Jewish community, essentially Alsatian, proud of its native status, Brill's family was part of a large influx of Russian-Jewish emigrés from czarist oppression who settled in the ghettolike, working class neighborhoods of Paris, who labored diligently and won the rewards that French freedom of opportunity offered. In the prelapsarian period of the family's

French sojourn, Joseph enjoyed the vitality of his immigrant neighborhood, where one heard the Yiddish dialects of Kiev and Minsk and Lithuania and where he freely studied Jewish and French culture. Like his biblical namesake, Joseph is violently separated from his family and betrayed by an unrequited lover. Joseph's family came to France to find freedom from persecution and economic opportunity and was betrayed by Vichy France. Just as the biblical Jews immigrated to Egypt seeking a better life and stayed long enough to be enslaved, the Brills' escaped from Russian oppression to French liberation, only to be enslaved again. France has become Joseph's Egypt.

Joseph's education in French anti-Semitism is initiated in childhood, advanced in the university, and completed in the Holocaust. The child of immigrants who fled the church-inspired, government-sponsored anti-Semitic pogroms of Russia, Joseph is moved upon reading a French street name commemorating the lost Temple of Jerusalem and concludes that French non-Jews have "reverence for the pieties and principles of an ancient people" (*CG*, 7). A French schoolmate laughs at Joseph's innocent joy over the Vielle du Temple street name and tells him of the collective punishment Jews suffered in a local blood-libel charge against Jonathan le Juif, who "having stolen the Host, the Body of God, boiled it and stabbed it; then the Host wept tears and cried for mercy in the Virgin's own voice" (*CG*, 7). For the child reared in traditional Catholic anti-Semitism, the mere record of punishment of the Jews is evidence of their guilt. So much for the distinctions between Russian-Orthodox-inspired pogroms and French-Catholic-inspired massacres. Astounded by Joseph's ignorance of the crusader knights, Jean-Lucas furthers the young Jew's education by lending him medieval romances. The crusader romance is the first of the novel's many richly suggestive literary references commenting directly or indirectly on Holocaust themes. In addition to authenticating the cultural index of the Jean-Joseph association, the allusion to the crusaders evokes historic Christian anti-Semitism and its specious gloss in romantic fiction, perhaps invoked by Ozick to parallel revisionists and obscurantist Holocaust whitewashes in our time. Sharing the Hebraic-Greek schizophrenia of Ozick's artists and intellectuals, Joseph is torn by the dichotomy of Jewish and Western values. Inextricably drawn to the beauty of literature and the visual arts, he is nonetheless guilty knowing that his parents consider these idolatrous and vain. When the young

Joseph overcomes his guilt and trepidation and visits an art museum, a "pagan hall . . . an offense to modesty and a scandal of piety" (*CG,* 9), he imagines himself like Jonathan le Juif, a violator of the sacred gentile world. Joseph's adoration of French literature grows, and he becomes ever more aware of his impure French: "The University inspired him to alter his diction . . . it was humiliating to be an immigrant's child and fill one' mouth with the wrong noise" (*CG,* 12) As with his early attraction to the visual arts, so Brill's pleasure with French literature causes him discomfort because his parents disparage secular literature as frivolous and void of moral significance.

Joseph's education in French anti-Semitism parallels his education in French literature and art. A university associate and literary aesthete, Claude mocks Joseph's parochialism and introduces him to the Louvre and the English homosexual literary society, admonishing him to "relinquish your stupid Israelite squeamishness" (*CG,* 13). When Joseph rejects Claude's homosexual advances, Claude responds not only as a rejected suitor but as a vicious anti-Semite, addressing the Jew as Dreyfus and encouraging their mutual friends to follow suit. Typical of Ozick's historicity, the Vichy government's betrayal of the Jews during the Holocaust is depicted as a continuation of French anti-Semitism displayed in the French Army's collusion prosecuting, sentencing, and imprisoning Captain Dreyfus on Devil's Island on a false charge of espionage. Although Dreyfus was eventually cleared after twelve years of unwarranted suffering and fierce controversy that divided France and involved widespread anti-Semitism,[35] it is clear from Claude's tone that the anti-Semitic fervor of the anti-Dreyfusards remains intact decades after the trials. Claude's insult, coinciding with Joseph's discovery of Voltaire's anti-Semitic writing,[36] sharpen the young Jew's feelings of exclusion from French society. Forty years after the Holocaust, when Brill thinks of the crucial experiences of his youth, he associates the destructive memories with anti-Semitism, "From the hour that Claude named him Dreyfus he had never been happy at the University" (*CG,* 107). Conversely, he associates happy memories with his Jewish experiences, "When he dipped his head down into the great tractates of Gemara; . . . when Rabbi Pult praised him" (*CG,* 107), and when he prayed deeply and with full devotion.

Ozick's juxtaposition of the Jean-Lucas/Claude antagonisms and the blood-libel/Dreyfus calumnies illustrates the correlation between historic French-Catholic anti-Semitism and the Vichy government's betrayal of immigrant and native French Jews. Just as Jean-Lucus heralds Claude, so the crude, religiously motivated blood-libel attack foreshadows the more sophisticated, politically motivated injustice to Dreyfus. The Dreyfus Affair reflected post-Enlightenment anti-Semitism in a nation that prides itself on liberty, equality, and fraternity, a modern Western nation that had granted Jews full citizenship. The Dreyfus riots, viewed by many as harbingers of German anti-Semitism, foreshadowed the abuses of National Socialism in Germany and Austria as well as the Vichy government's collaboration in Germany's implementation of the Final Solution. Thematically and structurally, these passages on French anti-Semitism foreshadow the narrative's Holocaust sequence.

The polar side of young Brill's education, under the direction of Rabbi Pult, is Hebraic. The rabbi's acerbic commentary on Voltaire and the French Enlightenment goes to the heart of unacknowledged borrowing from Jewish law by the Europeans: "the founder and purveyor of *fraternité* and *liberté* catching up eighteen centuries late . . . to the postulates and civilities of Hillel and Akiva" (*CG*, 7). Accustomed as Brill is becoming to Christian anti-Semitism, he remains puzzled by Voltaire's atheist anti-Semitism. Rabbi Pult's satiric analysis—"The Enlightenment engendered a new slogan: There is no God and the Jews killed him" (*CG*, 16)—addresses a common malady of secular anti-Semitism: residual prejudice resulting from the endemic anti-Semitism of the Christian tradition within which even secularists like Voltaire were nurtured. "Sick of human adventure," Joseph sacrifices the study of French literature and philosophy to pursue a degree in astronomy, a discipline he believes will be free from subjective prejudice. Vichy France soon disabuses the idealist. Joseph's major professor, whose brother-in-law is a Vichy official, dismisses him from the astronomy program.

Ozick separates the prelapsarian period from the Holocaust section of her novel with a brief look at the post-war American period in order to dramatize the impact of the Holocaust on the survivor. Just as Norma Rosen's Holocaust-sensitized women think in Holocaust diction and imagery in the Vietnam era, so Joseph Brill remains scarred by his losses, pained by an architectural configuration of buildings that evoke Holocaust memories "of a freight train on the move: three hapless boxcars" (*CG*, 17). Illustrative of the prolonged mental suffering of survivors, the boxcar vision provides a dramatic transition to the book's short Holocaust sequence. School architecture, like Proust's madeleine, sparks Brill's remembrance of times past: "boxcars rolling eastward had taken away Joseph Brill's mother, father, his brothers, . . . his little sisters, . . . his baby sister . . . and released their souls into an ash field" (*CG*, 17).

Ozick makes the transition from American school to Holocaust school through a reference to the dual curriculum, an educational theory Brill had developed while hiding in a French convent-school during the war. Brill hid first under the protection of four nuns in a convent school's subcellar and later like Singer's Herman Broder, in a hayloft under guard of an antagonistic farm couple. The nuns believed that "with God's help, he would end by turning Christian" (*CG*, 19), and to that end they fed and sustained him. They provided him with a dead priest's library, and he spent his confinement reading a rich store of novels, poetry, and drama, theology, and philosophy rather than listening to radio "rantings against the Jews." "If they did not hunt him out, if he lived, if the war ended and he survived it" (*CG*, 26), Brill vowed to teach, to establish a school devoted to a dual curriculum of European and Judaic cultures. Unlike James Joyce's young boy in "Araby" who remains essentially uninfluenced by the departed Irish priest's unusual library, Joseph Brill is intellectually moved by the deceased French priest's books and marginal notations. Most important to the young fugitive are the works of Edmond Fleg, an accomplished poet, playwright, and essayist, whose development led him from agnosticism to Judaism. Edmond Fleg was an important figure in "a new element of symbiosis" that emerged with the unprecedented return of prominent French-Jewish intellectuals to Jewish cultural interests in the aftermath of the Dreyfus affair.[37] Fleg wrote prolifically on Jewish themes in books such as *Ecoute Israel, Pourquoi, je suis Juif (Why I am a Jew)*, and *L'Enfant prophete (The Boy Prophet)* read by Brill during his confinement. The last title, a "romanticized account of a boy estranged from Judaism and rejected by Christian society describes how the child glimpses through the gloom of the Church a Jesus who is at once victim and persecutor, and how he at last seeks to revive his old faith through messianic expectation."[38] The first book is part of a four-part verse cycle spanning the whole of Jewish history up to the era of the reborn Jewish state, and the second book is an influential analysis of the young agnostic's spiritual return to Judaism and his recognition that French genius owes much to Israel. Ozick's reference to Fleg's *Pourquoi je suis Juif* unites and strengthens several strands addressing Hebraic influence on Western thought and vividly demonstrates parallels among Edmond Fleg, Rabbi Pult, and the unnamed priest. The priest's marginal note on Fleg's position echoes Pult's observation on the debt the French Enlightenment owes to Hillel and Akiva.

> The Israelitish divinely unifying impulse and the Israelitish ethical inspiration are the foundations of our French genius. Edmond Fleg brings together all his visions and sacrifices none. He harmonizes the rosette of the Legion d'Honneur in his lapel with the frontlets of the Covenant on his brow. (*CG*, 22)

Ozick refers by title to Fleg's *Ma Palestine (The Land of Promise)*, an essay in which Fleg "demonstrates the compatability of French patriotism and Western culture with Jewish values."[39] Inspired by Fleg's effort, "to establish a reconciliation between Paris and Palestine, between being a Frenchman deeply attached to Western culture and a Jew deeply convinced of Israel's mission to perfect the unity of man through the unity of God,"[40] Brill decides to establish a school devoted to a dual curriculum of European and Judaic cultures. From his consideration of the priest's meditations on Fleg's writings, Brill turns quite naturally to his own thoughts; he worries about his teacher, Rabbi Pult, whose parting gift, the treatise *Ta'anit*, Brill also keeps throughout his captivity and survival. Discussion of these libraries—the priest's safeguarded library and rabbi's burnt library—forms the narrative transition from Holocaust reflection to dramatic presentation.

A book burning evoking the *Kristallnacht* bonfires initiates the novel's Holocaust action. While Joseph is helping the rabbi pack his belongings to escape, French police surround the neighborhood. Joseph runs home to find "everything tranquil, everything in its place—the bread on the table, half sliced, . . . Everyone was gone" (*CG*, 23). In the twenty minutes it takes to return to Rabbi Pult's home, the scene has been transformed. The shop window below the rabbi's apartment is smashed, the rabbi's door is torn off its hinges, "all the books they had packed into suitcases the night before, dumped out. Some were burned to ash, some only charred. The invaders had made a bonfire" (*CG*, 24). The diction Ozick uses to describe the book burning—"ruin," "flame," "animal hides"—paints a visual image of *Kristallnacht,* and in her graphic presentation of the roundup of French Jews for the eastern death camps, she foreshadows the human carnage of the Final Solution.

> In the streets creatures like centaurs scuttled and scrabbled, flinging their rods, sticks, rocks, poles. Metamorphosis and shock. Fangs, hoofs, strange hairiness. Uniforms everywhere. Noble French youth. Gendarmes, patrolmen, baby-faced students from the police school, hundreds of cross-strapped blue shirts and armbands. The gutters of Paris a wilderness. (*CG,* 24)

In this powerfully evocative passage, Ozick uses overtones of myth to invoke a heritage of violence, comparing the Vichy French government with barbarians of a primitive era and suggesting the horror associated with the Paris roundup of 28,000 Jews for transport to the notorious French camp, Drancy, and ultimately to the death centers. Comparison of Ozick's account with those of historians reveals her attention to the details and ferocity of the July 1942 roundup that the historians' accounts lack:

> On the morning of 16 July, 9,000 French police went into action. The force was composed of gendarmes, gardes mobile, baliffs, detectives, patrolmen, and even students from the police school. Three or four hundred followers of Doriot's also turned out to help, wearing blue shirts, cross-straps, and armbands bearing the initials "PPF."[41]

Authorial and protagonist voices inform readers of the fate of Joseph's family, and in Ozick's documentary summation, we learn the fate of French Jewry. Fleeing through the streets of Paris, Joseph prays for the safety of three older sisters who had left home a month earlier and talked of escaping to Sweden. He worries about his family's welfare in Poland, but quickly recognizes the deception of "resettlement." In fact, Brill's family has been herded with thousands of other French Jews to the sports stadium where they will live for a week

> penned up in that spot without food or toilets, in the open, body jammed into body, under a devouring sun, squatting or sprawling among the faint and dying, day after day, . . . until the terrifying and delusive relief of the coming of the trucks—and then the loading and unloading, the brutal hiatus in Drancy, and again the loading

into boxcars, and again the unloading, the undressing, the run to the
false showers. (*CG*, 25)

In this short paragraph, Ozick summarizes the pitiful fate of many
French Jews, especially those of foreign origin like the Brills, who
in 1942 were rounded up and left to rot for five days in the summer sun with no food, water, or sanitary facilities at the Velodrome
d'Hiver. Ironically, the Velodrome d'Hiver was also the site of
numerous anti-Semitic demonstrations in 1937 and the site of the
temporary internment of Jewish refugees of German nationality in
1939 and, of foreign women in 1940.[42] Ozick counterpoints the
roundup drama with a *Ta'anit* tractate infusing the contemporary
scene with biblical import, adding layer upon layer of meaning.
The *Ta'anit* tractate is a rich composite of calamitous and restorative events in Jewish history: natural and man-made disasters
and examples of divine response to Jewish petition and efforts to
cope with tragedy. The passage Ozick fashions for Joseph's reading
is a composite of the *Mishnah* text regarding calamitous and restorative events in Jewish history, a passage filled with purgative and
restorative rain imagery, and a Talmudic narrative addressing the
nobility of a dedicated Jewish teacher winning his student to learning. Thus, in the span of two pages, Ozick carries the reader from
brutality of the Paris roundup to the *Mishnah Ta'anit*, legends of
miracles and the redemption of Jerusalem, in a book Joseph had
refrained from reading to protect its "sweet letters" from the offensive cellar smell. Euphoric over his Fleg-inspired decision to
establish a dual curriculum school, Joseph turns to study the *Ta'anit*
tractate that had been given to Rabbi Pult by his teacher.[43]

The idyllic security of Joseph's cellar sanctuary is lost when a
talkative girl, herself a fugitive, Renee Le Fevre, nee Levin, discovers Brill. Although Ozick did not intend it, she ironically be-
stows the name of a leading clerical anti-Semite on the Jewish
fugitive,[44] a third-generation Catholic with one Jewish grandparent. Fearful that Renee will inadvertently reveal Joseph's secret,
the nuns transfer him to a farm where conditions are considerably
more primitive and where he is in danger from his guardians as
well as the Nazis. During the transport to the farm, Joseph sees the
trappings of Nazism in the Paris streets, the "buntings, swastikas,"
and he worries again whether his sisters are alive or "dead, dying,
captive, escaped?"(*CG*, 32).

For the remainder of the war, Joseph is confined to the hayloft, but occasionally manages to sneak out to the barn floor where he flits

> like a barn wraith, beginning to believe himself invisible. . . . He ate what he found or filched. . . . He felt himself more and more turning into a beast of the field. . . . He had lost his will to read. . . . He lay passively for hours, testing the edge of his winter hunger. (*CG*, 32–33)

Greater deprivation and the primitive living conditions of the barn, more closely resemble the concentrationary conditions his fellow Jews are suffering than the relative luxury of his convent cellar.

With war's end, Brill discovers that most of his family has been killed and that only his sisters who escaped to Sweden survived. Although Brill regains his place at the university, he no longer feels equal to a career in astronomy and withdraws to make a new life in America. Fleeing his Egypt with the sponsorship of an American benefactress, Brill establishes the Edmond Fleg Primary School and institutes the dual curriculum, "the blessed renewing days of his invention" (*CG*, 56). At the opening of the novel, he has served as principal of the school for three decades and even his admirers believe his brilliance has dimmed and the dual curriculum has ossified. Part of Brill's Holocaust tragedy is that he does not live up to the inspirational motto, *ad astra,* that he adopted from Fleg. *Pourquoi je suis Juif* concludes with the line, "We are God's people, for we will it so, the stars our quest and truth our watchword still."[45] This is the philosophy Brill hoped to instill in his school through the dual curriculum. It is not until novel's end and Ozick's redemptive theme is sounded that Brill achieves full recognition of the *ad astra* motto.

Like other survivors Brill dwells on the void in his life, "loss after loss. Many and much. He counted over the many" (*CG*, 41). The Holocaust remains in Brill's thoughts, most persistently as the thief of his family, especially "his bleating baby sister Ruth in the Vel d'Hiv, Pult breathing gas in Poland" (*CG*, 57). On the rare occasions when Brill tries to articulate his Holocaust thoughts, he either meets an unreceptive audience or is trapped in his own limitations. Brill's young American wife is uninterested in the Holocaust. He never told her about his hayloft confinement,

> she knew he had been hidden in the war, but she was young, and all that seemed as distant to her as Attila the Hun. She was uninterested

in his recountings of old desolations. The nuns especially (he had
undertaken to tell about the convent) bored her. (*CG*, 115–116)

Neither is the Holocaust taught at his school. Even when Brill
returns to Europe to the site of his losses, his surviving sisters are
reluctant to talk with him about the family, and he recognizes the
distinction between them: "he had returned to Egypt only to count
his losses. . . . his sisters counted blessings" (*CG*, 133). Despite the
use of the word *blessing*, the sisters are neither religious nor spiritual; their blessings are adequate material possessions, blessings to
those who knew extreme deprivation. Brill dwells on the lost members of the family, *maman* and *papa*, Michelle, Leah-Louise, Rabbi
Pult, Ruth; their names have been a refrain through the novel, and
the list has always included the name of Brill's beloved teacher with
the family members. The trauma of Brill's Holocaust loss is far
greater than his grief for his sisters who died of natural causes forty
years after the war. When Brill realizes that his sister is too ex-
hausted, too "far from history," to talk with him or listen to his talk
about the war years, he makes a pilgrimage to the convent where
he was given sanctuary. To his dismay, the young nun who greets
him at the gate shows no interest in his story about the shelter and
the preservation he found in the convent. The bitter memories of
his French Egypt erupt, flooding his consciousness: Claude calling
him Dreyfus; his withdrawal from astronomy. When he retraces his
way to the museum that gave him such joy in his youth, he wanders
about the rooms unfulfilled and notes the absence of Hebrew art.
In this place, "it was as if there had never been a Hebrew people,
no Abraham, or Joseph, or Moses. Not a trace of holy Israel" (*CG*,
131). Evidence of denial is everywhere.

Brill wished to fuse Jewish moral genius and European
culture, the music of King David and Victor Hugo, the metaphysics
of Maimonides and Pascal, the poetry of Bialik and Keats. His
pedagogical ambition fails. Principal, faculty, and students are unequal to the rigor and grandeur of the project. After years of being
worn down by argumentative parents, mediocre teachers, and lackluster students, Brill abandons the standard of excellence he hoped
to achieve, but retains the dual curriculum and *ad astra* as the
school motto. In middle America, Brill's learning became stale.
Although memory serves him, when he reels off lines from
Baudelaire, Rimbaud, Mallarme, and Verlaine, he no longer reads
them seriously. Survival guilt compounds his feelings of failure:

> For this the nuns had kept him alive. For this the hayloft had kept
> him alive. . . . He feared for himself, because he was of the elect, the
> fearful elect who are swallowed up by a look at immortality. . . . He
> saw how he had not died in the middle of the time of dying. (*CG*, 45)

Into Brill's mundane American existence bursts a new spirit,
an imaginative linguistic logician, an intellectual luminary who has
come to enroll her daughter in the Edmond Fleg School. Brill is
intoxicated by the possibility of a prodigy, but Hester Lilt's
daughter, Beulah, is a dismal disappointment to her teachers and
principal. Judging the daughter ordinary, Brill is enthralled by the
mother's brilliance, fascinated and intimidated by Hester Lilt's intellectual superiority and, at the same time, offended by her indifference to his educational system and her disinterest in her daughter's needs. The remainder of the novel draws its tension from the
antagonism between Brill and Lilt—Brill's failure to realize his
intellectual promise juxtaposed to Lilt's many brilliant accomplishments.

Because Hester is a Holocaust survivor, Brill presumes compatability between them, "there ought to have been the bond of the
ravished" (*CG*, 82–83). During their first interview, Brill concludes
that he and Hester are "members of the same broken band, behind
whose dumb-show certain knowings pace and pitch" (*CG*, 49). Lilt
prefers silence about her Holocaust experiences, and she responds
minimally to Brill's probing, admitting to leaving middle Europe
on a children's transport, but resisting talk about what she endured. He becomes obsessed with Hester and wonders whether her
name signifies moral darkness, comparing it to the Hebrew word
for night "leyl," or Lilith, the night demon. Since by this point in
Brill's career we recognize that his ideas are often wrongheaded,
Ozick's intention might be that we dismiss Brill's hint and concentrate instead on the meaning of Lilt's first name. One interpretation relates her name directly to the Hebrew word *hester* as used in
the Hebrew expression describing the hiding of the face of God,
*hester panim*, and thus is relevant to the character's reluctance to
reveal her Holocaust history, "because more important than the
Jewish reality she represents is the mystery to be interpreted."[46]
Another possibility lies in a Mishnahic interpretation, especially in
light of the similarity to the destruction-restoration motifs of the
Book of Esther, which follows the *Ta'anit* tractate in the *Mishnah*.
Hester, a variant of Esther, offers appropriate correspondencies to

the novel's contexts. Esther's legendary reputation for sound judgment and self control is more analogous to Hester's persona than is the demon seductress of Brill's musings. Queen Esther, honored for her prudence, intelligence, and deep insight, qualities that scholar Lilt shares, is credited with saving Persian Jewry from annihilation.[47] Similarly, the celestial association of the name Esther complements Hester's role as dramatic foil to the lapsed astronomer.

Despite maintaining silence about her Holocaust history, Hester Lilt is significant among Ozick's survivor-mentors; she is transmitter of Jewish ideas, moral vision, and teaching style in the novel. The novelist associates Lilt with the teaching styles of the fictional moral register Rabbi Pult and the celebrated *midrashic* teacher Rabbi Akiva. Brill reads her books, attends her lectures, and occasionally is the beneficiary of her advice, including the recommendation that he read Andre Neher's *The Exile of the Word* and be guided by Neher's interpretation of Edmond Fleg. Presumably Lilt counsels him to read Neher because, having spent the war years with his father and brother in intensive Jewish studies, Neher emerged as an important thinker and spiritual leader of French intellectuals, preaching ideals of reasoned belief and of respect for tradition."[48] In *The Exile of the Word,* Neher commends the post-Holocaust writing of Edmond Fleg, *Nous de l'Esperance* [*We the Hopeful*]. This work posits "religious faith strengthened by testing and revolt, . . . whose last images seem to melt away into God,"[49] and turns "on the axis of hope."[50] Whereas Brill has read only Fleg's pre-Holocaust publications, Neher insists on Fleg's postwar advocacy of "Jewish hope gathered in the depths of disaster: the hope of Jeremiah who in the chaotic disintegration of the world suddenly saw a Genesis rise up, but a Genesis not at the beginning but at the end— . . . a 'return toward the Future,'"[51] and thereby supports Ozick's post-Holocaust vision. Furthermore, the Frenchman's allusion to the Jeremiah redemptive prophecy parallels Lilt's reference to the Zechariah restoration prophecy. Unlike Brill, who stopped too soon, with a limited vision of a diasporan dual curriculum, Edmond Fleg and André Neher look to a brighter Jewish future. The French-Jewish intellectuals rose from Holocaust ash to contribute to the Jewish redemptive vision. They both championed cultural symbiosis, affirming French and Hebrew culture, and both became ardent Zionists. Whereas Brill capitulated too soon, Hester Lilt, through association with Fleg's and Neher's postwar visions

and achievements on behalf of Jewish scholarship and their commitment to the State of Israel, contributes to a more vital Jewish
renaissance. Ozick joins Saul Bellow, I. B. Singer, Arthur Cohen,
and Chaim Potok in the creative interpretation of the Jewish moral
vision and a dedication to Jewish sources as an authentic Jewish
response to the Holocaust.

In a pivotal chapter of the novel, Lilt emerges as the shining
star of the *midrashic* method, thus associating her with a traditional
Jewish pedagogical style—with Neher's narrative style in *The Exile
of the Word* and with Ozick's celebrated "liturgical literature." With
Brill in attendance, Lilt delivers a university lecture using the
*midrashic* vehicle to make her point, uniting three apparently disparate stories, one from traditional Jewish lore about Rabbi Akiva,
one from the natural sciences, and one dealing with outer space.
Lilt relates the legend of Rabbi Akiva's enigmatic laughter in response to the destruction of the Temple, a story of the entelechy of
the bee, and a story of cannibal galaxies—"megalosaurian colonies
of primordial gases that devour smaller brother galaxies" (*CG*, 69).
The cannibal galaxies *midrash* illuminates the novel's title and the
Holocaust subject in its metaphoric allusion to the Nazi effort to
make Jewry an extinct race. The Akiva narrative comments on
every major aspect of the novel, from its cultural to its historic
indices. Akiva and his rabbinic companions respond to the destruction of the Temple and the desecration of its site in disparate ways.
Rabbi Gamliel, Rabbi Elazar, and Rabbi Joshua weep, but Rabbi
Akiva laughs and explains that the fruition of Uriah's prophecy of
the destruction of Jerusalem simply leads to the eventual fruition
of Zechariah's restoration prophecy, "Yet again shall the streets of
Jerusalem be filled with boys and girls playing" (*CG*, 68). Hester
cites Akiva's position as admirable pedagogy. She values Akiva's
instruction: "To predict not from the first text, but from the second. Not from the earliest evidence, but from the latest. . . . The
hoax is when the pedagogue stops too soon. To stop at Uriah
without the expectation of Zechariah is to stop too soon" (*CG*, 68).
The Akiva *midrash* confirms the Fleg-Neher theses and Lilt's advice
to Brill. Thus, Hester Lilt, secular linguistic logician, relies on the
*midrashic* method to illumine a spiritual leader's restorative response to destruction as a viable model for Jews to rebuild Judaism
and the people by renewing the tradition in expectation of
Zechariah's prophecy. Lilt's Akiva *midrash* provides a structural link
with Rabbi Pult's teaching of steadfast Judaism. In contrast to

Brill's mediocre effort to synthesize Western and Jewish cultures, Lilt perceives the significance of holy distinctions. She understands the lessons of Akiva and Pult concerning the necessity of honoring those distinctions; that is, it is only as a distinctive religious entity that Jews have survived efforts to transform or destroy them. Lilt uses the *midrashic* method to span the abyss between faith and despair, to make sense of tragic history. Although Lilt is silent about her Holocaust experience, her commitment to the Jewish way of learning refutes Nazism by confirming Judaism and the prophetic statements of Jewish revival. Furthermore, her silence adheres to Andre Neher's idea of a variant of holy silence, "silence weighty with meaning,"[52] the type of silence associated with Eli Wiesel's Holocaust writing, "the theological reality of the silence of God."[53]

Like Singer, Ozick relates the Holocaust to other catastrophes of Jewish history, but unlike Singer, who catalogues other examples, she achieves this historic recognition through allusion to the sacred texts of the Jews. She achieves both structural and thematic balance and unity by counterpointing Brill's *Ta'anit* with the implicit reference to Esther and the explicit prophecies of destruction and restoration in the Akiva *midrash*. Central to the tension between Brill and Lilt is their interpretation of theological and philosophic texts. We have seen how Joseph's dreams of astronomy and a superior dual-cultural educational system are overshadowed by the star-scholar whose thinking and methods are derivative of and openly identified with traditional Jewish sources, which she applies to Western philosphy and literature. A similar reliance on traditional Jewish materials distinguishes Ozick's literary treatment of the Holocaust. Although she continues her well-established conventions of documentary reference and delineation of survivor trauma, in this work she gives greater attention to the relationship of the Holocaust and other tragedies in Jewish history through allusive referents. Joseph Brill's perception of France as his Egypt parallels how the Jews were first welcomed to Egypt, but were later enslaved, as French Jews enjoyed citizenship, but were then betrayed by French Nazi collaboration. Similarly, Hester's allusive name evokes the period of Persian anti-Jewish oppression and Haman's aborted attempt to annihilate Persian Jewry. Through these historic and textual allusions, Ozick joins Singer, Wiesel, and Cohen in relating the *Shoah* to the history of Jewish martyrology, adding Hitler's name to Jewry's list of historic enemies, Pharaoh and Haman. Beyond biblical parallels, Ozick's introduction of the literature of the *Mishnah* serves doubly as character referent and Holocaust commentary.[54] The tractate *Ta'anit*, Rabbi Pult's gift to Joseph, and the Book of Esther are in adjacent positions in the second order of the *Mishnah*, the section *Mo'ed* dealing with festivals. Both tractates deal with calamities that befell the Jewish people, both contain prospects for restoration, and both explore the significance of prayer and fasting as vehicles of petition for divine deliverance from the enemies of the Jews. Historicity is evident in Ozick's *Ta'anit* selection. Brill's reading during his Holocaust confinement deals, in addition to fasts associated with drought, with the fast on *Tisha B'av*, commemorating such national tragedies as the destruction of both temples, the loss of national independence, and the expulsion from Spain. In contrast with this fast that commemorates historic tragedy, the fast of Esther commemorates the queen's fast before she petitioned the king on behalf of her people and also the three-day fast undertaken by the Jews of Persia for deliverance from Haman's plot. The *Ta'anit* and the Book of Esther also share restorative references, deliverances of life-giving rain, and royal deliverance. Whereas the *Ta'anit*/Esther parallels operate allusively in the novel, with Ozick depending on her readers' knowledge of the *Mishnah* to make these connections, she explicitly associates Hester Lilt's use of the destruction-deliverance theme with the traditional Akiva *midrash*. Hester's narration of Akiva's response to the destruction of the Temple and Zechariah's prophecy of restoration may be interpreted as Lilt's (and Ozick's) Holocaust *midrash*. As Zechariah foretells the restoration of Jews to Jerusalem, Ozick celebrates the triumphant restoration of Jerusalem as the capital of the modern State of Israel. Lilt's offering of the Akiva *midrash* is entirely consistent with her advice to Brill that he read Andre Neher's interpretation of Edmond Fleg, since both writers echo Zechariah's prophecy and each progresses from Holocaust despair to redemptive joy in the State of Israel. Similarly, Lilt's vision and Ozick's visions parallel restorative philosophies of Emil Fackenheim and Eliezer Berkovits. Lilt's use of the *midrashic* method dramatically confirms the vibrancy of Jewish learning and denies Hitler's dream of an extinct Jewish culture.

Although Ozick's 1983 fiction continues to explore and enlarge the Holocaust themes and strategies of the earlier works, she devotes more attention to dramatic contrasts of character survival and Holocaust response, often structuring the characters as dramatic survivor foils. She juxtaposes Hester's relative Holocaust silence with Brill's articulation of Holocaust suffering, and Brill's affinity for survivors coupled with his reluctance to discuss the Holocaust with nonwitnesses. Hester Lilt's silence is holy, "weighty with meaning." Brill's debilitation contrasts with Hester's restoration in creative work that benefits from and contributes to traditional Jewish scholarship and a dynamic Jewish civilization. It is only at the end of the novel—"in what is not to be construed as an ironic twist of fate but as a deliberate act of "penitence"—we learn that Joseph Brill has accomplished *t'shuva*"[55] (redemption) by determining that the school's *ad astra* award is to be given to the graduate with the most creative potential regardless of class standing. For Ozick the inner spirit of *The Cannibal Galaxy* is "the idea of redemptiveness. The opposite of Greek fate; that if we can change ourselves, we can change our character, and if we can change our character, we can change what appears to be our 'fate.' That destiny is not fixed. That Torah's gift is *t'shuva*."[56]

Cynthia Ozick dedicated *The Messiah of Stockholm*, her most recent Holocaust novel, to Philip Roth. She was introduced to the fiction of Bruno Schulz when Roth, in his capacity as editor of the Penguin "Writers From the Other Europe" series, invited her to review Schulz's *Street of Crocodiles*. Her 1977 essay characterized the Polish-Jewish writer as "one of the most original literary imaginations in modern Europe"[57] and she devoted as much attention to his Holocaust biography as she did to his fiction. The review is an elegy lamenting the loss of a great writer, "gunned down by a Jew-hunting contingent of SS men in the streets of an insignificant provincial town in eastern Galicia"[58] During a 1984 visit to Stockholm, Ozick heard a tale about the appearance of Bruno Schulz's manuscript for a novel entitled *The Messiah*. The report proved false, but Ozick remained intrigued and it served as the genesis of *The Messiah of Stockholm*.[59] What she thought would be a two week effort to complete a short story became a two year labor to complete a novel that took "many wrong turns."[60] The story of the discovery of a literary giant's lost manuscript offered her opportunity for powerful drama. Inclusion of Schulz's Holocaust history elevates the work to a level beyond fashionable self-reflexive fiction, advancing it to the liturgical sphere. Although Ozick's characters do not speak of their Jewish origins and have Swedish names, they are Jews obsessed with the era during which efforts were made to bring an end to Jewish history. Ozick asserts that she did not intend to write a Holocaust novel when she undertook *The Messiah of Stockholm* (1987).[61] Yet given her passion for "imaginary libraries,"[62] her devotion to Jewish history, and the circumstances of Bruno Schulz's murder, it is understandable that the novel is about the lost work of a writer murdered in the Holocaust.

Echoes from the literary heritage abound in *The Messiah of Stockholm*. The voice of Bruno Schulz reverberates throughout the work, as well as whispers from Henry James, I. B. Singer, Philip Roth, and Ozick herself. James's *The Aspern Papers* is echoed in the exploration of the moral implications of exploiting people to acquire a writer's private papers. Singer's *The Manuscript*—about a courageous woman who returns to occupied Warsaw to retrieve her lover's novel that was left behind as they fled the Nazi invasion—is echoed in the vengeful destruction of the *Messiah* manuscript. Roth's "The Prague Orgy"—the story of a Jewish writer's murder by a Nazi commandant's Gestapo antagonist as revenge for the commandant's earlier murder of a Jew the Gestapo officer was protecting—resonates throughout Ozick's book. The hint of literary usurpation by the writer of Bruno Schulz's murder intricately links "The Prague Orgy" with the *Messiah of Stockholm's* repeated speculation and ambivalence regarding the authenticity of the fictional *Messiah* manuscript. Another connection between the works of Ozick and Roth is Roth's literary resurrection of Franz Kafka and Anne Frank. In "Looking at Kafka," Roth transforms Kafka into a Newark Hebrew School teacher, and in *The Ghost Writer,* the guilt-ridden Nathan Zuckerman imagines a redemptive marriage to a surviving Anne Frank. Parallels exist between the quests of the Roth and Ozick protagonists for spiritual literary fathers; the ghost of Kafka informs Roth's sensibility, as the spirit of Schulz inspires the language and imagery of Ozick's *Messiah*. Finally, Ozick's own "Rosa," and the efforts of its protagonist to restore life that the Nazis have snuffed out, echo in the novel. Just as Rosa creates an imagined life for the infant she lost in the concentration camp, Lars Andemening invents a father to substitute for the parent lost to the Nazis. Ozick stated she was astonished to realize at work's end that all four of her major characters are impostors and attributed it to her fascination with imaginary fictions, imaginary writers, and imaginary libraries.[63] Although her imposter constructions lend intrigue to the literary mystery, they compromise the Holocaust import of the work.

The protagonist of *The Messiah of Stockholm,* Lars Andemen-

ing, shares with many of Ozick's characters an exemplary dedication to literature. He is the Monday literary critic for *Morgontorn,* a
Swedish daily newspaper, and brings to his column a particular
interest in the work of central and eastern European writers. Orphaned in World War II, Lars is a Polish refugee raised by a
Swedish foster family whose obsession with his foreign identity
causes him to leave their home. Twice divorced and estranged
from his daughter whom an embittered wife keeps from him, Lars
invents his own family. He "had an orphan's terrifying freedom to
choose. . . . his own history."[64] As one who gives all his power and
energy to reading, a man "chained to the alphabet, in thrall to
sentences and paragraphs" (*M,* 15), Andemening chooses to be the
son of Bruno Schulz, whose voice and vision he believes he shares.
Obsessed with Bruno Schulz, Lars learns Polish in order to read his
works in the original. Ozick conveys Lars's obsession through diction that evokes the Pole's Kafkaesque style in *The Street of Crocodiles:* "On account of his father Lars shrank himself. He felt he
resembled his father: all the tales were about men shrinking more
and more into the phantasmagoria of the mind" (*M,* 5). As his
Swedish name suggests, Andemening looks inward to his soul,
mind, and conscience to find meaning. He assumes the perspective
of his father's murdered eye and adopts the highly emblematic
name, Lazarus Baruch—a fusion of Jewish and Christian names
signifying a blessed resurrection to be manifested in the quest for
the *Messiah* manuscript. Lars seeks to give the *Messiah* new life.

Ozick implies the grievous Holocaust loss to civilization of its
Jewish writers, artists, philosophers, theologians, scientists, and
scholars in Lars Andemening's Swedish Academy revery:

> His father belonged there, in the ventricles of the Academy; . . . His
> father had been born to be of that pantheon—with Selma Lagerlöf
> and Knut Hamsun; with Camus and Pasternak. Shaw, Mann, Piran-
> dello. Faulkner, Yeats, Bellow, Singer, Canetti! Maeterlinck and
> Tagore. The long, long stupendous list of Winners. His father, if he
> had lived, would have won the great Prize—it was self-evident. He
> was of the magisterial company. (*M,* 16)

Mrs. Eklund, cocollector of Schulziana, recognizes Andemening's
passion for those lost in the Holocaust:

> He took on everyone's loss; everyone's foolish grief. Foolish because
> unstinting. Rescue was the only thought he kept in his head—he was

arrogant about it, he was steady, he wanted to salvage every scrap of paper all over Europe. Europe's savior! His head was full of Europe—all those obscure languages in all those shadowy places where there had been all those shootings—in the streets, in the forests. He had attached himself to the leavings of tyranny, tragedy, confusion. (*M*, 98)

Just as the protagonist of *The Cannibal Galaxy* is moved to make his survival meaningful through the influence of the French-Jewish writer Edmond Fleg, so Lars discovers his meaning in the liberating vision of a novelist.

Unlike Ozick's other protagonists who express definite feelings about being Jews, Lars "never thinks of himself as being Jewish and scarcely understands that his fantasy of being Schulz's son is a quest for a lost identity, for belonging to a people."[65] Although he has no connection to Judaism, Lars identifies with the Holocaust history of the Jews. With

A handful of other infants [he] had been spirited away from Poland—Poland overrun by the Nazis—and squeezed into Stockholm under the same auspices: a merciful Swedish traveler well-paid, under the protection of her government's neutrality. (*M*, 24)

When the elderly relative who cared for him, herself a poor, frightened refugee, passed away, he was sent to the household of foster parents who grudgingly raised him, despite the woman's dislike of "the looks of other nations, especially those more distant from the Arctic Circle then her own" (*M*, 24). Lars dwells, instead, on the details of his father's misfortune: "a murdered man, a man shot down in the streets over forty years ago, in Poland, while the son was still in the mother's womb. It was a thing he knew and kept buried" (*M*, 4).

In addition to the memory of Bruno Schulz, Ozick invokes that of Holocaust poet Nellie Sachs. As Lars walks to the bookshop that carries the Polish editions of his father's novels, he smells a burning in the winter air, a smell of something roasting: "O the chimneys. Quiet everywhere: here was the street where Nellie Sachs and her old mother had once lived. The poet's flat; the poet's windows. All moribund there" (*M*, 17). Minimizing mimetic recreation of the Holocaust universe in this book, Ozick evokes it indirectly through allusion to the graphic poetry of *O Chimneys*.

Through the narrative device of a confidante—a postwar

self-exiled German woman, Heidi Eklund, who is the proprietor of the bookshop catering to the international refugee community— Lars shares his feelings for Bruno Schulz and eventually shares his obsession for finding the *Messiah* manuscript. Heidi Eklund alternately plays Lar's Dopplegänger and foil, lending tension to the pilgrim's search for a spiritual father. Initially reluctant to accept his story about his relationship to Schulz, Eklund mocks him, explaining that half her clientele have fabricated their identities, claiming that they were famous professors, ambassadors, European nobility. She urges him to forget his quest, warning him to avoid dredging up the past, "nobody cares, old Nazi stories, you think anyone cares anymore?" (*M*, 25). But she eventually relents and agrees to find Lars a tutor. Becoming his "fellow collector" she retrieves letters and photographs of Schulz, but she is skeptical about recovering the lost manuscript. A German who spent the war years in close proximity to a concentration camp, Heidi Eklund entertains no illusions regarding the manuscript's safety. As tension mounts between the two, it becomes evident that the reviewer remains fascinated with the writer's work and Heidi with the biography, especially the manner of Schulz's death.

Reminiscent of Bellow's repetition of Sammler's fall into the mass grave, Ozick uses incremental repetition to tell the story of Schulz's death, each time adding more detail and intensity to the crime, making it the pivotal holocaustal scene of the novel. The first installment is brief and accounts for Eklund's agreement to help Lars.

> They shot him in the streets. Murdered. The underground got him false papers—in those times forgery was a sacrament. They had already found him a hiding place. But he wouldn't leave home. (*M*, 25)

In a passage fusing the surrealistic mode of Kafka, Schulz, and Kosinski, with the realistic documentary account of Nazi criminality she employed in *Trust* and the roundup scene of *The Cannibal Galaxy*, Ozick creates a Holocaust aura that Heidi Eklund remembers and Lars can only imagine through fiction.

> It was the shooting that drew her. The shooting; the murder. Shot in the streets! Lars suspected that Heidi cared more for his father's death than for his father's tales, where savagely crafty nouns and verbs were set on a crooked road to take on engorgements and

trasmogrifications: a bicycle ascends to the zodiac, rooms in houses are misplaced, wallpaper hisses, the calendar acquires a thirteenth month. Losses, metamorphoses, degradations. In one of the stories the father turns into a pincered crab; the mother boils it and serves it to the family on a dish. Heidi shouldered all that aside: it was the catastrophe of fact she wanted. Lar's father gunned down in the gutters of Drohobycz along with two hundred and thirty other Jews. A Thursday in 1942, as it happened: the nineteenth of November. Lars's father was bringing home a loaf of bread. (M, 32–33)

In this superbly crafted passage, Ozick draws upon her own review of *Street of Crocodiles,* evoking Schulz's diction and tone, and juxtaposes it with mimetic realism to convey the fragmentation and disruption the Holocaust wrought in the lives of ordinary people. The section is characteristic of Ozick's sustained invocation of the ghost of Bruno Schulz to preside over her manuscript. From the obvious newspaper office banter in which the secretaries are called "crocodiles," to the more subtle incorporation of the tone and imagery of Schulz's prose, the Polish Jew's voice haunts Ozick's *Messiah.*

As the cocollectors study scraps of Schulz's publications, private letters, photographs—materials Ozick received from Philip Roth and Lucjan Dobroszycki[66]—his romantic liaisons, family relations, and short trips away from the village to Warsaw, Lvov, and Paris, they reconstruct the novelist's Drohobycz life. Drawing again on her review of *The Street of Crocodiles* and some autobiograhical detail, Ozick simultaneously imagines the impact of Drohobycz on Schulz's writing and the Nazi desolation of his real and fictional community:

> The hasidim of the neighborhood—gone. Lars's father's father's shop—a drygoods business—gone. Nothing left; not a ribbon, not a thimble. Between Drohobycz and Lar's father there had occurred a mutual digestion. Street by street, house by house, shop by shop, Lars's father had swallowed Drohobycz whole; Drohobycz was now inside every tale. And Drohobycz had swallowed Lars's father also: a drab salary, a job he despised, a band of relatives to support—paralyzed, stuck, how was it possible to leave? Lars's father was a gargoyle on the flank of Drohobycz, a mole on its innermost sinew. (*M,* 35)

Just as Ozick's Rosa Lublin imagined an adult life for her daughter who died as an infant in a concentration camp,[67] so Lars and Heidi speculate, calculate, puzzle, and probe Schulz's history in an effort to give substance to ash. They trace every memoir, every note and letter about Schulz, even an unattributed American review that Lars retrieves from his colleague's wastebasket, an allusion to Ozick's own review for the *The New York Times*.[68] Tension between the two mounts as they vie with each other for greater understanding and capacity to locate material by or about Schulz. Ozick underscores the ferocity of the Lars-Heidi competition by structuring it as a verbal sparring match between German and Polish refugee antagonists, who spew accusations reminiscent of the repartee between the German and Jew in "The Suitcase."

> She punished him . . . by orphaning him; again and again she led him back to the shooting. She came to it by a dozen routes. Each time it was a surprise, an ambush. She could begin anywhere, and she still would smash Lars into Thursday, that Thursday, the Thursday of the shooting: Thursday the nineteenth of November. They discovered—Heidi's research—that the terrible day had a name among the Jews of Drohobycz: Black Thursday. And the hunt itself, the hunt for Jews in the streets was called "the wild action." No matter how wary Lars tried to be, Heidi was canny enough to catch him up in the wild action. Her snares were ingenious. Had Lars been mooning once more over the missing *Messiah*? It ended in the wild action; in a camp; in murder. It was known that Lar's father had handed over the manuscript—to whom? when?—for its preservation. What had become of *The Messiah* and its keeper? . . . Killed in the wild action, on Black Thursday? Or else deported, gassed. The corpse thrown into the oven; smoke up the chimney. And *The Messiah*? If its keeper was shot in the street, was *The Messiah* scattered loose in the gutter, to be chewed over by dogs, to rot in the urine of cats? Or was *The Messiah* shut up in an old dresser in a house in Drohobycz until this day? Or put out with the trash thirty-five years ago? Or left tangled between its keeper's coat and shoes in the mountain of coats and shoes behind a fence in the place of death? (*M*, 38–39)

This wrenching concentrationary evocation marshalls judgment against the Nazis for an unparalleled crime against Jews and Jewish civilization, and against all humanity for the loss it sustains when robbed of the Jewish consciousness. Discussion of Schulz's writing and his drawing always reverts to discussion of the shooting, each reference more intimidating, each more tragic as the artist-writer's life becomes more precious to the reader with growing knowledge of his genius. Then, when Ozick finally renders the murder most simply and directly, the brutal shock wounds the reader's sensibilities, and the reader is a paralyzed witness. On the day of the "wild action," Schulz had been given a temporary pass to leave the ghetto by a Gestapo officer who appreciated his art and, therefore protected him. "Lars's father was not shot randomly. An S.S. man recognized him as the Gestapo officer's Jew and gunned him down" (*M*, 39). Lars is so outraged by Heidi's ghoulish interest in the details of the murder rather than the missing manuscript that he accuses her of taking pleasure in the murder: "Maybe you like it that they shot him dead in the streets! Maybe you have affectionate feelings for the S.S.! Nostalgia for the Gestapo!" (*M*, 40). As they battle even more fiercely, Heidi shifts her argument from the moral aesthetic thesis of the *The Aspern Papers'* aggrieved Miss Juliana Bordereau, dismayed by a literary critic's crude exploitation, to the moral tone of a Holocaust-haunted survivor:

> She was all at once discomposed; . . . she was surrendering her own old landscape. . . . It was her life—the life before—she was giving him. . . . It appeared before him in the dark with the clarified simplicity of a charcoal drawing— . . . he traced her, there at the fence, heaving lumps over it to the shadows on the other side: as a young woman she had lived, she said in a village not far from one of those camps, and crept at night as often as she could without detection to throw food over the fence. It was like a cage in there, crammed with dying beasts. She heard their scratchings, clawings, mufflings, muzzlings; they were all shadows; they were afraid to come near. She heard them tear into the paper wrapping; then they stuffed the wrappings into their sleeves, into their shoes; she heard them gulp and chew. Occasionally they vomited, or exploded, with cries like muzzled beasts, into floods of diarrhoea; she made out all this in the blind night by the sound and the pestilential smell. Often she heard shooting; there was no sense to the shooting, she could not tell where or why. . . . And immediately after the war she . . . traveled north across the border, leaving Germany behind. She would never go back. (*M*, 42–43)

Heidi's intimate knowledge of camp hunger, disease, and hardships leads Lars to believe that she spent the war inside rather than outside the fence: "He supposed she was one of them, but hidden—one of the shadows inside" (*M*, 43). He concludes from her former name, Simon, that she was an escapee.

The mystery of Heidi's Holocaust experience is surpassed only by the appearance of a counter-claimant to the paternity of Bruno Schulz and *The Messiah* manuscript. A woman, calling herself Adela, the name of the maid in *Street of Crocodiles,* begs Lars to translate a manuscript she claims is Schulz's *Messiah.* Explaining that she is the illegitimate daughter of the art teacher and his young student-model who managed to flee the country, she claims to have retrieved the manuscript from a gentile, to whom it passed inadvertantly when the widow of its original peasant-protector remarried, sold her home, and moved to Warsaw. The new owner found the papers hidden under the house and initially assumed it was a Jewish will that would bring him a share in its fortune. Upon understanding his error, he decided that the frequent references to God in the manuscript suggested it was a blasphemous Jewish text and purged his house of it. Because his frugal wife stuffed wet shoes with the paper rather than discard it, Adela was able to recover the manuscript.

The passage Ozick creates for *The Messiah* sequence is essentially holocaustal and Schulzian in its Kafkaesque fantasy and language.

> No human beings remained in Drohobycz; only hundreds and hundreds of idols. A few were contemptibly crude and ill-constructed, but most represented the inspired toil of armies of ingenious artisans, and there was actually a handful of masterworks. . . . Since there were no human beings to worship them, there was some confusion about their purpose. The more diffident among them, accordingly, undertook to adore the more aggressive; but at first this was not very typical. Each was accustomed to being regarded as sublime, . . . but there were no longer any human beings anywhere in Dorohobycz. They had all gone on long, fatiguing journeys to other cities.
>
> More and more frequently there were sacrificial bonfires all over Dorhobycz. The taller and stronger idols began seizing the smaller and lesser idols and casting them into the flames. . . . Day and night honeyed swirls of hot incense and the acrid smoky smell of roasting metal circled over Dorhobycz. (*M*, 108–109)

The Jews of Drohobycz have been deported and replaced by Nazi idols who carry the "master race" ideology to its murderous conclusion, eventually destroying each other. Ozick complements the Schulzian phantasmagoria with an amended Drohobycz legend of Moishe the *tzaddik.* According to legend, Moishe was celebrated for his extraordinary charity to strangers.[69] Although Ozick resists the notion of Holocaust redemption, she invests the Messianic figure, who emerged from the cellar of the local synagogue, with a Noah-like bird that introduces a redemptive moment. It quenches the flames of the city, dissolves the idols, and leaves a town of total emptiness, "empty streets and empty shops and empty houses, and the flecks of sparks fading to ash" (*M*, 111). The redemptive moment is the legacy of Moishe; Jewish continuity will exist even after the desolation. Much as the Noah dove suggests biological survival, the *tzaddik's* bird implies the spiritual survival of Judaism after the false idols have been destroyed.

In language that foreshadows the fury of his reaction to Adela's manuscript: "Lars, looking with all his strength, felt his own ordinary pupil consumed by a conflagration in the socket. As if copulating with an angel whose wings were on fire" (*M*, 104). He is ecstatic at first to find the Adela of *Cinnamon Shops* and *Sanatorium* absent from *The Messiah*. Yet he has an uncomfortable recognition of her presence. As the Eklunds and Adela pressure Lars to introduce the manuscript through his column, he grows increasingly skeptical about its authenticity. The manuscript is composed so that it is possible to believe it is authentic and that it is Dr. Eklund's forgery. Readers must solve the mystery for themselves. Lars, however, concludes: "The *Messiah* went into the camps with its keeper. . . . The *Messiah* was burned up in those places. Behind those fences, in those ovens. It was burned" (*M*, 121). Convinced that the Eklunds are exploiting him and that the manuscript in Adela's jar is a forgery, Lars sets it afire—a terrible reminder of the burned Jews of Europe. Andemening's grief is no longer for the lost manuscript, but for the Jews destroyed in the Holocaust as represented by "the man in the long black coat, hurrying with the metal garter box squeezed under his arm, hurrying and hurrying toward the chimneys" (*M*, 144).

Unlike some contemporary writers who believe in "fiction that is self-referential, that what a story is about is the language that it is made out of,"[70] Ozick believes art should also be concerned with extraliterary values. Her work shares the historic sense, dense societal milieu, and the moral vision of the fiction of Saul Bellow and Bernard Malamud. Insistence on the relevance of the aesthetic to the exclusion of other values is idolatrous, creating "literature for its own sake, for its own maw: not for the sake of humanity."[71] Instead of "art for art's sake," Ozick writes "a redemptive literature, a literature that interprets and decodes the world, beaten out for the sake of humanity."[72] Her philosophy of redemptive literature is based on the traditional Jewish belief in *t'shuva,* the energy of creative renewal and turning, expressed in her fiction as "the notion that people and things are subject to willed alteration; . . . of turning away from, or turning toward; of deliverance; the sense that we act for ourselves rather than are acted upon; the sense that we are responsible."[73] Ozick's distinctive liturgical style makes her a major voice in contemporary American Jewish literature and contributes to her growing stature as a moral voice in world literature, a voice that reshapes the reader's thinking. As Ozick reminds us,

> Jacob did not become Israel until he fought all night and was not left whole. The angel, you remember, struck him in the sinew of his thigh. A Jewish literature is not a literature of wholeness; it too must have the angel's terrible mark left visibly in its sinew. A Jewish literature, like a Jewish life, should leave us with the sense of having been struck in the very meat of our being, altered by the blow.[74]

Ozick has achieved throughout the canon an authentic Jewish literature; that is, she has given a light to her readers, a literature that fuses Jewish and Western sensibilities of the sort Brill had dreamed of achieving and that Ozick commends in her recent manifesto, "Bialik's Hint": "this unimaginable fusion of what we are as the children of the Enlightenment, what we are as the children of Israel, and what we are to become when these learn to comingle."[75]

# CHAPTER EIGHT

*Eternal Faith, Eternal People: The Holocaust and*
*Redemption in Arthur A. Cohen's*
In the Days of Simon Stern

Arthur Cohen contends that all Jews, whether physically Holocaust-maimed or not, are psychological survivors. He maintains that the inheritors of Holocaust knowledge, whom he describes as "the generation that bears the scar without the wound,"[1] is obligated "to describe a meaning and wrest instruction from the historical."[2] In his theological interpretation of the Holocaust, Cohen writes:

> The *tremendum* is more than historical. It is an elaboration of the most terrible of Jewish fears—that the eternal people is not eternal, that the chosen people is rejected, that the Jewish people is mortal. If there is one incontestable article of the Jewish unconscious, it has been the mythos of indestructibility and the moral obligation of tenacity. Six years, nonetheless, nearly concluded three millennia of endurance. Is it a wonder that Jews should regard the *tremendum* as a caesural fissure that acquires with each decade a more and more profound metahistorical station as the counterevent of Jewish history, the source of its revisionist reconsideration and self-appraisal.[3]

279

His novel *In the Days of Simon Stern* (1973) is a rich, culturally textured, complex philosophic novel. It incorporates biblical legend, theological, Talmudic, and kabbalistic discourse, and dramatic enactment of the Messianic redemptive theory to "wrest instruction from the Holocaust." Praised by Cynthia Ozick for "a brilliance of Jewish insight and erudition to be found in no other novelist,"[4] Cohen masters the sacred, theological, and mystical texts of Judaism to present a mythic odyssey of the Messiah in the Holocaust era. The novel examines the European-Jewish experience from the perspective of refugees, survivors, and documentary studies. Like most American writers, Cohen does not focus directly on the concentrationary environment. Instead, he places the Holocaust within the context of Jewish persecution history in the mode of Andre Schwarz-Bart's *The Last of the Just,* chronicling specific examples from the Spanish Inquisition to Russian pogroms and incorporates testimony from public figures to supplement invented Holocaust histories for characters. More than any other American novel, *In the Days of Simon Stern* focuses on the Allied Powers abandonment of European Jewry and the failed efforts of the American Jewish leadership to bring the tragedy to public attention or to convince government officials of the need to counter its progress.

The novel's story line chronicles the efforts of Simon Stern, a Jew informed of a prophecy proclaiming him Messiah, with the task of rescuing and rehabilitating a group of death camp survivors. It spans a broad time frame, beginning in late nineteenth-century Poland with the prophetic announcement of the marriage of Simon's parents and their future son's messianic destiny, traverses the immigration to America, Simon's extraordinary rise to wealth and influence, and concludes in the postHolocaust period with Simon leaving the confines of the Lower East Side to extend his messianic influence. Significant among the novel's contributions to American Holocaust literature is its unique exploration of the

> bearing of the Holocaust upon the ancient Jewish idea that messianic redemption will come through historical catastrophe. Above all, it suggests a new future for American Jewish writing by opening the question of how to reorganize Judaism in the Diaspora after the European Diaspora has been destroyed.[5]

The novel is a compendium of Jewish religious thought, history, and sociology presented in various modes ranging from expository essay to tales within tales, dream-drama, sermons, letters, meditations, and commentaries—all bound by the scribe Nathan of Gaza, who presents himself as a hagiographer, chronicling the life and times of Simon Stern, messiah. Although allusively related to the seventeenth-century Nathan of Gaza, supporter of the self-proclaimed messiah, Sabbatai Zevi, Cohen never suggests that the modern day scribe is following a false prophet. Although Jewish literature is rich with stories of false messiahs, and Cohen's attribution of the name Nathan of Gaza to his messianic proclaimer raises doubts connected with the Sabbatain debacle, the fictional Nathan assures his readers that he has told the story of

> a real moment, never a psychological conceit. I think of Simon Stern as one correct moment. There are many times that need messiahs, but time skips over the moment, and the messiah, waiting ready in the shadows, does not appear. I have told you the story of a fulfilled moment. It is when God flees that we have tragedy. But it is as well the occasion when genius, risking the little that a man can share, holds back tragedy until God regains his courage and returns.[6]

A survivor of Auschwitz and Buchenwald, Nathan's authenticity stems from his Holocaust witness and his prewar career as Torahic scribe. Blinded in the Holocaust, he is endowed with moral insight.

Having developed Stern's messianic identity, Cohen introduces commonalities of traditional Christian and Nazi anti-Semitism in an internal narrative, "The Legend of the Last Jew on Earth," set in modern Spain at a time when the church has achieved "the conversion of all the world to the Catholic faith" (*D*, 119). The protagonist, Don Rafael Acosta, is technically Catholic, but is actually a secret Jew, the last survivor of many generations of the forced Conversos of Iberia. Structurally the legend foreshadows and introduces the novel's Holocaust sequence, and thematically it reveals both the similarities and distinctions between Roman Catholic and Nazi anti-Semitism. The section exemplifies Cohen's superb fusion of Jewish learning and artistic imagination.

The burden of "The Last Jew" is the inquisitional confrontation between Church and Jew. Although the specific time of Don Rafael's martyrdom is unspecified, it is evidently in the modern era since he is driven by automobile to the archbishop's residence, and the media is technically proficient in transmitting the news of the Jew's rejection of Catholicism. Acosta lives in the village of Gerona

on Calle de la Disputacion, which commemorates the medieval
debate between Acosta's kinsman Rabbi Moses ben Nachman and
the convert Pablo Christiani before King Alfonso and his court in
Barcelona.[7] Within the privacy of his home, Don Rafael lives as an
observant Jew honoring the pledge of the family patriarch, Solomon ben Juhudah, at the time of the massacres of 1391:

> to obey in continuity and to death the seven principles of the faith of
> Noah. Moreover and wherever possible, . . . the observance of the
> Sabbath and the Fasts of Av and the Day of Atonement. They were
> then commanded . . . to return in fulness and faith to all the remem-
> bered observances of the House of Israel, to remove from them-
> selves the deceiving guise of the Other Faith and to obey the God of
> their fathers until the time of the true Messiah—but this only when
> true service could be accomplished in peace, serenity, and without
> threat to life. (*D*, 120)

In Acosta lives the Golden Age of Spanish Jewry, its philosophers,
rabbis, poets, legists, mystics, and martyrs who flourished in Spain
and endured trials and torments at the hands of the Almohades
(Muslims who forced both their Jewish and Christian subjects to
convert to Islam) and the Inquisition. Cohen introduces the Holocaust theme and Acosta's own martyrdom by reference to the Jewish persecutions of the thirteenth- and fourteenth-century church,
"pogroms and desecrations, . . . the fiery preachers—converts and
Jew-haters all—who picked off, one by one, from the stock of
Israel the finest branches and grafted them forcibly to the num-
berless trees in the forest of Christendom" (*D*, 118). Even with the
introduction of religious toleration in Spain in 1868, "the spirit of
Spanish intolerance remained pure and uncorrupt" and the
Acostas continued to practice a secret Judaism. In the days of Don
Rafael's parents, Spaniards were no longer obliged by law to be
observant Catholics and the father began to educate himself and
his family more thoroughly in Jewish practices. Don Rafael gives a
priest and his parents hospitality when they are unable to start their
car. Taking offense at Acosta's Jewish observances, the priest reports him to the archbishop and thus begins his trouble—a modern
version of the Spanish Inquisition, including the public torment,
humiliation, and murder of the last Jew on earth who, with his
dying breath, repudiates Christianity and affirms loyalty to the God
of his ancestors. Don Rafael's final words at his Vatican exhibition

are clearly evocative of postHolocaust religious crises. Acosta argues, as do postHolocaust thinkers, for the continuation of Jews and Judaism despite God's silence in the face of destruction. This redemptive legend ends with the narrator's report of the regeneration of Jewry by Acosta followers, and it inspires Simon Stern to found the Society for the Rescue and Resurrection of the Jews.

Book One concludes with Simon Stern uncharacteristically venturing beyond the Lower East Side to hear an address by Chaim Weizmann in Madison Square Garden on March 1, 1943. As he approaches the Garden, Stern sees a woman carrying a placard with the grim admonition REMEMBER THE ST. LOUIS. In this fine visual prologue to the speech, Cohen alludes to the fate of 907 Jewish refugees from Germany aboard the *St. Louis* who were denied entry to any country, including the United States, and returned to Europe and so to death. It is at this meeting that Simon learns that the Nazis have already exterminated two million Jews and hears President Roosevelt's telegrammed assurance, "The Nazis will not succeed in exterminating their victims" (*D*, 153). More convincing are Weizmann's final words, "We're being destroyed by a conspiracy of silence" (*D*, 153).

Cohen introduces a dream following the Weizmann speech to chart Jewish frustration with American government disinterest in the Holocaust. Evoking the December 8, 1942,[8] meeting between a pleading Jewish leadership and an immune president; the dream suggests Roosevelt's physical paralysis is emblematic of the government's Holocaust passivity: "He sat becalmed by his power, sometimes forcing a crippled leg to shift its insensate weight, . . . lifting the leg like a dead member which clung to him but which he did not possess" (*D*, 154). The dream foreshadows America's separation of its war interests from those of the dying Jewish masses. The dream president challenges the authenticity of the petitioners' report, as the State Department chooses to disparage evidence of the magnitude of Jewish losses in 1942. Roosevelt points to Red Cross documents, noting "the camps to be clean, no maltreatment, no disease, and few deaths. Excellent medical facilities" (*D*, 155). He reads directly from the report:

> The camps in Eastern Europe are essentially detention camps while detainees await relocation to newer homes being constructed farther from the battle lines. It would appear the Germans are intent upon

resettlement of populations. Talk of liquidation is regarded as irre-
sponsible. (*D*,155)

Members of the delegation contradict the Red Cross reports, offering testimony from escapees, such as that transmitted through
Switzerland and the free Poles in London, that cite the truth of
German destruction.[9] The testimony distinguishes between the initial killings in the German camps where one and two hundred died
in a week and the Eastern European camps where the scale of the
massacres was far greater. The president counters that war brings
death to many and disregards the "alleged" reports of Jewish victims. The anguished Jew is unable to make the president acknowledge the distinction between those who die as combatants in war,
civilians who die in the confusion and chaos of war, and Jews who
are systematically selected for genocide. Simon appears in his own
dream pleading with the president to "Open the nation and ransom captives" (*D*, 156). Simon's dream supplication evokes the *St.
Louis* protest sign designating the United States Holocaust-era anti-
Semitic immigration policy, a policy that denied Jews entry into
America knowing that such denial helped assure the success of
Hitler's genocide program.[10] As the dream dialogue continues,
Simon contrasts the president's empty promises with the harsh
reality of massacre and the bare truth that the president has the
power to save them by ransoming them, taking them into this
country, and convincing the allies to allow immigration. The president's lame response is to query whether he should cable the Pope,
a fitting conclusion to a despairing dream since the president's
failure to act on behalf of the Jews is matched by Pius XII's. The
dream sequence is a rare instance of Cohen's use of irony.

The confluence of the Wiezmann speech, the Roosevelt
dream, and a visit from an old Hasid bearing the letter of Simon
Stern's messianic election crystallize Simon's purpose: "to begin the
work of redemption" (*D*, 161), to rescue Jews, in action independent of obstructionist government agencies. Simon Stern's messianic destiny is closely associated with the Holocaust. Simon's discovery of his election occurs in 1943 when an old Hasid delivers a
letter containing the prophetic proclamation written by his father
on the day of Simon's birth. The delivery of the letter coincides
with Simon's attendance at Chaim Weizmann's Madison Square
Garden announcement of the murder of two million Jews and the
peril of annihilation of European Jewry amid a conspiracy of si-

lence. Simon, therefore, begins his messianic mission with plans to rescue a Holocaust remnant. Until then Simon had given his energies to the accumulation of wealth through real-estate investment. Now he endows the Society for the Rescue and Resurrection of the Jews, which is to be dedicated to the spiritual restoration of survivors. In a Jewish community on the Lower East Side, Stern envisions and builds a Bene Brak, as in the days after the destruction of the Holy Temple, to bear testament to the endurance of Judaism and Jewry. In the shelter, shielded from a ritually impure world characterized by anti-Semitism,[11] Stern proposes to rehabilitate the European Jews not in the acculturated mode of American Jewry but in the manner of traditional Jewish learning and life. Although the major work of the society is to restore Jews in the context of Orthodox Judaism, its mission, and the novel's, is to bear Holocaust witness, to "testify to the world that it is a monstrous place . . . [to] hold up to the world the mirror of its desecration" (*D*, 253). This objective is pursued through penetrating exploration of the history and theology of Diasporan Jewry, examination of the historic correspondence of religious anti-Semitism and the racial model of National Socialism, concentrationary and holocaustal case histories, and documentation of American failure to counter the destruction of European Jewry.

Cohen looks beyond presidential and congressional disinterest in the annihilation of European Jewry to the American press's failure to report the magnitude of Jewish losses. Lackluster press coverage coupled with the State Department's suppression of reliable casualty reports speak to an extraordinary effort to suppress the truth:

> the news will go to Switzerland and from Switzerland to London and from London to New York. They prepare memoranda. Civil servants at hospitals and refugee centers in Switzerland take down information, write it up, mail it to the International Red Cross, and the International Red Cross speaks to London and says, "By the way, another ten thousand gone in Mauthausen and Treblinka. Tell New York, will you?" (*D*, 180)

The bitter tone of this speech reflects the frustration Jewish leaders feel in what appears to be a conspiracy of silence and inaction on the part of those in power. Only the Yiddish press covers the Holocaust with the urgency it requires, and although *The New York Times* occasionally publishes reports, it buries pertinent stories in the back pages of the paper. Corresponding to the efforts of Jewish leaders, Simon Stern and his assistant, Dr. Klay, publish announcements of the mounting death toll in the Yiddish press each month. They place statements coded to the weekly Torah readings:

> Go Forth (*Lech Lecha*)
>     How?
> Three million Jews are in Nazi
> prisons and cannot go forth
> (except to mass graves and lime pits)
>     UNLESS
> the Allies bomb the camps
>     NOW                (*D*, 202)

Simon Stern's program, formalized as "The Ratner's Declaration of Conscience," outlines his shattered belief in human dignity and focuses on the recognition of universal disinterest in alleviating Jewish suffering: "No man will help them to survive and no nation may be trusted. They must go it alone" (*D*, 198). Stern's certainty of Jewish isolation results in his resolution to create "a community within the community of Israel . . . an enclave in which to cultivate the resources of stubbornness, a remnant whose strength shall be in mutual love and helpfulness and disdainful removal and estrangement from all others" (*D*, 198). Years later, when Nathan asks Simon if he believed literally in the principles of the Declaration, Simon qualifies the language, but reaffirms his belief in its uncompromising ferocity.

Book Two ends with a reminder of the *St. Louis,* an allusion to the world's acquiescence to the destruction of the Jews. Here Cohen addresses the Allies' rejection of a 1944 Nazi offer to barter a remnant of Hungarian Jewry for trucks and other supplies. Cohen's attention to documentary evidence and thematic development is well served in his creation of a letter to Stern's society from Joel Brand, the Hungarian Jew who was dispatched by Adolf Eichmann near war's end to trade with the Allies one million Jewish lives for ten thousand trucks, food, and medical supplies. In a letter dated July 11, 1944, which arrives in November after being delayed in Washington and after thousands of Hungarian Jews have been killed, Brand pleads:

> I have told my story so many hundreds of times now, to so many officials, to so many governments, to so many emissaries, that with

each telling the story is condensed as the hope shrivels. It is the case that during the early part of April, while acting as a leader of the Jewish community of Hungary, I was approached by a high Nazi official, Adolf Eichmann, who was responsible for organizing the extermination of the Jews of Poland and Czechoslovakia. He offered to sell me the lives of one million Hungarian Jews. He demanded in return a quantity of foodstuffs, trucks, one truck for every ten Jews (ten thousand trucks), and as earnest of his seriousness he offered immediately upon confirmation that the transaction would take place to move one hundred thousand Jews to the border for passage into a neutral country. (*D*, 233–34)

The fictional letter describes the difficulty of dealing with officialdom, lists names of American and British representatives Brand actually met with, and details information about his detention by the British and the identification of historic figures with whom to negotiate the ransom of Hungarian Jewry. Incorporating the names of the historic players from Jewish agencies, Britain and America, Cohen indicts the British for their concerted effort to thwart the release of Jews bound for gas chambers by imprisoning Brand in Cairo and thereby preventing him from negotiating the exchange of people for equipment. Cohen's construction of the Brand petition evokes the historic obstacles put in Brand's way by the Allies, especially the British, making them partners with the Nazis in their willingness to abandon Hungarian Jewry to the crematoria. That American officials share the ignominy of their British colleagues is evident from Cohen's speculation that the letter may have been carried about by Roosevelt's emissary, coming to nothing "for higher than his good will had been the communications and signals exchanged by the warring allies to disregard his information" (*D*, 233), information following the known destruction of four million Jews by this time. In contrast to government inaction, Stern sends six million dollars to Switzerland to save the Hungarian remnant from the invading Russians and a million dollars in gold to Raoul Wallenberg to save a few Jews he might still have under Swedish protection.

Stern's dismay about Allied abandonment of the Jews is expressed in remarks to his colleague Dr. Klay: "We must begin by recognizing one fact: Jews are dispensable. There is no moral appeal possible for Jews. . . . Mass murder is a victorious crime precisely because its scale makes it unimaginable" (*D*, 195). Anticipating that as many as five million Jews will be murdered by war's end, Stern determines to concentrate their efforts on the rescue and restoration of the remnant, and to that end he creates a foundation called The Society for the Rescue and Resurrection of the Jews, to which he dedicates all his wealth. At war's end, Simon travels to Europe to bring a remnant of those surviving Dachau, Bergen-Belsen, Mauthausen, Auschwitz and other camps to the rehabilitation center he built. Thus, inversely parodying the Nazi death selections, the Jewish messiah now goes to Europe to make restoration selections, to select Jews of all classes and backgrounds, all professions, all capacities united by a passion for renewal "to do nothing but rebuild each other's flesh and spirit, . . . their productivity and confraternity—shall be a witness that despite all, everything, Jews will endure" (*D,* 252–53).

Cohen rarely uses satire, but he occasionally indulges in it to ridicule Allied indifference to the genocide of the Jews. Paralleling British and American suppression of news of the genocide during 1942–1943 is the mismanagement of the postwar refugee program under the United Nations Relief and Rehabilitation Administration. Cohen uses Dr. Klay's unwelcome presence at an UNRRA meeting to demonstrate the British lack of compassion for Jewry. The Americans are the butt of mild satire, presented as "energetic, concerned, pragmatic, and completely naive"; however, the British, who obstruct efforts such as Stern's to serve Jewish needs, are the target of the sharpest invective: "The English . . . are all splendid personages, incredibly correct, even right-headed, but stuffed with a kind of punctiliousness that makes even the Pharisees models of flexibility" (*D,* 247).

It is generally through the biographies of Simon's associates that Cohen introduces Holocaust documentation and commentary on the important link between pre-Nazi and Nazi anti-Semitism. A case in point is the history of Fisher Klay, an Austrian refugee who distinguishes the real Vienna from the romantic illusion, commenting that it is no surprise that Hitler was an Austrian. Contrasting the storybook, aristocratic Vienna of numerous concerts and operas and lavish ballrooms, and restaurants with the political realities of Vienna, he describes "popular Viennese anti-Semitism" rampant on the political right and left. He characterizes Vienna of 1938 as a city that tolerated daily riots, "Jews were being assaulted, humiliated, harassed. The National Socialists were upon us" (*D,* 187). In sharp contrast to Austria's postwar denial of its Nazi fervor and ardent anti-Semitism, Dr. Klay describes an Austria eagerly welcoming the Nazis:

> The streets were lined with cheering Viennese who put aside their cakes and excellent coffee long enough to shout '*Heil* Hitler.' . . . they organized a parade. All the local Gauleiters were out in their polished jackboots and the Hitler Jugend were commandeered as cheerleaders and traffic marshals. But the Viennese, the Jews among them (however much they quaked), maintained their decorum, taking their coffee in the cafés, reading their newspapers and magazines, even talking about literature and the arts. (*D*, 187–88)

Klay's emphasis on Austrian commitment to anti-Semitism and approval of Nazism is echoed by a Russian, Lazare Steinmann, who compares opposing totalitarian regimes and comments on pre-*Anschluss* Austrian attitudes:

> You remember that Austria was beginning to behave with good National Socialist fervor several months before it was actually taken over. There were three staged trials against Communists and other political agitators. . . . I was curious to see whether they would be like the Soviet trials of '36. More a question of comparative totalitarianism. . . . The same quality of cruelty and the same elevation of patriotic rhetoric. . . . Nazis wanted the credibility of the middle class smashed, wanted the school system which sustained the humanism of old Vienna demoralized. (*D*, 250)

Cohen turns to the history of a Russian Jew, Rabbi Lazare Steinmann, to enlarge the juxtaposition of Christian and Nazi anti-Semitism. Although he is a survivor of occupied Europe, Steinmann's Holocaust biography does not include ghettoization or concentration camp internment. A radical socialist exiled from Russia, he escaped first to Austria then to Switzerland and from there to London where he was attached to a Jewish communications network, monitoring broadcasts from underground and partisan groups in occupied Europe and maintaining a file on Nazi crimes. Steinmann's history illustrates historic anti-Semitic persecution of Russian Jews that was prelude to the twentieth-century European manifestations. Describing himself as "a Jew who has been on the losing side of every major conflict of the century" (*D*, 242), Steinmann suffered government-sponsored anti-Jewish terrorist actions and restrictions of residential confinement within the Russian Pale of Settlement.[12] The Mendel Beiliss blood-libel trial provided the occasion for the Black Hundreds to set fire to his father's warehouse and burn the entire business. The government reply to the

elder Steinmann's appeal for justice is advice from the czar's secret
police to leave the country. The victim exacts his own revenge by
burning a church, the prime Russian source of anti-Semitic fervor.
The son denounces this act as "a wasted gesture, a gesture of rage"
(*D*, 244). He has harbored other hopes for the improvement of
Jewish life in Russia, and while continuing his religious studies by
day, he serves radical socialists by night.

Unlike Epstein, Singer, and Elman who concentrate their
Holocaust delineation in one country, Cohen introduces a group of
survivors of differing nationalities, thereby enriching the fictional
canvas with wide-ranging Holocaust experiences. His approach
differs from the approach of others in its use of short glimpses of
survivor memories, which encapsulate the concentrationary universe rather than dramatizing it or inventing extensive memories.
Like Bellow's Sammler who returned to Poland from the relative
safety of England, Nathan's Holocaust history begins with an ironic
return to Hungary from the safety of prewar Palestine. Having
accompanied a blind uncle on a penitential trip to his parents'
birthplace in the mid-thirties, Nathan remained in Europe after his
uncle's death to study with a distinguished Hasidic *rebbe*. As did
most Hungarian nationals, he felt distant from the war while in his
remote village near the Rumanian border, and it was not until he
heard German bombers overhead and reports of Nazi parachutists
in the outskirts of Budapest that the war touched him. Three
months later, he was at a detention camp that held victims for
transfer to Auschwitz. Nathan characterizes his Auschwitz experience as "ordinary" and describes only one incident, his escape from
death in 1943, an event that reveals common camp experiences:
starvation, illness, and arbitrary death. Nathan's tone is always
somber in his discussions of collective Holocaust experiences, but
he begins his own story with an ironic contrast between the "efficiency" of the commandant's death selections and his own close call
with death by "overeating." As he elaborates, the joke turns sour
and the real tragedy of the concentrationary world emerges:

> We were starving to death most assuredly. To overeat was little more
> than finding a cache of food and eating it all at once. An elderly Jew
> from Posen died in the bunk next to mine. I watched him die. It was
> in the middle of the night. Under his pillow I found three boiled
> potatoes, the stump of a carrot, and a crust of bread. I ate them
> immediately, fearing that in the morning others might ransack his

> belongings looking for his food and strip me if they suspected I had
> hidden it. (*D*, 208)

The victim pays for his gluttony the next day with horrendous
stomach pains and spasms of diarrhea, which he fears to be dysentery. By the following morning he is too ill to stand for roll call.
Terrified of being reported sick and consequently sentenced to
death, he hides himself among the corpses, which generally remained untended for three or four days before collection for burning. In this way, he steals a day's rest. In a detail typical of camp
histories, he tells of prisoner bartering and methods for cheating
the Nazis of their Jewish prey; Nathan's absence is noted but not
reported by the kapo who is amenable to a bribe of three cigarettes,
which Nathan has hidden for such an emergency. We learn from
Nathan that he was moved from Auschwitz during the fall of 1944
when shipments of the lethal gas used in the extermination process
slowed. Mass firing squads were reintroduced for the weaker victims, and the stronger ones were marched across Poland to south-
eastern Germany and Austria to be used as slave laborers in the
Bavarian Alps. As the group marched toward Dachau, Nathan
seized the opportunity to fall into a cow pit, where he remained
hidden until the other prisoners were marched away. Hiding by
day and moving and searching for food at night, he managed to
remain free until January 1945 when he was found by three boy
soldiers who fortunately turned him over to their sergeant rather
than the Gestapo; from there he was sent to Buchenwald where
Simon Stern later finds him. By this time, concentration camp ravages had conquered his body. He hobbles, dragging behind him a
leg crippled by the commandant's wolfhound. He is also blind from
eye infections left untended. Like Bellow's Sammler and Wallant's
Nazerman, Nathan's perceptions are vivid, despite impaired vision.
His Holocaust experiences have provided him special insight into
the human condition.

Among the particularly memorable scenes of collective Holocaust suffering in American fiction are Bellow's and Epstein's Lodz
Ghetto and Wallant's and Cohen's Buchenwald. Nathan's description of the liberation of Buchenwald is a tale of continuing death:

> The process of mortification is not speedily reversed. Food does not
> feed; medicine does not cure; freedom does not liberate. The starv-
> ing, sick, and imprisoned have first to acclimate themselves to the

reversal. . . . We are conditioned creatures, and when we have made
a covenant . . . to die, it is not enough to announce its abrogation.
Learning must take place. (*D*, 260)

The starving had to learn to accomodate food. Nathan was fortunate to vomit his first mouthful of nourishing vegetable soup, unlike others who ate gluttonously and died from "gastric explosion."
Thousands of survivors died in the first months of liberation and
by the end of 1945, 150,000 survivors died.

Illustrative of Cohen's capacity to incorporate Holocaust topics normally absent from all but full-length accounts of the catastrophe are his two brief independent delineations of physical and
spiritual survival techniques. In addition to Nathan's description of
learning to take food successfully after starvation, he gives another
deceptively simple account of the daily grind of Buchenwald survival skills:

> All of us, those of us at Buchenwald and the millions of other cap-
> tives elsewhere throughout Europe, had grown accustomed to strug-
> gle each day for a bit of bread, a minute of rest, a moment in a quiet
> place, the sight of a bird or a clean, unsplattered blade of grass. A
> little thing would keep us going. A very little thing. You cannot
> imagine how little was our connection to life and how very little
> things managed to sustain that connection. The struggle was not
> against ideas, or people, or nations—that would return later. The
> struggle was against growing faint, losing weight, getting the runs,
> not being able to work. Those things meant death. Death was the
> enemy. And death was such an enemy that the meaning of life was
> bound up in the struggle against death. The struggle was every
> moment. (*D*, 264–65)

This passage effectively and simply demonstrates the Nazi policy of
complete humiliation and debasement of prisoners and the prisoners' struggles to live. Cohen captures the central paradox of
extremity—that life persists in an environment designed for
killing.

The society cook, whose Holocaust history includes three
years hiding in a basement, two years in forced labor, two years in
prison awaiting death, and rejection when she returns to the land
of her birth, tells how a Maidanek concentration camp prisoner
infamous for his cruelties to fellow inmates—for stealing bread
and tipping over soup—inexplicably befriended her and tried to

comfort her with stories about the poor people of Lodz, or with songs and occasional gifts of a cigarette or a potato with no expectation of payment. Her survival strategy consisted of looking at the crematorium belching smoke and imagining the ashes, "Not bodies, not faces, not children or women or young boys or old men, but names . . . just names going back to be remembered and used again (*D,* 383).

Although the Nazis were highly successful in ridding Europe of Jews, their bloodletting did not cleanse Europe of its virulent anti-Semitism. Despite all Europe knew of the death camps, the survivors were not welcome to return to their homes. Cohen, like Bellow and Epstein, illustrates Polish zeal in creating a postwar *Judenrein* Poland through the story of a displaced Jew's return to the village of his birth with "a Polish nationalist who had served as voluntary labor in a war factory in Düsseldorf" (*D,* 261). "The home of the Jew is occupied by a Catholic family which despises Jews. The Polish nationalist kills the Jew, and Poland is rid of one more Jew" (*D,* 261). The scene was repeated many times, and soon Jews despaired of returning to Catholic Poland, which loathed them as Jews, or to Communist Poland, which rejected them as Zionists. Instead, confirmed and reconfirmed in the knowledge of European anti-Semitism, they went to displaced persons camps to await emigration. Cohen's Jews have learned the lesson of the European Diaspora: "We are what we are—Jews. That was enough reason to deliver us to Hitler and kill us if we survived" (*D,* 261).

In keeping with most American authors, Arthur Cohen devotes little space to the delineation of Holocaust oppressors. His villain, among the most enigmatic, is neither a German racist nor an Arendt-type banal bureaucrat. On the contrary, he is the victim of sexual sadism and racist experimentation, a self-hating half-Jew, half-Romanian, shaped by a violent childhood and European anti-Jewish pathology. Cohen introduces Janos Baltar metaphorically— cast in the Satanic role in a production of Job. In the Edenic landscape of the Rothschild chateau gardens, Baltar is seen in rehearsal, "a moaning figure, slithering across the grass, his hands sliding down upon his drawn-up legs, . . . shimmying upon the ground, foot by foot, dragging himself . . . angling and turning his body like a man become serpent . . . a beast of the ages" (*D,* 276). Portraying himself as a concentration camp victim, Baltar approaches Simon Stern as a dissembling demon, asking to join Stern's society, to serve it. He fabricates a past of holocaustal suffering and devotion to a Hasidic *rebbe*: "I knew Bible, the Psalms by heart, backwards and forwards . . . *Shulhan Aruck*—all the useful laws and ways and means of interpreting them in good, solid style. I made myself helpful to small communities in Poland and Hungary, traveling around . . . preaching like a *maggid* and answering questions of law" (*D*, 288).

Exposition of Baltar's true biography appears more than 100 pages later, after we have witnessed intimations of his anger and after Simon Stern's key advisors, Nathan and Dr. Klay, have hired a detective to investigate his past. The detective describes Baltar as a frightening specimen, "a competent, skilled murderer, . . . [who] appears to think of himself as a kind of inverted Christ, a crucified man who has the responsibility of opening up the wounds of the world and forcing them to bleed again" (*D*, 399). Janos Baltar's speciality in his Ravensbruck incarnation was

> burning into victims the four wounds of Christ, and then as the blood would begin to flow and his victims groan in unendurable pain he would put a cloth soaked in vinegar upon them, he would bathe their heads, he would hold them in his arms until they revived or died. And then most curiously he would become deeply melancholic, weep pitiably, begin to recite snatches of Hebrew prayers it was not believed he knew and then disappear to sleep it off, and, upon reawakening, have no recollection of the torments he had inflicted. (*D*, 399–400)

Cohen follows this rare graphic depiction of concentration camp atrocity with a lengthy account of Baltar's life explaining his criminal personality. A product of European corruption and hatred, he was himself a victim of violence and, therefore, becomes a perpetrator of violence against the helpless. Born into a society that established opportunities on the basis of religious and ethnic identity, he was at a disadvantage. Since his father was a Jew and his mother a Christian, "he knew that according to the Jews he was no Jew,[13] and according to the Nazis completely a Jew. In short he belonged to no one" (*D*, 400). Shortly before the German invasion of Poland, an old Jew addresses Baltar as "Miserable Jew" and tells him that the birthmark on his forehead is an ominous sign of his violent character and begs him to "pray God to die before you kill" (*D*, 408). So traumatized is Baltar by this annunciation that he is removed to a sanatorium where he becomes the experimental subject for shock treatment, hydrotherapy, hypnosis, and psychiatric interviews, "conducted in a spirit of genial cruelty" (*D*, 409). He is the patient of a doctor deeply interested in race theory and purification, who "regarded Baltar's history as a splendid example of precisely the degeneracy and restoration which his political mentor, Alfred Rosenberg, obliged him to endorse in return for the annual state subsidy his institution received" (*D*, 409). Baltar is transformed according to Nazi racist philosophy, a monster created in the Nazi laboratory, "winnowed of his father's impurities and restored by medical treatment to an Aryanism which could be prudently employed by the Party" (*D*, 490). Upon his doctor's recommendation, he is admitted to the German army in 1941 and by 1942 works at Ravensbrück, "where he distinguished himself for . . . sadism" (*D*, 409). A Viennese who served with him described him as "a sadist, whose pleasure was to undertake the torture and then succor and ease the pain of the tortured" (*D*, 399). During the course of his Ravensbruck service, he is reported to have been responsible for the torturing and murdering of three inmates and the crippling of many more, "all of whom were found pierced with scalpel efficiency in the same manner as had been the crucified Messiah" (*D*, 409). Baltar's passion thus appears to include psychotic fusion of Christian and Nazi anti-Semitism. That his hatred does not end with the war is amply demonstrated in his contrivance to join Simon Stern's Society for the Rescue and Resurrection of the Jews in an attempt to exercise his homocidal mania in the context of a Jewish population. Balthar's postwar holocaustal ambition reflects Nazism's denial of Jewish life in any form and its use of modern technology to achieve the goal.

Baltar's character is a manifestation of Cohen's thesis that the evil of the Holocaust resonates endlessly.

> The evil of this age, . . . is crystallized as a symbolic cloture which however past, is not done. The Holocaust is fixed to a time but resonates endlessly and without end. It is seen as ultimate evil, intending by such ultimacy a consumate destructiveness. The Holocaust, in its immediacy, constellates everything that we mean by evil and, as such, is a perfected figuration of the demonic. In this respect, it is borne into the life of memory, . . . as an order of being which sinks roots deep into the human *passio* and, though cut off, lurks in the spirit available to succor and renascence. It is not, as were the earlier catastrophes of Jewish history, the concomitant of national

disaster or the aggravated *hubris* of a triumphant Church, but the expression of ordinary secular corruption raised to immense powers of magnification and extremity.[14]

Just as Simon Stern demands interpretation of the Elijah figure's "Legend of the Last Jew on Earth," so Cohen's Holocaust novel demands thought about the theological implications of the Holocaust. Although Cohen does not present the theological analyses and arguments of his expository works in the fiction, he weaves theological concerns into the narrative through the meditations of the scribe, dialogues between the messianic redeemer and his staff, and in a biblical play that is analogous to the medieval morality genre.[15]

The passage assessing Holocaust evil appears to be an early formulation of Cohen's *tremendum* philosophy positing a "transforming caesura," a break in interpretation of Jewish theology and history that denies the symmetry of Sinai and Holocaust: "it annihilates for us the familiar categories by which we have read and decoded our past. . . . The *tremendum* disallows traditional memory, obliging it to regard all settled doctrine anew, all accepted principle afresh, all closed truths and revelations as open."[16]

In keeping with the restorative and regenerative approaches to Holocaust tragedy espoused by Emil Fackenheim, Cohen's Jews respond to Holocaust loss by undertaking a major project of repair (*tikkun*) to strengthen Judaism and Jewry. In contrast to Baltar's destructive intention, Stern and Rabbi Steinmann build a fortress to house a rehabilitation center. Their model is the Akiva Bene Brak, rebuilding the remnant within the traditional Judaic system as a distinctive and separate religious entity. Unlike Singer's protesters and Elman's Yagodah, Cohen's Jews follow the tradition of the ancients, who refrained from blaming God for the destruction of the Temples, for the Exile, for the Diaspora, and for depredation, for the victory of Christendom and Islam. However, Steinmann departs from the ancient rabbis in his perception of the Diety and the covenant. To blame or try God is a futile gesture:

> No need for a trial. If that were all, He'd be condemned in a trice . . . what makes me weep is the confident knowledge that God couldn't help it. . . . He is the rapture of desire—of eternity and incompletion, without justice, incapable of politics and practicalities, but a dreamer of impassable visions, wanting to feel, but not feeling, desiring humanity, but unhuman. He is suffering perfection. (*D*, 255)

Steinmann does not expect God to think and respond in human terms; notions of human justice are irrelevant. "Justice," he claims, "is a human convention, a covenant of the fallible" (*D*, 255). Steinmann sheds no tears for humanity, but sheds tears for God because "He wants so much and can affect so little" (*D*, 255). Steinmann has arrived at a position that marks the Holocaust as an event so different, even from the previous Jewish disasters, that it must change our theological perceptions. To try God is to expect a participatory covenant and to expect God to respond to human petition. Steinmann's judgment anticipates the theological argument of *The Tremendum*, which insists on a break from past theology. In *The Tremendum*, Cohen argues, "the traditional God has no connection with the Holocaust despite the palpable fact that the immensity of the *tremendum* implies a judgment upon God.[17] Simon Stern and Steinmann herald Cohen's later insistence that "Jewish reality must account for the *tremendum* in its view of God, world, and man; it must constellate Jewish facts of practice and belief in such a way as to enable them to endure . . . the *tremendum* and withstand it and a God who creates a universe in which such destructiveness occurs."[18]

In sharp contrast to Rabbi Steinmann's capitulation to Divine mystery, Jonas Baltar presents a Job play calculated to undermine the survivors' faith in a just and benevolent deity. During his satanic role and narrative commentary, Baltar assumes an adversarial position, one that departs from the traditional Jewish interpretation of the Job legend and draws painful comparisons between the conclusion of Job and the conclusion of the Holocaust contrasting the restitution made to Job and the irretrievable losses of the Holocaust victims. His prologue establishes the ironic tone and juxtapositionary mode of the play. Like Milton's Satan, Baltar is often compelling. His Job is introduced as the millionaire of Uz, who erred, as did the Jews of Europe, because he kept wealth "in lives and tangible substance" and, therefore, suffered the tragedy "wrought upon him by a vain divinity unsure of his power" (*D*, 277). As the drama shows Job's physical trials and tribulations to the accompaniment of a passive God standing by weeping, the speaker questions, "Who the sinner and who the sinned against?" (*D*, 280). He challenges acceptance of the classical Jewish belief that the just suffer, their suffering being a test of their fidelity and the acceptance that man's finite mind cannot probe the depths of Divine omniscience. Baltar urges the audience to counter this view, because as Holocaust survivors, they know tragedy without Divine reversal—the faithful were not spared:

> Women sang to their children before the open pits, and fathers held the hands of their sons, but the finger pulled the trigger and we toppled over into our graves. Untragic! Who was there to have pity and fear? (*D*, 281)

Holocaust diction juxtaposed with biblical allusion highlights Baltar's peculiar equation of Job's endurance—which he interprets as an effort to embarrass God—with his advice to the survivors to "be proud and humiliate the world" (*D*, 281). As the play concludes with Satan's defeat, restoration of Job's sons and daughters, and the doubling of his wealth, Baltar maliciously juxtaposes Job's regeneration to the permanent loss of Holocaust victims.

> Yours are buried beneath the earth of Europe, and your sons and daughters, issue of your loins, are not restored to you. And there is no less righteousness in you. Our only sin, . . . is that we are not God but know well how true Gods should behave towards us. (*D*, 283)

Baltar offers an ironic closing hymn, inviting the audience to join him in praising "our Lord God, protector and sustainer of Israel." The hymn amounts to a celebration of the enduring people and denunciation of a God whom they honor but should not trust—the antithesis of the Jewish interpretation of Job, which advocates perfect trust. Unlike Rabbi Steinmann's Jobian acceptance of Divine mystery, Baltar's Job is in the tradition of countercommentary, an expression of Holocaust despair rather than Jobian faith. Baltar's proficiency for countercommentary is dramatized again in his teaching of the Jonah story. On the occasion of the Fast of the Ninth Day of Av, commemorating historic collective catastrophes in Jewish history, including the destruction of the first and second Temples, the fall of Bar Kokhba's fortress, and the expulsion from Spain, Baltar inverts the traditional Jewish teaching of the Book of Jonah as an illustration of human repentance and Divine mercy. Baltar drew "analogies between the ransoming of the penitent pagans of Nineveh and the destruction of pious Jerusalem—and lest his audience forget, the savaging of their own generation (*D*, 291).

Despite the caution expressed by his aides, their warnings of the "indefinable contagion of Baltar," and his own reservations, Simon Stern accepts Baltar's plea to join the survivor remnant in America. Stern explains his decision in kabbalistic terms that characterize Cohen's postHolocaust theodicy. This includes a perception of God as the creator of good and evil—"that God contains within Himself the possibility of good and evil" (*D*, 292). Simon concludes that Baltar comes to them because he senses in them the counter to his own villainy and they must, therefore, accept him. As the messianic figure, Simon addresses the heart of Jewish redemptive philosophy, the principle of *t'shuva*, which posits the view that to sin is to turn away from God, and to repent is to return to God. Cohen here plays on the word *turn* echoing the Hebrew redemptive diction:

> The very heart of the struggle between good and evil, between Baltar and ourselves, is that we are not all good and he could not be wholly evil. Repentance. Turning. Turning away. Turning back. Returning. These motions of regeneration are what the Jewish people must always stand for. (*D*, 296)

Simon speaks directly to the limitations of Jewish and non-Jewish philosophies that restrict God to being good and interpret evil as absence. He addresses the reality of evil in the universe, arguing that since its source is in divine creation it contributes to the complexity of creation and must be approached with the goal of repair. The assertion of evil's authenticity and power are repeated in Cohen's voice in *The Tremendum,* leading to his claim that too much effort may have been placed in preserving an outmoded theodicy without attending to the Holocaust-wrought need to rethink and redescribe both God and man. The vital question is how to affirm God meaningfully in a world where evil enjoys dominion.

Simon's comprehension that God embodies good and evil is manifested in his salvific effort to create a Bene Brak for the regeneration of the survivors and, after Balthar's eventual explosive destruction of the center, in his moving uptown to assume a larger messianic role. The blind scribe's assessment of Simon's move echoes Cohen's acceptance of contraries in his nonfictional exploration of postHolocaust theodicy, his understanding of the necessity of distinctions:

> First by separating the *tremendum* from all things and descending into the abyss, then by rejoining the *tremendum* to the whole experience of mankind as endpoint of the abyss and new beginning of the race, it is possible to link again the death camps, the *tremendum* of the abyss, to the *mysterium tremendum* of God who is sometimes in love with creation and its creatures and sometimes, it must initially be thought, indifferent to their fate.[19]

# CHAPTER NINE

*Eternal Light: The Holocaust and the Revival of
Judaism and Jewish Civilization
in the Fiction of Chaim Potok*

Chaim Potok is a rabbi, scholar, and novelist
whose philosophic and ethical views are derived from Torah and
Talmud and whose aesthetic theory is derived from Western philosophy, literature, and art. With Saul Bellow, Bernard Malamud,
Cynthia Ozick, Arthur Cohen, and I. B. Singer, Potok rejects alienation in favor of the affirmative position of Jewish idealism in the
face of evil and suffering. Jewish history, including repeated out-
breaks of anti-Semitism and its 1939–1945 genocidal manifestation, resonates throughout Potok's fiction. Because the author believes that "the Jew sees all his contemporary history refracted
through the ocean of blood that is the Holocaust,"[1] the *Shoah* is
always in the background of his fictional universe. Rather than
treating the Holocaust directly, Potok generally introduces the
topic indirectly and focuses instead on Holocaust restoration
through renewal of Judaism and Jewry in America and Israel.
Potok's characters are generally devout Jews, conversant in Jewish
theology, liturgy, Talmudic studies, and rabbinic commentary and
frequently presented in the context of synagogue, yeshiva, and

300

observant Jewish homes. Their pre-Holocaust mission—dedication to the religious life and adoption from and contribution to secular civilization—is enhanced by their postHolocaust mission—renewal of Judaism and Jewry in the Diaspora and creation and sustenance of a Jewish homeland in Israel. Potok's fictional heroes thus aspire, as the novelist does in *Wanderings,* "to rebuild . . . [Judaism's] core from the treasures of our past, fuse it with the best in secularism, and create a new philosophy, a new literature, a new world of Jewish art, a new community, and take seriously the meaning of the word emancipation."[2]

The year Potok's popular first novel, *The Chosen* (1967), was published, his short story, "The Dark Place Inside," appeared. "The Dark Place Inside" portrays an Israeli Holocaust survivor suffering the trauma of his losses sixteen years after their occurrence. On the joyous occasion of the birth of his fifth son, he mourns the loss of four sons who "had walked the narrow corridor and tasted the smoky waters of poison gas in the shower house, together with their mother."[3] We learn that Levi Abramovich escaped death in a mass shooting when he fell into heavy brush a moment before the bullets met their mark; he survived as a fugitive in the barn of a Polish peasant. He had been hunted like an animal by the Nazis: "They had smashed his face in the hunting and bayoneted him in the killing so that his blood had run in dark pools. . . . But the killing had been poorly accomplished; the peasant's herbs had sealed the wounds" (*DP,* 35). Holocaust memories become a dark force in Levi's being, generally suppressed, but occasionally emerging and overpowering his capacity for regeneration. Unlike the survivors in Potok's novels, who appear in brief cameos and largely in the restorative mode of commitment to Judaism and the Jewish community, Levi has not made peace with the God of the Holocaust. Like I. B. Singer's protestors, he voices his anger against the impotent or uncaring God: "I believe in God. I believe He is the paradigm for all the fools in the universe" (*DP,* 36). Receipt of his murdered wife's watch is the catalyst for Levi's transformation from a matter-of-fact dismisser of the ineffectual divine—"God is stupidity. God is comic. God is a fool" (*DP,* 36)—to the despairing protester. He is alienated from God and man: "There is no one to talk to now. . . . There is not even God to talk to he thought, trying to make it a calm thinking and failing miserably"(*DP,* 39). Tormented by the memory of four dead sons, he thinks the appearance of his dead wife's watch is an absurd cruelty and charges God accordingly: "Master of the Universe, . . . if You are truly real, then You are powerless and cruel. If You are able to prevent evil but are unwilling, You are cruel. If You are willing to prevent evil but are not able, then You are without power. And if You are able and willing, why then is there evil?" (*DP*, 39). Because Levi regards the sudden appearance of the watch as an extraordinary burden, he dismisses the possibility of its potential to make the present meaningful by evoking the past. Now he hates God, hates Him with a cold passionless contempt. He expresses the utter despair of the believer, "I believe in perfect faith that You are unworthy of my perfect faith. You no longer merit consideration" (*DP*, 39). No bleaker moment exists in Potok's fiction.

Much more typical of Potok's treatment of the Holocaust is *The Chosen*. The novel, set in the Williamsburg section of Brooklyn, is the story of two sets of fathers and sons and their practice and study of Judaism, set against the backdrop of the Holocaust and the establishment of the State of Israel. These historic forces remain in the novel's background while the religious issues dividing Jewish orthodoxy claim the novelist's central interest. Nevertheless, the *Shoah* remains a leitmotif and an important influence on the lives of the characters. David Malter, a yeshiva teacher, and his son Reuven are Orthodox Jews open to the influences of Western philosophy and scholarship. Reb Saunders, the dynastic Hasidic *tzaddik*, resists non-Hasidic thought and expects his son Danny to follow the prescriptions of the Hasidim and assume the religious leadership of his father's congregation. The novel's dramatic tension results from opposing interpretations of Jewish religious writing, worship, and practices by the groups. A measure of difference between the Orthodox and Hasidic fathers is the manner of their response to the Holocaust and the establishment of a Jewish homeland in Israel. Similarly, antithetical reactions to these two dimensions of twentieth-century Jewish history divide the sons.

In a rare instance of American fictional treatment of the Allies abandonment of the Jews, David Malter addresses Anthony Eden's 1942 House of Commons speech detailing the Nazi genocide plan and Eden's failure to move beyond rhetorical denunciation of the Final Solution. Malter is outraged by British moral failure:

> the whole machinery of democratic expression had been set in motion to impress upon the British Government the need for action—

and not a thing was done. Everyone was sympathetic, but no one was sympathetic enough. The British let some few Jews in, and then closed their doors. America hadn't cared enough, either. No one had cared enough. The world closed its doors and six million Jews were slaughtered.[4]

Although the Holocaust is not in the forefront of Potok's young protagonists' discussions, they are deeply concerned about Jewish losses and refer to Hitler's war against Jewry in the context of general war news. With the end of war and release of news of the concentration camps, Reuven expresses bewilderment at the immensity of the Nazi crimes against Jewry:

The numbers of the Jews slaughtered had gone from one million to three million to four million, and almost every article we read said that the last count was still incomplete, the final number would probably reach six million. I couldn't . . . imagine six million of my people murdered. . . . It didn't make any sense at all. My mind couldn't hold on to it, to the death of six million people. (*C*, 180)

Reb Saunders spoke "of the Jewish world in Europe, of the people he had known who were now probably dead, of the brutality of the world" (*C*, 180), interpreting this catastrophe historically, "the world drinks our blood" (*C*, 181). He laments the slaughter of the six million in the context of an extraordinary history of persecution. Although Saunders reluctantly accepts the Holocaust as "the will of God" (*C*, 181), a Divine mystery of inaction, he expresses his bewilderment and petitions the Almighty, "Master of the Universe, how do You permit such a thing to happen?" (*C*, 181). Departing from his characteristic tendency to explain Jewish beliefs and attitudes, Potok allows the statement to stand without pursuing its theological implications.

In contrast to many writers' focus on the atrocities of the Holocaust period and burdens of Holocaust survival, Potok generally concentrates on the possibilities of Holocaust restoration. David Malter rejects Reb Saunders' acceptance of the Holocaust as God's will, arguing instead "We cannot wait for God. If there is an answer, we must make it ourselves" (*C*, 182). Instead, he works for "the education of American Jewry and a Jewish state in Palestine" (*C*, 213). Reb Saunders, bound by the belief in a religious and holy state ushered in by the Messiah, rejects Zionism because it is a secular movement. For some Hasidim, the establishment of a secular state in Israel was regarded as a Torahic violation. For Malter, the way to derive meaning from the slaughter of six million Jews is for American Jews to replace the lost treasures of Judaism, to train teachers and rabbis to lead the people and to generate a religious renaissance among American Jews. He is heartened by a return to the synagogues, even by the Jewishly uneducated, believing that the mission of the religious is to educate the assimilated and return them to Judaism and to the Jewish people. In the immediate aftermath of the Holocaust and before the establishment of the State of Israel, Malter is convinced that Judaism must be rebuilt in America or perish. When Zionism is resuscitated, David Malter responds enthusiastically and works assiduously to realize Zionist goals. At a massive rally in Madison Square Garden, Malter argues the need to arouse the world to the desperate requirement for a Jewish homeland in Palestine, particularly as a haven for those "that had escaped Hitler's ovens" (*C*, 215). Furthermore, he counters that

> the slaughter of six million Jews would have meaning only on the day a Jewish state was established. Only then would their sacrifice begin to make some sense; only then would the songs of faith they had sung on their way to the gas chambers take on meaning; only then would Jewry again become a light to the world. (*C*, 215)

When the United Nations voted for the Partition Plan, Malter reacts with an exhuberance common in the American Jewish community:

> The death of the six million Jews had finally been given meaning. . . . After two thousand years, it had finally happened. We were a people again, with our own land. We were a blessed generation. We had been given the opportunity to see the creation of the Jewish state. (*C*, 226)

Sharing his father's dreams, Reuven endangers his own safety to load smuggled arms for the Jewish Army, which must meet the Arab threat to destroy the new nation as soon as it is established.

In deference to his father, Danny refrains from supporting the Zionist movement. As Arab anti-Jewish violence mounts and the toll of Jewish dead increases daily, Reb Saunders' league becomes silent in its opposition to the secular state. Moved by the similarity of Nazi and Arab anti-Semitism, Hasidic opponents lament Jewish blood being spilled again: "Hitler wasn't enough. Now more Jewish blood, more slaughter. What does the world want from us? Six million isn't enough? More Jews have to die?" (*C*, 227) Their pain over the new outbreak of violence against the Jews of Israel outweighs Hasidic opposition to the secular state, and they end their vocal campaign against the establishment and recognition of Israel.

The sequel to *The Chosen, The Promise,* continues to trace the lives of Reuven Malter preparing for rabbinic ordination and Danny Saunders pursuing a career in clinical psychology. Reuven is at the center of a theological conflict between fundamentalist-traditionalists and religious scholars who bring the tools of scientific textual criticism to the analysis of religious sources. The religious dichotomy dramatized between Hasidic and *Mitnagdic* orthodoxies in *The Chosen* is extended in *The Promise* to a philosophic conflict between Orthodox and Conservative approaches to Talmud study. The Conservative faction is represented by a new character, Abraham Gordon, and the traditionalist faction by several Holocaust survivors who teach at David Malter's yeshiva, and by Rav Kalman who teaches at Reuven's seminary. Gordon is an American scholar who suffered none of the European hardships that Kalman experienced. Yet the Holocaust changed the direction of his life. After experiencing a crisis of faith, Gordon went to Europe for two years of postdoctoral work in logic with the Vienna Circle positivists. He had been in Germany and reported that he "could smell the smoke of the crematoria even before anyone knew what a crematorium was."[5] Realizing that not many Jews would survive Hitler's Europe, Gordon rejected an invitation from Harvard University to teach logic and entered a seminary to aid in rebuilding American Judaism, a Judaism free of fundamentalist dogma that would appeal to progressive thinkers. Although David Malter remains in the Orthodox community, his scholarly techniques of comparative textual analysis and emendation, like Abraham Gordon's, are often discredited by fundamentalists and associated with progressive thinkers. Malter's major antagonist is his son's teacher, a rigorous European Talmudist who has dedicated his life to traditional Talmudic explication.

Unlike Bellow, Wallant, and Elman who focus on physical and psychological traumas of survivorship, Potok, like Singer, examines the religious and theological implications of the concentrationary experience. The reader perceives the survivors through Reuven's impressions of their responses to the unorthodox scholarship of Abraham Gordon and David Malter. Reuven attributes religious zeal of the neighborhood to the influence of the concentration camp traditionalists: "everything traditional was being drawn to-ward . . . zealousness. They had changed everything merely by sur-viving and crossing an ocean. They had brought that spark to the broken streets of Williamsburg, and men like Rav Kalman who were not Hasidim felt swayed by their presence and believed themselves to be equally zealous guardians of the spark (*P*, 195).

The survivors of the "sulfurous chaos of the concentration camps . . . eyes brooding, like balls of black flame turned inward upon private visions of the demonic" (*P*, 13), remain steadfast tra-ditionalists, staunchly opposed to modern tampering with ortho-dox worship, practice, and scholarship. Undefeated by the physical enemy in Europe, they are prepared to do battle with those they perceive to be Judaism's spiritual enemies in America. Representa-tive of the survivors' intolerance for other expressions of Jewish learning and worship are the "newcomers" at David Malter's yesh-iva, who denounce his publications as a threat to scripture and support Abraham Gordon's excommunication. Reuven's teacher, Rav Kalman, also rejects other methods in fealty to his teachers and students who died martyrs' deaths. The survivor-purists perceive American Jewish schools, where students do not wear skullcaps and teachers do not believe that the Torah was given to Moses by God, as being ritually "unclean." Such a school in their opinion is "a desecration of the name of God." Potok's survivors bear witness to the Holocaust through their determination to live religiously pure lives, to live according to the commandments, to defend the Torah, and to revitalize the *Yiddishkeit* (Jewishness) that the Nazis sought to destroy. Against the Nazi program of death and destruc-tion, these Jews defiantly stand for the sanctity of life. Potok's sur-vivors are engaged in the restorative process, regenerating Judaism and the Jewish people.

> Here, is Williamsburg, they set about rebuilding their burned-out world. Families had been destroyed; they remarried and created new families. Dynasties had been shattered; elders met and formed new dynasties. Children had been killed; their women now seemed forever pregnant. (*P*, 13)

Unlike the survivors in Singer's fiction who rant against an unjust God, the characters in Potok's novels neither protest God's Holocaust silence nor question their faith in God and dedication to Torah Judaism. As zealous "guardians of the spark," they may be disruptive to progressive American Jewry but even those Americans who have the most to lose from their irresoluteness, understand the zealots' determination to guard the Torah their comrades died for. Despite Hitler's racial ideology, Potok's characters never speak of Jews dying in Hitler's racial war. Their perception is religious, and the victims died *kiddish ha-Shem,* religious martyrs sanctifying God's holy name.

Rav Kalman, the only survivor individually developed by Potok, fiercely protects his scholarly approach to the sacred texts in order to honor God's word and the memory of those Jews who lived their lives and lost their lives in devotion to Torah and God. Through student speculation about his past, we learn that he had been a teacher in a highly reputed yeshiva in Vilna, a city famed for the superiority of its Jewish institutions of learning. It is known that he spent two years in a German concentration camp in northern Poland, the rest is rumor. Some think storm troopers shot his wife and three daughters before his eyes in the woods outside Warsaw. Other speculations focus on his escape and capture:

> he had escaped from a concentration camp, been caught, and escaped again; he had crossed the Polish frontier into Russia and fought with Russian partisans for a year. One rumor had it that he had organized a group of Orthodox Jewish partisans that specialized in blowing up the tracks of German trains carrying Jews to the concentration camps. Another rumor had it that he had been concealed in a bunker for more than a year by a Polish farm family, had been discovered, had been forced to watch the execution of the family, and had somehow escaped again. He was said to have made his way across northern Russia into Siberia and from there to Shanghai, where he had waited out the war under the eyes of the Japanese, who were not possessed of Hitler's feelings toward Jews and who left the few Jews under their rule alone. According to this version of the life of Rav Kalman, he was brought to America by the administration of Hirsch University and was promptly invited to teach in the rabbinical department. (*P*, 117)

In marked contrast to the fictional characters of Wallant, Malamud, and Singer who either speak directly of their Holocaust experiences or think about them, in Potok's fiction nonsurvivors speculate about the Holocaust suffering of survivors. It is unclear why Potok includes these student speculations rather than incorporating direct survivor commentary. Perhaps they offer the writer a means of briefly referring to multiple holocaustal experiences and avoiding the need to create other characters with full biographies and dramatic roles in the manner of Singer, Bellow, and Cohen. Rather than dwell on past atrocities, Potok's survivors concentrate on living. Reuven's father verifies the Shanghai episode. The elder Malter comments on the excellence of Rav Kalman's Talmudic reputation and cites Kalman's establishment of a yeshiva in Shanghai as the cause of delay in bringing him to America where his services were coveted as "a great Talmud scholar" and "one of the great men in Orthodoxy" (*P*, 200).

David Malter, who served as Potok's voice of reason in *The Chosen,* continues in that fashion in the sequel, and it is his observation that Kalman is to be respected as a champion of the Torah. Malter draws an analogy between Kalman's resistance to Nazism and his resistance to weakened religious observance: "He was not of those who believed in going willingly to the crematoria. He was with the partisans and killed German soldiers for Torah. Now he defends it with words" (*P*, 280).

Just as we discover Kalman's heroism, first in student speculation and later confirmed by David Malter, so we also first learn of Kalman's suffering under Nazi medical experimentation through an exchange he has with Reuven's friend Danny Saunders regarding his treatment of a withdrawn patient. Kalman becomes rigid at Danny's mere mention of the word *experiment* to explain Michael Gordon's psychological therapy. Later we learn that because of the experiments he endured Kalman has not remarried and started a new family. This indirect means of suggesting holocaustal atrocity is typical of Potok's reluctance to use graphic description of torture or direct or dramatic references to the concentrationary universe. The reader can assume from ample historic reference the types of medical experiments Kalman may have witnessed and endured. In addition to Kalman's response to the word *experiment* and speculation about that which he experienced, one of the novel's most sympathetic characters, the modern scholar and victim of Rav Kalman's fierce orthodoxy, Abraham Gordon, addresses the philosophic implications of Kalman's Holocaust suffering:

The concentration camps destroyed a lot more than European Jewry. They destroyed man's faith in himself. I cannot blame Rav Kalman for being suspicious of man and believing only in God. Why should anyone believe in man? There are going to be decades of chaos until we learn to believe again in man. (*P*, 315)

The progressives of Potok's fiction, like their Orthodox and fundamentalist brothers, consistently respond to the Holocaust with determination to rebuild Jewry through a revitalized and strengthened Judaism. Unlike the debilitated survivors of Wallant's, Bellow's, and Singer's novels, Potok's survivors are developed not in terms of their physical and psychological disabilities but as Jews strengthened in their commitment to Judaism. They are ever vigilant, ever dedicated, whether as rabbis, scholars, or Zionists, to the survival and flourishing of Judaism and the Jewish people. Beyond Holocaust horror looms a Jewish renaissance.

Potok's fourth novel, *In the Beginning*, continues to evidence his interests in Judaism and Jewish history. The subject is the Jewish encounter with anti-Semitism, including European, Arab, and American variations. Like Bellow, Epstein, Wallant, and Singer, Potok makes a strong case for a causal relationship between the Holocaust and historic Christian anti-Semitism. He departs from some of the others in the extent to which he develops the American and Arab varieties. Although the Holocaust was of import in the earlier fiction, Potok had presented it as a haunted presence in the lives of American Jews and survivors and as further motivation for their commitment to Judaism and Zionism. *In the Beginning* brings historic anti-Semitism, "the dark underbelly of Western civilization,"[6] and its holocaustal manifestation to the thematic core and dramatic center of the novel. Addressing the importance of anti-Semitism and the Holocaust on the American-Jewish consciousness, Potok said:

Probably the American Jew feels . . . quite guilt-ridden. . . . For whatever reason, he never did enough at a crucial point in time by way of an effort to get the thing stopped, or to protest it. . . . I don't see how it is possible to think the world through Jewish eyes without having the blood-screen of the Holocaust in front of your eyes as part of the filtering. I'll go even further and say that for thinking people, Jew or non-Jew, I don't think it is possible to think the world anymore in this century without thinking Holocaust.[7]

Readers of Potok's earlier novels will find much that is familiar in the fourth work: narrative that is presented from the point of
view of an intelligent, sensitive young boy; a positive and supportive relationship between two males; and vital father-son and
teacher-student character constructs. Departure from the previously established patterns is seen in a sustained antagonism between two boys and the significant intrusion of the secular world in
terms of economic depression and social conflict.

David Lurie, the first-person narrator tells his story chrono-
logically from childhood through early adulthood revealing his
initiation to anti-Semitism through his father's European memories
and his own victimization at the hands of anti-Semitic neighborhood bullies. The narrative is set in an immigrant Bronx neighborhood where transplanted Europeans have retained their Old
World fears and prejudices and passed them on to their American-
born children. Here Potok offers an unusual double exposure to
anti-Semitism, superimposing a child's American experience on
the adult European manifestations. The bustling multiethnic
neighborhoods of the Bronx, where Potok spent his childhood,
provide the realistic backdrop for antagonistic encounters between
Jew and gentile. Urban experience impinges more forcefully on
David Lurie than it had on Reuven Malter, Danny Saunders, and
Asher Lev. In addition to a yeshiva classroom, a synagogue, and an
observant home, the novel's settings include streets, schoolyards,
business districts, and a local zoo. Eddie Kulanski, son of Polish
immigrants, is described by his Jewish victim as hating Jews with "a
kind of mindless demonic rage."[8] Although still a child, this hoo-
ligan acts like an adult, expressing prejudice that "bore the breed-
ing of a thousand years" (*IB*, 11). The novel's Jewish protagonist,
named for an uncle who died in a pogrom, has been educated in
the history of European anti-Semitism and knows of his family's
persecution, but is nevertheless surprised to find it prevalent in
America. Eddie learns that David's family is from Poland and he
spews the Old World venom in his mother tongue, using the Polish
epithet *Anonymowe Panstwo*, ("Anonymous Empire") reiterating the
slander outlined in *The Protocols of the Elders of Zion*—namely, that
Jews secretly conspire first to destroy Christian countries and then
to dominate the world. Exemplifying Potok's method of using the
novel to inform the reader of Jewish history is the expository
speech on the Jewish conspiracy by David's older cousin, Saul:

This group is supposed to be able to make all kinds of problems for the goyim because it owns most of the banks and newspapers in the world. These old Jews can do almost anything because they have so much money and control the news and what people say and think. They have plans for all the goyishe governments to get into such bad trouble that they'll fail—and then these Jews can take over the world. My teacher said that in Poland they call this secret organization *Anonymowe Panstwo*. It's even in the Polish dictionary, he said. Almost everyone in Poland believes it. (*IB*, 62)

Variations of anti-Semitic attitudes expressed in all historic periods reappear in the microcosm of David's childhood world. In a scene that would be comic were it not for its sinister implications, David is watching his sleeping infant brother when Eddie and an older cousin, who shares his anti-Jewish prejudices, insist on inspecting the baby's horns. Disappointed to find the child hornless, they question David about the age at which he lost his horns. Eddie parrots the oft-repeated Christian charge of Jewish influence and affluence, albeit in childish overtones: "You own all the money, but you don't own this here sidewalk" (*IB*, 55). Paralleling the European model, but on a smaller scale, violent words lead to violent action. After David accidentally rides his tricycle over Eddie's hand, which was poised on the sidewalk in a street game, Eddie seeks revenge. Nothing short of David's Jewish life will suit him. He tries repeatedly to push the tricycle and rider into oncoming traffic. Unable to inflict his murderous desire on David because an adult intervenes, Eddie arranges for his cousin to slash the tire of David's tricycle. On another occasion Eddie and his cousin conduct a surrealistic chase and assault on David, in an environment suggestive of primitive brutality. The cousins ambush the unsuspecting David in the Bronx Zoo. With the rallying cry "for Christ's sake," they molest David, satisfying their lurid curiosity about the appearance of a circumcised penis. During the attack, David suspects the young anti-Semite's pleasure in Jewish pain and asks rhetorically: "Eddie. Have you seen a concentration camp? Did they look good, all those corpses of dead Jews?" (*IB*, 400)

Emphasizing the Christian source and sustenance of anti-Semitism that is dramatically manifested in the conflict between the boys, a Christian neighbor cites the deicide libel as the fuel for nearly 2000 years of murderous Christian anti-Semitism and informs the Jewish innocent of church doctrine and books that per-petuate the infamy. David is persistently puzzled by the motivation for Christian anti-Semitism. As he looks out the window of his small synagogue at a large local church, he wonders "how a statue whose face was so full of love could be worshipped by someone whose heart was so full of hate" (*IB*, 121). To understand why Christians hate Jews so vehemently, David goes to the library to read the New Testament, the ur-text for anti-Semitism. In Mat-thew, he finds "rage and scorn directed at the scribes and Phar-isees. The rabbis of the Talmud . . . called hypocrites! . . . the word *Jews* in the account of the crucifixion (*IB*, 305). In Mark he finds further expression of hatred for the Pharisees and similar invec-tives on the crucifixion in Luke and John. Further, David finds corroboration for early Christian anti-Semitism in current Catholic textbooks that he finds in the playground of a nearby parochial school. In *Religion: Doctrine and Practice* by Francis B. Cassilly, S. J., he reads "The widespread popularity enjoyed by this text since its appearance in 1926 is evidence that our Catholic schools consider the fundamental truths of Faith essential to the high-school course in religion" (*IB*, 307). He turns to the index to search for references to Jews and finds the following: "The Jews as a nation refused to accept Christ and since His time they have been wanderers on the earth without a temple or a sacrifice, and without the Messias" (*IB*, 307). Next he finds a Catholic distortion of the Jewish rejection of Jesus: "The Jews rejected Christ mainly because they expected Him to found a never-ending kingdom, as was foretold in the prophecies. This He really did, but the kingdom He founded—the Church—was a spiritual one, not a temporal one such as the carnal Jews were hoping for" (*IB*, 307). The causal link between Catholic anti-Semitism and the success of the Holocaust is manifested in Potok's documentary incorporation of propaganda disseminated by Father Charles Coughlin and his supporters during the Holocaust.

Potok skillfully juxtaposes David's American anti-Semitic ex-periences with his father's European encounters, demonstrating how each generation is shaped by this social pathology. Although Max Lurie's animosity for Christians has been regularly and amply refurbished through repetitions of anti-Jewish actions, the Tulchin massacre looms largest in his consciousness as a touchstone of Christian betrayal of Jewry and Jewry's misplaced trust in Christian decency. Max begins his account of the attack on the city objectively and concludes in a passionate denunciation:

> There were in it Jews and Poles. Cossacks attacked it. The Jews fought well. The Poles wanted to surrender. The Jews could have taken over the city from the Poles and continued fighting. But their rabbi would not let them do it. He was afraid that Poles all over Poland would take revenge on all the Jews in Poland. So the Jews of Tulchin gave all their possessions to the Poles to give to the Cossacks. They hoped the Cossacks would take the money and jewels and gold and not destroy the city. The Cossacks took it all from the Poles and then asked the Poles to hand over the Jews. They handed over the Jews, the same Jews who had fought with them to defend the city. The bastard Poles. . . . A nice story, yes? The courageous Jews! What Martyrdom! They could have lived if they had converted to Christianity. Not one of them accepted the offer. What was there in Christianity? It is the idolatry of butchers and murders. (*IB*, 117–18)

It is from this experience that Max knows it is naive for Jews to expect help from gentiles in the Nazi era. As a descendant of a Tulchin massacre survivor, Max rages against the passive Jewish mentality, which tries to negotiate peace when armed resistance is needed to counter enemies bent on slaughtering Jews. Max Lurie shares the contempt for Poles that is common among many of Singer's Jews, because of their extensive experience with Polish anti-Semitism. Certainly the bitterness of Lurie's tone is unprecedented in the fiction created by American-born novelists, but it is authentic in light of Polish-Jewish history. Lurie rages equally against Catholic murderers and Tulchin's rabbi, who trusted Christians to be true to their Jewish neighbors and prevented the Jews from defending themselves.

The ex-machine-gunner spares no details when telling his son of the wholesale butchery of Polish Jews by Russians, Ukrainians, and fellow Poles during World War I. He teaches David about Jewish suffering under Marshall Pilsudski, a national hero, who refused to discomfort Polish peasants by interfering with their violence against Jews. Like Potok's father, Max Lurie returned from serving his country in World War I to the native enemy eager to exercise its anti-Semitic prejudices.[9] Emblematic of traditional Polish anti-Semitism is the scar Max bears from a wound he sustained on a postwar troop train. The train was detained by bandits who stole only from Jewish soldiers. Max refused to surrender his prayer shawl, and a bandit slashed his face. Not one comrade with whom Max served came to his assistance. It is this kind of pervasive Polish anti-Semitism that leads Max to unite the surviving Jews of his unit into the *Am Kedoshim* Society, a Jewish self-defense group. For Max Lurie, two thousand years of Christian betrayal and indiscriminate slaughter of Jews make the formation of aggressive Jewish self-defense units the only viable response to anti-Semitism.

Photography and the visual imagination offer means through which David Lurie engages in his people's suffering. The *Am Kedoshim* photograph and the history it represents serve for Potok as connective tissue for David's comprehension of historic anti-Semitism and as a structural link connecting the microcosm of Lurie family history to collective Jewish experience. Lurie founded the society in the aftermath of World War I to combat Polish anti-Semitism. Opposing passive acceptance of persecution, the men of *Am Kedoshim*

> learned never to forget the harm our enemies inflict upon us. We have learned that when we work together we can defeat our enemies. We will not stand by with our arms folded when our enemies attack us; nor will we do as some of our families did almost three hundred years ago in Tulchin when they decided not to attack the Poles in that city because they feared what Poles in other cities might do to Jews. We leave such righteousness to other Jews, . . . to Jews whose pure souls make them unable to shed goyishe blood. (*IB,* 71)

Growing Depression-era anti-Jewish violence and the rise of Nazism lead the *Am Kedoshim* to send a representative to get Jews out of Europe and to assist those facing the mounting terror.

David's education in anti-Semitism takes a particularly sinister turn with the news of the Hebron Massacre. He expects outbursts of persecution against Jews in Europe, but he is astonished by the slaughter of Jews in Palestine. Although he learns of violence against Jews in Jerusalem, Safed, Tel Aviv, and Haifa, it is the Arab massacre of yeshiva students in Hebron that troubles David most intensely. Max makes the historical analogy between the Tulchin rabbi and the Hebron Jewish leadership. He voices ire against the Hebron leaders who had anticipated Arab violence, yet refused the protection of the Jewish self-defense organization in order to avoid antagonizing the British commander who guaranteed community safety on the condition that the Jews do nothing to provoke the Arabs. As Lurie's response to Hebron becomes a free association with Tulchin, the novelist superimposes a foreward glance at the Holocaust in the Hebron Massacre:

On the fifteenth of August, Tisha B'av, there had been Arab disturbances in Jerusalem. The British said these had been in reaction to the demonstration staged by the followers of Jabotinsky at the Western Wall protesting new British regulations that interfered with Jewish religious services at the Wall. But we knew all about the British, he said. Our dear friends, the British. They announced that they washed their hands of the Jews as a result of this demonstration, and the Arabs took the hint. The day after the demonstration, on Tish B'av, a group of Arabs beat up Jews gathered at the Wall for prayers, and then burned copies of the Book of Psalms. . . . Then the Mufti of Jerusalem spread the rumor that the Jews were ready to capture and desecrate the holy mosques on the Temple Mount in Jerusalem. The Arabs began coming into Jerusalem from all over the country. In Hebron, Arabs who were friends of the Jews reported that messengers of the Mufti had been in the city and had preached in the mosque . . . that the Jews had attacked Arabs in Jerusalem and desecrated their mosques.

The leaders of the Jewish community of Hebron met secretly. They were informed that the Jewish self-defense organization had sent a message from its headquarters in Jerusalem that it was prepared to dispatch a group of armed young men to defend the Jews at Hebron. At the same time, the leaders were informed that the British district commander had guaranteed the safety of the Jews of Hebron on condition that the Jews do nothing to provoke the Arabs and that no one who was not a resident of the city should enter it. . . . The Jews decided to reject the offer of the self-defense organization. They believed the goyim. They were possessed by the mentality of Tulchin. . . . A band of Arabs returned to Hebron from a mass meeting led by the Mufti and his followers in Jerusalem. They ran through the city attacking Jews. They killed a student they found in the yeshiva. . . . On Shabbos morning, . . . Arabs began coming into the city from all over. They carried rifles and revolvers and knives and swords. The Jews locked themselves in their houses. The police warned the Jews to remain inside. Like sheep, they remained inside. And like sheep, they were slaughtered. They were shot and stabbed and chopped to pieces. They had their eyes pierced and their hands cut off. They were burned to death inside their homes and inside the Hadassah Hospital in Hebron. (*IB*, 162–64)

Bernard Malamud's treatment of the Russian persecution and incarceration in the Beiliss case is an analogue for the Holocaust. So, too, Potok's description of the Hebron Massacre includes elements in common with the Holocaust. Lurie's description of the Hebron Massacre incorporates all the elements of European Holocaust betrayal. False claims of Jewish intent to destroy Islamic holy places parallels Nazi lies about undue Jewish political and economic influence in Europe. Staging the attack on *Tisha B'av,* a day of fasting, mirrors Nazi "special actions" on Jewish holy days—like the Passover offensive against the Warsaw Ghetto. Britain's betrayal of Jews in Hebron foreshadows Britain's betrayal of the Jews in the concentration camps and Britain's sabotage of the Joel Brand mission to save a small portion of Hungarian Jewry in 1944. Potok's lengthy history lesson, like I. B. Singer's use of the Chmielnicki Massacre in *The Satan of Goray,* corresponds to the holocaustal violence and the methods of deceit used to stir up violence against the Jews—the attacks with armed units, which are then protected and inspired to further atrocities by the government in power.

The recitation of anti-Semitic history and David's experience of anti-Jewish street violence converge in the recesses of his imagination as he juxtaposes his father's militant response with his impotent fear. Introduction of the Holocaust in this novel is an organic outgrowth of Potok's focus on Polish and Arab anti-Semitism. Representative of the novelist's increasing skill and sensitivity for integrating liturgy and theme is his invocation of the Holocaust theme in relation to a Yom Kippur memorial service. As David chants a lament for Torah sages martyred during Roman dominion, he grieves for an anonymous Jew, whose murder in Berlin by uniformed Nazis was witnessed from a passing cab by an *Am Kedoshim* member. The witness later read that "the man, a Jew, was found dead the next morning in an alley near a bookstore" (*IB,* 223). During a subsequent trip to Germany to help Jews, the Nazis inform the witness that they will look kindly neither upon his presence in Germany nor his efforts to rescue Jews. American Jewish efforts to aid European Jews is given scant attention in American Holocaust fiction, but Chaim Potok, like Arthur Cohen, acknowledges the central role of immigrant Jews in this endeavor.

Complementing the theme of the continuum of anti-Semitic persecution through reference to the lamentation liturgy is the introduction of biblical and folkloric material. *Am Kedoshim's* foiled efforts to save Jews, culminating in Max Lurie's rage, find parallel in David's withdrawal into biblical and mythological constructs. He conceives of a flood that would cleanse Lemberg, Warsaw, Lodz, the cities of ancestral persecution, and then the site of his own victimization. Rather than a destructive flood, however, it would be a purging flood in whose aftermath "everything outside would be clean and white and the Angel of Death would have less of a job to do because goyim would not kill Jews and the entire world would be free of accidents. Perhaps the Angel of Death himself would die in the flood; the only one to die" (*IB*, 96). On the occasion of the Hebron Massacre, David retreats into a stream of consciousness revery in which he assumes his father's militant personality, raging as his father has against Jewish passivity in the face of gentile violence. Recalling Russian and Polish anti-Jewish atrocities, the boy soldier rants against the Cossacks, for having "Jewish blood on their sabers. And the Jewish flesh on their whips" (*IB*, 166). He also rebukes the Jews: "You are going to sit there reciting Psalms? When did a Psalm prevent a throat from being torn open?" (*IB*, 166). David imagines taking his father's role: the Jew who fights the oppressor, the machine-gunner and cavalryman, the founder and organizer of the *Am Kedoshim* Society, a holy order for the defense of the Jewish people.

In *The Last of the Just*, Andre Schwarz-Bart incorporates the legend of the thirty-six righteous men as a means of relating the history of anti-Semitic persecution from the eleventh to the twentieth century, culminating in the Holocaust. Potok takes a similar approach in his incorporation of the Golem of Prague myth. Jewish folklore created a mythic *golem*, fashioned from lifeless, shapeless matter by a person who knew God's ineffable name and who could, by its mystic means, breath life into the homunculus. The sixteenth-century *golem* was characterized as a huge and very strong figure with a propensity for exercising its physical power, even in indiscriminate destruction. Although the oral tradition inevitably generates variations, most share commonalities including the *golem's* supernatural capacity to discover and foil anti-Jewish violence and the *golem's* enormous strength, used most often to protect powerless Jews from potent enemies. Viewed within the historic frame of European anti-Semitic terror, it is the *golem's* protective role that appealed to the collective imagination of an oppressed people. For his *Legend of the Golem of Prague*, Rabbi Loew endowed the figure with communal responsibility and moral conscience and thus fashioned "a national protector of persecuted Jews, a God-sent Avenger of the wrongs done to a helpless people."[10]

David's *golem* fantasies coincide with the Third Reich's heightened anti-Jewish violence. Gazing into the dark rectangle of his window shade David imagines a Nazi demonstration, flags and banners waving, torches smoking, and twenty-thousand brown-shirted men shouting and saluting. As the news from abroad becomes more violent, ever more menacing visions appear in David's window shade. He consults with the *golem* and envisions himself performing heroically, shouting down the Nazis, quelling demonstrations, and spying on Nazi strategy sessions. The shadow glows red and the boy imagines a German building ablaze. Another time, he imagines a holocaustal conflagration, a synagogue aflame, and himself plunging swiftly through smoke and fire toward the ark to save the endangered Torah scrolls:

> Golem, look what they've done, the brown-shirted servants of the Angel of Death. We must save the Torah scrolls! He came then out of the invisibility in which I had left him and stood beside my bed in the darkness. He bowed in mute acknowledgment of my words, bringing his face close to mine, the face I had molded, my face; then he straightened his massive seven-foot frame and in a leap my eyes could barely discern was suddenly inside the window shade. . . . Through the flames! Into the smoke and through the flames! The flames tore at me but I felt nothing and I moved swiftly through smoke-filled corridors and burst into the heart of the synagogue where the pews were burning and the flames licked at the curtain of the Ark. . . . I tore at the flames with my fingers, beating them away from the sacred words. I gathered the scrolls into my arms and left them with startled sleepy-eyed men on the street. The flames roared in my ears. I slipped from the rectangle and lay in my bed listening to the long clattering of an elevated train. You did well, I murmured. Slowly, the Golem bowed. (*IB*, 254–55)

Dreams commonly used in European Holocaust literature here, too, reflect anxieties of the impotent while adding mythic elements to link historic brutality and contemporary travail. As Nazi harassment of German Jews escalates, the *golem* recedes. During the Passover season—the celebration of the deliverance of the Israelites from Egyptian bondage—David retreats into silence. The *golem* having failed, David now longs for another Moses to deliver the Jews from the German Angel of Death. Potok closes this section of the novel by juxtaposing the end of the *golem* reveries with the German invasion of Poland and cessation of the delivery of mail to or from the family in Poland. "The silences deepened and grew lengthier as the Nazi darkness spread itself across Europe" (*IB*, 322).

The final segment of the novel, set in the Holocaust era and its immediate aftermath, deals with heightened American anti-Semitism as exemplified by the followers of Father Charles E. Coughlin and his Social Justice Movement. Coughlin spewed anti-Semitic propaganda on his regularly scheduled radio broadcasts and in his tabloid, *Social Justice*. As with the Third Reich, rhetoric inspired action. Roaming gangs of American hooligans ambushed yeshiva boys and old Jews: "platoons of goyim numbering about twenty-five each walking the streets of New York looking for Jews. They would try to sell a copy of *Social Justice* to someone who looked Jewish and if he refused to buy it they would start taunting him and pushing him and then they would beat him and run off" (*IB*, 289). Max Lurie had assured his son that the great difference between European and American anti-Semitism was that anti-Semitism was supported and sponsored by the government in Europe, but the American government rejected such behavior. Yet David is a witness to the collaboration of police officers' anti-Semitism, when they passively stand by as a Jew is assaulted in a blatant anti-Semitic attack. Incorporation of the Father Coughlin episode suggests both the Christian foundation upon which Nazi racial anti-Semitism thrived and the support given the Nazis' program of genocide by the churches in Europe.

While hooligans attacked Jews in American streets, genteel anti-Semites in Congress blocked Jewish immigration despite their knowledge of the mass murders occurring in Europe. Although Potok fails to develop this matter at length, he alludes to it in the *Am Kedoshim* rescue worker's assessment of Jewish emigration from Nazi-occupied Europe: "Europe and England will take in a few. So will America. But no country will want many of them" (*IB*, 300).[11] As Germany's Final Solution becomes ever clearer, Max's despair gives way to fatalism. In response to his son's inquiry about assistance for the Jews, Lurie explains: "It is not officially known as yet. When it becomes officially known, then governments will meet and decide that nothing can be done" (*IB*, 335). Since the Jews of America can do little during the war to save European Jewry, the

members of the *Am Kedoshim,* like Arthur Cohen's Jews of the
Society for the Rescue and Resurrection of Jewry, begin to plan
their strategy for helping the surviving remnant. Max advocates
the need for a Jewish army in Palestine to counter the anticipated
British resistance to Jewish immigration.

Through David's mother, Potok registers the impact of the
Holocaust on American-Jewish immigrants whose families were
being destroyed in Europe. Ruth Lurie continues to care for her
American family's physical needs, but withdraws from them emotionally. Having failed to convince her parents to come to America
from Poland when they actually had visas and when exodus was
possible, she fears they will not survive the war. Eventually Ruth
stops reading the old letters from her parents and, for periods
lasting several days, avoids speech. The Luries knew during the
second year of the war of the massive death toll of Eastern European Jewry, but it is at war's end that they learn the full impact of
the concentration camp atrocities and mass murders. Confirmation
is received that the families were transferred from Auschwitz to
Bergen-Belsen and no one survived. Over 150 family members
perished, a fate similar to that which the Potoks suffered. The
novelist, who was David's age at war's end, draws on his own history
for David's reaction to "newspaper photographs, the memorial assemblies, the disbelief in the faces of friends, the shock as news
came of death and more death."[12] Potok writes, "I remember my
father's rage, my mother's soft endless weeping."[13] Predictably,
Max rages and Ruth weeps.

Only when he writes of the Bergen-Belsen photographs does
Potok treat Holocaust atrocities graphically. "Grotesque forms with
skeletal arms and legs and rib cages and heads lay stacked like
macabre cordwood on a stone ramp" (*IB,* 408). The enormity of
the crime is suggested by "hills of corpses, pits of bones, the naked
rubble of the dead and the staring eyes and hollow faces of the
survivors" (*IB,* 400). David is overwhelmed by a photograph of
dead children, "eyes and mouths open, bodies twisted and frozen
with death" (*IB,* 400). From the photographs, David understands
the truth of his teacher's assessment of the German contribution to
the technology of death and the full implications of the Nazi crime
against Jewry: "They destroyed an entire civilization. The Nazis
have taught Western civilization that not only making cars but also
committing murder can become a mass production industry" (*IB,*
401). In addition to realistic rendering, Potok composes an imag-

istic revery in which David imagines the Bergen-Belsen newsphotos while walking along a parapet overlooking the Hudson River. As he looks at the railroad tracks and a shanty town across the river, he falls down a rocky bluff and cuts his finger, which bleeds profusely. The river begins to flow red—all the world is red. As a freight train passes, he imagines the central holocaustal vision of the trains that crisscrossed German-occupied Europe, behind whose sealed doors he envisions "a multitude of writhing human beings packed together riding in filth and terror" (*IB*, 412). The photographs of Bergen-Belsen atrocities catapult David from traditional to secular biblical scholarship and to a determination to dedicate his life

> to fighting what these accident-makers are doing with . . . the most beautiful photograph of all; that is to say, the picture of my people in the Bible. As a result of the fusion of these two metaphors, he leaves his Orthodoxy, enters one of the metaphors: the secular world, in order to understand better the other metaphor: the photograph, the Bible, which is the picture of his people at a certain period of time.[14]

The final confrontation with anti-Semitism comes to this boy from modern Bible criticism.[15] David follows the path of Potok's colleagues who entered the field of Bible scholarship "to change the attitude of that discipline toward Jews."[16] He loves the Torah and decides to join the ranks of its detractors to prove them wrong, to discredit their insertion of anti-Semitic innuendo in their writing, to use textual criticism—the scholarly method abhorrent to traditionalists—to save the Torah from its detractors. The child who sought to save the Torah from the flames of the anti-Semites in his *golem* fantasies has matured and found a substantive way to contribute to Torahic preservation. However, his method distresses his father who objects to textual criticism because of its association not only with all that he hates about modern Germany but with nineteenth-century German Jewish scholars' creation of Reform Judaism, which he regards as the destruction of Torah Judaism.

The novel's final Holocaust reference appears in the postwar era. David, a biblical scholar, travels to Germany to inspect a manuscript. There he sets out on his quest "into the final beginnings" of his family. In the land of annihilation, standing at the entrance to Bergen-Belsen, David is seized by paralytic terror. Inclined to flee, he is urged forward by his Uncle David's voice and by a vision of his teacher commanding him to view the remains of a family devoted to Torah. Out of the wind, his Uncle David, the victim of the Lemberg pogrom, urges him to a new beginning, implying that out of the ashes Judaism will arise again. For David the revitalization takes the form of biblical scholarship. He reads the numbers of the dead, the dead in the hundreds of thousands in Bergen-Belsen, and laments his family losses: "Who lies beneath my feet? I am walking on the dead of my family's beginnings" (*IB*, 431). In this place of barbarism, Potok celebrates Jewish dignity in a superimposed dialogue between Max and his brother, David. They celebrate the living David, who, carrying his uncle's name, will bring new life to old roots. In an allegoric juxtaposition, Potok contrasts the poison of one civilization with the fruit of its victims. Germany's use of modern technology to exterminate millions of Jews and the millions they would have begotten is contrasted with the ancient Jewish Leverite marriage, which symbolizes Judaism's will to survive despite the world's effort to destroy it. Young David is living testimony to the Torahic encouragement that a childless widow may marry her husband's brother and name the first son of the union for the dead husband, thereby perpetuating his name in Israel. David follows his uncle's scholarly path and is perceived by the family as "the resurrection of the dead" (*IB*, 219). Unlike the ghost of the murdered in Renaissance and Jacobean drama who returns to demand vengeance, Uncle David's ghost demands devotion to Judaism and Jewry. At Bergen-Belsen Uncle David strengthens his nephew's commitment to Jewish scholarship. The novel concludes with David's recitation of the Mourner's Kaddish, a prayer for the dead, but a prayer filled with hope for Jewish survival on the site that witnessed the murder of so many Jews.

The continuity suggested by David's incantation of the Kaddish is given dramatic realization in this novel, as in all Potok's fiction, through the renewed vigor of Jewish-American education, manifested in David Lurie's scholarship, and through building and sustaining a vibrant Israel, the mission Max Lurie adopts as his own. Recalling David Malter's turn from Holocaust defeat to Zionist promise in *The Chosen*, Max Lurie rejects passivity in the wake of the European debacle. Like Potok's father, Max is also a fervent Irgunist and supporter of Vladimir Jabotinsky's militant approach to Jewish immigration and survival in Israel. "With grim and silent satisfaction" that Benjamin Max Potok possessed,[17] Lurie supports Irgun raids for Jewish rights in Palestine.

Illustrative of Potok's growing craft as a novelist is his successful integration of biblical and sacred textual matter with the historic themes of the novel, particularly the incorporation of Genesis subjects, language, and imagery. The Genesis parallels operate structurally, thematically, and allusively. The title is derived from the first word of the Hebrew Bible, *Bereshith*. As Genesis traces the history of the Israelites and their relations with other peoples, so too does Potok now abandon the closed societies of his early fiction, the parochial enclaves of Williamsburg and Crown-Heights, for a multiethnic Bronx neighborhood; this neighborhood serves as a microcosm for twentieth-century Jewish interaction with the gentile world. Toward the end of Genesis, Joseph recapitulates the lesson of his career: that God brings good out of evil, and that He will bring the Jewish people out of Egypt and to the land He promised the patriarchs. Potok invokes this redemptive voice to celebrate the remnant's emergence from European Holocaust bondage and its going forth to rebuild and to restore the land and people of Israel. Similarly, during the worst period of Holocaust suffering, the nineteen-year-old David recalls his *Bar Mitzvah* Torah reading: the entry of the Jews into Egypt and its accompanying prophetic reading from Amos regarding restoration of the fortunes of the Jewish homeland and those who would rebuild the ruined cities and inhabit them. Potok's Jews, survivors and American Jews, are determined to make a new beginning after the Holocaust, a beginning that rejuvenates Judaism and Jewry. Whether the new beginning is in Israel or in the Diaspora is unimportant to them; however, that it support Israel as the Jewish homeland and maintain Judaism in Israel and in the Diaspora is of paramount significance. Chaim Potok's dedication to the State of Israel, Jewish scholarship, and the creation of fiction addressing the dynamics of Jewish civilization testify to his celebration of Judaism and Jewry. Potok adds his voice to Emil Fackenheim's affirmation for Holocaust restoration through commitment to Judaism and Jewry, since, like Fackenheim, Potok believes that "the alternative [to Jewish commitment] is to say Hitler succeeded, that everybody really died for nothing."[18]

# CHAPTER TEN

*Nazism on Trial: The Holocaust Fiction of*
*George Steiner*

Because his family left Vienna in 1924 and fled France in 1940 to immigrate to America, George Steiner escaped the assemblies in public squares of Jewish children awaiting deportation, escaped being forcibly separated from his parents when the trains reached their destinations, and escaped the concentration camp selections, slave labor, starvation, and death. He did not, however, escape survivor guilt. Steiner considers himself "maimed for not having been at the roll call."[1] The tragedy that befell the Jews of Europe colors his attitudes toward his own children, his views of language, literature, politics, and the human condition.[2] He writes "My own consciousness is possessed by the eruption of barbarism in modern Europe; by the mass murder of the Jews and by the destruction under Nazism and Stalinism of . . . the particular genius of 'Central European humanism.'"[3] Because the Holocaust rose from within and from the core of European civilization, because "the cry of the murdered sounded in earshot of the universities; the sadism went on a street away from the theaters and museums,"[4] Steiner has sought to explain the relationship of the historic event to its cultural context—specifically to the language and literature of the perpetrators of the Final Solution.

To one who thinks seriously about the Holocaust, all hitherto fixed ideas undergo change. Notions of God, of humanity, of law, of place and time are altered. Regarding himself, "an exile everywhere."[5] Steiner differentiates normal time and Holocaust time:

> If we reject some such module, it becomes exceedingly difficult to grasp the continuity between normal existence and the hour at which hell starts, on the city square when the Germans begin the deportations, or in the office of the *Judenrat* or wherever, an hour marking men, women, children off from any precedent of life, from any voice "outside," in that other time of sleep and food and humane speech. . . .

> This notion of different orders of time . . . may be necessary to the rest of us, who were not there, who lived as if on another planet . . . to discover the relations between those done to death and those alive then, and the relations of both to us; to locate, as exactly as record and imagination are able, the measure of unknowing, indifference, complicity, commission which relates the contemporary or survivor to the slain.[6]

Steiner's literary criticism is premised on the view "that literature deals essentially and continually with the image of man, with the shape and motive of human conduct."[7] To believe that Auschwitz is irrelevant to the life of the imagination is fallacious. For Steiner it "puts in question the primary concepts of a literary, humanistic culture."[8] The following are recurrent themes in his essays: an explanation of anti-Semitism arguing that the Jews, as the embodiment of conscience, became intolerable to Christian Europe, which sought to rid itself of this visible reproach to its pagan spirit; the relationship of the corruption of the German language to the Third Reich's criminal behavior; international complicity and culpability for Holocaust crimes; repudiation of German Holocaust amnesia; vigorous exposure of postwar German lies regarding Holocaust-era knowledge of Nazi atrocities; and denial of the right of any except survivors to forgive Holocaust crimes.

In *Language and Silence* (1967) Steiner explicitly examines the relationship of the Holocaust and the culture that produced it. His interest is in language and the damage it has sustained through corrupt service to political depravity. Steiner contends that language has the capacity to

> absorb masses of hysteria, illiteracy, and cheapness. . . . But there comes a breaking point. Use a language to conceive, organize, and justify Belsen; use it to make out specifications for gas ovens; use it to dehumanize man during twelve years of calculated bestiality. Something will happen to it. Make of words what Hitler and Goebbels and the hundred thousand *Unterstrumführer* made: conveyers of terror and falsehood. Something will happen to the words. Something of the lies and sadism will settle in the marrow of the language. Imperceptibly at first, like the poisons of radiation sifting silently into the bone. But the cancer will begin, and the deep-set destruction. The language will no longer grow and freshen. It will no longer perform, quite as well as it used to, its two principal functions: the conveyance of humane order which we call law, and the communication of the quick of the human spirit which we call grace.[9]

Writing about the Nazi corruption of German, Steiner observes that it is one of the peculiar horrors of the Nazi period that the Nazis themselves recorded the atrocities they committed:

> In Gestapo cellars, stenographers . . . took down carefully the noises of fear and agony wrenched, burned, or beaten out of the human voice. The tortures and experiments carried out on live beings at Belsen and Matthausen were exactly recorded. The regulations governing the number of blows to be meted out on the flogging blocks at Dachau were set down in writing. When Polish rabbis were compelled to shovel out open latrines with their hands and mouths, there were German officers there to record the fact, to photograph it, and to label the photographs.[10]

Steiner acknowledges a measure of validity in Elie Wiesel's call for fictional Holocaust silence and argues, "The best *now,* after so much as been set forth, is, perhaps, to be silent; not to add to the trivia of literary, sociological debate, to the unspeakable".[11] However, in the end he, like Wiesel, rejects this view in favor of the effort to understand, to learn from, and to keep faith with the victims, to bear witness to the appalling crimes of Nazism and to testify to the complicity of non-Germans in those abominations. Steiner contributes significantly to the Holocaust fictional canon with three novellas collected under the title *Anno Domini* (1964) and

*The Portage to San Cristobal of A. H.* (1982). Evading dramatic presentation of the ghettos and camps, Steiner approaches the conditions of these institutions through character judgments against the Nazis and their collaborators. Occasionally through survivor flashbacks and judgments and through self-incrimination of the villains, but more often through choral judgmental voices, George Steiner's fiction operates as a tribunal, where history's actors stand convicted of crimes against humanity. Whether the scene is a French seaside village, a country mental asylum, or a Brazilian jungle, metaphorically the Steiner stage is the Nuremberg courtroom. Steiner writes like a prosecutor subjecting the witness to historic, psychological, and moral scrutiny.

The stories of *Anno Domini* explore memories of the war years, the need to keep the memories alive, and the aftermath of a vanished moment of heightened awareness triggered by the war experience. Each story shares the common theme of coping with the delayed disturbance of a man who has suffered psychologically during the war. The Jewish experience emerges in two of the three selections—albeit briefly and somewhat peripherally to the narrative's central focus.

In "Return No More," a Wehrmacht officer—now a prosperous industrialist—returns to the Normandy farmhouse where he was billeted during the war to win a daughter of the family in marriage. Despite his protestations to the contrary, Falk is not sufficiently contrite to suit the family whose son he ordered hanged from their own ash tree. In an effort to convey his own and Germany's wartime suffering, Falk tells the French family of the Hamburg bombing and fire storm when he joined a Gestapo euthenasia squad killing phosphorus burn victims, including a young woman whose face was too severely burned for positive identification, but whom he thought was his sister. Claiming to have learned the value of life in the rural French village, Falk contrasts its idyllic life and his own unsettling experience as a Hitler youth and young soldier in Germany.

> I grew up in a kind of very loud bad dream, . . . I cannot remember a time when we were not marching or shouting and when there were no flags in the street. When I think of my childhood all I can remember distinctly are the drums and the uniform I wore as a young pioneer. And the great red flags with the white circle and the black hooked cross in the middle. . . .

School was worse. The drums beat louder and there were more flags. On the way home we played rabbit hunt and went after Jews. We made them run in the gutter carrying our books and if they dropped any we held them down and pissed in their faces. . . . I never finished school. I suppose my final exam came in Lemberg when they told me to clean out a bunker with a flame thrower. I had my graduation in Warsaw, marching with the victory parade. Now the drums never stopped.[12]

Believing the German people have built a wall of lies to avoid facing their Holocaust crimes, Falk recalls his own period of service in Norway and Utrecht with dismay, the wounds he sustained in Salonika and Kharkov, and admits Nazi atrocities in Salonika, "where he hanged the partisans on meat hooks" (*R*, 34). This confession to the people he has robbed of a son and a brother is difficult, and Falk responds to their hatred by explaining how easy it would be for him to remain in Hamburg or Hanover, marry a widow with a pension, and be like most Germans who refrain from speaking of the past. "We all have amnesia or perhaps someone put an iron collar around our necks so that we can't look back" (*R*, 42). Falk's observations echo those Steiner offered in his controversial essay, "The Hollow Miracle," which contrasts the early postwar German acknowledgment of the events of the Hitler era with the post-1948 era and the initiation of economic recovery. The focus on work, productivity, and economic and industrial restoration heralded a new German myth, a myth that denied the crimes of the Nazi past, claimed that the horrors had been grossly exaggerated, expressed ignorance of the Nazi atrocities, and zealously dedicated itself to the principle of forgetting the past. Because Falk shares these Steinerian views and loves the French girl and the serene life she represents, he comes to France to face the horrors, to remember the dead on both sides.

Reactions vary. Eager for reparations, some villagers entertain the idea of accepting the German for a price. Others reject him outright. An aunt, perceiving England, not Germany, as her country's real enemy, welcomes Falk into the family with ceremony and honor. The French girl's embrace of her brother's murderer and her parents' acceptance of their son's assassin strains credulity. At the country wedding celebration, only the bride's surviving brother and his cohorts stand to the side muttering their dissatisfaction. Finally, in an abrupt conclusion, they demand that the lame bridegroom dance and join him in the dance macabre, administering the punishment he may have unconsciously sought by trampling him to death. The thematic burden of "Return No More," despite its sympathetic rendering of the German, posits that there is no forgetting and no forgiving Nazi atrocity.

The second story, "Cake," is presented from the point of view of an innocent American caught in the Nazi nightmare. He is a graduate student working in Europe on his dissertation when war breaks out. Disgusted by what he perceives to be his own cowardice, he agrees to carry messages for the Resistance. As the Gestapo closes in, the American is hidden in an insane asylum under the protection of an anti-Fascist doctor. There he falls in love with a Jewish girl who is also concealed, until she is denounced by a jealous old patient who fancies the American.

The Jewish tragedy is more prominent in "Cake" than in the other stories of the collection. The story is told through flashbacks of the American as he returns to the asylum after the war; the Jewish material is a recollection of what the narrator witnessed prior to his asylum sanctuary: the Holocaust history of his lover's family as she revealed it to him and his witness of the Gestapo action at the asylum.

Initially the American is not inconvenienced by the German occupation of France. He secures travel permission to Paris so he may work in the rare book room at the Bibliotheque Sainte-Genevieve, and for him life goes on as usual. His first encounter with Nazi brutality occurs in a train compartment when an SS patrol removes two Jews. The American watches intently as the guards tear an old man from his seat, "not in rage, but with venomous pleasure. They pushed him down the steps of the railway car. . . . They struck him with unhurried blows, let him lurch to his feet and kicked him to the ground again."[13] The frightened witness looks on as the girl traveling with the old man lunges at the Nazis, who in turn "held her down and rubbed cinders in her face till it was black and raw" (*C,* 72). The image of the men rubbing cinders into the girl's hair and mouth, then stripping off her coat as the train pulled away lingers with the American who assumes something beastial will take place in the wood. The American becomes sick to his stomach witnessing the SS tactics. Yet in time he comes to envy the old man and girl, "the torments being wrought on them. Of what I supposed had been done to them once they had been dragged to the SS barracks, and then afterwards" (*C,* 73).

This odd envy is not based on ignorance for it is the summer of 1941 and people know that those detained by the Gestapo often turn up in the Loire, "their faces and bodies torn" (*C*, 73). Like the tourist who wants to experience the real Europe, this man feels deprived to be missing the pain in his flesh that others are feeling daily. He scans the censored newspapers for references to hostages, deportations, and the increasing ferocity of German reprisals for French resistance. No longer content to spend his efforts on the violence in literature when real blood flows all around him in the prison camps and Gestapo cellars, the American suppresses his fear and becomes a courier for the underground.

Steiner reveals the special actions taken against Jews in France through the narration of Rahel Jakobsen, the young woman whom the narrator meets in the asylum. Adhering to the traditional pattern of Holocaust realism, he delineates the pre-Nazi normality, its piecemeal disruption, and the horrors of the Final Solution. The Jakobsens were prosperous assimilated Jews living in Brussels. Their home evidenced the cultured life of its inhabitants—a music stand with Chopin études, Chagall paintings, and books in many languages. The family "still went to the synagogue once or twice a year, but in black English homburgs" (*C*, 89). Encroachments by the Reich first manifested themselves when an uncle and aunt were forced to leave Frankfurt and were allowed to take only one suitcase. Others emigrate. Eventually Rahel was kept home from school and her father stayed home from the Bourse, passing the time tutoring his sons. The servants departed, one marching off with Mrs. Jakobsen's furs. Indignities mounted: in place of milk bottles, the family found parcels of excrement on the door step. The prelude to the end of their charmed existence was when Rahel's mother sewed yellow stars on all their coats and jackets. A man appeared to tell her father that lists of deportees had already been composed, that the destruction of the Jewish community was imminent, and that plans had to be made to try to save the children. Although Rahel begged that her younger brother be taken to safety since his survival would mean continuation of the family name, and only a male is allowed to lead the prayers for the dead in the synagogue, she was chosen for rescue. Her father and older brother were summoned to the Gestapo and presumed lost. At the time of her departure, she had no knowledge of the whereabouts of her mother and younger brother.

In the asylum Rahel frets most over the younger brother,

imagining him being sent to those places, unable even to name the dreaded camps. Despite what he hears from Rahel and his own witnessing of violence, the American strives to comfort Rahel with pipe dreams of a civilized Germany, "the land of Schiller and Beethoven; it spoke the language of Rilke" (*C*, 92). He reminds her of the excesses of World War I anti-German propaganda in an effort to give her hope that Nazi atrocities are exaggerated and that her mother and brother may still be alive, indeed that she will see her whole family again. The American innocent remains undaunted.

Bearing witness to the murder of European Jewry is a common theme in Holocaust literature. Steiner incorporates it in "Cake" through Rahel's plea that the American remember the details of her family history. She made the telling and listening a holy service, for in her anticipated American retelling of the history "she and her family were to have their only survivance" (*C*, 99). Defying those who swore "that no one would even recall the names of the dead, that their sum would be ash, . . . [that they] would have neither graves nor the fitful resurrection men are allowed in the remembrance of their children" (*C*, 99), Rahel solemnly narrates the family history for perpetuity. In a beautiful image evoking the Jewish practice of lighting annual memorial candles for the dead, the narrator reflects on Rahel's efforts with great solemnity: "One by one she lit in me the candles for her dead" (*C*, 99).

Like most of the writers in this study, Steiner raises in this Holocaust story the subject of traditional pre-Nazi anti-Semitism. He introduces the topic through a warning to the American from an elderly female patient who believes he is being deceived and is, therefore, forming an alliance with "a dirty little Jewess." The admonition is a catalyst for the American's spontaneous recollection of the anti-Semitism he witnessed in upper-class America—the enrollment quotas restricting Jews in prestigious private schools, their exclusion from social clubs, the Harvard social prejudice, and finally the ironic recognition that if he lived to preserve Rahel's history, it would be in his mother's Belmont home and in "cousin Peyton's library on Mt. Auburn Street, in the Somerset Club . . . [places where] "living Jews have small welcome" (*C*, 99). Indeed, the narrator faces his own anti-Semitism, which he characterizes as a universal attitude: "Like most people, I found that Jews left me uncomfortable; I parted from them as from a stiff chair" (*C*, 94). Defending this statement, he cites one of Steiner's oft-repeated theses explaining a root cause of anti-Semitism: "By their unending misery, the Jews have put mankind in the wrong. Their presence is reproach" (*C*, 95). This is an allusion to Steiner's theme that the Jewish insistence on moral perfectability is a threat to the non-Jewish world, which defies it through their periodic destruction of Jews.

Another recurrent topic in Steiner's essays, the significance of language to human behavior and psychology, finds expression through gentile attitudes toward the Jew's use of a non-Jewish language. A student of literature, the narrator was particularly aware of the significance of the Jewish contribution to language and literature. Yet his recognition smacks of hostility, a common phenomenon among educated anti-Semites. The narrator, like George Steiner in his essays and Jean Paul Sartre in *Jew and Anti-Semite*, observes:

> No one can engage in literary studies without being made cognizant of their seducer's gift for language and their ironic devotion to the abstract. The Jew makes of language a place. He is not really at home in it (how could he be, lacking that tenebrous, immemorial complicity with the stone, leaf and ash of a land, which give to speech its precedent, unspoken meaning?). But he masters it with the nonchalant adroitness of a privileged guest; he chucks it knowingly under the chin. (*C*, 94)

The narrator's education in anti-Semitism is brief but pointed. His memory of Rahel and her family remains with him after the girl is forcibly removed from the asylum by the Gestapo, acting on information supplied by the jealous old woman. In his postwar visit to the asylum in the company of his aristocratic, unsympathetic mother, the narrator goes to Rahel's room hoping against credulity to find her alive. Here he confronts the truth about his Jewish encounter and expresses his grief in a Holocaust image: "I would cry out to her that since she had left me, my life was ash" (*C*, 111).

*The Portage to San Cristobal of A.H.* opens with a startlingly dramatic scene: the discovery of Adolf Hitler, in the Amazon Jungle, by a group of Israeli Nazi hunters. The plot centers on removing Hitler from the jungles and swamps to San Cristobal for judgment. Echoing in fragmentary sentences the argument he made in "The Hollow Miracle," Steiner returns to his theme of Nazism's pervasive corruption of the German language as manifested in Hitler's transformation of words into weapons: "They say your voice could . . . Burn cities. They say that when you spoke. Leaves turning to ash and men weeping. They say that women just to hear your voice, . . . Would tear their clothes off."[14] The leader of the search team warns the men by radio not to allow Hitler to speak during their jungle trek lest they succumb and respond to him sympathetically. Referring to a theory of dichotomies, the team leader, Emmanuel Lieber, advises:

> All that is God's . . . must have its counterpart, its backside of evil and negation. So it is with the Word, with the gift of speech that is the glory of man and distinguishes him everlastingly from the silence or animal noises of creation. When He made the Word, God made possible also its contrary. . . . He created on the night side of language a speech for hell. . . . Few men can learn that speech or speak it for long. It burns their mouths. It draws them into death. But there shall come a man whose mouth shall be as a furnace and whose tongue as a sword laying waste. He will know the grammar of hell and teach it to others. He will know the sounds of madness and loathing and make them seem music. . . . Do not let him speak freely. (*P*, 45)

Steiner parallels the portage through the Amazonian swamps and jungles with allegoric and historic journeys, charting the Holocaust terrain traveled and interpreted by its victims, its criminal perpetrators, and their acquiescent and passive partners. Like Joseph Conrad's allegoric use of the jungle in *Heart of Darkness*, Steiner's jungle/swamp setting signifies "the inaccessible mystery of what . . . [Hitler] did and who he was, and bringing him out of the jungle means gaining the attention of a forgetful world, long since stricken with historical amnesia."[15]

The premise of Steiner's fantasy is based on the myth that the Fuhrer did not perish in his bunker by suicide, but escaped from Germany to South America. The novel's structural pattern juxtaposes scenes of the jungle with those from the civilized world. Its rhythms shift from tense altercation between the Jews and the Holocaust architect to the sedate, supercilious, passionless German, French, Russian, British, and American voices of the international intelligence agencies analyzing the advantages and damages that might accrue to their respective nations should Hitler still be alive and returned to civilization.

Although the only overt trial in *Portage* is Hitler's, the international community is also on trial and judged corrupt through authorial selection. Indifference and acquiescence of the great powers to Jewish annihilation, a recurrent theme of Holocaust literature, is effectively shown through postwar vignettes of the intelligence services. Steiner's representation of multinational intelligence officers—which often verges on caricature—renders distinctive national sensibilities, political agendas, and idiosyncratic historic interpretations of Hitler's career and the Holocaust. The British concern is primarily forensic; the German concern is legal; the Russian concern is political; the French concern collaborational; the American opportunistic; and the Israeli punative. These passages are extensions of Steiner's long-term examination of language as a mirror of human psychology. It is through the international characters' use and abuse of language that their national purposes are revealed.

British and American interests in Hitler and the Holocaust are minimally treated. The focus is on Israeli, Russian, German, and French concerns, which relate largely to their desire to conceal past and present collaboration and errors in judgment. The chapter devoted to British interests also develops crucial expository material from the point of view of Evelyn Ryder, a forensics expert who identified Hitler's remains and whose conclusions were generally accepted. In Ryder's dialogue, Steiner reviews the Hitler survival myth: a double is killed in place of the Fuhrer, and Hitler escapes and prepares for a second coming, when the Reich would rise again in response to his voice. Ryder's summary of the nature and progress of the Israeli mission for the benefit of his young colleague provides readers with the historic background of the Israeli mission. Protective of his own reputation for forensic expertise and angry with Israeli persistence in tracking Nazi criminals, Ryder prefers to believe that the team is in error about their captive's identity. His refutation, however, focuses not on forensic science but on Hitler's psychology and style:

> I don't see it. Using a double at that point, where it mattered so that the ghastly show be done right. The high note and Valhalla. And how could he be that sure of any other human being, leaving another man to step into his own fire? When everything around him was betrayal. . . .
>
> I don't suppose he wanted time to go on, not after him. . . . In the last fire. Sardanapalus. There's a lot of that in German romantic poetry, you know. And he was a romantic. A romantic mountebank. Mad to the heart but with a brightness. (*P*, 11–12)

Ryder's interest is in the Israeli trackers, in forensic detail, and not in the historic significance or moral import of the Holocaust or the chase. The Briton's remarks on the Holocaust are negligible, passionless, and amoral and as such are representative of his government's Holocaust-era attitude toward the genocide program.

Steiner introduces Holocaust history through Ryder's recollection of one of the Israelis, Isaac Amsel, whom he knew during the war. While serving under the British command, Amsel managed to get in and out of Poland and tried, to no avail, to persuade the British to bomb the rail lines to the concentration camps. Without a trace of moral consternation, Ryder notes that Amsel tried to get him to "go to the old man and tell him about the ovens. The old man wouldn't have believed me you know. Not his kind of war really" (*P*, 9–10). Ryder's apparent failure to transmit the message says as much about his character as it does about the British high command. Ryder's tone here is supercilious; he is completely indifferent to his failure even to bring the matter before the British command and indifferent to British immorality in having full knowledge of the genocide plan in 1942 and yet choosing to suppress it. Ryder's acknowledgment that the same Israeli left the British service to work against their efforts to prevent Holocaust survivors from immigrating to Israel further indicts British policy in the face of Jewish tragedy. The British officer's unintentional self-incrimination creates a dramatic impact. His inability to recognize the immorality of the position, even in the postHolocaust period, bespeaks continued British reluctance to recognize its Holocaust-era crime and admit its shameful postwar hindrance of survivors' immigration to Palestine. Britain's failure reflects the moral question Steiner pursues in "A Kind of Survivor"—the complicity of non-Aryans in the destruction of the Jews. In the essay, he condemns the Americans and the British for failing to bomb the rail lines to the death camps and the Russians for failing to send advance warning to Jewish communities when they knew of the mass killings in regions already invaded by the Nazis.

Americans surpass the British in greed and ineptitude. In the first instance, an American agent posing as a public relations man gains the cooperation of the spy who is tracking the Israeli team for the British. In the latter case, government officials are the object of Steiner's satire in a news conference where they qualify and modify every sentence to evade disclosing the truth. Dismayed at being caught off-guard, the Americans determine to honor protocol rather than the moral significance of the capture. Sensitive to the wishes of the nations party to the Berlin agreements and Nuremberg tribunal, as well as the newly established regimes in Austria, the German Federal Republic and the German Democratic Republic, the Americans consider turning the investigation over to the United Nations. The only interests the Americans fail to recognize are Israel's, the nation representing the people who suffered most from Hitler's policies. The American official maliciously complains of the Israeli government's lack of cooperation with American requests and its silence about its recruitment or support of the search team. To the Israeli reporter's question regarding Israel's successful movement of Hitler to Israel to stand trial, the American offers an unsympathetic comparison to the Eichmann kidnapping. Typical of Steiner's satiric treatment of the United States' failure to act on the moral and historic implications of bringing Hitler to trial, and the particular significance of this event to Israel, is a discussion of Israel's response in the event of the United States interception of the mission and its concern for providing Hitler legal aid for his defense.

The Russian section as well is void of any mention of Hitler's crimes. Here Steiner concentrates explicitly on Russian totalitarianism and the Russian attitude toward Hitler's death in the bunker. The chapter's tension arises from the exchange between a Soviet intelligence officer and a Russian citizen being encouraged, in light of the Israeli discovery, to retract his earlier coerced recantation on the demise of the German leader. The terrified citizen had been tortured and imprisoned in a Siberian camp for eight years for doubting the authenticity of the body presented as Hitler's corpse. Having learned the Gulag lesson sufficiently, the man attributed his doubt to Western propaganda and recanted. Prompted by memories of beatings and freezing temperatures in Siberian camps that achieved his previous false recantation, the citizen willingly obliges his interrogators and concludes in despair: "Hitler was alive. They knew it now. And they wanted him. . . . Because he is they ripped out my nails, and sent me to the ice forest" (*P*, 39). The chapter is an indictment of Soviet manipulation of Holocaust history to suit its political objectives. Truth is lost in the process.

Steiner presents the French position, written in diary form, from the perspective of a self-serving career intelligence officer of a Fascist family that served the Vichy government. In addition to blocking Israel's victory in bringing Hitler to trial, the diarist's greater interest is in avoiding any dishonor to France. He asserts that "the Jewish organization" has neither privilege over Hitler's person nor the right to bring him to Israel; since that nation had no status "at the time of the said crimes or of the Nuremberg trials . . . [it] cannot be considered a party to the case, though possibly a 'friend of the court' or 'interested observer'" (*P*, 139). The Frenchman's disregard for the crime against Jewry and the justice of Israel's cause in bringing Nazis to trial exemplifies Western arrogance. Concluding that the only appropriate place to hold the trial is France, he then questions the advisability of a trial because the proceedings could turn farcical, and more to the point, France could be embarrassed.

> Why open the old wounds? Things would get said, which all of us know and can, therefore, let be. That Vichy was not his creation, but a structure out of the heart of French history, out of an agrarian, clerical, patriarchal France which has never accepted the Revolution, which loathes the Jew and the Mason, which would, with a shrug, consign Paris to the devil. That to so many of my beloved countrymen—including my esteemed father and Uncle Xavier—it was the wrong war in the first place. . . . "Perfidious Albion" and Jewish finance being the real enemies. . . . And the larger design: a more or less united Europe, with strong central organs. . . . Chancellor Hitler's dream and our current ideal, . . . Drieux's testament; still worth reading. 'Millions will have died through a hideous misunderstanding before Europe moves toward that unity which Fascism envisioned, that unity of the Teutonic-Latin genius in the face of the materialist barbarism of the United States and its grotesque imitator, the Soviet Union.' Do we really want that stuff pouring out over the front pages once again, reminding us of our grosser indiscretions? The mass killings—for that's what they were—at the time of the "liberation"? The betrayals before that? The years of the *milice*, no Germans in that bunch, and of the French camps? (*P*, 140)

To the Frenchman, who views the mass murder of Jews as a minor indiscretion, the French political image is sacrosanct. Throughout this chapter one hears Steiner's moral indictment of the Vichy government and its continued cover-up.

Counterpointed with French arrogance is German sentimentality. The German perspective is introduced in a scene that evokes the image of the Nazi capacity to enjoy Goethe and Rilke, to admire Bach and Schubert, and yet to work the torture chambers and gas chambers of Auschwitz. Dr. Rothling, who had been exhilarated by the triumphs of the Third Reich, now despairs at the timidity and caution of his daughter's generation; he disdains those who "pretend that they are carrying our national burden, that the past lies on their shoulders and the blood on their forehead" (*P*, 114). Like his countrymen who proudly served Hitler, Dr. Rothling prefers to erase Nazi crimes from history, to enjoy sweet amnesia, to protect Germans at the expense of discrediting Nazi victims. He regards a Hitler trial negatively, much as the Frenchman does, and is opposed to exposing criminals who have evaded punishment and have successfully integrated into the postwar German society and economy. Rothling tries to discredit those who expose hidden Nazis, charging them with

> mere hysteria. Melodrama. Whoever was not in it can have no real knowledge of what it was like, of why we acted or did not act. Those who claim they feel remorse on our behalf are swindlers. They invested nothing of their own conscience in that terrible account. What right have they to draw on it? Any man can say *Auschwitz*, and if he says it loud enough everyone has to cast their eyes down and listen. . . . So easy to do if you were a child at the time or not even born. (*P*, 114)

In a prologue to Hitler's defense, Rothling expresses neither personal responsibility nor remorse for his embrace of an immoral regime. Instead, he invokes the "innocent" bystander rationale to defend his colleagues:

> When you can have no idea of what it was really like, for most of us, for the decent educated class trying to survive on that other side of the moon. Go ahead, say Auschwitz, Belsen, what have you, put ash on your head, shake your fists in our faces and demand that we do eternal penance. There's a tidy sum in remorse, TV serials to be produced, books for the autumn trade. . . . What would you have done, what fine words would you have cried out at the time? When the brown men stomped by, the bravest of us wet our pants. (*P*, 114)

This self-serving excuse is not only immoral but reveals the obscenity of the German's nostalgia for the war years. Dr. Rothling recalls with perverse pleasure the combination of violence and beauty during the occupation of Holland: the people hanging from "two perfect rows of poplars, one on each side of the canal. The vesper bells rang from somewhere in the town. The sound and the fallen leaves came toward me down the dusky water" (*P*, 115). Similarly, he describes the beauty of the spring light in Norway and crows who "had been at the partisans' eyes and stripped their cheeks" (*P*, 115). He found these mutilated faces "beautiful to look on, marbled, folded in sleep" (*P*, 115). He despairs of Germans who wish the Third Reich had never materialized. For him it was an opportunity to live history fully, to live heroically, to "have crossed and recrossed Europe like Napoleon's hordes, have seen Salonika burning and the face of an old man floating, in the Grand Canal. . . . A thousand year Reich inside each of us, a millennium of remembered life" (*P*, 117). Unlike the repentant German of "Return No More," Dr. Rothling's immorality is measured by failure to feel remorse for German crimes against humanity. He expresses regret only for the diminished lives of postwar Germans who inherited the Nazi ashes. This regret is minor, for Dr. Rothling concludes his ecstatic revery by admitting that he would not trade the past. He regrets only German defeat, not the philosophy or the sins of the Reich. Rothling's thoughts are accompanied by his daughter's music, a dreadful reminder to the reader that a great culture was also a great criminal state, a reminder that Jews heard music as they were shoved into the gas chambers. Thus, this brilliant episode serves simultaneously to link Nazism to the culture from which it emerged and to suggest postwar German nostalgia for the Hitler period.

The press of current affairs interrupts Rothling's revery. He must examine Germany's legal options should Hitler be alive and study the questions of national versus international jurisdiction. He had been asked by his government, in the wake of the Eichmann trial—"that disorderly escapade in Jerusalem" (*P*, 122)—to study the law in the unlikely eventuality that the rumors that Hitler was still alive prove to be true. He consults a younger lawyer who suggests an international tribunal composed of people who had no direct part in the events, those who were either too young or not yet born. The lawyer suggests that Hitler's advanced years make judicial retribution unlikely and that Hitler "stands outside the norms of law either common or specifically promulgated" (*P*, 126). Rothling is astounded that a younger man takes this position and argues, "If the codex does not apply to Herr Hitler, . . . then he was absolutely right in claiming that he was above the law, that the law is a bundle of mouse-eaten parchment with no authority over

the superman or the will of the *Volk*" (*P,* 126). Although this outburst appears, at first glance, a criticism of the young lawyer's
thinking, it is not, for the older man says he finds it noble, but
dangerous. A legalist, Rothling is prepared to manipulate the law
to his purpose. Reminiscent of German lawyers and doctors who
had no compunctions about cheating and torturing Jews as long as
it served the Reich, Rothling balks only at the notion of disobeying
established laws. Ethics are irrelevant. Uncomfortable with the
management of the Nuremberg hearings, Rothling insists that
forms, traditions, and correct judicial procedures be fully exercised
should Hitler come to trial. The young lawyer's intent, however,
appears more wide-ranging. He worries not only about one individual but about many who could be subject to retribution:

> The rise and deeds of Nazism involved the active support, the ini-
> tiative of many other men, perhaps millions. It was the relationship
> of Hitler's person to that support, the way in which he obtained and
> harnessed it, the question of whether responsibility could ever be
> localized which needed clarification. (*P,* 127)

The lawyers do not resolve the legal questions; they take refuge in
the thought that the rumors of Hitler's survival are unfounded and
hence the dilemma merely hypothetical. Eager to dismiss the implications of a trial against Hitler, the Germans seek comfort in
evasion, and comfort in the conviction that the importance of
Hitler has been exaggerated, and sentimentalized and that there is
no need to worry about how or why Nazism dominated Germany.
They conclude with the worst kind of arrogance, an arrogance that
was at the heart of Aryan racism. They condemn those who persist
in raising questions about the past: "They think they're making
deep and terrible statements on behalf of the dead. They aren't.
They're puffing up their own little lives. Oh it was hell; we were in
it up to our eyes—while it lasted. And for a few years more. . . . But
now, looking back, . . . I can't help wondering whether it was very
important" (*P,* 129).

In dramatic contrast to the many national voices that focus on
the more exciting aspects of tracking Hitler, but have little concern
for the crimes or the victims, the Israeli team is the novel's moral
register, obsessed with Holocaust loss and bringing its architect to
justice. The team includes both choral and primary voices addressing the essence of Holocaust history and its crucial aftermath. Emmanuel Lieber, the team's leader who directs the operation by

radio from Tel Aviv, has worked on the project from its inception thirty years prior to the Hitler discovery, guiding the team from London, Turin, and Tel Aviv. The little that Steiner divulges of Lieber's Holocaust background appears in the meditation of Simeon, the field leader. We learn that Lieber crawled out from under burnt flesh in a death pit, having witnessed "the fires of Bialka, the children hung alive, the bird droppings glistening on the shorn heads of the dying" (*P*, 17). Those memories are the well-spring of his dedication to bringing Nazi criminals to account. The tattoo on the forearm is but an emblem of the inner marking the Holocaust has indelibly inscribed on its victims. They are "marked by the things seen. . . . [marked by] a perception so outside the focus of man's customary vision" (*P*, 17) as to identify them as a special order of consciousness. Lieber and the others share a solemn oath "to find him, be it at the cost of their lives. Not to return until they had found him or had absolute proof that he was dead" (*P*, 19). This resolve was taken after years of hunting and shared, but unspoken, doubt about the plausibility of the mission and an even graver doubt about the international reaction if they should succeed. After years of fighting the natural tribulations of jungle, swampland, and human obstructions—such as Stroessner's hooligans—the Israelis fear that even if they manage to get Hitler out of the jungles and swamps alive, nations will either be reluctant to take him or will not know how to deal with him; they will be reluctant to confront the Holocaust and its political and human significance. The national vignettes amply demonstrate the Israelis' foresight.

The Israelis pass the time during their jungle ordeal imagining judgment and retribution. Each man, certain of the immensity of Hitler's crimes and society's inability to exact commensurate punishment, conjures up his own retribution. Gideon Benasseraf, who is just beginning to use future tense verbs and who is burdened with the memory of seeing one of his children burnt alive and the other led by its mother into the gas chamber, would allow Hitler freedom of movement throughout Israel, "Every single time he wanted food or water or shelter he'd have to ask for it and say who he was" (*P*, 62). Isaac Amsel, whose father was brutally murdered and who lost three of his own children declares all punishment inadequate:

> Because we've got Hitler and can tear his nails out and wait for them to grow again the dead will sit up and give themselves a dusting. They won't. Not one of them. Not if you parade him over every

grave, over every ashpit, not if you dip him in boiling oil six million times. Do you really believe a man can get even for the murder of his children? For what a six year old girl saw before she died. . . . (*P*, 63)

Amsel resists execution because that would satisfy history and nations would claim the accounts settled, when they can never be settled. Execution would vindicate those who want to forget their own complicity in Nazi crimes against Jewry and attribute all the blame to Hitler. Steiner moves from this view to one that echoes his earlier essay analyses of the roots of Christian anti-Semitism and adapts it to postHolocaust rationale: "First they nailed up Christ and now Hitler. God has chosen the Jew. For his hangman. Let them carry the blood. We're in the clear" (*P*, 64).[16]

The most religious of Steiner's characters, Elie Baruch, whose name evokes images of the priesthood and blessings, responds to Hitler's judgment as one would expect of an Orthodox Jew, leaving the matter to God's superior judgment. Appropriately, his memory of the Holocaust occurs in the context of a philosophic meditation on the nature of evil. Reviewing various theories about God purposefully allowing one small error in the Torahic text—an "unfathomable error, the breach through which evil has rushed on man" (*P*, 86)—he recalls his own teacher's theory and in turn the dreadful memory of the righteous man's brutal death in the Nazi fire pit at Grodny. Like the author who expresses a measure of guilt for missing the roll call of his peers, Elie laments that he ought to have been with his teacher in death, where at least his death would have been quick, rather than this slow deterioration in the Amazon jungle. Elie refrains from speculating on punishment for Hitler. He prays that God will make the team His instrument, but not His substitute: "Do not ask of us, O Lord, that we do vengeance or show mercy. The task is greater than we are. It passes understanding. And whom Thou hast now delivered into our hands, may he be Thine utterly" (*P*, 22). As Elie and the others discuss carrying the aged Hitler out of the jungle and swamp on their backs if necessary, Elie contrasts the care the Jews must exercise on Hitler's behalf with the barbarism the Nazis inflicted on old Jews:

> Men and women ninety years old. The crippled and the blind and the ones spitting blood. They made them walk barefoot, over the cobbles. And whoever fell behind, they threw water over their feet. So that they would freeze to the stones. And stand there till they

died. Burning alive in their skins. At Chelmno, there was a rabbi, a man of wonders. A hundred years old. And they tore out his tongue . . . and made him hold it before him, and walk. A mile. More than that. Till he came to the fire pit. And they told him: Sing. Sing you man of wonder. (*P*, 23)

The grotesquery and sadism of the Nazi war against the Jews is treated briefly in the fragmented memories of the survivors and is occasionally relieved by gallows humor, as when the team is discussing carrying Hitler and one member declares, "We'll take turns carrying him. Like the ark" (*P*, 23). Steiner incorporates Holocaust-era agonies into the postwar context by comparing the jungle slime, disease, physical peril, and general travail the team is undergoing to the recollected suffering in Europe. As he cuts his way through vines, lice-infested plants, and rat-infested swamps, Isaac remembers maneuvering in the sewers under the ghetto wall, all the while fearful that when he raised the cover there would be a Nazi boot in his face.

Isaac Amsel, whose sewer reverie stalks his jungle trek, fantasizes about a painful death for Hitler, a prolonged agony commensurate with what European Jews suffered:

I'd do it so that he knew it was being done. Every thousandth of a second. And done many times. Not all at once. Snap and it's all over. So he'd wonder about the next time. . . . I'd chain him to a stake on top of a pile of wood. So high that he could see beyond the city. And lay a trail of powder or a wick a hundred miles long, winding through every street and coiling around the square. And light it. He'd see the flame traveling nearer. He'd have to watch it for hours. Closer and closer. Just before it reached the faggots I'd jump in front of the crowd and stamp it out. . . . Or hang him on a pulley just above a vat of acid. Each day someone would come, . . . and turn the crank so that some bit of him would dip in the acid. One turn if you've lost a wife, two for each child. I'd jam a prop in his mouth so that he couldn't scream. Till his eyes burst. Or set his balls in a carpenter's vise. For a few minutes each day. Until he fainted. Putting a timetable on his wall so that he would know exactly when the next session came. And skin his leg to make the lampshade in his cell. (*P*, 61)

This gruesome catalogue is of course a grotesque accumulation, the rantings of a vengeful imagination, but it replicates some of the atrocites the Nazis inflicted on their Jewish victims. His compatriots point out the absurdity of this fantasy, which leads Isaac to add that he would execute such a plan if he could and keep Hitler alive in order to repeat the process, much as the Nazis sought to degrade, humiliate, and torture the Jews before they killed them.

Worried that they will die before extricating Hitler from the jungle, the team members also fear losing Hitler to other nationals should they survive and succeed. Using an example that is characteristic of the Eastern block's denial of the particularity of Jewish suffering in the Holocaust,[17] one Israeli notes the official Polish biased assessment of Auschwitz:

> "Here perished the heroic Polish combatants against Fascism. Here the vanguard of the heroic Communist partisans were executed." And then in the corner: "Eighty Jewish women from the Warsaw Postal Service were deported here and died." *Eighty.* No. He'd be their's to try, or parade around the world, or pension off. They wouldn't let us near him. . . . "Now we take over. . . . We might call you to say your piece. Or we might not. . . ." Subtract eighty from six million, and what do you get? Zero. The mathematics of the *goy.* (*P*, 26)

John Asher, whose interest began when he heard rumors about the capture of Martin Bormann, is the only member of the team who had no direct Holocaust experience. An English schoolboy during the war, he enjoyed relative safety. The closest he came to experiencing the tragedy the others suffered was playing Macduff in a school production. Leiber selected Asher precisely because he was unmaimed and could therefore be an objective counterbalance to the Holocaust victims on the team. "He was the one in whom interest was stronger than love or hatred or hunger" (*P*, 134).

In dramatic contrast to John Asher's detachment is Emmanuel Leiber's passionate obsession with Hitler and the Holocaust. Although we never see Leiber, it is his voice and purpose that directs the team and the reader's perceptions of other characters. His is the voice of historical memory and moral imperative. Leiber's narrative argument is a moral, thematic, and stylistic *tour de force* and would have been even more glorious and dramatic had Steiner chosen it to conclude the novel rather than Hitler's speech. The chapter shifts from biblical diction and cadence to graphic realism and symbolic fragmentation charting the disruptive impact of Nazism on civilization and the human psyche. Leiber responds to the team's discovery with a prayer of thanksgiving, praising God for prevailing. His anticipation of bringing Hitler to justice is rendered in images of light: light shinning over Gilead and Hebron, light radiating to the ends of the earth supplanting the images of darkness associated with Nazism, "Darkness unmoving. Over us and our children"(*P,* 44).

Returning to the language theme introduced at the beginning of the novel, Leiber ascribes to the belief that all that is God's has its counterpart,

> its backside of evil and negation. So it is with the Word, the gift of speech that is the glory of man. . . . When He made the Word, God made possible also its contrary. Silence is not the contrary of the Word but its guardian. No, He created on the night side of language a speech for hell. Whose words mean hatred . . . Few men can learn that speech or speak it for long. It burns their mouths. It draws them into death. But there shall come a man whose mouth shall be as a furnace and whose tongue as a sword laying waste. He will know the grammar of hell and teach it to others. He will know the sounds of madness and loathing and make them seem music. Where God said, let there be, he will unsay. And there is one word . . . one word amid the million sounds that make the secret sum of all language, which if spoken in hatred, may end creation, as there was one that brought creation into being. . . . Perhaps he knows that word, he who very nearly did us to death, who deafened God so that the covenant seemed broken and our children given to ash. (*P,* 45)

Because he has elevated language to these mythic and cosmic proportions, Leiber urges his men to resist listening to Hitler's speech. He urges them to anticipate his every need and provide it, to gag him, and to stop their own ears as Ulysses did, rather than chance succumbing to the demonic voice, thinking him a man and forgetting his crimes. "That he almost drove us from the face of the earth. That his words tore up our lives by the root" (*P,* 46).

Structurally this chapter works as the legal prosecution that Hitler evades in the novel as he evaded it in history. Leiber's powerful litany of the tortured and murdered Jews functions both as an indictment of the criminal and a memorial to the martyrs. Its language evokes the concentrationary world of excrement and extremity recorded in such works as Terrence Des Pres' *The Survivor.* Steiner's selection details aspects of atrocity perpetrated against the Jews to degrade and humiliate them prior to their murder. Illustrating individual suffering, he makes the destruction of the six million comprehensible, while conveying the immensity of the Holocaust through reference to the genocidal mass murders. In a lengthy passage that is similar to but more graphic than Cynthia Ozick's catalogue of the dead in *Trust,* Leiber asks for remembrance:

> Tell me that you remember. The garden in Salonika, where Mordechai Zathsmar, the cantor's youngest child, ate excrement; the Hoofstraat in Arnhem where they took Leah Burstein and made her watch while her father; the two lime trees where the road to Montrouge turns south, 8th November 1942, on which they hung the meathooks; the pantry on the third floor, Nowy Swiat xi, where Jakov Kaplan, author of the *History of Algebraic Thought in Eastern Europe 1280–1655,* had to dance over the body of; in White Springs, Ohio, Rahel Nadelman who wakes each night, sweat in her mouth because thirty-one years earlier in the Mauerallee in Hanover three louts drifting home from an SS recruitment spree had tied her legs and with a truncheon; the latrine in the police station in Wörgel which Doktor Ruth Levin and her niece had to clean with their hair; the fire raid on Engstaad and the Jakobsons made to kneel outside the shelter until the incendiaries; Sternowitz caught in the woods near Sibor talking to Ludmilla, an Aryan woman, and filled with water and a piano wire wound tight around his; Branka seeing them burn the dolls near the ramp and when she sought to hide hers being taken to the fire and; Elias Kornfeld, Sarah Ellbogen, Robert Heimann in front of the biology class, . . . so that Professor Horst Kuntzer could demonstrate to his pupils the obvious racial, . . . Lilian Gourevitch given two work passes, yellow-colored, . . . for her three children in Tver Street and ordered to choose which of the children was to go on the next transport; . . . George Benjamin Dorfmann, collector of prints of the late seventeenth century, doctor and player on the viola, lying, no kneeling, no squatting in the punishment cell at Buchenwald, . . . watching the pus break from his torn nails and whispering the catalogue numbers of the Hobbemas in Albertina, so far as he could remember them in the raw pain of his shaven skull, until the guard took a whip; . . . Hagadio, who in the shoe factory of Treblinka was caught splitting leather, sabotage, and made to crawl alive into the quicklime while at the edge Reuben Cohen, aged eleven, had to proclaim "so shall all saboteurs and subverters of the united front." (*P,* 46–47)

Steiner's catalogue, composed as one long sentence of fragmented phrases, creates a breathless surge of emotion. His pattern of con-

cluding each entry without finishing its descriptive phrase encourages the reader to complete the thought and reflects the violent
disruption in the victims' lives. Reminiscent of traditional Hebrew
lamentation poetry, Leiber exclaims and laments the Holocaust
with tragic dignity. Like Cynthia Ozick's concentration camp litany
in *Trust,* Leiber's discourse counts in a sacred litany and, "like Cel-
an's stuttering and hallucinatory lyricism" [in "Todesfuge"], it also
drives language into and beyond ellipsis, finding in fragments of
speech a literary form to encompass and express brokenness."[18]
Psychological abuse, public humiliation, rape, torture, mutilation,
starvation, suicide, and variations of murder abound in this seemingly endless catalogue of Nazi atrocities. Lieber's speech, outlining
the gratuitous terror that constituted the Nazi universe, shares
qualities similar to Steiner's own discussion of death and concentration camps in *Bluebeard's Castle,* where he illustrates the similarity of
the Nazi universe to Western civilization's artistic and literary visions of Hell. Comparing Canto 33 of Dante's *Inferno* with the Nazi
camps, Steiner writes:

> They are the transference of Hell from below the earth to its surface.
> They are the deliberate enactment of a long, precise imagining.
> Because it imagined more fully than any other text, because it ar-
> gued the centrality of Hell in the Western order, the *Commedia* re-
> mains our literal guidebook—to the flames, to the ice fields, to the
> meat hooks. In the camps the millenary pornography of fear and
> vengeance cultivated in the Western mind by Christian doctrines of
> damnation was realized.[19]

The problem of Holocaust transmission, which appears as a
minor theme in many fictions, is raised here, too. Leiber doubts
whether we are capable of ever comprehending the mass killings:
"unspeakable because beyond imagining, . . . we can imagine the
cry of one, the hunger of two, the burning of ten, but past a hundred there is no clear imagining" (*P,* 49). Yet it would be immoral
to speak only in terms of comprehensible numbers. Thus, he recites the awesome list of death camps and suggests their tragic
proportions by referring again to individual losses:

> at Maidanek ten thousand a day; . . . in one corner of Treblinka
> seven hundred thousand bodies, I will count them now, Aaron,
> Aaronowitch, Aaronson, Abilech, Abraham, I will count seven hun-
> dred thousand names and you must listen, . . . I will say Kaddish to

the end of time and when time ceases shall not have reached the millionth name; at Belzec three hundred thousand, Friedberg, Friedman, Friedstein, the names gone in fire and gas, ash in the wind at Chelmno, the long black wind at Chelmno, Israel Meyer, Ida Meyer, the four children' at the pit at Sobivor; four hundred and eleven thousand three hundred and eighty-one in section three at Belsen, the one being Salomon Rheinfeld who left on his desk in Mainz the uncorrected proofs of the grammar of Hittite . . . the one being Belin the tanner whose face they sprinkled with acid from the vat and who was dragged through the streets of Kershon behind a dung cart but sang, . . . the one being David Pollachek whose fingers they broke in the quarry at Leutach when they heard that he had been first violin . . . the one not being Nathaniel Steiner who was taken to America in time but goes maimed nevertheless for not having been at the roll call. (*P*, 48–49)

In this painful litany of names and places of death, Steiner returns the dignity that the Nazis tried to steal from the Jews before murdering them. Jewish family love and devotion, Jewish scholarship, music, decency, and hard work, attributes of the apostrophes, are dramatically juxtaposed to apostrophes citing German sadism and murder. The passage is aptly introduced and concluded with examples of Jewish veneration for life. Preceding the catalogue is a brief tale of parents who throw their child from a transport with money sewn in his jacket and a note begging for help, parents who know they are destined for the gas, but hope their child will be saved. An epilogue to the sequence is the judgment that Hitler has "made ash of prayer," and until each victim's name is recalled and spoken "man will have no peace on earth, . . . for when spoken each after the other, with not a single letter omitted, . . . the syllables will make up the hidden name of GOD" (*P*, 50). At the center of the catalogue is an autobiographical reference to the Steiner family's escape from the physicality of hell and, nevertheless, an explicit recognition of being maimed by the Holocaust.

Leiber's speech encapsulates most of the novel's themes, including that of non-Aryan complicity in the Final Solution as illustrated by the fate of the child thrown from the death camp transport: betrayed by peasants who took his money and laid him on the railtracks, gagged, feet tied, to await the next train. As Leiber reminds the team that the man in their custody is responsible for all this evil, he also reminds them of the willing collaborators and bystanders to the tragedy:

Oh they helped. Nearly all of them. Who would not give visas and put barbed wire on their borders. Who threw stones through the windows and spat. Who when six hundred escaped from Treblinka hunted down and killed all but thirty-nine—Polish farmers, irregulars, partisans, charcoal burners in the forest—saying Jews belong in Treblinka. He could not have done it alone. I know that. Not without the helpers and the indifferent, not without the hooligans who laughed and the soft men who took over the shops and moved into the houses. Not without those who said in Belgravia and Marly, in Stresa and in Shaker Heights that the news was exaggerated, that the Jews were whining again and peddling horrors. Not without D. initialing a memo to B-W. at Printing House Square: *no more atrocity stories. Probably overplayed.* Or Foggy Bottom offering seventy-five visas above the quota when one hundred thousand children could have been saved. (*P*, 50–51)

In this economical speech, Leiber summarizes some of the many sins of the Allies and the Axis sympathizers in their abandonment and betrayal of the Jews—matters others have taken chapters and entire novels to dramatize. The uniquely Steinerian aspect of this assessment is its connection to traditional anti-Semitism and interpretation of the cause of Christian anti-Semitism, "Because we foisted Christ on them" (*P*, 51). Leiber, like Steiner in *Bluebeard's Castle*, views anti-Semitism as the rebellion of natural man against the abstractness of monotheism and the Jewish moral imperatives Jesus repeated in his teachings.

Had Steiner concluded the novel with Leiber's speech, some sense of justice would have prevailed. Instead, we are left with the affront to justice that marked the Holocaust, an affront to reason and morality that characterized Hitler's war against the Jews. The novel's final speech is Hitler's. Perhaps Steiner's strategy reflects his assessment of the way in which the Germans and the international community dealt with the implications of the Holocaust in the post-war era. Hitler's speech is outrageous. It testifies to the failure of the world to learn from the Holocaust and testifies to the persistence of anti-Semitism, which reached new dimensions posing as anti-Zionism.

Alvin Rosenfeld demonstrated, in *Imagining Hitler*, that the architect of the Holocaust is strangely absent from most Jewish Holocaust literature. Although Hitler's name occasionally appears as the butt of a curse, in aggressive ghetto wit, in allusion or abstraction, "the principal perpetrator of the war against the Jews is for the most part missing from the corpus of serious Holocaust literature."[20] George Steiner ended that silence. Not only does Hitler's shadow loom over Steiner's novel, his person is the center of the novel's focus, his crimes the *raison d'être* for all the characters, his diatribe the novel's climactic speech.

Steiner alone among the authors in this study treats the personality of Adolf Hitler and concentrates his novel on the themes of Holocaust culpability and bringing Nazis to justice for crimes against the Jews. For this reason, *The Portage to San Cristobal of A.H.* is constructed as a thriller, with the genre's interest in crime and punishment. Yet Steiner minimizes his use of conventions normally associated with mysteries to pursue a Dostoevskian quest for understanding.

Steiner's demonstration of the relation between Holocaust barbarism and the corruption of language finds dramatic expression in the novel's final chapter. Under the pretense of prosecuting the criminal before the world powers can abduct him, the Israelis prosecute Hitler in the jungle. Ignoring Lieber's instructions to keep Hitler's speech to a minimum, the team allows him opportunity to speak at length. Given Steiner's thematic focus on the corruptive power of language, perhaps it is fictionally mandatory that Hitler speak, but it is equally unfortunate that Steiner awards him the final chapter of the novel. Lieber's dire predictions of the consequences if the villain is permitted to speak are realized, and thus the novel concludes as a demonstration of language gone awry through a villain's malice. A.H. uses language as Hitler did in his Holocaust career, to lie, to distort, to misrepresent, to defile Jews and Judaism.

Characteristic of the fraudulent essence of Hitler's speech is the claim that he learned his racist philosophy from Judaism, specifically from Jacob Grill, a defrocked priest who was the son of a Polish rabbi.[21] Steiner's outline of Grill evokes the historic Christian exploitation of converts to denounce Judaism in public forums. To alert the reader to the bogus quality of Hitler's speech, Grill's ignorance of Judaism is established in an obviously erroneous reference to seventy-two hidden saints of Jewish lore. Given this overt signal and his reputation for distorting language, one may discredit much of Hitler's commentary on Jewish matter as illustrative of ignorance or evidence of malice. The capacity for distortion is amply illustrated in the comparison of his doctrine of Aryan racial superiority to the Judaic principle of convenantal election—his fallacious comparison of his *Ubermenschen* with the chosen people. When Steiner addresses this issue in essay form, the tone is quite different and the distinctions between the two positions are clearly enunciated:

> By one of the cruel, deep ironies of history, the concept of a chosen people, of a nation exalted above others by particular destiny, was born in Israel. In the vocabulary of Nazism there were elements of a vengeful parody on the Judaic claim. The theological motif of a people elected at Sinai is echoed in the pretense of the master race and its chiliastic dominion. Thus there was in the obsessed relation of Nazi to Jew a minute but fearful grain of logic.[22]

Hitler's second thesis is biblical justification for genocide. He claims to have learned from the Bible "a device to alter the human soul" (*P*, 163)—that is, "To slaughter a city because of an idea, because of vexation over words" (*P*, 163). Here the language changes from biblical diction to racial propaganda, so characteristic of the historic figure's speech. He asks "what is the Jew if he is not a long cancer of unrest?" (*P*, 164). Even more authentic is his fusion of the disease metaphor and vermin/sanitation idiom to characterize Jews: "Three times the Jew has pressed on us the blackmail of transcendence. Three times he has infected our blood and brains with the bacillus of perfection" (*P*, 166). Here Hitler's speech, evoking the Fuhrer's vocabulary of disease and corruption, is linked with Steiner's own theories of the causes of anti-Semitism. Hitler blames the Jews for their idealism, whether it be in the form of monotheism, ethical perfection, or social and economic equality. Hitler's understanding that anti-Semitism is directly related to gentile hatred of the Jewish inventions of God and conscience—affronts to Western paganism—echoes Steiner's own essays. Compare Hitler's words—"Was there ever a crueler invention, a contrivance more calculated to harrow human existence, than that of an omnipotent, all-seeing, yet invisible, impalpable, inconceivable God" (*P*, 164)—and Steiner's remarks in *Bluebeard's Castle:*

> It seems to me incontrovertible that the holocaust must be set in the framework of the psychology of religion, and that an understanding of this framework is vital to an argument on culture. . . . The holocaust was not the result of merely individual pathology or of the neuroses of one nation-state. . . . There are parallels [to other massacres] in technique and in the idiom of hatred. But not on-

tologically, not at the level of philosophic intent. That intent takes us
to the heart of certain instabilities in the fabric of Western culture, in
the relations between instinctual and religious life. Hitler's jibe that
'conscience is a Jewish invention' provides a clue. . . . Historians of
religion tell us that the emergence of the concept of the Mosaic God
is a unique fact in human experience, that a genuinely comparable
notion sprang up at no other place and time. The abruptness of the
Mosaic revelation, the finality of the creed at Sinai, tore up the
human psyche by its most ancient roots.[23]

Similarly, Hitler echoes Steiner's observations that the Jewish code,
setting forth a system for attaining moral perfectibility, affronts
man's natural inclination to evil:

> We must bottle up our rages and desires, chastise the flesh and walk
> bent in the rain. You call me a tyrant, an enslaver. What tyranny,
> what enslavement has been more oppressive, . . . than the sick fan-
> tasies of the Jew? You are not God-killers, but God-makers. And that
> is infinitely worse. The Jew invented conscience and left man a guilty
> serf. (*P*, 165)

Building his case against the Jews, he cites the moral and social
demands of two Jews: Jesus who demanded man be more altruistic
and self-denying and Marx who called for a classless society providing for each according to his needs. This argument also echoes
Steiner's analysis of the root causes of anti-Semitism:

> Monotheism at Sinai, primitive Christianity, messianic socialism:
> these are the three supreme moments in which Western culture is
> presented with . . . "the claims of the ideal" . . . Judaism produced a
> summons to perfection and sought to impose it on the current and
> currency of Western life. Deep loathing built up in the social sub-
> conscious, murderous resentments. The mechanism is simple but
> primordial. *We hate most those who hold out to us a goal, an ideal, a
> visionary promise which, . . . we cannot reach, . . . yet, and this is crucial,
> which remains profoundly desirable, which we cannot reject because we fully
> acknowledge its supreme value.*[24]

Hitler defends himself on the basis of shared guilt. His argument amounts to an indictment of his collaborators. "When I
turned on the Jew, no one came to his rescue. No one. France,
England, Russia, even Jew-ridden America did nothing. They were
glad that the exterminator had come. . . . Secretly they rejoiced" (*P*,

167). Hitler describes himself as a man of his times, not a demon, not the quintessence of evil. It was his ordinariness, he claims, that gave him a following of millions who found in him the reflection of their own desires. This assertion is prelude to his final perversion of reason: that he is to be revered as the father of Israel since the Holocaust was the vehicle responsible for the creation of the State.

> Would Palestine have become Israel, would the Jews have come to that barren patch of the Levant, would the United States and the Soviet Union, . . . have given you recognition and guaranteed your survival, had it not been for the Holocaust? It was the Holocaust that gave you the courage of injustice, that made you drive the Arab out of his home, out of his field, . . . because he was in your divinely ordered way. . . . Perhaps I am the Messiah, the true Messiah, the new Sabbatai whose infamous deeds were allowed by God in order to bring His people home. (*P*, 169)

Although postwar sympathy for the creation of a Jewish homeland is an undeniable legacy of the Final Solution, it is absurd for Hitler to take credit as a founding father of Israel. Characteristically, Steiner's A.H. formulates statements that contain an iota of truth and distorts them to deceive his audience.

Simply put, the speech is disturbing because it echoes neo-Nazi and New Left propaganda. However, it is at the same time a cunning combination of truth, half-truth, perversions, grotesqueries, outright misrepresentations, and lies. In the fashion of Milton's Satan, A.H. argues his evil is benign because it served to generate good, and he was therefore God's instrument. Steiner designed this speech as the essence of evil. It is. In that regard it is artistically successful. Because it deals with a topic of recent history that so traumatized the victims and so changed our perceptions of the human condition, it is painful. Many who respect Steiner's essays on the Holocaust, his literary criticism and much of his fiction, recoil in horror at the literary license he took with Hitler's character. Representative of the detractors' opinion is their concern that

> the impact is not in the world of apocalypse, as Steiner intended, but in the world in which we live, where arguments of the kind A.H. uses are believed quite seriously by educated people; where propaganda is continually going on to diminish the significance of the Holocaust by blaming the Jews themselves for it in various ways; where, in fact,

the chief effect of Hitler's peroration, presented with an air of awe and unanswerability, may well be to send away some from the theater with anti-Jewish prejudices reinforced.[25]

Steiner's basic composition strategy for Hitler's speech, fusing A.H. distortions with material from his own essays, leads to the reader's dismay. The artistic flaw inherent in such strategy is the subject of several critical reviews. The most thorough and eloquent are analyses by Hyam Maccoby and Alvin Rosenfeld. Macoby observes that in playing the Devil's advocate Steiner risks attributing convincing arguments to Hitler that, apart from being uncharacteristic of the historic prototype's racist demogoguery, might be misinterpreted as valid.[26] Alvin Rosenfeld strenuously objects to Steiner's attribution of "the authority of his own essayistic voice, but pitched now to express an exuberant mockery of his Jewish adversaries—indeed, a mockery of every major aspect of Jewish antecedence."[27] Rosenfeld's criticism is devastating, contending that

> the appeal of Steiner's Hitler, in short, is the appeal of cleverly formulated Nazi apologetics in combination with stridently stated anti-Semitic invective, a potent combination in Hitler's day and, if George Steiner's novel is any indication, still available for imaginative appropriation and revivification today.[28]

Although Hitler has the last speech, his self-description as the Sabbatai links him to a historic false messiah who converted from Judaism to Islam to save his life. The false messiah allusion serves also as a link to Lieber's reference to Nathaniel of Mainz, describing the voice and language of a counter-Messiah negating the Bible and "banishing God from creation," a voice remarkably similar to the fictional Hitler's:

> A man whose mouth shall be as a furnace and whose tongue as a sword laying waste. He will know the grammar of hell and teach it to others. He will know the sounds of madness and loathing and make them seem music. Where God said, let there be, he will unsay. (*P*, 45)

Perhaps Steiner should have adopted Lieber's advice and circumscribed Hitler's speech. Given Steiner's distinguished canon on Nazism, malice cannot reasonably be imputed to him. Instead, an aesthetic defense is sought for a device that fails. If Steiner's intention is to demonstrate Hitler's facility for manipulating language to distort truth, he succeeds. If his goal in this novel is to convey the tragic dimensions of Jewish suffering and Nazi evil, his success is diminished by the concluding speech. Steiner's critical evaluations of literature invariably consider aesthetics in relation to political and social values. It is surprising, therefore, that he evidences so little sensitivity to the political implications some readers will draw from the A.H. diatribe. Because the speech is left unanswered, readers too remain trapped in the morass of the dark jungle.

# CONCLUSION

*In 1948, Issac Rosenfeld wrote.*

> How is it possible that thousands of men, women, children, and infants should be lined up in a field, to be shot before an open ditch, and that their screams should not be heard? That furnaces should be stuffed with human beings? That thousands should be marched into air-tight chambers, to be gassed or steamed to death, their naked bodies stuck together by the pressure and the heat? . . . We cannot understand, we are as numb as the perpetrators of the crime. Our knowledge should shock us, it should stir up deeply, it should make our life impossible, subjectively, as it is impossible in fact.[1]

Twenty years after Isaac Rosenfeld asked and answered these questions, Lothar Kahn observed in 1969, "No Jewish writer of today . . . has written a book without the memory of Auschwitz propelling him to issue warnings."[2] Whether Kahn's assessment will continue to characterize Jewish American literature remains to be seen. It is already evident that the works of fiction examined in these chapters constitute a substantial subgenre of Jewish American fiction addressing the Holocaust as a central reference point for Jews and establishing the Holocaust survivor as a recognizable persona in our literature.

Like their European colleagues, the Americans are inextricably engaged in the tragedy that changed forever the way we view human capacity for good and evil. Artists and scholars overcame their early reluctance to address events that cast into doubt everything we believed, events often perceived as being beyond imagination and language. Immediate postwar numbness, willed amnesia, and self-imposed silence have given way to pain, recollection, and expression. Echoing Elie Wiesel's reproach to the free world for its acceptance of Jewish genocide in "A Plea for the Dead," the Americans—especially Epstein, Elman, and Singer—carefully delineate the respite between one phase of the Holocaust and the next, between the Nuremberg Laws and *Kristallnacht,* between expropriation of Jewish property and deportation of Jews, between ghetto and concentration camp construction and liquidation, between deportations and gas chamber annihilations. And like the historians, the novelists demonstrate how the world-wide silence following each atrocity against the Jews confirmed the German belief that there was implicit international approval for the Final Solution. American literary voices have been among the most vocal in denouncing the Nazi legacy, mourning its victims and celebrating the survival of Jews and Judaism.

As we have seen, common themes and stylistic strategies have emerged in American Holocaust fiction. Although the novelists dramatize the repercussions of the legalization of the *Rassenkunde* theory as manifested in the Nuremberg Laws of German-occupied Europe, they give limited attention to the pseudoscientific determinist racial theory that dominated Nazi Germany. Instead, they emphasize the relationship of traditional European Christian anti-Semitism and Nazism, paralleling the institutional manifestations of the Reich's anti-Jewish policies with centuries of Christian teaching about Jews and Judaism, the long history of church inquisition and pogrom that provided the prototype for genocide. The fiction abounds in analogies between Church-propagated canards of deicide, poisoned wells, and blood lettings and Nazi propaganda charging Jews with political and economic conspiracies to destroy Europe. Early American Holocaust fiction drew muted analogies between Christian and Nazi anti-Semitism, as exemplified by Edward Wallant's crucifixion scenes in *The Pawnbroker* and Saul Bellow's yellow, train, and gas images in *The Victim.* Later works render the connections explicitly, either dramatically—as in Leslie Epstein's parodic morality play and Christmas Mass and Arthur Cohen's parable, "The Legend of the Last Jew on Earth"—or through protagonist polemics in the works of Singer, Bellow, Potok, Ozick, and Steiner. One may safely speculate the recent Holocaust scholarship and the reemergence of violent anti-Semitism in Europe, America, and the Middle East provided the vital impetus for the explicit artistic portrayal of the common goals of traditional and Nazi anti-Semitism, despite the claim of the former to foster only the destruction of the religion and the latter's enthusiastic destruction of the people. Employing parody, allusion, and metaphor, the writers link the success of the genocide program with the failure of Christians to fight against the Nazi policy of Jewish annihilation in their nations. More damning, they illuminate the role of anti-Nazi Europeans in abetting the smooth operation of the Final Solution. American writers thus charge that the free world's repeated failure to thwart German Holocaust policy is nothing less than complicity in the Nazi crime.

The canon is replete with Holocaust experience, from its onslaught in 1933 through its culmination in 1945. Unlike their European colleagues, Americans rarely elect to dramatize Holocaust-era degradation and atrocity. They often convey the range of experience in fragments of survivor memories, nightmare vision, and European flashbacks. With the exceptions of Elman and Epstein, who set their works in the European sphere during the Holocaust, most American writers portray the Holocaust universe through memories and dreams to integrate past experiences and contemporary trauma in the lives of characters. Confrontation of the past and present takes center stage in the survivor's consciousness. Survivor-witnesses in American fiction often refer to contemporary documented reports or newspaper accounts of camp existence, discuss aspects of the Nazi occupation, or suffer nightmares that illuminate isolated incidents of the concentrationary universe. Whether they rely on present tense dramatization or retrospective revery, the Americans use the European model: contrasting prewar Europe with Hitler's hell; conveying the historic record and ambiance of the Nazi period by chronicling the systematic destruction of European Jewry through economic deprivation, civil disenfranchisement, and collective humiliation of the Jews in the occupied countries. They document the increasingly brutal, incremental process of subjugation: directives that Jews wear identity badges, refrain from travel on public vehicles without permits, and attending public parks and entertainments; prohibitions against marriage between Jews and non-Jews; expulsion from schools and hospitals; dismissal from the labor force, businesses, and the professions; deprivation of food and medical services; arrest without warrant; impressment in rural and urban slave-labor brigades; and, finally, isolation and incarceration in ghettos and concentration camps as a prelude to mass murders in the forests, lime pits, gas chambers, and crematoria.

Equally characteristic of American fiction is the delineation of the aftermath of the catastrophe. Focusing on survivor trauma— manifested as physical and psychological debilitation or spiritual malaise—the secular Jewish writers concentrate on survivor syndrome and the meaning of the Holocaust in the creation of a new social consciousness. Although the religiously oriented writers also incorporate survivor syndrome and address the postHolocaust consciousness, they achieve it through a theological and historic Judaic framework and often include the crisis of faith as part of survivor trauma. Usually the secular characters' recovery is circumscribed. Those steeped in Judaic religious sources and Jewish history progress more readily to spiritual and cultural postwar restoration, despite ongoing physical and psychological suffering.

Among the most important themes in American Holocaust fiction are postHolocaust theology and the survival of Judaism in the face of the unprecedented evil of the Holocaust. These are major chords in the fiction of Singer, Cohen, Ozick, and Potok and minor chords in the works of Bellow, Malamud, and Elman. Like the philosophers and theologians (Rubenstein, Fackenheim, Greenberg, and Berkovits), the novelists studied here reject outright the retributive *mi-penei hata' einu* postulate. The theological responses of American survivor-protagonists range from Rubenstein's radical renunciation (articulated by Singer's Freidl and Wallant's pawnbroker) and temporary renunciation (as in the cases of Singer's Broder, Elman's Yagodah, and Bellow's Bruch) to traditional protest against God's passivity in the face of evil (Cohen's Stern and Steinmann, Potok's Lurie, and a chorus of Singer characters). Singer, Potok, Ozick, and Cohen posit the traditional *hester panim* (hidden face) theory of God's acceptance of evil and combine that with the precept of *tikkun* advocating man's responsibility for Holocaust repair. *Tikkun* is illustrated by the return of lapsed Jews to Judaism (Singer's Broder, Tamara, Fietzelzohn, and Shapiro;

Bellow's Sammler; and Ozick's Bleilip, Vand, and Lilt), or by reconfirmed dedication of the religiously observant (Singer's Shifrah Puah and Nissen; Cohen's Stern, Klay, and Steinman; Potok's Malters and Luries; Steiner's Lieber). *Tikkun* is communal in the work of Malamud and Potok where the focus is on building the faith and the identification of American Jews with Holocaust survivors who serve as mentors. Although Malamud's characters refrain from theological dispute and formal evaluation of God and Judaism in Holocaust history, his survivors teach American lapsed Jews the values of the Jewish ethical code and act as mentors to innocent Americans on matters of Jewish identity and history. Exemplifying Malamud's affirmation of the validity of Jewish values for the postHolocaust age are the lady of the lake's insistence on marrying within the faith, thereby perpetuating the Jewish people, and the last mohican's education of an American Jew in Holocaust history and the codes of charity. Even the fixer, whose torment is a symbolic prelude to the Holocaust experience, strengthens his loyalty to the Jewish community as a result of his imprisonment for the crime of being Jewish. The survivors of Cohen's fortress and the teachers in Potok's religious schools are dedicated to creating a new Jewish civilization in America in order to commemorate that destroyed in Europe. The principle of *tikkun* is expressed thematically in the establishment of the State of Israel in Potok's and Steiner's works and as antithesis to the hidden face theory in the works of Singer, Potok, and Steiner.

A corollary to the religious theme is the American writer's progression from destruction to renewal, which echoes the traditional Hebrew dirges that progress from the theme of First and Second Temple destruction to redemptive visions of Jerusalem rebuilt. While rejecting the idea that a precondition of the rebirth of Israel was the destruction of European Jewry, Potok, Singer, and Steiner recognize the paradoxical link between destruction in Europe and revival in Israel. Support for Israel's survival finds expression in much American Holocaust fiction. Potok's David Malter and Max Lurie work in America for the establishment of Israel, making speeches, providing funds, supplies, and moral support. Bellow's Sammler travels to Israel during the Six Day War under the auspices of the press, but his primary purpose is to be with the threatened population—rather than safe in America— when Arabs have threatened a second Holocaust. Bellow uses this sequence to iterate the thesis that once again the world is indif ferent to Jewish suffering, that governments, churches, political and religious leaders are again prepared to silently acquiesce to the genocide of the Jews. Elman's Yagodah vacillates between negative and positive group identification—symptomatic of his anti-Semitic victimization—and similarly vacillates between supporting Israeli militancy and castigating it. Steiner's Nazi hunters are illustrative of the impact of the Holocaust on Israeli political consciousness. While Singer's secular Jews address the political and military viability of Israel in the context of Holocaust history, his penitent, immigrates to Judaism's spiritual center to live as a devout Jew in a Jewish nation.

In Singer, Steiner, and Potok one finds the conviction that Israel exists to heal the survivors physically and spiritually, a theme common to Israeli literature. Singer's *Shosha* concludes with a survivor asserting pride in the transformation of the meek diasporan Jew into the assertive Israeli. Similarly, Max Lurie shares his pride in the Irgunist rejection of passive acceptance of Arab violence, a sharp contrast to the passive Tulchin mentality he scorned in Europe. Steiner's Nazi hunters address the issue in their compulsion to bring Nazis to trial in Israel as part of the collective healing process. Singer's Shapiro is less vocal about the physical assertion of the Holocaust survivor in Israel than he is about the diasporan Jew's spiritual renewal in the land of the patriarchs. Shapiro frees himself from the diasporan assimilationist mentality to seek spiritual repair through religious Jewish life in Jerusalem. Although these writers meticulously avoid any suggestion that God presided over the destruction of six million European Jews so that He might resurrect the Jewish people in their homeland, they celebrate the ideal of national and religious redemption for a shattered people.

Tadeusz Borowski's sardonic wit finds clear echo in the expressive anger and satiric barbs of Epstein's and Elman's protagonists. Yet the dominant nihilistic mood of Borowski's *This Way for the Gas, Ladies and Gentlemen,* Jakov Lind's *Soul of Wood,* Jerzy Kosinski's *The Painted Bird,* and Piotr Rawicz's *Blood from the Sky* is mitigated in American fiction. The American writers characteristically affirm the fundamental worth of life and the possibility of human decency through the restorative careers of their survivors. Although the survivors are forever wounded by their Holocaust experiences and suffer perpetual physical and psychic pain, some eventually achieve a small measure of restoration. Nazerman gradually abandons his isolation from others to protect the weak, the sick, and the oppressed. Sammler moderates his disdain for the less intelligent and sophisticated and agrees to counsel those who seek his opinions. Yagodah resolves his ambiguous relationship to Judaism and the Jewish State and establishes a separate peace for himself, incorporating communal tolerance and family responsibility. Broder recants his Holocaust oath and fathers a child for this less than perfect world. Shapiro abandons American hedonism for a Hasidic life of piety in Israel.

The writers whose works are considered in this volume have embraced the arduous task of addressing questions confronting humanity in the postHolocaust age—questions that go directly to the heart of the human condition. Writing from the premise that the Holocaust has changed forever our perception of humanity, these writers strive to understand why and how the Holocaust happened and what it means to civilization. Just as the archivists, historians, poets, and novelists in the occupied territories, ghettos, and concentration camps wrote as an act of resistance and faith to transcend the Nazi hell, to bear witness for future generations, so, too, contemporary writers bear witness and raise their voices against radical evil. By adding to the Holocaust testimony, these American-Jewish writers join their European and Israeli colleagues to honor the dead, to preserve the collective memory, and to offer warnings for the future.

Out of the tragedy has arisen a commemorative literature that honors the victims and warns of the human capacity for evil lest a similar catastrophe again envelop us. Ours is a volatile political era in which nations operate torture factories and control their citizenry by fear, a time when terrorists humiliate and manipulate legitimate governments, a time when hijackings and hostage-takings dominate the news. Isaac Rosenfeld's questions are still our questions. Ignoring the moral urging of large segments of the American public, an American president travels to Bitburg to pay tribute to fallen Germans, including those who served the Nazi cause. Like his wartime predecessor, insensitive to Jewish Holocaust trauma, a pope officially welcomes Kurt Waldheim to the Vatican. Isaac Rosenfeld's questions remain. Under the guise of scholarship, revisionist historians campaign to deny the Holocaust. We must persist in asking Rosenfeld's questions. Anti-Semitism flourishes in its traditional trappings and under new guises. Rosenfeld's plea, "our knowledge should shock us, it should stir us deeply," demands our attention.

As the Jew is enjoined to active remembrance of the central experience of slavery in ancient Egypt, so Elie Wiesel has written of Auschwitz, "Every Jew, again, must feel that he himself was there."[3] American creative writers have made lasting strides toward that objective and have dramatized the central role the destruction of European Jewry plays in our lives. Geographically and existentially distanced from the ghettos, transports, concentration camps, gas chambers, and crematoria, these writers' creative testimony has succeeded in extending Holocaust boundaries. Remembering yesterday's crime, they endeavor to transform humanity so that such criminality will never again be tolerated. They help ensure that the smoke and ash of European Jewry can be neither forgotten nor forgiven, that the murdered Jews of Europe live on in the minds and hearts of succeeding generations. Witnesses through the imagination, these American Jewish writers spiritually resist Nazism and celebrate Jewish survival and regeneration.

# NOTES

## Preface

    1. Norman Rosen, "The Holocaust and the American-Jewish Novelist," *Midstream* 20 (October 1974): 58.

    2. Sidra Ezrahi, *By Words Alone: The Holocaust in Literature* (Chicago: University of Chicago Press, 1980), 2.

    3. I will examine *Touching Evil* and *Anya* in a forthcoming book. See S. Lillian Kremer, "The Holocaust in our Time: Norma Rosen's *Touching Evil*," *Studies in American Jewish Literature* 3 (1983): 212–22.

## Introduction

    1. Hannah Arendt, *The Origins of Totalitarianism* (New York: Harcourt, Brace and World, 1951), 3:142.

    2. Isaac Rosenfeld, "Terror Beyond Evil," in *An Age of Enormity: Life and Writing in the Forties and Fifties* (New York: The World Publishing Co., 1962), 197; reprinted from *The New Leader* (February 1948).

    3. Ibid., 199.

    4. Lionel Trilling, *The Liberal Imagination* (Garden City, N. Y.: Doubleday, 1953), 256.

    5. Alfred Kazin, *New York Jew* (New York: Vintage Books, 1979), 39.

    6. Ibid., 51.

7. George Steiner, "A Kind of Survivor," in *Language and Silence: Essays on Language, Literature, and the Inhuman* (New York: Atheneum, 1977), 143–44.

8. Robert Alter, "Confronting the Holocaust: Three Israeli Novels," *Commentary* 41 (March 1966): 67. Reprinted in *After the Tradition: Essays in Modern Jewish Writing* (New York: E. P. Dutton, 1969), 163.

9. Lothar Kahn, "The American Jewish Novel Today," *Congress Bi-Weekly* 36 (5 December 1969): 3.

10. Emil Fackenheim, quoted in Alvin Rosenfeld, "The Problematics of Holocaust Literature," *A Double Dying: Reflections on Holocaust Literature* (Bloomington: Indiana University Press, 1980), 17–18.

11. Alan Mintz, *Hurban: Responses to Catastrophe in Hebrew Literature* (New York: Columbia University Press, 1984), 10.

12. See Yehuda Amichai's *Not of This Time, Not of This Place,* Yoram Kaniuk's *Adam Resurrected,* and Haim Gouri's *The Chocolate Deal.*

13. Anti-Semitism raised to a legal status is not a Nazi innovation. Parallels between anti-Semitic canonical laws and Nazi measures are obvious. However, the 1935 Nuremberg Laws defined the Jew negatively, as someone ineligible for German citizenship, and marked a dramatic progression toward persecution culminating in the Final Solution.

14. See Henry James Cargas, ed., *When God and Man Failed: Non-Jewish Views of the Holocaust* (New York: Macmillan, 1981).

15. Robert F. Drinan, S. J., "Transcendental Anti-Semitism of Hitler's Third Reich," *When God and Man Failed* (New York: Macmillan, 1981), 17.

16. Nora Levin, *The Holocaust: The Destruction of European Jewry 1933–1945* (New York: Schocken Books, 1973), 10.

17. Dorothy Bilik, *Immigrant Survivors: Post-Holocaust Consciousness in Recent Jewish-American Fiction* (Middleton, Conn.: Wesleyan University Press, 1981), 49.

18. For an extended discussion of the distinctions between the pre- and postHolocaust immigrants of American-Jewish literature, see Dorothy Bilik, *Immigrant Survivors.*

19. Bilik, *Immigrant Survivors,* 46.

20. Elie Wiesel, *The Gates of the Forest* (New York: Avon Books, 1966), 195.

21. Richard Rubenstein, *After Auschwitz: Radical Theology and Contemporary Judaism* (Indianapolis: Bobbs-Merrill, 1966), 68.

22. Ibid., 119.

23. Emil Fackenheim, *God's Presence in History,* 11, quoted in Steven T. Katz, *Post-Holocaust Dialogues: Critical Studies in Modern Jewish Thought* (New York: New York University Press, 1983), 152–53. I am indebted to Steven Katz for theological interpretation.

24. Ibid., 153.

25. Ibid., 154.

26. Ibid.

27. Eliezar Berkovits, *Faith After the Holocaust* (New York: KTAV Publishing 1973), 89.

28. Ibid., 89.

29. An extended analysis of the *hester panim* concept may be found in Andre Neher's *The Exile of the Word: From the Silence of the Bible to the Silence of Auschwitz,* trans. David Maisel (Philadelphia: Jewish Publication Society, 1981).

30. Berkovits, *Faith After the Holocaust,* 156.

31. Irving Greenberg, "Cloud of Smoke, Pillar of Fire: Judaism, Christianity, and Modernity After the Holocaust," *Auschwitz: Beginning of a New Era?,* ed. Eva Fleischner (New York: KTAV Publishing, 1986); quoted by Eva Fleischner in "The Crucial Importance of the Holocaust for Christians," *When God and Man Failed,* 34.

32. A. Alverez, "The Literature of the Holocaust," *Commentary* 38 (November 1964): 67.

33. David G. Roskies, *Against the Apocalypse: Responses to Catastrophe in Modern Jewish Culture* (Cambridge: Harvard University Press, 1984), 226.

34. Primo Levi, *Survival in Auschwitz: The Nazi Assault on Humanity*, trans. Stuart Woolf (New York: Collier Books, 1959), 22.

35. Alverez, "Literature of the Holocaust," 67.

36. Roskies, *Against the Apocalypse*, 20.

37. Ibid., 20.

38. Ibid., 30.

39. Alvin Rosenfeld, *Double Dying*, 31.

40. Arthur A. Cohen, *The Tremendum: A Theological Interpretation of the Holocaust* (New York: Crossroad, 1981), 2.

## Chapter One

1. Saul Bellow, *To Jerusalem and Back* (New York: Avon Books, 1976), 35–36.

2. Bellow has explored historic varieties of anti-Semitism: the concept of Jew as Christ-killer in *The Adventures of Augie March* (1953); cultural and institutional anti-Semitism in *The Victim* (1947) and *Humboldt's Gift* (1973); economic and social anti-Semitism in "The Old System" (1967); and violent anti-Semitism in *Herzog* (1964), "Mosby's Memoirs" (1968), and *Mr. Sammler's Planet* (1970). In addition to the fictional use of historic anti-Semitism, Bellow has expressed anxiety regarding the continuing threat to the survival of the Jewish people in essays, letters, and in *To Jerusalem and Back*. Illustrative of Bellow's recognition of the pervasive nature of anti-Semitism was his censure of New Left anti-Jewish propaganda during his Noble Prize acceptance speech. He warned his audience that there was no simple choice between "the Children of Light and the Children of Darkness," that good and evil are not clearly distributed along political affiliations, that anti-Semitism is prevalent in German Fascist and Communist political propaganda; he quoted Ulrike Meinhof of the West German Red Army, particularly in regard to the movement's approval of "revolutionary extermination." "For her German anti-Semitism of the Hitler period was essentially anti-capitalist. 'Auschwitz,' she is quoted as saying, 'meant that six million Jews were killed and thrown on the waste heap of Europe for what they were, money Jews' (*geldjuden*)." Saul Bellow, "The Nobel Lecture," *American Scholar* 46 (Winter-Autumn 1976–1977): 320–21.

3. Saul Bellow, *Herzog* (Greenwich, Conn.: Fawcett Publications, 1964), 37.

4. Saul Bellow, *Humboldt's Gift* (New York: Avon Books, 1976), 156.

5. Chester Eisinger, "Saul Bellow: Love and Identity," *Accent* 18 (Summer 1958): 189.

6. Saul Bellow, *The Victim* (New York: New American Library, 1965), 139. Subsequent quotations are from this edition, identified as *V* in the text.

7. Josephine Knopp, *The Trial of Judaism in Contemporary Jewish Writing* (Urbana: University of Illinois Press, 1975), 129.

8. See Jean Paul Sartre, *Anti-Semite and Jew* (New York: Schocken Books, 1948).

9. According to sociologist Willam Ryan blaming the victim is crucial to isolating the minority group from the dominant society. Allbee attempts a form of this strategy, implying with his repeated phrase "you people" and his frequent declarations that Jews are different, that they think and feel differently from the rest of society. Allbee insists that Jews cling to different goals and learn different truths. See William Ryan, *Blaming the Victim* (New York: Pantheon Books, 1971).

10. It is fitting that Bellow's twentieth-century religious bigot should be a direct descendant of Governor Winthrop of Massachusetts. Winthrop, a religious zealot of the seventeenth century, supported the banishment of Roger Williams from Boston, fought the Antinomians, and harassed Anne Hutchinson. Colonial Massachusetts was notorious for its demand for uniformity in culture and religion. Allbee's intolerance is part of his Puritan legacy.

11. In his analysis of French anti-Semitism, which appeared one year before *The Victim* was published, Jean Paul Sartre treats the problem of cultural anti-Semitism in a similar manner. Sartre contends that the anti-Semite tries to persuade the Jew that he is incapable of understanding the true sense of the host culture. In this way the Jew is made to feel an intruder, an alien always: "there is formed around him an impalpable atmosphere, which is the *genuine* France, with its *genuine* values, its *genuine* tact, its *genuine* morality, and he has no part in it" (82). Sartre points also to the French anti-Semite's jealous protection of the French language (24–25).

12. For a good discussion of the use of dream in European Holocaust literature, see Lawrence L. Langer, *The Holocaust and the Literary Imagination* (New Haven: Yale University Press, 1975).

13. Saul Bellow, *Mr. Sammler's Planet* (Greenwich, Conn.: Fawcett Publications, 1970), 84–85. Subsequent quotations are from this edition, identified as *MSP* in the text.

14. Elie Wiesel, "The Firey Shadow: Jewish Existence Out of the Holocaust," *Jewish Existence in an Open Society* (U.S.A.: Jewish Centers Association, 1970), 43.

15. Bellow, *To Jerusalem and Back*, 78.

16. L. H. Goldman, *Saul Bellow's Moral Vision: A Critical Study of the Jewish Experience* (New York: Irvington Publications, 1983), 183.

17. Knopp, *The Trial of Judaism*, 150–51.

18. Alan L. Berger, *Crisis and Covenant: The Holocaust in American Jewish Fiction* (Albany: State University of New York Press, 1985), 107.

19. For a discussion of the novel's parallel to Ecclesiastes, see Goldman, *Saul Bellow's Vision*, 157–58, 166.

20. Goldman, *Saul Bellow's Vision*, 159.

21. See Terrence Des Pres, *The Survivor: An Anatomy of Life in the Death Camps* (New York: Oxford University Press, 1976), 51–73.

22. Ibid., 59.

23. Eugen Kogan, *The Theory and Practice of Hell*, trans. Heinz Norden (New York: Farrar, Straus, & Giroux, 1953), 56; quoted in Des Pres, *The Survivor*, 59.

24. Eugene Weinstock, *Beyond the Last Path*, trans. Clara Ryan (New York: Boni and Gaer, 1947), 157–58; quoted in Des Pres, *The Survivor*, 59.

25. Leonard Tushnet, *The Pavement of Hell* (New York: St. Martin's Press, 1972), 61.

26. George Steiner, "K," *Language and Silence: Essays on Language, Literature and the Inhuman* (New York: Atheneum, 1977), 123.

27. See Daniel Fuchs, *Saul Bellow: Vision and Revision* (Durhamn, N.C.: Duke University Press, 1984), 226.

28. Robert Boyers, et al., "Literature and Culture: An Interview With Saul Bellow," *Salmagundi* 30 (1975), 16–17; noted in Judi Newman, *Saul Bellow and History* (London: Macmillan, 1984), 136.

29. Saul Bellow, *To Jerusalem and Back*, 184.

30. Saul Bellow, "Israeli Diary," *Newsday*, 1967; reprinted in *Jewish Heritage* 10 (Winter 1967–1968): 32–43.

31. Dorothy Seidman Bilik, *Immigrant Survivors: Post-Holocaust Consciousness in Recent Jewish American Fiction* (Middleton, Conn.: Wesleyan University Press, 1981), 149.

32. Alvin H. Rosenfeld, *A Double Dying: Reflections on Holocaust Literature* (Bloomington: Indiana University Press, 1980), 32.

33. Ibid., 32.

34. Saul Bellow, "Thinking Man's Wasteland," *Saturday Review of Literature* 48 (3 April 1965).

35. Saul Bellow, "The Writer as Moralist," *Atlantic Monthly* 211 (March 1963).

36. Saul Bellow, "Distractions of a Fiction Writer," *The Living Novel: A Symposium,* ed. Granville Hicks (New York: Macmillan, 1957), 12.

37. Saul Bellow, "Some Notes on Recent American Fiction," *Encounter* xxi (November 1963): 22–23.

## Chapter Two

1. Edward Lewis Wallant, *The Pawnbroker* (New York: Harcourt Brace Jovanovich, 1961), 37. Subsequent quotations are from this edition, identified as *P* in the text.

2. Thomas M. Lorch, "The Novels of Edward Lewis Wallant," *Chicago Review* 19 (1967): 80.

3. William V. Davis, "Learning to Walk on Water: Edward Lewis Wallant's *The Pawnbroker*," *The Literary Review* 17 (Winter 1973–1974): 154–55.

4. Nicholas Ayo, "The Secular Heart: The Achievement of Edward Lewis Wallant," *Critique* XII (1970): 91.

5. Jonathan Baumback, "The Illusion of Indifference: *The Pawnbroker* by Edward Lewis Wallant," *The Landscape of Nightmare: Studies in the Contemporary American Novel* (New York: New York University Press, 1965), 145.

## Chapter Three

1. Daniel Stern, Interview, "The Art of Fiction," *Paris Review* 61 (Spring 1975): 56.

2. Michiko Kakutani, "Malamud Still Seeks Balance and Solitude," *New York Times,* 15 July 1980.

3. Ibid.

4. Bernard Malamud, "The First Seven Years," *The Magic Barrel* (New York: Avon Books, 1980), 17.

5. Bernard Malamud, "The Loan," *The Magic Barrel,* 170–71. Subsequent quotations are from this edition, identified as *TL* in the text.

6. Bernard Malamud, "The Lady of the Lake," *The Magic Barrel,* 96. Subsequent quotations are from this edition, identified as *LL* in the text.

7. Edward Alexander, "The Holocaust in American-Jewish Fiction: A Slow Awakening," *Judaism* 25 (Summer 1976), 323.

8. Bernard Malamud, "The Last Mohican," *The Magic Barrel,* 147. Subsequent quotations are from this edition, identified as *LM* in the text.

9. Michael Brown, "Metaphor for Holocaust and Holocaust as Metaphor: *The Assistant* and *The Fixer* of Bernard Malamud Reexamined," *Judaism* 29 (Fall 1980), 480.

10. Bernard Malamud, "The German Refugee," *Idiots First* (New York: Delta Books, 1965), 198. Subsequent quotations are from this edition identified as *GR* in the text.

11. Analyzing Malamud's metaphoric evocation of the Holocaust in *The Assistant,* Michael Brown astutely observes:

Morris's ultimate economic ruin is caused by new competition in the neighborhood, a delicatessen owned by a German. Frank Alpine and the upstairs tenants who exploit Morris's kindness by accepting cheap rent but buying their food in another shop, are Italians. The woman for whom Bober gets the roll each morning is a taciturn Pole, whom both Morris and Frank assume to be an anti-Semite. The Germans and their World War II allies conspire against Bober, the Jew. Where the Bobers live there are but three Jewish families. During the course of events the store of one of them is burned to the ground, leaving in charred ashes one-third of the Jewish community, a parallel with the Holocaust, which destroyed one-third of world Jewry. Less obviously but more significantly, the neighborhood in which the Bobers reside is reminiscent of Holocaust Europe. It is bleak and hopeless. There is no escape from it. It is removed from reality, much like the reservations established for the Jews of Nazi Europe. And Morris Bober himself is a dead man, going nowhere, inhabiting a world which is his tomb. At one point Morris goes to the barber, returning to find Alpine dipping into the till. Frank remarks in unwitting quadruple entendre, that Morris looks 'like a sheep that had the wool clipped off it.' Morris has been shorn by the barber; he has been shorn of his money by Frank; the wool has been lifted from his eyes, and he now sees Frank as a wolf in sheep's clothing; but he is also like the Jews of the Holocaust who, according to popular myth, were led 'like sheep to the slaughter.' The grocer's face turns 'ashen' at the analogy. Later he gets pneumonia, brought on by inhaling gas from a radiator he has forgotten to ignite, surely a reference to the fate of the Jews in Auschwitz and other camps. (Michael Brown, "Metaphor for the Holocaust and Holocaust as Metaphor: *The Assistant* and *The Fixer* of Bernard Malamud Reexamined," *Judaism* 29 [Fall 1980], 483–84)

Malamud's last novel, *God's Grace* (1982), is set in the postnuclear period, and its protagonist, the only human survivor, Calvin Cohen, refers to the Nazi Holocaust to comment on the devastating failure of humanity and God. As a descendant of a line of rabbis, Cohen, who had himself studied for the rabbinate, contends with God in the tradition of Jewish protest. Malamud's most religiously oriented novel, *God's Grace*, makes more overt use of Jewish theology, Hebrew liturgy, and Torahic commentaries than the earlier works of the canon. Through Cohen's objection to God's Holocaust-era silence, Malamud echoes the Holocaust protests of Elie Wiesel and I. B. Singer. The Nazi Holocaust was an orienting event in Cohen's Jewish consciousness, he thinks of the nuclear holocaust as an extension of the Nazi outrage. Further, he perceives a direct linkage from Russian pogrom to Nazi Holocaust to nuclear holocaust.

12. Bernard Malamud, quoted in Haskel Frankel, "One Man to Stand for Six Million," *Saturday Review* 10 September 1966, 39.

13. Leslie and Joyce Field, "An Interview with Bernard Malamud," *Bernard Malamud: A Collection of Critical Essays* (Englewood Cliffs, N.J.: Prentice-Hall, 1975), 10.

14. Robert Alter, "Jewishness as Metaphor," *Bernard Malamud and the Critics*, ed. Leslie A. Field and Joyce W. Field (New York: New York University Press, 1970), 38.

15. Bernard Malamud, *The Fixer* (Middlesex, England: Penguin Books, 1967), 141. Subsequent quotations are from this edition, identified as *F* in the text.

16. Earl H. Rovit, "Bernard Malamud and the Jewish Literary Tradition," *Critique* 3 (Winter 1960): 10.

17. Josephine Knopp, *The Trial of Judaism in Contemporary Jewish Writing* (Urbana: University of Illinois Press, 1975), 116.

18. Tony Tanner, "Bernard Malamud and the New Life," *Critical Quarterly* 10 (1965): 167.

19. Bernard Malamud, "Speaking of Books: Theme, Content and the New Novel," *The New York Times Book Review*, 26 March 1967, 2.

20. Alvin Rosenfeld, *A Double Dying: Reflections on Holocaust Literature* (Bloomington: Indiana University Press, 1980), 68.


## Chapter Four

1. Samuel Taylor Coleridge, *Biographia Literaria* (London: Dent, 1962) 167.

2. Leslie Epstein, "The Reality of Evil," *Partisan Review* XLIII (1976): 639.

3. Author interview with Leslie Epstein, 6 June 1985.

4. Author interview with Leslie Epstein, 6 June 1985.

5. Gerald Reitlinger, *The Final Solution: The Attempt to Exterminate the Jews of Europe 1939–1945* (New York: A. S. Barnes, 1961), 63–64.

6. Reitlinger's *Final Solution* is probably the source of many character details and names. The narrator's first name, Nisel, was probably Anglicized from Dr. Nyiszli, whom Reitlinger identifies as a survivor-physician who "noticed the famine-striken condition of the Lodz Jews, even when compared to Auschwitz inmates (303). The fictional American relief-worker, Faulhaber, probably owes his name to Cardinal Faulhaber, a bishop who protested the early euthenasia program practiced against Germans (131). In addition, Reitlinger's discussion of the Rievesaltes internment camp for French Jews is doubtless the source of the infamous police chief's name (75), and the fictional ethnic German, F. X. Wohltat, bears the name of Helmuth Wohltat, identified by Reitlinger as the head of the Foreign Credits Control Office (20, 46).

7. Among the historians and novelists who have treated the career of Rumkowski and the operation of the Lodz Ghetto are Lucjan Dobroszycki in *The Chronicle of the Lodz Ghetto 1941–1944*, Gerald Reitlinger in *The Final Solution*, Isaiah Trunk in *Judenrat: The Jewish Councils in Eastern Europe under Nazi Occupation*, and Leonard Tushnet in *The Pavement of Hell*. Fictional interpretations of Rumkowski and the ghetto appear in Jarek Becker, *Jacob the Liar;* Saul Bellow, *Mr. Sammler's Planet;* Primo Levi, *Moments of Reprieve;* and Adolf Rudnicki, "The Merchant of Lodz."

8. Lucjan Dobroszycki, ed. Introduction to *The Chronicle of the Lodz Ghetto 1941–1944* (New Haven: Yale University Press, 1984), xxix.

9. Primo Levi, *Moments of Reprieve*, trans. Ruth Feldman (New York: Summit Books, 1985), 165.

10. Ibid., 165.

11. Saul Bellow, *Mr. Sammler's Planet* (Greenwich, Conn.: Fawcett Publications, 1970), 211.

12. Leonard Tushnet, *The Pavement of Hell* (New York: St. Martin's Press, 1972), 9.

13. Ibid., 7.

14. Leslie Epstein, *King of the Jews* (New York: Avon Books, 1979), 35. Subsequent quotations are from this edition, identified as *KJ* in the text.

15. Alvin H. Rosenfeld, *A Double Dying: Reflections on Holocaust Literature* (Bloomington: Indiana University Press, 1980), 149.

16. Ibid., 149.

17. Reitlinger, *The Final Solution*, 64.

18. Ruth R. Wisse, "Books in Review," *Commentary* 67 (May 1979): 76.

19. See Edith Milton, "Looking Backward: Six Novels," *The Yale Review* 69

(October 1979): 95. See also Ruth R. Wisse, "Books in Review," *Commentary* 67 (May 1979): 76.

20. Leslie Epstein, "Eichmann and Other Matters," *New York Times Book Review*, 21 January 1979. Review of Hannah Arendt's *Jew As Pariah*.

21. Dobroszycki, Introduction to *Chronicle of the Lodz Ghetto*, xxxiv-xxxvi.

22. The methodical path to annihilation was outlined by Reinhardt Heydrich in his 21 September 1939 Berlin memorandum "Concerning: The Jewish Problem in the Occupied Zone." A copy of this memorandum may be seen in Helen Fein, *Accounting for Genocide: National Responses and Jewish Victimization During the Holocaust* (New York: The Free Press, 1979), 121–22.

23. Tushnet, *The Pavement of Hell*, 66–69.

24. Ibid., 66–69.

25. See Reitlinger, *The Final Solution*, and Tushnet, *The Pavement of Hell*.

26. Tushnet, *The Pavement of Hell*, 21.

27. Ibid.

28. Ibid., 22.

29. Before the German occupation, David Gertler had been a secret police agent for the Polish Internal Revenue Service. His job then was to ferret out materials on which no tax had been paid. Under the Nazis, he became a trusted Gestapo agent. (Tushnet, *The Pavement of Hell*, 62)

30. Tushnet, *The Pavement of Hell*, 62.

31. Excrement removal as punishment is noted in Mendel Grossman, *With a Camera in the Ghetto*, ed. Zvi Szmer and Alexander Sened (New York: Schocken Books, 1977), and noted specifically as a smuggling punishment in *The Chronicle of the Lodz Ghetto*, 391.

32. Tushnet writes, "No organized resistance movement against the Germans or against Rumkowski as the transmitter of German orders ever developed in the Lodz Ghetto, as it did in Warsaw and Vilna" (*The Pavement of Hell*, 64). He explains further, "For a short period before the 1940 strikes and demonstrations, the proletarian parties (Bund, Right and Left Labor Zionists, Communists) got together in a United Front to coordinate their activities and Rumkowski used their hunger and ration cards to break down morale" (*The Pavement of Hell*, 64).

33. Ibid., 26.

34. Ibid., 26.

35. "The Madagascar Plan was meant to serve as a cloak under which the preparations for the physical extermination of all the Jews of Western Europe could be carried forward. . . . No such cloak was needed for the Polish Jews." Hannah Arendt, *Eichmann in Jerusalem: A Report on the Banality of Evil* (New York: Viking Press, 1963), 71.

36. Tushnet, *The Pavement of Hell*, 45. See also *The Chronicle of the Lodz Ghetto*, entry of 20 December 1941, 96–97.

37. A delegation of four rabbis came to Jacob Gens to protest his participation in the selections for Ponary. In addition to quoting Maimonides, the rabbis advised Gens that according to Jewish law, a Jew could be surrendered to a governing authority only if he were personally guilty of a crime, not merely because he was a Jew (Tushnet, *The Pavement of Hell*, 160).

38. Wisse, "Books in Review," 76.

39. Tushnet, *The Pavement of Hell*, 160.

40. In *Eichmann In Jerusalem*, Arendt points out that the Nazis regarded *Judenrate* cooperation as the cornerstone of their Jewish policy. "Jewish officials could be trusted to compile the lists of persons and their property, to secure money from the deportees to defray the expenses of their deportation and extermination, to keep track of vacated apartments, to supply police forces to help seize Jews and

get them on trains" (104). Epstein's admiration for Hannah Arendt may be seen in his review of her book *The Jew As Parriah* (*New York Times Book Review*, 21 January 1979, 10, 30) in which he reviews the two major controversial issues of *Eichmann in Jerusalem*, namely, the banality of evil thesis regarding the Germans and the failure of the Jewish leadership to serve its constituency, and traces these themes in her earlier work.

41. Tushnet, *The Pavement of Hell*, 169–70.

42. Rosenfeld, *A Double Dying*, 174.

43. Tushnet, *The Pavement of Hell*, 45.

44. Ibid.

45. Tadeusz Borowski, "This Way for the Gas, Ladies and Gentlemen," *This Way for the Gas, Ladies and Gentlemen*, trans. Barbara Vedder (Middlesex, England: Penguin Books, 1976), 111–12.

46. Leo Baeck "refused to disseminate news of extermination at Auschwitz while he was interned in Theresienstadt; he had been cognizant of similar reports earlier but hoped they were rumors or 'the illusion of a diseased imagination.'" (Fein, *Accounting for Genocide*, 138) Admitting cooperation in the Vilna Ghetto selections, Jacob Gens said: "I stand and count off at the gate, but do you know how hard that is for me? People ask me where they're going and I don't tell them because I know where they're going. I want to save a few, and if possible the best, the most useful, so that they can renew our people." (Tushnet, *The Pavement of Hell*, 161).

47. Grossman, *Camera in the Ghetto*.

48. Further internal evidence of Epstein's familiarity with Grossman's book appears in the similarity of his description of a linen sorting session in the Church of the Virgin Mary. See and compare Epstein, *King of the Jews*, 100–101, 206 to Grossman, *Camera in the Ghetto*, 103.

49. Grossman, *Camera in the Ghetto*, 101.

50. Ibid., 102.

51. Ibid., 103.

52. Ibid., 101.

53. Ibid., 107.

54. David G. Roskies, *Against the Apocalypse: Responses to Catastrophe in Modern Jewish Culture* (Cambridge: Harvard University Press, 1984), 205.

55. Tushnet, *The Pavement of Hell*, 62–63.

56. Author interview with Leslie Epstein, 6 June 1985.

57. See Lucien Steinberg, *The Jews Against Hitler*, trans. Marion Hunter (London: Gordon & Cremonesi, 1974).

58. See Michael Checinski, "How Rumkowski Died," *Commentary* 67 (May 1979): 63–65.

59. Author interview with Leslie Epstein, 6 June 1985.

60. Milton, "Looking Backward," 95 and Wisse, "Books in Review," 76.

61. Alvin Rosenfeld, *A Double Dying*, Wisse, "Books in Review," and Milton, "Looking Backward."

62. Author interview with Leslie Epstein, 6 June 1985.

63. Author interview with Leslie Epstein, 6 June 1985.

64. Author interview with Leslie Epstein, 6 June 1985.

65. Oscar Rosenfeld (1884–1944) was a major contributor to *The Chronicle of the Lodz Ghetto 1941–1944*. Rosenfeld, a noted writer and publicist was deported from Prague to the Lodz Ghetto in October 1941 and frequently contributed supplementary articles and essays entitled "Sketches of Ghetto Life," recording the mood of the ghetto population. As a committed Zionist, Rosenfeld's tone is generally bitter in its critical presentation of *Judenrat* capitulation.

66. Leslie Epstein, "Holocaust and the Imagination." Speech delivered at Conference on the Holocaust, Millersville University, 21 April 1985.

67. Roskies, *Against the Apocalypse,* 212.
68. Ibid.
69. Author interview with Leslie Epstein, 6 June 1985.
70. Leslie Epstein, "Round Up the Usual Suspects," *New York Times Book Review,* 10 October 1982, 28.
71. Robert Alter, "A Fable of Power," *New York Times Book Review,* 2 February 1979, 44–45.
72. Ibid., 44–45.
73. Terrence Des Pres, Jacket Notes for *King of the Jews.*

## Chapter Five

1. Whereas most American novelists take the Polish-Jewish tragedy as their paradigm of Holocaust atrocity, Richard Elman selected the atypical Hungarian-Jewish experience for his historic trilogy. By selecting the distinctive Hungarian situation, Elman was able to focus on several peculiarly shocking circumstances that resulted in the destruction of a Jewish population in mid-1944, in full view of the world. The genocide of Hungarian Jewry occurred in Hitler's final year of power, in an Axis universe already close to defeat. Among all the Jews of Europe, the Hungarians, while still relatively safe, had ample warning and full knowledge of the German intent to create a *Judenrein* Europe. Further, the Hungarian deportations were openly conducted in full view of the Allied nations who had documentation of Polish-Jewish genocide and yet stood by and watched as the Axis powers applied the Final Solution to Hungarian Jewry. Historian Helen Fein writes: "Although in 1944 Hungarian Jews were still unsegregated, in 1941 the alien police agency expelled about 15,000 to 20,000 non-Hungarian born Jews from Transylvania. . . . These people were driven across the border to Poland, where they were massacred. News of general extermination came with the return of some escapees of this group and from Polish Jews fleeing into Hungary. . . . The Jews in Hungary were nominally free until 1944, except for the men up to the age of 48 who were compelled to serve in the labor brigades as compulsory alternative to military service. Because of the punitive conditions and sometimes torture imposed by their commanders, they ran a high risk of death." *Accounting For Genocide: National Responses and Jewish Victimization During the Holocaust* (New York: The Free Press, 1979), 107.
2. Raul Hilberg, *The Destruction of the European Jews* (Chicago: Quadrangle Books, 1961), 511.
3. Author interview with Richard Elman, 6 April 1987.
4. Author interview with Richard Elman, 6 April 1987.
5. Richard Elman reports that his father, a lawyer, showed him documents of "a will contested by the Romanian government because they wanted the dollars." Elman notes that he used the will for "the dramatics of the way people argued," rather than for its specific content. Author interview with Richard Elman, 6 April 1987.
6. Richard M. Elman, *The 28th Day of Elul* (New York: Charles Scribner's Sons, 1967), 12. Subsequent quotations are from this edition, identified as *E* in the text.
7. Eliezer Berkovits, *Faith after the Holocaust* (New York: KTAV Publishing, 1973), 68.
8. Richard Elman, note to author, 6 April 1987.
9. Hannah Arendt, *Eichmann in Jerusalem: A Report on the Banality of Evil* (New York: Viking Press, 1963), 177.
10. For a complete discussion of the concentrated and methodical deportation and massacre of Hungarian Jews, see Gerald Reitlinger, *The Final Solution: The*

*Attempt to Exterminate the Jews of Europe 1939–1945* (New York: A S Barnes & Co.,
1961), 412–47; and Arendt, *Eichmann in Jerusalem*,) 122–32, 176–84.

11. See Raul Hilberg's detailed documentation of Hungarian Jewry's loss of
civil rights, beginning with the 1938 definition of *Jew* in the first anti-Jewish law, to
the final destruction in 1944. *The Destruction of the European Jews* 509–54.

12. See Nora Levin, "The Brand Mission," *The Holocaust: The Destruction of
European Jewry 1939–1945* (New York: Schocken Books, 1973) 619–37. Joel Brand
was a Hungarian Labor Zionist and founder of the illegal Jewish organization
*Vaadah Ezra Hazalah (Vaadah)*. Unlike the Jewish Councils, the *Vaadah* had no illusions about German plans to annihilate European Jewry. The organization sent
people into the Hungarian provincial camps to warn Jews that the deportations
equalled death sentences. It forged baptism and Palestine emigration certificates to
rescue Jewish refugees from Poland, Slovakia, Yugoslavia, and Romania and smug-
gle them into Palestine. Brand negotiated with Eichmann for the lives of one million
Hungarian Jews. Eichmann offered to sell Brand a million Jews in exchange for
10,000 trucks complete with spare parts and equipped for winter conditions by the
Allies. To that end Eichmann kept Brand's family hostage while permitting him to
travel to Istanbul to contact Jewish Agency and Allied representatives. Although
Brand did not expect the Allies to exchange trucks for Jews, he thought an alternative could be found. Eichmann refused Brand's plea to halt deportations while he
tried to negotiate with the Allies and promised instead that 12,000 Jews would be
deported daily. Eichmann's only concession to Brand was that he would transport
some to Austria rather than Auschwitz to await news of Brand's mission. British
manipulation and sabotage, ranging from bureaucratic delays and prevention of his
travel in Turkey, to detaining him in Syria to gain vital information about German
positions and then placing him in protective custody in Cairo, assured the failure of
Brand's mission. The British refused to accept the German offer to exchange Jews
for trucks and did everything they could to foil his efforts with the Americans.
Brand eventually understood that the British were as much his enemies as the
Germans.

13. Richard Elman acknowledges using Raul Hilberg's *The Destruction of the
European Jews*, and notes that he interviewed the historian in 1981. Author interview
with Richard Elman, 7 April 1987.

14. Among the actions taken to curb Jewish liberties was the dismissal of
journalists, civil servants, lawyers, and accountants. Jews were required to register
their property. The Ministry of Trade ordered Jews to close their stores, offices, and
warehouses. Of the 40,000 reported Jewish businesses most were to remain closed,
and the few that were permitted to reopen did so under the trusteeship appointed
by local officials. The government closed Jewish bank accounts, confiscated Jewish
property, including art objects, automobiles, radios, telephones, books, and clothes.
The Food and Agriculture Ministry took over 600,000 acres of land that had been
owned by Jews. The Food Ministry issued instructions to deprive Jews of butter,
eggs, and spices commonly used in Jewish cooking; they restricted their meat supply
to a few ounces per week, and reduced allocated quantities of sugar, fat, and milk.
Legislation was enacted to forbid intercourse and marriage between Jews and non-
Jews and the employment of non-Jews in Jewish households. Jews were subjected to
Jewish Councils, ordered to wear identity stars; their movement was restricted,
subject to curfews, and finally they were ghettoized in designated apartments, city
districts, and cities. Hungarian territory was divided into five zones and the city of
Budapest, where Jews were systematically rounded up and ghettoized for expeditious deportation to labor and death camps. (Hilberg, *The Destruction of the European
Jews*, 531–35). "Two Hungarian Nazis, Laszlo Baky and Laszlo Endre, who became
secretaries in the new pro-Nazi Ministry of the Interior, worked with Eichmann to
plan the ghettoization and deportation of Hungarian Jewry. On April 7 instructions

were sent to the provinces to move the Jews into ghettos; implementation began on April 15. . . . On April 27 and 28 two trains carrying four thousand persons left for Auschwitz. Then, by province, between May 15 and July 9, 437,000 followed. Approximately 100,000 who were capable of work were sent to the labor camp in Auschwitz or to other camps in Germany. Some 75 percent were gassed immediately on arrival. Because the crematoria could not handle such volume, open pits were again resorted to." Yehuda Bauer, *A History of the Holocaust* (New York: F. Watts, 1982), 314.

15. Bauer, *A History of the Holocaust*, 312.

16. See Hilberg, *The Destruction of the European Jews*, 552.

17. In the early years of the Axis, Hungarian-Jewish war veterans and their families were exempted from quotas thereby reducing the Jewish economic presence (Hilberg, *The Destruction of the European Jews*, 5ℨ). Also, when the 1944 decree ordering Jews to wear identifying stars was issued, wives, widows and children of exempted veterans were excused from wearing the demeaning badges (Ibid., 534).

18. Deportees were not given tattooed numbers prior to arriving at the concentration camp according to Eli Weisel, "Legacy of Evil," *The New York Times Book Review*, 28 May 1967, 4.

19. Dr. Rezso (Rudolf) Kastner, a Labor Zionist and leader of the *Vaadah* movement warned Brand to be wary of the British and deal directly with the Jewish Agency and Chaim Weizmann to save Hungarian Jewry. Kastner served the rescue effort by negotiating with other Zionist groups, the official Jewish leadership, and Hungarian politicians. While Brand was abroad trying to negotiate with the British to reply positively to the Eichmann proposal, Kastner convinced Eichmann to move 1,709 Jews from the Bergen-Belsen transport to safety and 18,000 Jews from Budapest and the provinces to Austria rather than Auschwitz where they would be held awaiting the outcome of Brand's mission. In this way many of the 18,000 survived. Kastner was instrumental in other *Vaadah* rescue efforts. Levin, *The Holocaust*, 640–41. See Levin for further discussion of Kastner's role in efforts to save Hungarian Jewry.

20. See "After the Deluge," *Times Literary Supplement*, 21 September 1967, 833; John Leonard, "Books of the Times: Complicity and Consequences," *New York Times*, 13 September 1968; and Frederic Morton, "When Yagodah Glimpses His Fate, His Humanity Vanishes: *The Reckoning*," *The New York Times Book Review*, 14 September 1969, 5, 20. In contrast to these criticisms, Elie Wiesel's analysis is more understanding of the complexities of Holocaust behavior, noting that Elman, "sparing no one, . . . provides disturbing insight into the traumatic psychology of certain survivors—who, caught in webs of universal betrayal, are forced into total alienation." "Legacy of Evil," *The New York Times Book Review*, 28 May 1967, 34.

21. Jean Amery, *At the Mind's Limits: Contemplations By A Survivor On Auschwitz And Its Realities* (Bloomington: Indiana University Press, 1980), 65.

22. Elman now regrets the Israeli frame of *The 28th Day of Elul* and would omit it if writing the book today. He wrote it when he had limited knowledge of Israel and feels he did not do the section very well, claiming, "I was writing over the top of my head." Author interview with Richard Elman, 6 April 1987.

23. Alan L. Berger, *Crisis And Covenant: The Holocaust in American Jewish Fiction* (Albany: State University of New York Press, 1985), 162.

24. Elman's note to author, 8 April 1987.

25. Elman's letter to author, 8 April 1987.

26. David G. Roskies, *Against the Apocalypse: Responses to Catastrophe in Modern Jewish Culture* (Cambridge: Harvard University Press, 1984), 20.

27. Ibid.

28. Richard Elman notes that he was also thinking of the French historian Jacques Ellul when he selected his title. Elman's note to author, 8 April 1987.

Among the Ellul works translated into English prior to publication of the first volume of the trilogy are *The Technological Society* (1964); *Propaganda* (1966); *The Political Illusion* (1967); and *The Presence of the Kingdom* (1967).

29. See Philip Birnbaum, *A Book of Jewish Concepts,* rev. ed. (New York: Hebrew Publishing Co., 1964), 35–36.

30. *Likkutei Torah, parshas Re'eh,* 32a; quoted in "The King in the Field: Preparing for Elul," *Wellsprings* 2 (August–September 1986): 5.

31. Birnbaum, *A Book of Jewish Concepts,* 35–36.

32. Author interview with Richard Elman, 6 April 1987.

33. Christopher Koch, *Lilo's Diary, Commonweal* 89 (17 January 1969): 505.

34. Richard Elman, *Fredi & Shirl & the Kids: The Autobiography in Fables of Richard M. Elman* (New York: Charles Scribner's Sons, 1972), 153.

35. Richard M. Elman, *Lilio's Diary* (New York: Charles Scribner's Sons, 1968), 43. Subsequent quotations are from this edition, identified as *LD* in the text.

36. See Hilberg, *The Destruction of the European Jews,* 534, 539–40.

37. Just as the trilogy's hostile family relationships, particularly that of the father and son, reflect Elman's family portrait in *Fredi & Shirl & the Kids,* so do the trilogy's ambivalent male-female relationships mirror situations in the autobiographical fable.

38. Andre Schwarz-Bart, *The Last of the Just* (New York: Atheneum, 1961), 374.

39. Morton, "When Yagodah Glimpses His Fate," 20.

40. Richard M. Elman, *The Reckoning: The Daily Ledgers of Newman Yagodah Advokat and Factor* (New York: Charles Scribner's Sons, 1969), 4. Subsequent quotations are from this edition, identified as *R* in the text.

41. Hannah Arendt, "Anti-Semitism"; quoted in Ron H. Feldman's Introduction to Hannah Arendt, *The Jew as Pariah: Jewish Identity and Politics in the Modern Age,* ed. Ron H. Feldman (New York: Grove Press, 1978), 18.

42. Arendt, *Jew as Pariah,* 68.

43. Ibid.

44. See Lawrence L. Langer, *Versions of Survival: The Holocaust and the Human Spirit* (Albany: State University of New York Press, 1982), 42.

45. Ibid., 49.

46. Ibid., 54.

47. Ibid., 85.

48. Elie Wiesel, *The Accident,* trans. A. Brochardt (New York; Hill & Wang, 1962), 79.

49. Wiesel, "Legacy of Evil," 4.

## Chapter Six

1. Edward Alexander, *Isaac Bashevis Singer,* Twayne's World Authors Series (Boston, Mass.: Twayne Publishers, 1980), 103.

2. Edward Alexander, *Resonance of Dust: Essays on Holocaust Literature and Jewish Fate* (Columbus: Ohio State University Press, 1980), 149–50.

3. Isaac Bashevis Singer, *The Family Moskat,* trans. A. H. Gross (Greenwich, Conn.: Fawcett Publications, 1950), 604. Subsequent quotations are from this edition, identified as *FM* in the text.

4. Isaac Bashevis Singer and Joseph Landis, trans. *"The Family Moskat:* Chapter 65," *Yiddish* 6 (Summer-Fall 1985): 106. Subsequent quotations from this Yiddish edition are identified as *YFM* in the text.

5. Isaac Bashevis Singer, "Author's Note," *Enemies, A Love Story* (New York:

Farrar, Straus, & Giroux, 1972). Subsequent quotations are from this edition, identified as *E* in the text.

6. Alexander, *Isaac Bashevis Singer,* 99.

7. Leslie Fiedler, "Isaac Bashevis Singer, or the Americanness of the American Jewish Writer," *Studies in American Jewish Literature* 1 (1981): 130.

8. Edwin Gittleman, "Isaac Bashevis Singer," *Dictionary of Literary Biography: American Novelists Since World War II,* vol. 6, ed. James Kibler (Detroit: Gale Research Company, 1980): 312.

9. Alexander, *Isaac Bashevis Singer,* 103.

10. Richard Rubenstein, *After Auschwitz: Radical Theology and Contemporary Judaism* (Indianapolis: Bobbs-Merrill, 1966). "When I say we live in the time of the death of God, I mean that the thread uniting God and man, heaven and earth has been broken. We stand in a cold, silent, unfeeling cosmos, unaided by any purposeful power beyond our own resources. After Auschwitz what else can a Jew say about God? . . . I see no other way than the 'death of God' position of expressing the void that confronts man where once God stood" (49). Rubenstein rejects God and the covenant with Israel: "If I believe in God as the omnipotent author of the historical drama and Israel as His Chosen People, I had to accept [the] . . . conclusion that it was God's will that Hitler commited six million Jews to slaughter. I could not possibly believe in such a God nor could I believe in Israel as the chosen people of God after Auschwitz" (47).

11. Emil Fackenheim's often-quoted dictum—"Jews are forbidden to hand Hitler posthumous victories!"—posits the thesis that, particularly after the Holocaust, Jews are under a sacred obligation to survive as a people, and that entails loyalty to God and Judaism. See Emil Fackenheim, *God's Presence in History: Jewish Affirmations and Philosophical Reflections* (New York: New York University Press, 1970).

12. Eliezer Berkovitz, *Faith After the Holocaust* (New York: KTAV Publishing, 1973), 106–7.

13. Ibid., 90.

14. Richard Burgin, "Interview: Isaac Bashevis Singer's Universe," *New York Times Book Review,* 3 December 1978, 52.

15. Ibid. Also noted in Author's note in *The Penitent,* 1968.

16. Elie Wiesel, *Night,* trans. Stella Rodway (New York: Hill & Wang, 1960), 53.

17. Byron Sherwin, "Elie Wiesel and Jewish Theology," *Judaism* 18 (Winter 1969): 46.

18. Grace Farrell Lee, "Seeing and Blindness: A Conversation With Isaac Bashevis Singer," *Novel* 9 (Winter 1976): 156.

19. Sherwin, "Elie Wiesel," 40.

20. Lee, "Seeing and Blindness," 156.

21. Alexander, *Isaac Bashevis Singer,* 109.

22. Ibid.

23. Nili Wachtel, "Freedom and Slavery in the Fiction of Isaac Bashevis Singer," *Judaism* 26 (Spring 1977): 171.

24. Ibid., 172.

25. Shosha was Singer's childhood friend on Krochmalna Street in Warsaw. For a biographical discussion of Singer's Warsaw circle described in *Shosha,* see Paul Kresh, *Isaac Bashevis Singer: The Magician of West 86th Street A Biography* (New York: Dial Books, 1979).

26. Isaac Bashevis Singer and Richard Burgin, *Conversations with Isaac Bashevis Singer* (Garden City: Doubleday, 1985), 139.

27. Ibid.

28. Isaac Bashevis Singer, *Shosha*, trans. Joseph Singer and Isaac Bashevis Singer, (New York: Farrar, Straus & Giroux, 1978), 206. Subsequent quotations are from this edition, identified as *S* in the text.

29. See Emil Fackenheim, "The Holocaust and the State of Israel: Their Relation," reprinted from *Encyclopedia Judaica Yearbook* in *Auschwitz: Beginning of a New Era? Reflections on the Holocaust*, ed. Eva Fleishner (New York: KTAV Publishing, 1974), 205–17. See also Eliezer Berkovits, *Faith After the Holocaust* (New York: KTAV Publishing, 1973), 111–12, 134, 144–69.

30. Isaac Bashevis Singer, "The Mentor," *A Friend of Kafka and Other Stories*, trans. Isaac Bashevis Singer and Evelyn Torton Beck (New York: Dell, 1962), 98. Subsequent quotations are from this edition, identified as *TM* in the text.

31. Isaac Bashevis Singer, "Hanka," *Passions and Other Stories,* trans. Isaac Bashevis Singer, and Blanche and Joseph Nevel (New York: Farrar, Straus & Giroux, 1970), 13. Subsequent quotations are from this edition, identified as *H* in the text.

32. Edwin Gittleman, "Dybbukism: The Meaning of Method in Singer's Short Stories," *Contemporary American-Jewish Literature*, ed. Irving Malin (Bloomington: University of Indiana Press, 1973), 248.

33. Isaac Bashevis Singer, "A Wedding in Brownsville," *Short Friday and Other Stories*, trans. Chana Faerstein and Elizabeth Pollett (Greenwich, Conn.: Fawcett Books, 1961), 229. Subsequent quotations are from this edition, identified as *WB* in the text.

34. Joyce Paula Penn, "Some Major Themes in the Short Fiction of Isaac Bashevis Singer" (Ph.D. diss., Stanford University, 1975), 152.

35. Isaac Bashevis Singer, "The Cafeteria," *A Friend of Kafka and Other Storeis,* trans. Isaac Bashevis Singer and Dorothea Straus, 77. Subsequent quotations are from this edition, identified as *C* in the text.

36. Penn, *Some Major Themes* 158.

37. Ibid., 157.

38. Isaac Bashevis Singer, *The Penitent* (New York: Farrar, Straus & Giroux, 1983), 42. Subsequent quotations are from this edition, identified as *P* in the text.

39. Joseph C. Landis, "I. B. Singer—Alone In The Forest," *Yiddish* 6 (Summer-Fall 1985): 7.

40. Isaac Bashevis Singer, "Nobel Lecture" (Nobel Foundation, 1978), reprinted in *Yiddish* 6 (Summer-Fall 1985): 171.

41. Misgivings about the value of assimilation has been Singer's obsession. In an autobiographical account of his early years in the company of Jewish writers in Warsaw, Singer describes his admiration for Hillel Zeitlin's belief that "modern Jewishness . . . that lacked religion was a paradox and an absurdity . . . that Jewishness without religion—a Jewishness based on language or even upon a nation— lacked the force to keep the Jews united." Isaac Bashevis Singer and Ira Moskovitz, *A Little Boy in Search of God: Mysticism in a Personal Light* (Garden City, N.Y.: Doubleday, 1976), 157.

42. In brief, Lurianic kabbalists believe in a mystical interpretation of the Bible, which explains the connection between God and creation, the existence of good and evil, and the way to spiritual perfection. Among the basic precepts of the kabbalists is *Tsimtsum*, the contraction of God into Himself to yield space for creation. Creation is believed to have been preceded by voluntary divine self-limitation of the infinite (*En Sof*) in order to make room for the finite world. God sustains the world by spiritual beams of light. Some of the vessels meant to contain God's light did not sustain the rush of light and therefore shattered. The "breaking of the vessels" caused deterioration and chaos in the world, ushering in evil. Human purpose in this context is described as *tikkun*, the restorative task of liberating the fallen divine sparks through devotion to moral perfection and intense prayer (*kavanah*).

43. Richard Burgin, "Interview: Isaac Bashevis Singer's Universe," 52.

44. Isaac Bashevis Singer, "Author's Note," *The Penitent,* 169.

45. Isaac Bashevis Singer and Ira Moskovitz, *A Little Boy in Search of God,* 179–80.

## Chapter Seven

1. Cynthia Ozick, "Toward a New Yiddish," *Art and Ardor: Essays* (New York: Alfred A. Knopf, 1983), 174–75.

2. Ibid.

3. Cynthia Ozick, "The Evasive Jewish Story," *Midstream* 12 (February 1966): 79.

4. S. Lillian Kremer, Interview with Cynthia Ozick, 28 December 1986.

5. In a letter to Victor Strandberg, Cynthia Ozick wrote, "I care more for *Trust* than for anything else I have written." Victor Strandberg, "The Art of Cynthia Ozick," *Texas Studies in Literature and Language* 25 (1983): 292.

6. Diane Cole, "Cynthia Ozick," *Dictionary of Literary Biography: Twentieth Century American-Jewish Fiction Writers,* ed. Daniel Walden 28 (Columbia, S.C.: Bruccoli-Clark Publishers, 1984), 214.

7. Cynthia Ozick, *Trust* (New York: The New American Library, 1966), 62. Subsequent quotations are from this edition, identified as *T* in the text. Reprinted by permission of the author.

8. Cynthia Ozick, "Four Questions of the Rabbis," *Reconstructionist* 38 (18 February 1972): 23.

9. Cynthia Ozick, Preface to *Bloodshed and Three Novellas* (New York: Alfred A Knopf, 1976), 4. Copyright © by Cynthia Ozick.

10. Philip Birnbaum, *A Book of Jewish Concepts* (New York: Hebrew Publishing, 1964), 24.

11. Cynthia Ozick, "The Biological Premises of Our Sad Earth-Speck," *Art and Ardor: Essays,* 235.

12. Ibid., 236.

13. Cynthia Ozick, "Remembering Maurice Samuel," *Art and Ardor: Essays,* 212.

14. Cynthia Ozick, Untitled essay, *Response* 6 (Fall 1972): 92.

15. Alan L. Berger, *Crisis and Covenant: The Holocaust in American-Jewish Fiction* (New York: State University of New York Press, 1985), 5.

16. Ibid.

17. Arthur A. Cohen, *The Tremendum: A Theological Interpretation of the Holocaust* (New York: Crossroad Publishing, 1981), 2.

18. Ozick, "Toward a New Yiddish," 157.

19. *Pentateuch and Haftorahs,* ed. J. H. Hertz, 2d ed. (London: Socino Press, 1979), 18.

20. John D. Davies, *The Westminster Dictionary of the Bible,* ed. Henry Snyder Gehman (Philadelphia: Westminster Press, 1944), 165.

21. Quoted in Strandberg, "The Art of Cynthia Ozick," 268.

22. Author interview with Cynthia Ozick, 26 December 1986.

23. Cynthia Ozick, "A Bintel Brief for Jacob Glatstein," *Jewish Heritage* 14 (September 1972): 60. Quoted in Deborah Heiligman Weiner, "Cynthia Ozick, Pagan vs Jew (1966–1976)," *Studies in American Jewish Literature* 3 (1983): 187.

24. Cynthia Ozick, "Envy; or, Yiddish in America," *The Pagan Rabbi and Other Stories* (New York: Alfred A Knopf, 1971), 42. Subsequent quotations are from this edition, identified as *E* in the text. Copyright © by Cynthia Ozick.

25. Cynthia Ozick, "The Suitcase," *The Pagan Rabbi and Other Stories,* 103.

Subsequent quotations are from this edition, identified as *S* in text. Copyright © by Cynthia Ozick.

26. Cynthia Ozick, "A Mercenary," *Bloodshed and Three Novellas* (New York: Alfred A Knopf, 1976), 13. Subsequent quotations are from this edition, identified as *AM* in the text. Copyright © by Cynthia Ozick.

27. Cynthia Ozick, Interview with Kay Bonetti, American Audio Prose Library, no. 6092.

28. Ibid.

29. Ozick's despair over the United Nations' flagrant anti-Israeli policy, published the same year as "A Mercenary," appears in her exposé of the United Nations' silence about Arab aggression against Israel during the Yom Kippur War and its sudden censuring voice when the tide turned toward Israeli victory. Ozick explicitly accuses the United Nations of anti-Semitism veiled as anti-Zionism: "Meanwhile, outside of Israel, the Zionism that was meant to end anti-Semitism became an equivalent for 'Jew' in all its ancient resonances. It is no good for anti-Semites to pretend anymore that they are 'anti-Zionist' but not 'anti-Jewish,' or that the two notions can be kept separate" (105). See "All the World Wants the Jews Dead," *Esquire* 82 (November 1974): 103–7, 207–10.

30. Cynthia Ozick, "All the World Wants the Jews Dead," 207.

31. Cynthia Ozick, "Bloodshed," *Bloodshed and Three Novellas*, 59. Subsequent quotations are from this edition, identified as *B* in the text. Copyright © by Cynthia Ozick.

32. Abraham Chill, *The Mitzot: The Commandments and Their Rationale* (New York: Bloch Publishing, 1974), 203.

33. Cynthia Ozick, "Levitation," *Levitation: Five Fictions* (New York: Alfred A Knopf, 1982), 7. Subsequent quotations are from this edition, identified as *L* in the text. Copyright © by Cynthia Ozick.

34. Cynthia Ozick, *The Cannibal Galaxy* (New York: Alfred A Knopf, 1983), 3. Subsequent quotations are from this edition, identified as *CG* in the text. Copyright © 1983 by Cynthia Ozick.

35. The anti-Semitism unleashed during the years of the Dreyfus Affair became a significant political issue in France and throughout Europe. At the time, the French Army was the stronghold of royalists and Catholics who preferred to cover up their original blunder and the framing of Dreyfus rather than convict the real traitor about whom they had ample evidence. Fanned by its own anti-Semitism and that of the royalist-Catholic press, the Army knowingly moved for a second miscarriage of justice at the retrial in 1899. Liberal reaction to this verdict in France and the rest of Western Europe was emphatic, leading to a pardon for Dreyfus by the liberal new president of the French Republic.

36. See Arthur Hertzberg, *The French Enlightenment and the Jews* (New York: Columbia University Press, 1968).

37. See Paula Hyman, *From Dreyfus to Vichy: The Remaking of French Jewry* (New York: Columbia University Press, 1979), 42–44.

38. *Encyclopedia Judaica* 12 (Jerusalem: 1972): 1340–41.

39. *Encyclopedia of Zionism and Israel*, ed. Raphel Patai (New York: 1971), 328–29.

40. *The Universal Jewish Encyclopedia*, ed. Isaac Landman (New York: 1941), 322.

41. Claude Levy and Paul Tillard, *La Grande Rafle du Vel d'Hiv* (16 juillet 1942) (Paris: 1967), 23, 37–38. Quoted in Michael R. Marrus and Robert O. Paxton, *Vichy France and the Jews* (New York: Basic Books, 1981), 250–51. Ozick confirmed her use of *Vichy France and the Jews*, in author interview with Cynthia Ozick, 26 December 1986.

42. Marrus and Paxton, *Vichy France and the Jews*, 250–51.

43. In a post *Cannibal Galaxy* publication letter from Andre Nehre, Ozick learned that the only book he had while hiding during the Holocaust was the *Ta'anit* tractate. Author interview with Cynthia Ozick, 28 December 1986.

44. In the course of a long career, Monsignor Justin Fevre turned toward policies and actions tainted by anti-Semitism, such as praising a book on the ritual murder canard. During the Dreyfus Affair, he wrote: "Under penalty of treason, we ought all to be antisemitic, Catholic, and French. We ought to have only one flag, only one battle cry, 'Down with the Jews!'"; reported in Robert Francis Byrnes, *Anti-Semitism in Modern France: The Prologue to the Dreyfus Affair* 1 (New Brunswick, N.J.: Rutgers University Press, 1950): 189–90. In response to the author's question about her ironic use of the Le Fevre name, Ozick replied that she was unaware of the Fevre history. Author interview with Cynthia Ozick, 28 December 1986.

45. Quoted in Berger, *Crisis and Covenant*, 135.

46. Joseph Lowin, "Cynthia Ozick's Memesis," *Jewish Book Annual* 42, (1984–1985): 85–86.

47. Esther intervened with King Ahasuerus, who made her his queen, and with the aid of her uncle, Mordechai, succeeded in averting the annihilation of the Persian-Jewish community planned by the Hitler of their period, Haman, the king's advisor. The significance of the Esther story to Jewish history stems from its symbolic value to a persecuted people of the ultimate triumph of truth and justice. Esther is still commemorated in the annual Festival of Purim, for saving her people.

48. *Encyclopedia Judaica* 12 (Jerusalem: 1972): 94.

49. Andre Neher, *The Exile of the Word: From the Silence of the Bible to the Silence of Auschwitz* (Philadelphia: The Jewish Publication Society of America, 1981), 144.

50. Ibid.

51. Ibid., 144–45.

52. Ibid., 215.

53. Ibid.

54. The *Mishnah* is the transcription of oral law, a collection of Jewish laws and ethics. It is divided into six parts known as *sedarim* (orders), each of which is subdivided into tractates. The *Mishnah* comprises sixty-three tractates. Despite its religious influence, the *Mishnah* is not a religious authority. Unanimous and dissenting rabbinic opinions are given; the laws in the work are not creed or dogma.

55. Lowin, "Cynthia Ozick's Memesis," 90.

56. Ibid.

57. Cynthia Ozick, "The Phantasmagoria of Bruno Schulz," *Art and Ardor*, 224; reprinted from *The New York Times Book Review*, 13 February 1977.

58. Ibid.

59. Cynthia Ozick, Response to audience question, Modern Language Association Convention, 28 December 1986.

60. Ozick, Commentary, Modern Language Association Convention, 28 December 1986.

61. Author interview with Cynthia Ozick, 8 April 1987.

62. Ibid.

63. Ibid.

64. Cynthia Ozick, *The Messiah of Stockholm* (New York: Alfred A Knopf, 1987), 102. Subsequent quotations are from this edition, identified as *M* in the text. Copyright © 1987 by Cynthia Ozick.

65. Harold Bloom, "The Book of the Father," *New York Times Book Review*, 22 March 1987, 36.

66. Author interview with Cynthia Ozick, 8 April 1987.

67. Cynthia Ozick, "Rosa," *The New Yorker*, 21 March 1983, 38–71.

68. Cynthia Ozick, Commentary, Modern Language Association Convention, 28 December 1986.

69. Ozick reports hearing the story of Moishe the *Tzaddik* from a Drohobycz survivor. Author interview with Cynthia Ozick, 8 April 1987.

70. Cynthia Ozick, "Innovation and Redemption: What Literature Means," *Art and Ardor,* 246.

71. Ibid., 247.

72. Ibid.

73. Ibid., 245–46.

74. Cynthia Ozick, Untitled essay, *Response,* 93.

75. Cynthia Ozick, "Bialik's Hint," *Commentary* 75 (February 1983): 28.


## Chapter Eight

1. Arthur A. Cohen, *The Tremendum: A Theological Interpretation of the Holocaust* (New York: Crossroad Publishing, 1981) 2.

2. Ibid.

3. Ibid., 53.

4. Cynthia Ozick, *"In the Days of Simon Stern,"* The New York Times Book Review, 3 June 1973, 6.

5. Edward Alexander, "The Holocaust in American-Jewish Fiction: A Slow Awakening," *Judaism* 25 (Summer 1976): 330.

6. Arthur A. Cohen, *In the Days of Simon Stern* (New York: Random House, 1972), 451. Subsequent quotations are from this edition, identified as *D* in the text.

7. Pablo Christiani (d. 1274) was a convert to Christianity and anti-Jewish polemist. In Barcelona he debated with Nahmanides, trying to prove the validity of Christianity from the Talmud.

8. The December 8, 1942, meeting with Jewish leaders was the only one President Roosevelt held with Jewish leaders concerning the Holocaust. See David S. Wyman, *The Abandonment of the Jews: America and the Holocaust: 1941–1945* (New York: Pantheon Books, 1985), 72.

9. Ibid.

10. Ibid., 5–6, 124–37.

11. Cohen develops the notion of Orthodox separation from secular society in a scene where the thirty-year-old Stern recalls his mother's admonition to keep his distance from "the forbidden world" and his association of that world with anti-Semitism. As he stood on the border between neighborhoods, he heard himself described as a subject of interest among non-Jews, often noted contemptuously: "sheeny, kike, yid (generic forms of designation; like simple denotative nouns, they pointed out without describing), but cockcutter, bloodeater, waterpoisoner, Christ killer, these were more, particular, sharp, combining the absolute unbearable monotone of history . . . with desperate particularity: Shimon the killer, the poisoner, the cutter, the Christ killer. In those childhood days Shimen would run home, tears rushing down his face" (95).

12. The Pale of Settlement refers to approximately 400,000 square miles in czarist Russia, where by 1897 approximately five million Jews were permitted to live. This system was introduced when partitions of Poland brought Jews into the area of the Russian state in 1791 and was abolished *de facto* in 1915 and absolutely in 1917. Borders were changed arbitrarily, causing great hardships for the Jews confined to this area. Only certain categories of Jews—those whose work, talents, or money were needed by the czarist regime—were exempt from living in the Pale.

13. According to Orthodox law, a child's mother must be Jewish for the child to be legally Jewish.

14. Cohen, *Tremendum,* 48–49.
15. See Arthur A. Cohen, *The Myth of the Judeo-Christian Tradition* (1970); *The Natural and the Supernatural Jew* (1979); *The Tremendum: A Theological Interpretation of the Holocaust* (1981); Arthur A. Cohen, ed. *Arguments and Doctrines: A Reader of Jewish Thinking in the Aftermath of the Holocaust* (1970).
16. Cohen, *Tremendum,* 80.
17. Ibid., 81.
18. Ibid., 82.
19. Ibid., 26.

## Chapter Nine

1. Chaim Potok, *Wanderings: Chaim Potok's History of the Jews* (New York: Alfred A Knopf, 1978), 398.
2. Ibid.
3. Chaim Potok, "The Dark Inside," *Dimensions in American Judaism* (Fall 1967): 35. Subsequent quotations are from this source, identified as *DP* in the text.
4. Chaim Potok, *The Chosen* (Greenwich, Conn.: Fawcett Publications, 1967), 186. Subsequent quotations are from this edition, identified as *C* in the text.
5. Chaim Potok, *The Promise* (New York: Fawcett Publications, 1969), 294. Subsequent quotations are from this edition, identified as *P* in the text. Copyright © 1969 by Chaim Potok.
6. Chaim Potok, "Judaism Under the Secular Umbrella," *Christianity Today* 22 (8 September 1978): 18.
7. S. Lillian Kremer, "An Interview With Chaim Potok, July 21, 1981," *Studies in American-Jewish Literature* 4 (1984): 91–92.
8. Chaim Potok, *In the Beginning* (Greenwich, Conn.: Fawcett Publishing, 1975), 11. Subsequent quotations are from this edition, identified as *IB* in the text. Copyright © 1975 by Chaim Potok.
9. Benjamin Max Potok, who "saw himself mirrored in the eye of most American gentiles as a Jewish Caliban," (*Wanderings,* 379) is a clear model for Max Lurie. The novelist's father learned while wearing Poland's uniform that his gentile countrymen did not consider him a full-fledged citizen, but merely a proper subject for exploitation and victimization, the subject of their suspicion, hatred, and violence. Max Lurie founds the Am Kedoshim Society just after World War I to fight Polish anti-Semitism. The wave of pogroms in Poland between 1917 and 1921 inspired the creation of many Jewish self-defense groups.
10. Nathan Ausubel, ed., *A Treasury of Jewish Folklore* (New York: Crown Publishers, 1948), 605.
11. For a good brief discussion of American anti-Semitism consisting of youth gang attacks and police negligence, as well as the anti-Semitic bias of the immigration policy in this period, see David S. Wyman, *The Abandonment of the Jews: America and the Holocaust 1941–1945* (New York: Pantheon Books, 1984), 9–11.
12. Potok, *Wanderings,* 388.
13. Ibid.
14. Harold Ribalow, Interview with Chaim Potok, *The Tie that Binds: Conversations With Jewish Writers* (New York: A S Barnes, 1980), 134.
15. Potok, "Judaism Under the Secular Umbrella," 20.
16. Ibid.
17. Potok, *Wanderings,* 388.
18. Ribalow, *The Tie that Binds,* 124.

## Chapter Ten

1. George Steiner, quoted in *Time,* 29 March 1982.
2. See George Steiner, "A Kind of Survivor," *Language and Silence: Essays On Language and Literature and the Inhuman* (New York: Atheneum, 1977) 140–54.
3. George Steiner, Preface to *Language and Silence,* viii.
4. Ibid.
5. Steiner, *Time.*
6. Steiner, Postscript to *Language and Silence,* 156–57.
7. Steiner, "Human Literacy," *Language and Silence,* 4.
8. Ibid., 4–5.
9. Steiner, "The Hollow Miracle," *Language and Silence,* 101.
10. Ibid., 99–100.
11. Steiner, Postscript, 163.
12. George Steiner, "Return No More," *Anno Domini Three Stories* (London: Faber and Faber, 1980), 34. Subsequent quotations are from this edition, identified as *R* in the text.
13. George Steiner "Cake," *Anno Domini,* 72. Subsequent quotations are from this edition, identified as *C* in the text.
14. George Steiner, *The Portage to San Cristobal of A.H.* (New York: Simon & Schuster, 1982), 7–8. Subsequent quotations are from this edition, identified as *P* in the text.
15. Morris Dickstein, "Alive and 90 in the Jungles of Brazil," *New York Times Book Review* (2 May 1982), 13.
16. See George Steiner, "A Kind of Survivor" and "A Season in Hell," *In Bluebeard's Castle: Some Notes Towards the Redefinition of Culture* (New Haven: Yale University Press, 1971), 29–56.
17. See Lucy S. Davidowicz, *The Holocaust and the Historians* (Cambridge: Harvard University Press, 1981).
18. Alvin Rosenfeld, *Imagining Hitler* (Bloomington: Indiana University Press, 1985), 88.
19. Steiner, "A Season in Hell," *Bluebeard's Castle,* 54–55.
20. Rosenfeld, *Imagining Hitler,* 82.
21. See Rosenfeld, *Imagining Hitler,* for a discussion of Jacob Grill, 96–97.
22. Steiner, "A Kind of Survivor," *Language and Silence,* 153.
23. Steiner, "A Season in Hell," *Bluebeard's Castle,* 34, 36–37.
24. Ibid., 44–45.
25. Hyam Maccoby, "George Steiner's 'Hitler': Of Theology and Politics," *Encounter* 58 (May 1982): 31.
26. Ibid., 27–34.
27. Rosenfeld, *Imagining Hitler,* 101.
28. Ibid., 101–2.

## Conclusion

1. Isaac Rosenfeld, "The Meaning of Terror," *Partisan Review* (January 1949), reprinted in Isaac Rosenfeld, *An Age of Enormity: Life and Writing in the Forties and Fifties* (New York: World Publishing, 1962), 207.
2. Lothar Kahn, "The American Jewish Novel Today," *Congress Bi-Weekly* 36 (5 December 1969): 3–4.
3. Elie Wiesel, "The Fiery Shadow—Jewish Existence out of the Holocaust," *Jewish Existence in an Open Society: A Convocation* (USA: Jewish Centers Association, 1970), 44.

# INDEX

385

S. Lillian Kremer teaches in the department of
English at Kansas State University. She received her
M.A. degree from City University of New York, and
her Ph.D. from Kansas State University. Her study
of Chaim Potok was included in the Dictionary of
Literary Biography: Twentieth-Century
American-Jewish Fiction Writers. Dr. Kremer's
articles and reviews on Jewish-American and
Holocaust writers and literature have appeared in
such journals as Studies in American Jewish
Literature, Saul Bellow Journal, Holocaust
Studies Annual, and Modern Jewish Studies
Annual.

The manuscript was edited for publication by Jana
Currie Scott. The typeface for the text is Baskerville
and the display is Palatino Bold. The book is printed
on 55-lb Glatfelter text paper and is bound in
Holliston Mills' Roxite Linen.
Manufactured in the United States of America.